ETHICS, POLITICS, AND SOCIAL RESEARCH

Ethics, Politics, and Social Research

Edited by
GIDEON SJOBERG
University of Texas

SCHENKMAN PUBLISHING COMPANY, INC.
Cambridge, Massachusetts

Library of Congress Catalog Card #67–29320

Copyright © 1967
by Schenkman Publishing Company, Inc.
Cambridge, Mass. 02138

CONTENTS

v

PART II   VIEWS FROM THE INSIDE

PREFACE

I want to thank the contributors for being so patient with my efforts. More specifically, I want to thank Richard Colvard for his assistance. I have for years carried on a dialogue with him concerning many of the issues considered in this volume. His constructive suggestions concerning the book's organization were very useful. He also read and commented on several chapters.

In addition, I wish to express my sincere appreciation to Jo Lewis for her valuable editorial assistance. She read many of the chapters and her critical evaluations concerning the arguments of the various authors were forwarded to them.

And I must thank my wife, Andrée F. Sjoberg, who took time out from her own work to put her excellent editorial talents to use on this book.

In the end my own efforts will have been worthwhile if this book results in some long-overdue debate on the ethics and politics of social research.

GIDEON SJOBERG
July, 1967

CONTRIBUTORS

J. KENNETH BENSON, *Department of Sociology, University of Missouri,* Columbia, Missouri.

RICHARD A. BRYMER, *Research Sociologist, Wesley Youth Project, Wesley Community Centers,* San Antonio, Texas.

LEONARD D CAIN, JR., *Department of Sociology, Sacramento State College,* Sacramento, California.

RICHARD COLVARD, *Department of Sociology, State University of New York at Buffalo,* Buffalo, New York.

ARLENE KAPLAN DANIELS, *Department of Sociology, San Francisco State College,* San Francisco, California.

BUFORD FARRIS, *Project Director, Wesley Youth Project; and Director, Wesley Community Centers,* San Antonio, Texas.

FRED H. GOLDNER, *Graduate School of Business, Columbia University,* New York, New York.

IRVING LOUIS HOROWITZ, *Department of Sociology, Washington University,* St. Louis, Missouri.

T. N. MADAN, *Senior Fellow, UNESCO Research Centre on Social and Economic Development in Southern Asia,* Delhi, India.

JOAN W. MOORE, *Department of Sociology, University of California,* Riverside, California.

HAROLD ORLANS, *Senior Staff, The Brookings Institution,* Washington, D.C.

JANE CASSELS RECORD, *Department of Economics, University of Portland,* Portland, Oregon.

GIDEON SJOBERG, *Department of Sociology, University of Texas,* Austin, Texas.

JAMES OTIS SMITH, *Project Director, Timberlawn Foundation Research Project: Social Epidemiology of Psychiatric Illness,* Dallas, Texas.

PIERRE L. VAN DEN BERGHE, *Department of Sociology, University of Washington,* Seattle, Washington.

TED R. VAUGHAN, *Department of Sociology, Ohio State University,* Columbus, Ohio.

INTRODUCTION

It is hoped that this book will contribute to a fuller understanding of the methods of social research and the social organization of scientific activity. The essays collected here focus attention upon the status, power, and moral dimensions of the social scientist's role in modern society.

The specific goals of the volume were outlined in a prospectus sent to each of the contributors. In part, this prospectus reads as follows:

Ethics. A major theme of this volume . . . concerns the ethics of social research. One of the book's scholarly aims will be to clarify and objectify certain neglected issues in this area. . . .

The question of ethics in social research has been brought to the fore in recent years by the efforts of various scientific associations to create codes of ethics for their membership. . . .

Some of the observations by the Committee on [Professional] Ethics, American Sociological Association, highlight some of the conflicting opinions concerning the relationship of ethics to social research. The Committee claimed it became aware of two rather divergent views:

> The first stands for the proposition that sociologists inevitably intervene in the situations that they study, that a research problem is always framed from a particular perspective and its results always reflect that perspective. This amounts to saying that there is no such thing as the role of an objective sociologist because our values enter into the manner in which we pose research projects. Holders of this view believe that any Code of Ethics . . . is flying in the face of reality.
>
> The other negative standpoint does not so much criticize the nature of the Code as hold it to be unnecessary. The partisans of this view believe that we are primarily scientists, that the American Sociological Association is a learned society, and that we have no ethical problems not shared by all scientists.[1]

Actually this statement far from exhausts the variety of arguments in this area. One has been expressed by Howard Becker in his chapter in

Vidich *et al., Reflections on Community Studies.*[2] Although from one point of view his argument would seem to fall into the Committee's second category, from another perspective it is rather distinct. Becker seems to avow that in the writing of, say, a research report, the ethical canons "must remain a matter of individual judgment." Some of you may agree with this, but it seems to me that researchers' ethical decisions are the products of broader values and belief systems — whether these stem from the "scientific community," from particular political ideologies, or whatever.

Another position regarding ethics (and politics) in research is my own. Although some of you may well disagree with it, I would like to think that it serves as a rationale for the volume itself. My position runs somewhat as follows: ethical and political considerations invariably enter into the research design and the execution of the project, and in the social sciences such factors are far more pervasive than in the natural sciences. Yet, one can reduce biases and increase objectivity within social science. However, such cannot be achieved through repetition of the formula, "I am objective," but through examination of the impact of ethical and political decisions upon social research. My view, then, seems to straddle those laid down by the aforementioned Committee on Ethics.

I hope that in your particular chapters some of you will take stands on the aforementioned differences of opinion among social scientists in the realm of ethics and social research. Here I think it is of interest that sociology has lagged behind psychology and anthropology in encouraging public discussion of these issues. Some of you may wish to re-read the Report of the Committee on Ethics of the ASA and perhaps use part of this material as a basis for your comments. [This Report was a "first draft" effort, and the "proposals" of this Committee were ultimately shelved by the Council of the American Sociological Association.] Personally I am convinced that this Committee "put the cart before the horse," . . . Codes are being developed on the basis of insufficient data. Codes, if they are to be created at all, should be based on discussions of the kind in which we are here engaged — with attention paid also to research in other cultural settings. . . .

Politics. The political issues are, in my judgment, closely associated with the ethical ones. Only on an analytical, rather than an empirical, plane is it possible to distinguish between the two. Actually, some of you may in the context of your own topic want to consider more specifically the relationships of ethics and politics.

The effects of politics upon research can be analyzed on at least two levels — the ideological and the structural. The researcher's political ideology (viewed broadly) does much to influence his selection of a topic, the formulation of his research design, and, of course, the research findings. So too, structural factors — e.g., the position of the researcher in the social order and the informal or formal controls exerted upon him by various groups in the society — influence the course of the research.

In your analyses of the political (as well as ethical) factors affecting the research process I hope you will keep the following "reference groups" in mind: the academic community (as a whole) and the university setting (in particular); the scientific community and the professional associations; the sponsors of the research; the group (or groups) being studied; and the impinging local, national, and even international political systems. Although topics are so structured that in most instances one or two groups will be given primary attention, I hope that your discussion will mention others, if only in passing.

May I elaborate upon some of the aforementioned groups. The university or broader academic system structures research efforts in numerous ways. One's own colleagues exert considerable controls over one's research. Then there are issues relating to co-authorship, to the amount of credit to be given student assistants, etc. Related to the university system is the broader "scientific community" — which is international in character — as well as the various scientific associations that support the scientist's professional activities. It is my impression that some researchers distinguish between "scientific" values and the more narrowly defined "professional" ones.

Several chapters will consider the impact of the scientific community and/or professional associations upon social research. . . . Leonard Cain will discuss the manner in which professional associations became involved in the controversy surrounding the publication of the results of an old-age study by two Emory University sociologists. And Pierre van den Berghe in his discussion of his research in South Africa will have much to say about the differing impact of the broader scientific value system and the national power structure.

I definitely hope most of you will give some attention to the values and beliefs — and the political power situation — of the groups under study, and that you will discuss how these factors have influenced the research findings or the structuring of the research report itself. The power position of the group being researched vis-à-vis the researcher seems to have affected the results of numerous studies, including the ethical decisions of the researcher. Germane to this subject also is the question of the manipulation of individuals or groups by social researchers. What kinds of manipulation are involved in social research? To what extent can one justify the manipulation of one's subjects in the cause of science? I hope the last question will be faced directly in the chapter on the Harvard Drug Case and in Richard Colvard's discussion of protecting one's informants in the writing of a research report.

Then there is the matter of the ideology and power position of local and national governmental units — and even of power systems on the international level. Several chapters will undoubtedly consider the relationship of the political structure to social research. Vaughan, for example, in his chapter on the Wichita jury trial, will discuss the ethical issues involved in "bugging" juries as well as the situation wherein the U.S. Congress held hearings and passed a law making it illegal for social researchers to record jury deliberations in Federal courts.

Finally, there are questions such as: What is the responsibility of the scientist to his various publics? How far should scientists proceed in opposing various groups or accommodating to their particular pressures?

Conclusions. Overall I hope that the matter of politics and ethics in social research will not be discussed as ends in themselves but that an effort will be made (wherever feasible) to show how these decisions affect the end-product of investigation. . . .

By way of a postscript, I would observe that some of my early intentions were modified as the book evolved. Originally I had planned to include chapters that focused only upon specific case studies, but it became necessary to include a few of a more general nature. Then too, I had hoped to include two additional chapters on the ethical and political problems of research in other societies, but the authors were, for personal reasons, unable to complete these. However, this situation permitted me to encourage a few contributors to elaborate more fully on their subjects than would otherwise have been possible.

The chapters have been grouped in two main sections: "Views from the Outside" and "Views from the Inside." Although the authors in the first section occasionally draw upon their own experiences for illustrative material, these chapters are written from a "third person" perspective. The chapters in the second section reflect a more personal view of the research process.

Perhaps not all of the initial objectives of the volume have been attained. Nevertheless, some unanticipated outcomes have led to major gains. I did not foresee, for example, how effectively the contributors would employ concepts and ideas in social science to clarify ethical and political issues in social research. As cases in point, Benson and Smith are able to bring a strikingly different perspective to bear upon the widely discussed Harvard Drug Case, and Goldner is able to clarify his own struggles to establish a research role in a large corporation through his concept of "the ethics of ambiguity."

Nor did I foresee the extent to which the various topics would result in the development of similar themes or meaningful contrasts. A review of some of these should prove useful:

1. The highly significant essays by Orlans and Record examine two important aspects of the structure that supports much of present-day research. While other authors have touched upon the ethical and political dimensions of the grantor-grantee relationship and of research institutes, none have done so in as wide-ranging a manner as have Orlans and Record.

2. In a broad sense, there is a dialogue between Orlans and some of the authors who follow in the first section. For many of the latter consider problems that arise in institutionalized, large-scale research efforts. On the other hand Madan highlights the difficulties that researchers encounter when support for research is limited. While we may question the manner in which social research in America is underwritten, the absence of any supportive structures would make large-scale research projects impossible to sustain.

We should also recognize that Orlans in general analyzes the typical case, whereas Record, Benson and Smith, Cain, Vaughan, and Sjoberg focus upon "deviant cases," upon research projects that have "failed." Although we can learn much from the study of problem cases, we must also recognize the dangers of generalizing from these to more normal situations.

3. The chapters by van den Berghe and Horowitz examine issues that no social scientist can ignore. Pierre van den Berghe brings to the fore his struggles to carry out field work within a totalitarian order (South Africa) and frankly justifies his actions in terms of his search for scientific knowledge. Irving Louis Horowitz vividly recounts the impact of his ideology and his intellectual and personal commitments on the making of his book on Brazil. Social scientists are prone to see the role of ideology in structuring the work of their colleagues; it is rare for an author to examine the place of ideology in his own analysis.

4. Several chapters provide the basis for comparing the problems that

scientists encounter when they study groups to the problems when they study individuals. Joan Moore effectively documents the role of an "organized ethnic group" in structuring the ethical and political decisions in an action-oriented research project. Contrast the impact of this organized group with that of the individuals in the projects discussed by Benson and Smith and Brymer and Farris. Some of the authors — e.g., Madan, Goldner, and Colvard — consider the relationship of the investigator to both groups and individuals.

5. The relationship of the researcher to his informants is viewed differently by Daniels, Colvard, and Farris and Brymer. Daniels apparently sees the researcher as a stranger vis-à-vis the informants in her study; Colvard regards the researcher as always more than a stranger; Brymer and Farris seem to stand between these two positions. As a result, the different authors tend to view ethical and political problems in somewhat differing lights.

6. We can also compare the roles played by Daniels and by Goldner and the political and ethical consequences thereof. Daniels dramatically portrays her encounters with the military establishment, a "secret society" into which she could never be integrated; Goldner, on the other hand, was clearly part of the system he studied.

7. In a number of chapters a "negotiation model" becomes the basis for resolving the ethical and political dilemmas posed by particular research situations. The essays by, for example, Orlans, Moore, Goldner, and Brymer and Farris all suggest, albeit with varying emphases, that the scientist is only one player in a highly pluralistic setting and that he must work out compromises with nonscientists if he is to attain some of his objectives.

8. Another theme that should not be overlooked relates to the many problems involved in the analysis, the writing up, and the publication of one's results. Horowitz provides us with a clearer understanding of how a writer must cope with a "mass audience." Cain, in turn, calls attention to the ethical and political ramifications of the mass media's diffusion of a particular set of findings, whereas Record, Goldner, Brymer and Farris, and Colvard consider the analysis and the writing of reports from still other perspectives. It is quite transparent that the analysis and the publication of data is a neglected, yet crucial, segment of the research process.

9. The ambiguities and the tensions that social scientists experience as a result of the political and ethical decisions they inevitably must make are pointed up by Cain's, and especially Colvard's, shifting positions over time. Using an exchange of letters with one of his editors as a backdrop, Colvard engages in a soul-searching dialogue with self in an effort to resolve the

conflict between his own concept of man and the premises of the scientific method.

I have kept this introduction brief, lest I appear to speak for any of the contributors. They ably speak for themselves. As for my own views on the ethical and political dimensions in social research, some of these appear in the prospectus that follows and others in my reflections on "Project Camelot."[3] How I came to be concerned with the ethics and politics of social research must await another essay.

GIDEON SJOBERG

NOTES

1. Committee on Professional Ethics, American Sociological Association, *Code of Ethics* (First Draft) (Washington, D.C.: American Sociological Association, 1964), 3.

2. Howard S. Becker, "Problems in the Publication of Field Studies," in Arthur J. Vidich *et al.* (eds.), *Reflections on Community Studies* (New York: John Wiley & Sons, 1964), 267–84.

3. Originally, I had planned to write a chapter on the controversy surrounding the translation and publication of one of Hsiao-tung Fei's books. But this did not prove to be feasible; for one thing, I was unable to secure permission to reproduce certain key materials — itself an interesting problem in social research.

PART
I
VIEWS FROM THE OUTSIDE

CHAPTER ONE

Ethical Problems in the Relations of Research Sponsors and Investigators

HAROLD ORLANS

It is said to be more blessed to give than to receive. Both givers and recipients of social research funds, however, are often troubled by misunderstandings and a sense of unfulfilled expectations that may lead readily enough to moral recriminations.

This paper will discuss some of the more common ethical problems that thereby arise in the sequence from the application for research funds through their use, and to the completion of a research report. To be more exact, it will discuss some of the problems commonly cast in moral terms by one or the other party to a research grant. By "moral" I mean simply conduct deemed proper and principled, good, honest, right, and equitable. As I will present no further definition, and little evidence that is not drawn from my limited experience, it should be clear that this will not be an empirical report but an essay, a personal appraisal of selected issues. To add to these limitations the object of repeating only popular views would be to accomplish nothing at all; therefore, I may dwell somewhat more fully on the views of administrators than on those of applicants (with which, I assume, most readers are already sympathetic). Before an academic audience, administrators are underdogs; and to those with a true interest in what is true, that is sufficient cause to present their case with special care.

Accordingly, I start with the assumption that *they* (who give) are as moral as *we* (who receive); or, that *they* (who ask) are as well-intentioned

3

and honest as *we* (who bestow). The assumption derives not so much from direct observation (though my observations support it) as from the reflection that the men on both sides of the relationship come from comparable professions and share many of the same goals and standards; at least the more sophisticated recognize that they are likely to have a variety of continuing contacts throughout their careers — they may, indeed, occasionally exchange roles — and long-term comfort and effectiveness require a basic measure of integrity and mutual confidence.

Doubtless, a number of knaves may prosper on deception. Telling half the truth, after all, can be charitable as well as self-serving; it is an art gentlemen as well as opportunists cultivate, and the test of its moral acceptability — in whose interest is it not to tell the other half? — is not readily determinable in any single instance. America is a large country and a man who changes projects, institutions, and sponsors often enough may keep ahead of the game for a while. So there are career opportunities for knaves who comport themselves as gentlemen. But that is not the way the game of research grants is normally played. In any event, knavery — lying, bad faith, conscious misrepresentation to get money, or the deliberate breach of the terms on which it was obtained — poses a practical rather than a moral problem. The offense is clear; the only question is if it will be detected or punished.

The persistent ethical dilemmas in sponsored research are those in which the right course of action is *not* clear, in which honorable men may differ and no consistent rule obtains. They involve issues in which what is reasonable to one man is ignoble to another; in which honesty must be reconciled with tact and effectiveness; in which the disinterested pursuit of innocent truth can abet the interested selection of useful knowledge; in which the judgment of the pragmatic man of affairs confronts that of the academic moralist.

Money Does Not Come Free

The basic source of most of the problems we will examine is obvious enough, although (with as human a sentiment but as odd a logic as if physicists disliked gravity) many scholars consider it pernicious: money is not a free good, available for any scholarly purpose, and those with funds to dispense do so for purposes and under conditions of their own choosing. This is inevitable and it is fruitless to lament it. Too often, the politics of research patronage — i.e., the choice of particular scholars to conduct particular studies likely to advance particular social objectives — is confused with its morality. But to confuse politics and morality is to demean both. It is almost a definition of civilized (or democratic, as distinct from revolutionary or totalitarian) politics *not* to impugn the integrity of one's opponents and *not* to equate the political interests of a group with its moral virtuousness or viciousness. In the sphere of research financing the conclusion that follows is: if you disagree with the objectives of an agency, don't decry the morality of its staff but try to change their objectives and, in the interim, don't take their money.

It is regrettable that more investigators do not adopt this evident course. A league of eminent men conducting only research that meets their own standards and can be supported with their own resources would enhance the respect and self-respect of individual research and perhaps even the modest financing it requires. Too many prefer the pains of having money to those of not having any; it takes a mighty self-confidence (or a marked record of success) to resist the feeling that exclusion from grantsmanship circles is a result of forced rather than free choice.

Across the academic spectrum, the frequency of application for research funds is patently related to the frequency of successful application which, in turn, is determined by opportunity and, to varying degrees, outlook and special kinds of ability. Thus, as of 1961, roughly three-quarters of natural scientists, under half of social scientists, and less than a fifth of humanists at major American universities had ever applied for federal research funds; but, of these, nine-tenths of the scientists, eight-tenths of the social scientists, and seven-tenths of the humanists had secured at least one award.[1] As of then, it might be said that virtually all scientists who applied for funds could expect to get some at *some* time; though humanists had such slight opportunities that few had ever bothered to ask, surprisingly, most of these had also been rewarded, which suggests that they had had either prior encouragement to apply, or talents specially suited to available programs. The level of support for the social sciences has fallen between that for the natural sciences and that for the humanities, but the larger volume of funds for selected purposes or quantitative approaches has posed divisive issues — particularly in sociology, social psychology, political science, and economics.

The question may appear irrelevant to some, but it is worth raising at the outset, if only to indicate the self-centered character of much moral judgment: *Should* so much money be spent on research, when not new knowledge but food and peace and medical care are needed to maintain the lives of thousands of Americans and millions of non-Americans? It is easy for economists or sociologists to complain that they are not getting as much money as physicists; for low energy physicists, that they are not getting as much as high energy physicists; and for high energy physicists, that they are getting less than movie stars or prizefighters. Having wearied of fruitless complaints about the volume of military research and development (now accepted as unpleasant but unavoidable a fact of contemporary life as death or taxes), the attention of many critics has focused on the entrancing and expensive enterprise of landing a man on the moon. Of this, Lord Bowden, British Minister of State for Education and Science, has observed:

> The US National and Aeronautics Space Administration is already deploying resources which might feed and clothe half the underdeveloped world. It is attracting engineers and technologists from the undeveloped countries which need them and cannot spare them, and it is producing a world-wide drift of men which we in Britain have come to call the "brain drain."
> Will a 20th-Century Voltaire ever say of NASA, "Ecrasez l'infame"?[2]

Such criticism can, of course, be part of a convincing political philosophy; but it is morally suspect to demand of others what one is not oneself inclined to offer. The thorny crown of righteousness must be awarded to the generals who protest arms budgets, the rocket engineers who decry space exploration, the biologists who oppose much biomedical research, and the sociologists who would convert their expenditures on sample surveys and computers into wheat for the hungry and wool for the cold. With comparable, transitory righteousness, Levin, thrust by marriage from the countryside into the world of the Moscow gentry, reckons how much labor goes into a footman's livery and how many bushels of oats could be bought for the cost of his family's dinner. In absolute moral terms, Levin is undoubtedly right and our contemporary scientific gentry wrong; but it may be noted that, like the latter, he grows accustomed soon enough to his new style of life.[3] Even the most religious only tithe; charity begins, and often ends, at home; it is both natural and convenient to serve others while serving oneself. We do not usually seek (like a saint, or a revolutionary) to build the world afresh, distributing its resources in some principled manner among the unfathomable range of human needs.

On Small Grants and Large Purposes

Although I have suggested that more social scientists should voluntarily operate outside the project system, I do not imagine very many will do so happily. A more practicable solution would be to enlarge alternative systems of support, offering the freedom investigators want with at least some of the money and recognition they also desire. One way to do this is to increase the funds available to universities and research institutions for their own allocations; and, in point of fact, government policy has been moving in this direction with the growth of National Institutes of Health and National Science Foundation institutional grants, and comparable programs of several other agencies. Another way is to enlarge the number of post-doctoral and senior faculty fellowships and to liberalize their terms, making more adequate provision for research expenses.

To William Whyte's charge that most foundations prefer large-scale projects to the support of individuals (the Guggenheim Foundation is generally cited as the most notable exception), several foundation officials have replied that wholesalers cannot run a retail business efficiently; this is the job of foundation-sponsored bodies like the Social Science Research Council, the Center for Advanced Study in the Behavioral Sciences, and other enterprises off and on campus.[4] Though the argument has merit, it is noticeably incomplete. The right of an agency to make only grants above, or below, a designated amount cannot reasonably be disputed. However, few of the major granting agencies do, in fact, so confine themselves (though many limit the size of awards that staff can make without approval of superior officers or the board). The most important agencies supporting social science research (such as the National Science Foundation, the Departments of Defense, and of Health, Education and Welfare, the Ford Foundation, and the Carnegie Corporation) give many small as well as large grants.

It may, therefore, more accurately be said that they do not so much refrain from making small grants as from making them directly to individuals and for purposes outside their defined compass. Foundations are purportedly wary of what Flexner called "scatteration" — the dispersion of funds in small concentric circles like sparklers that light up the night air evanescently but mark out no path in any direction. And both private and public agencies commonly award grants only to responsible nonprofit institutions, partly in recognition of the associated financial and educational benefits that accrue to these institutions — with which most of their applicants are, in any event, affiliated — and partly for the administrative and intellectual services they render (not to mention the protection they provide against the potential embarrassment depicted in the *New Yorker* cartoon of a partying professor in a girl-packed convertible, living it up upon receipt of a grant). In the rare cases in which grants are made directly to individuals, they are usually bonded.

The supposedly high cost of administering small grants casts more doubt on the efficiency of the granting agency than on the feasibility of such grants, for any necessary costs are no smaller (though they can be less apparent) when delegated to another organization. But if larger grants to fewer institutions produce no net reduction in overhead, clearly they do produce a closer and more continuing association between the granting and the recipient organizations, and a more decisive movement in an agreed direction.

Some agencies may favor large projects for another reason. It is difficult, at best, for any study of a controversial social problem to yield results and recommendations that will be accepted by all parties, and the conclusions of a single investigator may, with relatively little effort, be controverted by another. As the mere weight of a large staff and a ponderous methodological machinery renders a study more unique and less subject to such controversion, it serves to give its conclusions a weight they would otherwise lack.

Boycotting Certain Programs

Instead of remaining outside the system or waiting for it to be changed, many scholars and some institutions prefer the compromise of working only with certain agencies and having nothing to do with others. Most significant of these alternatives is the boycott of selected programs, such as those of the military or those subject to security or other administrative restrictions.

Thus, the Institute for Policy Studies accepts no federal projects, so as to avoid becoming financially dependent on government,[5] a policy differing only in degree from that of the Brookings Institution which accepts some government funds but rejects far more and strives to keep government financing down to a fraction of its research budget (it was under 20 percent in 1964 and 1965). As both organizations are engaged primarily in studies of government policies, it is important to both to maintain not only their freedom of inquiry (ensured in the last analysis not by the source of funds but by the terms under which they are obtained) but also the *credibility* of that freedom. In addition, private financing reduces the hazard of political attack to which those who conduct social research with public funds are especially vulnerable. Without in any way condoning the narrowness in scope and method of the social research that many government agencies will sponsor, it must be recognized that there is much work that it would be foolhardy for them to support — for example, studies of Congressional or Presidential politics; the voting behavior of religious groups; the political proclivities of civil servants, scientists, FBI agents, or any other honorable and putatively apolitical group; the sexual or other private activities of virtually any identifiable group of nondefenseless men; and many urgent problems of current social concern. The periodic furor caused by the revelation that one or another government agency has been sponsoring a study of some potentially awkward subject (such as nudism, wiretapping, the conditions under which a nation might surrender in a war, or possible sources of rebellion in a friendly nation) attests to the need for greater discretion by public than by private agencies.

The aversion of some scholars to conducting research under Defense Department auspices is often regrettable, not always well founded, and usually understandable. The fear of restraints on the direction of inquiry, and of administrative rigidities and follies, while warranted with some military agencies is unwarranted with others such as the Office of Naval Research, which pioneered the liberal policies later adopted by so model a civilian agency as the National Science Foundation. If able men do not work on military problems less able men may, to the detriment of those national interests that the Department serves;[6] and the idea that the unwillingness of a few to do what many are ready to undertake will lead to its curtailment is hardly borne out by experience. Nonetheless, it is understandable that conscientious objectors or critics of specific military policies, for example, should be unwilling to associate themselves with these policies even in a tangential way.[7] This is clearly their privilege, as it is the privilege of their colleagues to associate themselves with policies they favor, and there is no evident ground for deeming either faction nobler than the other.

Shortly after World War II, the issue of conducting classified research on campus was of greater practical importance than it is today, when both government and university officials concede that it is preferable, in peacetime, not to do this work in a setting designed for unfettered inquiry and instruction. In any event, the volume of classified work at universities has declined and alternative sites for its prosecution have increased, so that the problem has dwindled. More important now, and more neglected, is the issue of proprietary work that we will discuss later.

The list of administrative restrictions that have led individual investigators and, at times, institutions, to shun various government programs is long but not nearly long enough, for complaints have come more readily than action, the private action of individuals has been more frequent than their united public resolve, and rarely have many institutions jointly refused to participate in a program until designated restrictions were removed. A notable exception was the refusal of some thirty universities and colleges, a few years back, to accept from the U.S. Office of Education loans for students predicated on the students' certifying that they did not subscribe to the overthrow of the government by force, violence, or illegal or unconstitutional means. (An additional eighty institutions took the money though protesting the regulation.) The International Cooperation Administration (subsequently, the Agency for International Development) was repeatedly excoriated by university representatives for its apparent inability to comprehend what a university was about and to adjust its research and educational programs accordingly, but this did not lead to any widespread refusal by universities to cooperate with ICA. When the medieval provisions of the Arms Control and Disarmament Agency's grants — more restrictive by far than those of any other federal research grants — were promulgated in 1963, they evoked (so far as I know) no public protest (though one university spokesman privately doubted that many schools could legally accept some provisions).

A great deal has been said for and against grants and contracts, faculty often preferring grants for their administrative simplicity and flexibility, while university business officers may prefer contracts, which have reimbursed a fuller range of direct and indirect costs; rarely has either position been carried to the point where a faculty has refused to accept contracts or a university has refused to sanction grant applications (though some have encouraged faculty to apply first for a contract). This issue also is losing force as the cost policies and red tape of granting agencies approximate those of contracting agencies.

Perhaps I am making too much of the notion of manifest protest against objectionable requirements. Of course, an enormous amount of formal and informal discussion and consultation between government and university representatives goes on all the time, leading to constant modifications in administrative regulations and to compromises in the demands of each side. The point to be stressed is that many of the ethical and practical problems that may arise in the course of research can be foreseen and should be resolved before the work is begun. This is the time for negotiation or, if necessary, withdrawal. To assume a commitment one does not propose to honor is to head for a deserved fall.

In some respects, a research contract poses fewer dilemmas than a grant, precisely because it is normally subject to more detailed negotiation. A government cost contract can be tedious, pedantic, legalistic, and full of clauses irrelevant to the matter at hand. Nevertheless, the key passages — the statement of work, the conditions under which it will be regarded as satisfactorily completed, and the disposition of the final report — are the product of repeated review and explicit consent. By contrast, a grant is more one-sided, both in the initial, unsolicited request for funds and in the eventual letter that provides them on terms spelled out separately (by the National Science Foundation in a brochure, and by the Public Health Service in a compendious looseleaf book) but not normally negotiated or adjusted to the circumstances of each case. And, being more one-sided, the process of applying for, and living with, a grant can pose more subtle quandaries.

Unfortunately, the code for successful applications may not be disclosed (for if it were, granting agencies would only change it). Certain scholars at élite institutions believe they have broken it, but they are mistaken, since the secrets of grantsmanship, like those of nature, can never be entirely fathomed. Always, some impeccable applicant will be refused, others frustrated, and most mystified in one respect or another, while the staff, advisory committees, or board go through the occult consultations and internal struggles that are their birthright, since freedom of choice is as essential to their self-respect as it is to the applicant's. Even the untoward request of a President of the United States has been refused by a private agency, and delayed, if not forestalled, by a public one.

Choosing a Subject

The choice of a subject and method of inquiry is the quintessential problem. Every active researcher has an extensive agenda of work he would like to do sometime, but how often are his priorities the same as those of granting agencies, and how far should he accept theirs? Should an anthropologist who would rather go to Alaska be lured into fieldwork in Africa because the Carnegie Corporation or the State Department believe that it is in the nation's interest to familiarize more scholars with that continent? Should an economist emphasize the contribution to basic knowledge and play down the immediate usefulness of his findings in an application to the National Science Foundation — and do the reverse when applying to an industrial foundation? How many references to anxiety can a student of class structure honorably incorporate in a proposal to the National Institute of Mental Health? Should a political scientist who really wants to do a lot of reading on a public issue cook up a questionnaire about it because a quantified approach may yield a grant from the National Science Foundation?

These decisions can be aggravating, but the aggravation is personal; the man proposing to do something his heart is not really in may be unhappy as a result, but so long as he does what he says he will do, it is hard to call him dishonorable.

More satisfactory (to the investigator, at any rate) is the practice Peter Rossi has called "robinhooding," in which the investigator "agrees to do something in return for support to do something else in addition." As examples, Rossi cites a federally financed survey of recruitment in the natural sciences, medicine, and education that the National Opinion Research Center extended to the humanities "because we were able to convince the clients that it was more expensive for technical reasons to restrict the research . . .;" and a study of adult education that was broadened to include other leisure activities after NORC persuaded the Carnegie Corporation that it was more fruitful to examine adult education in that context.[8] The success of this strategy is, of course, dependent not only upon its cogency, but upon the investigator's bargaining power.

Accomplices

Morally more dubious is the practice of receiving funds for one purpose but using them at least in part for another, with the private but not public approval — that is, the complicity — of key granting agency staff. The situation commonly arises when staff (and perhaps the agency head) condone the auxiliary purpose but cannot acknowledge this openly because it may be illegal, be inconsistent with agency policy, encourage too many grantees to do likewise, or prove politically embarrassing. Thus, one senior foundation official invited a social scientist he respected to submit a proposal in line with one of the foundation's published program interests and then use the grant for a different purpose (which, as it happened, the man declined to do). Common forms of what may be called either duplicity or political finesse are the titling and description of government grants by their most saleable, popular, or obscure features, and an emphasis upon the possible usefulness of basic research that belies the equal likelihood that results will interest only scattered academicians. Both the investigator and the agency staff commonly share responsibility for thus merchandising humdrum intellectual wares.[9]

In recent years, the diversion of federal research funds to educational purposes has been widespread, with the complicity of responsible university and federal officials and congressmen, as some have frankly acknowledged. ". . . our medical schools lean heavily on the use of so-called research funds to accomplish their prime function of medical education. This is morally indefensible and legally sanctioned, thanks especially to the wisdom of the so-called bureaucrats who administer the federal programs in support of medical research," so one scientist and National Institutes of Health adviser,

Philip Handler, has observed[10] with commendable frankness but evident inconsistency, for if this diversion were explicitly sanctioned by law and administrative regulation, why was it "morally indefensible"? In my opinion, the legal sanction is (or *was,* because government policy has been moving toward formal endorsement of the educational use of some research funds) more questionable than the moral, though *that* is questionable too. However, questionable as the legal or moral sanction may have been, the political or social sanction was *not,* for little or no punitive action against such diversion has been taken either in Washington or on campus.

(Out of courtesy to Handler, this may be a suitable occasion to note that, outside of communion in the church of our choice, those indispensable adjectives collated in the preceding sentence — legal, moral, political, social — represent something less than the irrefragable lines at which the vaults of the heavenly kingdom intersect the earthly domain. What is "legal" is, in each instance, determined by the words on a piece of paper and those which are spoken, in elucidation of them, by two specific lawyers, a specific judge, and twelve selected citizens; what is "moral" are the words from on high which we hear far below; what is "political" advances the interests, as what is "social" defines the standards, of designated people. It follows that what is legal may not be moral, what is moral may be politically unwise, what is socially desirable may be politically impossible, and what, in each of these respects, is entirely right for one person may be very wrong for another.)

Conflicts of Interest

If some diversion of research funds to aid education has been widely sanctioned, the diversion of educational resources to aid research has for longer years been regarded by many faculty as their seigniorial right. The principal resources diverted are the amount of time faculty are supposed to devote to students and to course preparation, and the time graduate students would otherwise devote to their own, rather than their professors', purposes. These common forms of white-collar crime, unindictable in the courts and materially rewarded by most professions and universities, are punishable, if at all, principally by administrators — department chairmen, deans, vice presidents, mayhap even business officers — not normally extolled for upholding the moral standards of academic institutions. André Danière has rightly remarked that "the stealing of time that belongs properly to students — the chipping away of scheduled office hours, tutorial duties, planning and preparation for lectures, etc., to add more footnotes to a forthcoming publication . . . should not be confused with the exercise of essential academic freedoms" and has called for "the more stringent enforcement of better spelled working rules by the colleges and universities concerned."[11]

The conflicts between the interests of faculty and of their students are matched by comparable conflicts between the interests of faculty and of their institutions. Common examples are the use by faculty of secretarial and other institutional services, supplies, and facilities to assist in remunerative professional activities such as the writing of articles, books, and speeches, consulting and editorial work, or the conduct of nonprofessional business.

Finally, there are visible conflicts between the interests of faculty and of granting agencies, the most persistent and intransigent of which lie at the heart of the prevailing system of research support. Such is the dilemma of the man who serves both as an adviser to a granting agency and a recipient of its funds for his own, or his institution's, activities. Indeed, in some cases the same man may determine an agency's policies and programs and even authorize its grants, urge Congress to approve these programs and to appropriate funds for them, and then benefit directly or indirectly from the awards. The uncomfortable position in which eminent professional men and university presidents have thereby been placed was noted by President Truman. Explaining his veto of the first National Science Foundation bill, Truman observed that, under its terms, most members of the Foundation board "would be individuals employed by institutions or organizations eligible for . . . grants. Thus, there is created a conflict of interests which would inevitably give rise to suspicions of favoritism, regardless of the complete integrity of the [board] members . . ."[12] These terms were not, however, altered in the eventual National Science Foundation Act, nor are they essentially different at many other public and private agencies, for the conflict of interest problem is eased legally, but not morally, by designating as "consultants" or "advisers" (rather than as officials with formal policy responsibilities) men who benefit from funds they help to dispense.

No clean solution to this problem is feasible. The men most expert in a particular field are those best qualified to evaluate work in it; hence, to deprive research agencies or Congress[13] of their judgment is to enhance the danger that funds will be ill-spent. Yet to rely on their judgment is to foster a system in which, as Alvin Weinberg has put it, "judge, jury, plaintiff and defendant are usually one and the same."[14] The wisest course may be to require those who render advice to give those who receive it a full statement of their interests so that these can be discounted. Though it cannot be required, it can also be hoped that fewer experts will take a sanctimonious view of their specialty, and more will be able to distinguish its interest to themselves from its usefulness to society.

Malpractices

Simpler to correct are a number of malpractices that have marred the administration of research. One is the receipt of funds for the time a professor devotes to research (which may go either to him as additional income, e.g., for work in the summer or as a consultant's fee, or to his institution for relieving him of real or ostensible teaching responsibilities), when the budgeted time is *not,* in fact, devoted to that research. The wisdom of segmenting a professor's time and salary and collecting bits and pieces of it from different sources may be questioned; but it has swelled the coffers of many universities and professors, and it is only right for them to render fair value for the money received. Nor is it necessary that faculty punch time clocks to abide by this principle. A joint statement issued by the Council of the American Association of University Professors and the American Council on Education has set forth the principle clearly as well as a way to implement it:

> There are competing demands on the energies of a faculty member (for example, research, teaching, committee work, outside consulting). The way in which he divides his effort among these various functions does not raise ethical questions unless the Government agency [or private agency, we may add] supporting his research is misled in its understanding of the amount of intellectual effort he is actually devoting to the research in question. A system of precise time accounting is incompatible with the inherent character of the work of a faculty member, since the various functions he performs are closely interrelated and do not conform to any meaningful division of a standard work week. On the other hand, if the research agreement contemplates that a staff member will devote a certain fraction of his effort to the Government-sponsored research, or he agrees to assume responsibility in relation to such research, a demonstrable relationship between the indicated effort or responsibility and the actual extent of his involvement is to be expected. Each university, therefore, should — through joint consultation of administration and faculty — develop procedures to assure that proposals are responsibly made and complied with.[15]

Often well-intentioned but of dubious propriety (though sanctioned and even encouraged by some agencies) is the nominal proposal by established investigators on behalf of junior men. And there is the Very Important Professor, either a scientist or an entrepreneur at heart, who has so much research parcelled out to so many students and hirelings that some proposal and some report is always coming out of the communal mill; but to establish *which* report represents the outcome of *which* proposal (and, hence, what work should be budgeted to what project) is a considerable feat. Operating more modestly on a similar principle is the man who sells the same work to different clients, which, I suspect, a moderately eminent acquaintance accomplished by first reporting his highly potent findings in confidence to one sponsor and then, in revised (and subsequently published) form, to another. Not knowing the precise terms of each commitment, I would hesitate to charge him with more than shrewd business practice. How many intellectuals can say that they have never sold the same idea and the same, or similar, words to different audiences or publishers?

The Sanctity of a Proposal

How much sanctity should be attached to a proposal, and how much subsequent freedom should the investigator have to modify the proposed research design?

I first encountered this problem when attempting to conduct an "anthropological" study of an English community, for which I had received, in 1948, a fellowship from the Social Science Research Council. Before long, the enormity and vanity of the task appalled me. I felt like the Frenchman "who, having been three weeks here, proposed to write a book on England; who, after three months, found that he was not quite ready; and who, after three years, concluded that he knew nothing about it."[16] What passed for anthropological "theory" and "method" served well enough, perhaps, their original function of surveying for a Western audience grosser aspects of the life of illiterate peoples unable to correct the errors that thus became enshrined as scholarship. But their utter inadequacy for the analysis of the life of a sophisticated, literate people was patent.

Having reached this conclusion, I should doubtless have discussed it, and the alternative study I proposed to conduct, with the SSRC. They were, however, remote, whereas a distinguished British anthropologist was at hand. He assured me that changes of this sort were commonplace, and that I should have no compunction about changing my initial goal. He was a man of experience, disinterest, and distinction, and I took his advice. Probably he was right, particularly as mine was a "research training fellowship" which put "great emphasis . . . on getting predoctoral students 'out of their ruts' in both a geographical and a disciplinary sense . . .,"[17] a purpose, if anything, better served by the study I eventually completed. But I have always felt somewhat incredulous and guilty about the episode.

On the current research scene, this problem has proved troublesome to Federal agencies for a complex of legal, administrative, moral, and scientific reasons. Clearly, it makes no sense for an investigator who gets into a *cul de sac* to stay there because that is where his original proposal has led him. But it does not follow that all investigators should therefore be free to change their methods and objectives without their patron's consent. The latter view is approximated by some, as Jeanne Watson suggests in her account of the 1955–59 "sociability project" directed by Nelson Foote and David Riesman:

> Foote and Riesman both seem willing to discard the specific proposal if a better one can be devised, and they say that NIMH [the National Institute of Mental Health], also, encourages grantees to do what seems reasonable and not to be bound by what they have put in writing. (NIMH policy is explicit that a research proposal is not a contract and that grantees have discretion to change it as the work develops.) [18]

By contrast, Raymond Woodrow, Director of Research Administration at Princeton, and highly experienced in these matters, asserts,

> It is naive for any scientist or institution to expect freedom to change drastically the whole scope or purpose of either grant or contract without approval of the sponsoring agency. To act otherwise would make a mockery of the elaborate reviewing system used to decide whether a research proposal warrants support. [19]

With appropriate interpretations of words like "specific," "reasonable," "discretion," "drastically," and "whole," these two positions are not as contradictory as they appear; and, in part, their divergence reflects a tightening of regulations from the days of the Foote-Riesman project to 1964, when Woodrow was speaking. But there remains a delicate line between permissible and impermissible changes that the unwary may cross. The only safe course one can advocate is: When in doubt, *ask*. The same principle applies to shifts in the use of government grant funds from the budgetary lines (for salaries, equipment, travel, publication, overhead, and the like) designated at the time of the award. As private foundation grants and lump sum government contracts commonly afford more financial flexibility, they are often preferred.

The Course of Research

Most of the troubling ethical problems that arise during the course of research, in my experience, involve the investigator's relations with his informants rather than with his sponsor. These include such questions as whether full honesty about his purpose is practicable (it may take more time than is available to explain, or require specialized knowledge the informant lacks; and, when gathering information, the investigator may not even know the use to which it will later be put) or compatible with that purpose (if personal sympathy with an informant is necessary to elicit honest information, by the same token that information becomes a form of affectionate response and its subsequent use in an "objective" — i.e., depersonalized — context can constitute a kind of emotional betrayal).[20] We cannot do more than refer to these problems here; they have been discussed by a number of writers, including, recently and forcefully, Edward Shils.[21]

Something more may, however, be said about the investigator's communications with his sponsor as the research progresses. The communications often diminish after the award is made and subsist at a low ebb until the report-writing stage is approached.[22] Money and recognition in hand (if, perhaps, less of each than had been hoped for), the investigator proceeds with his work which, in the natural course of (historical, personal, and scientific) events, takes turns that had not and could not have been envisaged when the proposal was drafted. The obvious rule for meeting resultant contingencies is to take them up with the sponsor and reach an agreed solution. Often enough, this can be done quite satisfactorily: neither side has an interest in failure; each has reason to respect the other, and small problems can be brushed away and larger ones resolved by honest confrontation. I have seen (or, more strictly, heard) a critical problem disposed of, thus, in a candid two-minute telephone conversation between the head of a research institution and the head of a granting agency; and another project was hobbled by a similar conversation between two other men, one of whom had needlessly yielded the issue before he picked up the phone. In these relations between grantee and grantor there is, in a final sense, no simple rule as to who will prevail: one party may be consistently dominant, but ascendancy shifts with the issue and circumstances, and a process of continuing, mutual accommodation ensues.

In the case of a contract, contacts are usually frequent enough to provide a realistic appreciation of the status of the work and the degree to which it is meeting original expectations. But this is less likely to be true in the case of a grant, with its principled separation of sponsor and grantee.

Instances are known in which, after receiving an award, an investigator was never heard from again. The situation is awkward but not unprecedented. Inability to perform and the embarrassment of acknowledging it can produce a painful silence and a lack of response to the polite inquiries of the sponsor who merely financed the work and would like to know what has happened to it.

It is because foundations and government agencies have had sufficient experience with the man who produces nothing, or far less than he sold, that they prize highly those with a record of delivery. In this respect, almost any established research institution has an advantage over the academic investigator, since its officers assume a greater responsibility for the completion of work than do university officials. Unfortunately, that very responsibility may lead to the salvage of work that should be discarded, rather than to a frank acknowledgment of failure and the return of unexpended funds to the sponsor.

It is the investigator's frequent conceit that he knows what should be done and that his sponsor must be tolerated only because he signs the checks. Such an attitude may be deplored on intellectual grounds, for it precludes learning anything from the sponsor, which can be done only by listening to his requests with an open mind.

As an example, I will cite an experience in a 1960–62 study of the effects of federal programs on higher education, which I conducted under a contract that the U.S. Office of Education had signed with the Brookings Institution. Federal programs being heavily concentrated at universities, it was difficult, at best, to investigate their indirect effects on colleges, and to do so adequately complicated the work for which relatively little time and money were available. I therefore recommended that the study be confined to a dozen universities receiving large sums from the government and a dozen receiving smaller sums, and that the dozen liberal arts colleges that were to have been included be omitted. This recommendation the commissioning official at the Office of Education rejected. As it turned out, he was, I think, entirely right. Inclusion of the colleges rendered the work technically more difficult and less tidy, but decidedly more relevant to major issues of government policy; and in passing, I learned something about a significant sector of higher education of which I had previously been ignorant.

The Final Report

This chronicle of moral quandaries may now turn to the final quandary: should the report be published and who should decide what it contains?

The status of the final report is perhaps the single provision that it is most vital to define unequivocally before work is begun. It is perfectly reasonable for a report to be proprietary, though this is not the norm in

academic circles, and there is a tendency to believe that what is not customary in one's circle is wrong for everyone. Many, probably the great majority,
of the most influential reports (i.e., those whose conclusions lead to visible
action) are initially confidential, if we include under the rubric of professional "reports" not only accounts of formal research by accredited social
scientists but comparable, if less stilted, work of staff and advisers to men
managing large affairs. Some of the most professional and effective social
research is conducted on a proprietary basis by organizations like Rand,
the Institute for Defense Analyses, the Psychological Corporation, the Stanford Research Institute, Arthur D. Little, National Analysts, and innumerable
other reputable groups devoted to commercial polling, operations analysis,
economic and stock market forecasting, investment counselling, management
consulting, and so forth. The distaste of many professors for this kind of
arrangement is evident, but then, they should not enter into it. (The
Brookings Institution, by the way, undertakes no proprietary work and reserves the right to publish all reports.)

Freedom to publish is seldom a problem in research grants, which normally anticipate and even finance publication in regular professional channels. Difficulties arise in contracts under which a report may be viewed as
the property of the commissioning agency, as if it were a bolt of cloth that
can be cut and sewn to suit. A writer can prevent the misuse of neither his
proprietary nor published work, but he can disclaim responsibility for views
falsely attributed to him, and, in cases of major abuse, demand a retraction
or take legal action to protect his interests. The best way to deal with these
problems is to forestall them during contract negotiations by such a provision as, for example, requiring that any public report attributed to the
investigator must receive his prior concurrence. The reverse provision, which
requires that publication receive the prior approval of the sponsor, is a common trap in which investigators may be snared.

In Sum

I have sought to review some of the ethical problems that may beset the
relations between those who support and those who conduct research. I do
not share the view that all virtue lies with the pursuit of academic knowledge, all vice with the use of knowledge for practical purposes, and that the
main problem demanding attention is how to get social scientists more money
with fewer restraints. The sponsors of research are not only as human but
as moral as we who ask for money; their native and ineradicable offense is
not their wickedness but their power.

Overall, inexperience, naiveté, and the misapplication of principle are, with little doubt, responsible for more difficulties than downright unscrupulousness. A lot of bargaining goes on in a research relationship, and the sophisticated investigator can strike a better bargain than the novice. Once a bargain has been struck, it should be kept. In an honorable and mature relation between consenting adults, the terms are, as far as possible, understood at the outset, and problems which arise thereafter are faced frankly and jointly resolved.

Notes to the Chapter

1. As reported by faculty at 24 universities. See Harold Orlans, *The Effects of Federal Programs on Higher Education* (Washington, D.C.: Brookings Institution, 1962), 312–13.

2. Lord Bowden, "Expectations for Science," *New Scientist,* 27 (September 30, 1965), p. 853.

3. "Only during the very first days in Moscow had the unproductive but inevitable expenditure, so strange to country folk, yet demanded on all sides, startled Levin. Now he was used to it. In this respect the thing had happened to him which is said to happen to drunkards. 'The first glass you drive in like a stake, the second flies like a crake, and after the third they fly like wee little birds.' When he had changed the first hundred-rouble note to buy liveries for the footman and hall porter, he had involuntarily calculated that those useless liveries — which, however, were absolutely necessary, judging by the surprise of the old Princess and Kitty at his hint that one could do without liveries — would cost as much as the hire of two labourers for the summer months, that is, of one for about three hundred working days . . . — and each a day of heavy labour from early morning till late in the evening. He parted with that hundred-rouble note not without a struggle. The next such note he changed to buy provisions for a family dinner, costing twenty-eight roubles; and though he remembered that twenty-eight roubles was the price of nine chetverts of oats mown, bound into sheaves, threshed, winnowed, sifted, and shovelled with sweat and groans, nevertheless it went more easily than the first. The notes he now changed no longer evoked such calculations, but flew away like wee birds." Leo Tolstoy, *Anna Karenina,* the Maude translation, Vol. II (London: Oxford University Press, 1939), 274–75.

4. "We do try and take care of the individual, but it's hard in a foundation of this size. It's very hard to support individuals without a staff of about one thousand, so we prefer to rely upon other institutions to provide this service for us," Rowan Gaither, President of the Ford Foundation, is quoted as saying. William Whyte, *The Organization Man* (New York: Simon and Schuster, 1956), 231.

A very similar argument was made to the writer by a senior officer of another major foundation.

5. "It is the policy of the Institute that the Fellows themselves frame the research questions they pursue, and that they be able to take independent and critical positions. Since it has seemed essential that the Institute not be financially dependent on government, neither the Institute nor any full-time Fellow may accept a contract or grant from the Federal government." *The First Year 1964* (Washington, D.C.: Institute for Policy Studies, 1964), 2.

6. Cf. the episode recounted by David Riesman: "A friend of mine, who shares the most critical perspectives on Vietnam . . . was asked by a very dedicated and obviously disinterested representative of the Department of Defense to submit proposals for research on Asia which would be in no way classified or restricted as to outcome. . . . Later the same man suggested that my friend go to Saigon and interview Viet Cong prisoners and defectors. My friend . . . on declining was told that this would leave the work in the hands of reactionary people, for it was obvious and was made plain that the declination was on grounds of moral repugnance. . . . My friend was confronted with a good deal of moral ambiguity here, and wasn't sure that the decision not to go may not have been based more on what was convenient and immediately defensible to self and colleagues than on what was right." *Trans-action,* 3 (January–February, 1966), p. 2.

To men of the left, like C. Wright Mills and Alfred Kazin, who criticized intellectuals serving the government (in this instance, the Kennedy administration, but it might have been any other) on the ground that the intellectual's role should be "unremitting hostility to power," Arthur Schlesinger, Jr. has observed that "if intellectuals decided to abandon government to non-intellectuals, they would have only themselves to blame for the result." *A Thousand Days* (Boston: Houghton Mifflin, 1965), 744.

7. E.g., "Believing that research grants from the Department of Defense are a threat to free academic inquiry and inconsistent with the peace principles of the Society of Friends, Haverford College has decided not to accept money from the Department, even for non-military research . . ."*Bulletin of the Atomic Scientists,* 20 (January, 1954), p. 64. Lord Hailsham, the first British Minister for Science, has voiced (but not acted upon) a similar attitude, ". . . that, in the long run, the marriage between science and defence is corrupting, and will at best turn science from a liberating to a destructive force, and at worst dry up the wells of inventiveness in the scientist himself." *Science and Politics* (London: Faber and Faber, 1963), 15.

8. Peter Rossi, "Researchers, Scholars and Policy Makers: The Politics of Large Scale Research," *Daedalus,* 93 (Fall, 1964), p. 1157.

9. Robert Sproull, then Director of the Defense Department's Advanced Research Projects Agency, has observed: ". . . the recipient of Federal funds should

keep himself informed of how his work is being described and defended through the Federal budget process, including the presentation to Congress. It may happen, for example, that basic research is being defended as imminently applicable to practical problems. If the fund recipient believes the defense is wrong he has basically three choices: (1) He can suggest the defense be changed, accepting the risk that funds may be cut. (2) He can go to a different agency. (3) He can continue to accept support on these terms, accepting the risk that a 'day of reckoning' may come. It follows that he should not cry 'foul' and weep crocodile tears if after the best efforts of the Government agency program manager, the program and his part of it are cut." Robert Sproull, "Science and Technology, Government and Private," address at the Symposium Dedicating the Research and Engineering Center of the Xerox Corporation, Webster, New York, November 12, 1964.

10. See the *Journal of the American Medical Association* (June 3, 1961), p. 764.

11. André Danière, *Higher Education in the American Economy* (New York: Random House, 1964), 76–77.

12. *Congressional Record,* November 17, 1947, 10568. Cf. Don Price's comment on this issue: "Any board of part-time general advisers is almost necessarily drawn from the institutions that must benefit from such grants, or from among the professional colleagues of leaders in those institutions. To put such men in a position of complete executive responsibility for the program is to ask them to stand before the Appropriations Committees of Congress and defend a program of grants to themselves or to their friends." *Government and Science* (New York: New York University Press, 1954), 53.

13. Amitai Etzioni, for example, has called for "a new code of ethics . . . to forbid scientists who directly or indirectly receive research funds from a federal agency to testify on its behalf, or — at least — require a full statement of their ties to the agency before testimony is given." *The Moon-Doggle* (New York: Doubleday, 1964), 64. The disclosure requirement, which is practicable and reasonable, should be distinguished from the proposed ban on the testimony of interested experts, which is impracticable (since their views can hardly be suppressed or kept from Congress, even if they are not permitted to testify) and unreasonable (Why should their views not be made known? Even if the objective is to discount their advice, it can only be accomplished by first ascertaining what it *is*).

14. Quoted by Gerard Piel in "The Treason of the Clerks," address at the Annual Meeting of the American Philosophical Society, Philadelphia, April 22, 1965.

15. *On Preventing Conflicts of Interest in Government-Sponsored Research at Universities* (Washington, D.C.: American Council on Education, December, 1964).

16. Herbert Spencer, *The Study of Sociology* (New York: D. Appleton & Co., 1929), 91.

17. *Fellows of the Social Science Research Council 1925–1951* (New York, 1951), vi.

18. David Riesman and Jeanne Watson, "The Sociability Project," in Philip Hammond (ed.), *Sociologists at Work* (New York: Basic Books, 1964), 245 and 317. The sentence put in parentheses appears in the text as a footnote on p. 317.

19. Raymond Woodrow, "Grants vs. Contracts in Government-Sponsored Research," address to American Council on Education Conference on Research Administration in Colleges and Universities, Mayflower Hotel, Washington, D.C., October 8, 1964.

20. Cf. the perceptive observation of Father Fichter, the sociologist and priest: ". . . is it morally permissible for the sociologist to report *all the truth* he has discovered in his investigation, or are there certain boundaries of human decency which he may not cross? . . . The personal decision on how far to go in scientific objectivity seems to depend on the scientist's own sense of decency, which in turn is undoubtedly influenced by the prevailing values in the culture and in the practices of fellow-scientists . . . complete objectivity, or telling all the truth in all circumstances, is not necessarily a morally good act." Joseph H. Fichter, *Social Relations in the Urban Parish* (Chicago: University of Chicago Press, 1954), 219–20, 225. The abortive "Code of Ethics" drafted a few years ago by a committee of the American Sociological Association notably failed to heed this point, advocating lax moral standards so long as they served to advance the truth.

21. Edward Shils, "Social Inquiry and the Autonomy of the Individual," in Daniel Lerner (ed.), *The Human Meaning of the Social Sciences* (New York: Meridian Books, 1959), 114–57.

22. Arthur Vidich and Joseph Bensman: "It is part of the rhythm of the total research cycle that the sponsor recedes as an important reference group after the grant has been received and is only again reasserted as a significant other when findings are to be discovered, written, and reported." Arthur Vidich *et al., Reflections on Community Studies* (New York: John Wiley & Sons, 1964), 325.

CHAPTER TWO

The Research Institute and the Pressure Group

JANE CASSELS RECORD

Case One[1]

A mature graduate student works part time as a research assistant in the industrial relations institute of a Midwestern university. His assignment is to study the hiring hall of a local craft union, giving particular attention to the role of the business agent. He finishes the study and writes a manuscript which implicitly praises the union for the efficiency of its dispatchers, the honesty of its officers, and the breadth of its peripheral services to members. One chapter, however, questions the concentration of power in the hands of the business agent; important though it may be for controlling employment and policing work standards, is the concentration compatible with internal democracy?

The institute sends a copy of the manuscript to the business agent and asks for his comments. His response is explosive. He interprets the remarks about internal democracy as a reflection on his integrity as a union leader; he insists that the manuscript, if published as is, will give aid and comfort to "union-busting" employers and place the institute in the ranks of "labor baiters."

A few days later the director of the institute gets a phone call from a national officer of the union, who is on the institute's community advisory committee and has been helpful in recruiting union participants for several educational conferences which the institute sponsors periodically as part of its community service program. He points out that the business agent runs an honest, effective local, as the study itself has concluded; certainly there have been no complaints about his leadership from the members. Why stir up controversy? Why is the institute willing to jeopardize the good which the union can continue to do for workers in the craft?

The research co-ordinator of the institute tells the research assistant about the protests and asks how he would feel about deleting the chapter on internal government. The assistant objects with vigor. The matter is placed before the institute's executive council, composed of senior associates. They agree that the manuscript must not be amended under pressure, but one council member suggests that because the rest of the study can stand on its own, without the offending chapter, no great harm would be done by eliminating it, particularly if it might more suitably be incorporated in another project which is already being discussed: a comparative survey which will focus specifically on the problem of internal democracy in various kinds of union structure. The suggestion is accepted unanimously.

A decade passes. The study of union democracy has yet to be begun.

Case Two

An Eastern university has a research institute in the field of public administration. The institute signs a contract with an established scholar from another campus, who is to examine a problem concerning local governments. The published study will carry the institute's imprimatur.

Several years earlier the contracting scholar wrote a book which contained some implicit criticism of the incumbent administration of one city to be covered in the institute study.

Between the signing of the contract and the commencement of the research the mayor of that city learns of the contract and makes known his displeasure. He expresses it not directly to the institute director but to a mutual acquaintance. The city in question is one of several which have contributed public funds and personnel to institute programs, although the mayor makes no mention of that fact during his conversation with the mutual acquaintance. The latter relays the mayor's discontent to the institute director, who is now in a bind. How can he appease the mayor without offending the scholar and violating academic freedom? A happy solution occurs to him. He telephones the scholar and tells him of the mayor's objection. He assures the scholar that the institute and the university are prepared to stand firm on principle; however, the mayor's opposition has raised some tactical problems. Given the politician's attitude, will the scholar be able to gain access to the kinds of material he would need to do an adequate study?

The scholar thinks he can and says so. The director continues to express qualms. The scholar finally backs away and returns the contract.

Case Three

A young man who has just completed the doctorate accepts an appointment as lecturer in an academic department and associate in one of the research centers of a Western state university. His first project at the center is a study of the collective bargaining relationship of a small union of highly skilled technical employees and a medium-sized industrial corporation. After a year of research he concludes that the relationship has many elements of paternalism and that the concessions the union has gained from management are somewhat inferior to those obtained for similar employees by industrial unions in other plants.

Both company and union expressed concern at the outset of the inquiry about the ability of an "outsider" to get "all the facts straight." They were promised an opportunity to comment on the empirical accuracy of the manuscript, to aid the researcher as well as to safeguard the parties. Now representatives of both company and union protest the researcher's conclusions as "factually unsound." A top management representative, active in the political party currently in power in the state, threatens to "take the matter up with higher authorities." A long conversation between the top manager and the institute director about the distinction between statements of fact and reasoned conclusions as objects of criticism comes to naught. Then the institute director makes a proposal: because extensive revision of the manuscript will be necessary to incorporate the suggestions of several academic critics, and because publication is therefore not imminent, it may be a good idea to table the parties' objections, with the understanding that the discussions will be resumed before the manuscript is sent to the publisher.

Meanwhile the author of the manuscript has begun work on another research project. The institute director suggests that he finish that before revising the first manuscript, to allow time "for tempers to cool." Two years pass. The young research associate accepts a job offer from another university. In the two years he has worked on several studies which fully absorbed his time. The first manuscript, when it was occasionally mentioned in conversations with the institute director, was always referred to as if its revision and publication had been temporarily postponed and would be actively pursued as soon as time permitted. Now that he is leaving, the author asks if he may publish the material as a journal article, without reference to the institute. The director says no; he considers the manuscript to be the property of the institute and says he hopes to issue it eventually, in revised form, as an institute publication.

Another six years pass. The manuscript is now badly out of date. No move has been made to revise it.

Case Four

A federal agency has money for a research project in a metropolitan area. The project will study intensively a minor social problem and develop several experimental programs for remedying it. The agency approaches the research center of a small private university. It happens that two sociologists at the university have done some preliminary work on that problem and are designing a more extensive inquiry, for which they hope to get a foundation grant. The research director sees the possibility of a co-operative venture and invites the two sociologists and several men from other disciplines to discuss with agency representatives the possibility of a research contract. It quickly becomes apparent that the government men want to define the area of inquiry too narrowly. The academicians advise that little confidence can be placed in the findings unless the study has a wider scope. The federal men are adamant. Their insistence puzzles the social scientists because broadening the survey would increase the cost insignificantly in this case. Finally the agency representatives reveal that some of the peripheral areas are "politically untouchable for the present."

As the colloquy proceeds it becomes clear that the agency wishes not only to restrict the scope but also to make certain that it will have considerable control over the findings, particularly where they may refer to its own past activities. The agency would expect to be "consulted on methodology" and kept "informed as the results develop," though it would, of course, "not interfere with the academic objectivity of the research." An economist who has followed the conversation with quiet incredulity asks why the agency does not simply hire its own social scientists to do the study. "We're not in the research business," is the reply; "we want to make use of your know-how and reputation."

The government men leave. The economist argues forcefully against accepting the project. "They made it patent, without actually saying so, what they want us to find and not to find." A political scientist argues against the project on other grounds: even if the center were given a free hand, the time spent on red tape and administrative chores for a project of that size might better be used in individual inquiry by the academicians concerned.

The research director was brought to the campus to build up the center so that bright young academicians with a research orientation could be recruited for the faculty. He needs money. The agency has indicated it can spend $150,000 on the initial study and program design — possibly a great deal more "if things develop well." The research director says he believes the center can retain enough control over the project to make it "academically justifiable."

The contract is signed. One of the sociologists, who has raised some sharp questions about the value of the project and about its administration but who has said he would be willing to work on it at least during the first stages, to see how much sound inquiry might be salvaged, is never asked to participate, although the subject area is one in which he has something of a national reputation.

The Incidence and the Question

The events described in these four cases raise serious ethical questions about the relationships of academic research institutions to the special interest groups, private or public, whose policies and practices become the object (and sometimes the source) of inquiry. How often such groups have attempted to frustrate inquiry, to dictate its shape, to suppress or modify its findings, and with what degree of success, are difficult to determine or even to estimate with confidence. My own file of cases now exceeds a dozen. The fact that so many cases could come, unsought, to the attention of a single person in less than fifteen years, through personal observation or by the careful reporting of colleagues whose high repute evokes confidence in their accuracy, suggests that the incidence is not negligible.

Moreover, the disquieting impact of individual cases is not assuaged by close examination of what has happened during the past twenty years to the organization of scholarly inquiry and to the structure of many special interest groups which scholars have attempted to study. One salient development, for example, is the replacement of the individual by the team, the group, the institute as the dominant unit in academic research. The *reasons* for that development are well known, having been discussed extensively in the technical journals and elsewhere. Less attention has been paid to the *implications* which the institutionalization of research may have for the scope and quality of inquiry, particularly in sensitive areas of the social sciences. Certainly the question of whether an institute is even more sensitive to the disapproval of increasingly sophisticated interest groups, more vulnerable to their pressure, and more accommodative of their needs than an individual researcher would be has educed small discourse. Yet that is a question which should be discussed with candor.

Institutional Vulnerability

The institute has several needs which make it vulnerable to the pressure of special interest groups. The first of the needs is money. Large-scale research is expensive. If the institute is part of a state university, some of its money comes from the legislature, as part of the approved budget of the university. Just as the institute may be competitive with other sectors of the university for a greater share of the university budget, the university is competitive with other public institutions for a greater share of the total budget. In fact, one campus may compete with another for public funds. Even if the institute relies more heavily on federal and private funds than on state appropriations, it is part of the university and can be "gotten at" by interest groups within the state. Moreover, neither federal money not private grants are beyond the reach of partisan interests.

Naturally institutions of higher learning seek friends in the larger community. But powerful allies can become powerful enemies. A political administration that has been generous to the university may find its enthusiasm dampened by an institute study which indicates that some of the local party councils have been infiltrated by radical rightists or leftists. A large industry enjoying special tax treatment may resist having the subsidy examined by sharp young economists. Pluralist groups whose particularistic interests could be contravened by critical inquiry not only carry weight with state legislators but may even be represented on the university's board of trustees.

One way that the research institute may win public acceptance is to demonstrate its usefulness to the community by subsidiary public service projects such as training programs and educational conferences for union leaders, company executives, government officials, school administrators or similar groups. To help recruit for such programs — and for other purposes — the institute often establishes a community advisory group, to which it becomes indebted; and that debt may make its research program more vulnerable to pressure.

The degree to which academicians have become sensitive to the importance of a favorable image for gaining financial support is illustrated by a recent incident. A new campus of the state university had been established in a large midwestern city. The social science division proposed a research center for the interdisciplinary study of urban problems, and an interdepartmental committee was appointed to draft a detailed plan. At its first meeting the committee discussed methods of inducing the local business community to throw its weight behind greater legislative appropriations for the new campus, including funds for establishing the research center. Someone suggested that it would be helpful if key persons in the local power structure could be made to see that the proposed center might serve their interests. One committee member went so far as to propose that the university's public relations officer, a skilled politician who had the confidence of the business community, be consulted on the matter.

A political scientist expressed the fear that community support might be purchased at the expense of the research program's integrity. "Would getting business backing for the center mean that we couldn't touch the problem of housing, for example, because one of the most powerful of the local bigwigs is a slum landlord?"

There was general agreement that there must be no hobbling of objective research but that it might be "realistic to go slow on controversial subjects until the center is firmly established," with enough prestige and momentum to withstand the efforts of interest groups to influence its direction.

Though state universities and their research institutes are especially assailable, private institutions are far from free of pressure. They, too, need money, which often comes from sensitive groups or from individuals associated with such groups. The governing boards and fund-raising committees, to say nothing of alumni organizations, are reflective of, and may be the vehicles of pressure from, special interests.

What about the private foundations which support research; are they not above the fray? Not always, unfortunately. Sometimes the uses to which funds may be put are restricted by the founders. Some years ago a young sociologist asked a small social welfare foundation for a grant to study the employment experiences of several ethnic groups. His application was approved by the academic advisory committee and he was notified that the grant would be awarded, only to have it withdrawn shortly thereafter. The foundation administrator explained that the heirs of the original donor were "quite conservative" and preferred to finance research in other subject areas.

Even if founders give administrators a free hand, the foundations are institutions with internal needs of their own, which are not necessarily consonant with the requirements of scholarly research, as borne out by the experiences of an academician in a project financed by a prominent foundation. A large grant had been given to public and private agencies working in concert to arrest the cultural deterioration of an old neighborhood near the heart of an Eastern city, where rapid in-migration was taking place. One of the strings attached to the grant was the requirement that an experienced scholar be employed to evaluate the effectiveness of the co-ordinated remedial programs of law enforcement groups, schools, social work agencies, and other participants in the project.

After considerable delay a university professor was employed with the understanding, at least on his part, that he would be given a free hand to set up the research program. He soon discovered, however, that many of the agencies were reluctant to make their records available unless they could "see" in advance any reports he might make of their activities. Indeed, the project's executive council, composed of the heads of the co-operating agencies, eventually passed a resolution requiring that the reports of the research director be approved by the council before they were submitted to the foundation.

Unfortunately, lines of authority had not been spelled out in the project charter. The first grant had been for two years, subject to renewal for another three years if the achievements of the agencies during the initial period appeared to warrant the extension. More than a year had passed before the research director was hired. As the time for evaluation of the first two years neared, the research director urged the foundation to make renewal of the grant contingent upon the agencies' acceptance of an independent research program. But the agencies had qualms not only concerning frailties which the researcher might reveal to the foundation about the project as a whole but also concerning interagency comparisons which might become known to "outsiders" locally.

The project had received a great deal of favorable publicity nationally. Not to renew the grant would call for explanations, perhaps would precipitate controversy, with considerable unpleasantness. It is not difficult to understand why the foundation renewed the grant without clarifying the role of the research director. Administrators generally abhor conflict. Dissent and controversy are inimical to order and stability, which are the norms of efficient administration. Furthermore, once a large grant has been given to a project, the foundation and its staff have an equity in the project's "success." For the project to fail or to abort would call into question the efficacy of the original plan, and, by implication, the judgment of the foundation administrators.

The research director presented the issue to the project's academic advisory committee, a group of distinguished academicians from local campuses, who had agreed to meet periodically to give counsel for the project as a whole but particularly for the research program. The research director urged the committee to protect the contribution which objective scrutiny of the experimental programs might make to knowledge in the critical field of urban problems. He also pointed out that if the advisory committee did not insist upon removal of the research function from the authority of the project's executive council, the prestige of the academic community might be extended to "captive" research.

The advisory committee after long discussion declined to take action. It would be naive to attribute their failure to act to their interest in per diem fees. The committee members were busy men. To have engaged the issue would have meant involving themselves in distasteful, time-consuming, energy-draining altercation.

Some of the committee members headed or were closely associated with research institutes on their respective campuses — institutes which had developed various interrelationships with several of the project agencies, as sources of research data or of participants in service programs. Pursuit of the issue in question would have risked alienation of the agencies, to say nothing of the foundation.

The research director resigned and the job was redefined as "advisory" to the agencies in setting up their own evaluative surveys. As a concession to "objective research" the foundation decided to let specific contracts to academic research institutes to study particular aspects of the project; however, before any studies began, the designs would be submitted to the project executive council by the research institute for approval or rejection. The head of the institute which signed the first research contract explained to the former research director of the project that, though the project's research arrangements raised some serious ethical questions, the research institute, which was relatively new, badly needed the funds.

Money and public favor are not the only needs which make research institutions vulnerable to the pressure of special interests. Research centers also need access to sources of information, as indicated earlier, and some of the sources are special interest groups, whose primary reason for being is not to provide subject matter for scholars; in truth, their particularist interests may be antithetical to objective research in specific instances.

Unlike the individual researcher, who is apt to define his relationship to an interest group in the context of a single study, the research institute needs to develop continuing associations, to maintain open pipelines over long periods of time. The individual scholar may move on, but the institute remains. Its purposes, needs, reputation, image, and rationale are closely bound up with, yet distinct from, the purposes, needs, reputation, image, and rationale of its individual staff members at any one moment and certainly of the personnel as it changes over time.

Interviews, the provision of file materials, and other accommodations of research are encroachments on the time of busy staff members in the organization being studied. Why should they take the time if the results might bring disfavor on the organization in any way? Even the rare executive who views the accommodation of objective research as a social responsibility or as a valuable contribution to the improvement of his own organization may have institutional responsibilities which would compel him to try to exercise some control over the shape and use of the final report. No interest group can afford to be indifferent to what the researchers may find. Because he understands this, the research administrator may agree to submit the first draft of the manuscript to the organization for its appraisal. He needs to do that anyway, as an aid in freeing the manuscript of factual error and misinterpretation of historical material. But the hazards of the situation are patent, even in those cases where the research institute stated from the outset that it would not be bound by the organization's suggestions.

Perhaps the single most important determinant of the degree of cooperation an institute can gain for new studies is its reputation for "responsibility" and "trustworthiness" in previous projects. To maintain access to organizations in its area, the institute must develop a working relationship which embodies mutual confidence. Often the institute's community advisory committee helps it to gain entree to specific groups and to achieve "respectability" among the organizations which operate in its fields of study. By their explicit or implicit endorsement committee members risk the displeasure of their community associates, even the reprimand of their own organizations, if friction develops between those groups and institute researchers; protection of committee members therefore may become an additional charge upon the institute.

Institutional Accommodation

When the individual researcher working independently accedes to pressure from a special interest group, the moral implications are difficult to ignore. If the manuscript belongs to him, the choice is his; and he cannot escape responsibility for the decision.

Within an institutional setting, on the other hand, the locus of responsibility is often not so clear. If the research is paid for by the institute, the manuscript belongs to it rather than to the researcher, unless a contrary arrangement was made in advance. If the institute owns the manuscript, the ultimate decision about whether to publish it immediately in its original form or to amend, delay, or withhold it resides in the institute. The separation of the actual research function from control over the findings is a key to the research institute's capacity to accommodate pressure. For just as the researcher is not likely to have the same sense of identity, commitment, and responsibility that the top administrator feels toward the institute, the administrator is not likely to have the same sense of identity, urgency, commitment and confidence that the researcher feels toward the manuscript.

In the institutional setting scholarly inquiry may become not a first principle — the *sine qua non,* the *raison d'être* — but merely one of many values to be represented in the final decision. In addition to career advancement, obligation to family, and professional ethics there is the welfare of the institution (the university as well as the research institute) with which the institute administrator must concern himself. The result is apt to be a compromise of the competing values.

Often the issue is eventually defined as the researcher's interest in the integrity of a particular manuscript versus the institute's survival, rather than as the institute's interest in research integrity versus the institute's survival. If the question is posed in the first manner, the answer is virtually inevitable (just as the answer was inevitable when the pre-Warren Supreme Court defined civil liberties issues as the individual's right to freedom of speech versus the public interest in national security rather than as the public interest in freedom of speech versus the public interest in national security.)

The director of an institute may be a scholar, but he also heads a bureaucracy, and an administrator does not become the first minister of an institution in order to preside over its liquidation, or even its diminishment. In time he tends to identify his own needs and interests with those of the institution, and they become so identified in the eyes of others. To the degree that the administrator takes pride in the achievements of an institution he is likely to react defensively to anything which threatens it. In his state of alarm he tends to magnify the threat. If it can be removed or averted by a small compromise, why not? What are a few paragraphs in a single manuscript compared to all the good which the institution has done — and can continue to do, if its sources of funds and access to information are not impaired by reprisals from pressure groups? The fact that such decisions are seriatim rather than simultaneous contributes to accommodativeness because the choice which confronts the administrator in each instance is between the welfare of the institute and a single compromise. In other words, the accommodation is piecemeal rather than all of a piece. The issue is never posed as the institute's preservation versus the totality of compromises.

Thus even when a challenge is met head-on, the result is likely to be appeasement. But a second key to the institution's capacity for accommodation is its ability to blunt, to blur, to dilute, to divert, to evade, to defer, to diffuse (or de-fuse) the issue. No manuscript, for example, is perfect; there are almost always suggestions for revision from academic appraisers who have been asked to read it critically. The line between that kind of criticism and the protest of special interest groups as a rationale for discarding or tabling a manuscript can become hazy. Moreover, once a decision to delay is made, the lapse of time itself often takes care of the matter; the material becomes dated, the author may move on.

Indeed, there may be no need for an edict to delay. Getting a study into published form entails positive, often grueling effort. Dust has gathered on many a manuscript which never evoked the slightest controversy. Sometimes the suppression of a manuscript may require no negative act of censorship but merely the absence of a positive commitment to bring the manuscript to fruition.

The institutional milieu recruits its personnel selectively. What kind of person, for example, gravitates toward the top administrative post in an academic research institute? It is the man who can make the necessary kinds of decisions with least discomfort, the man who can take comfort in salvaging something for principle out of the conflicting needs and values which converge upon him. The idealist, the hair-splitter, the cross-grained individualist tends to resign, to be eased out, or never to have been attracted to the directorship — perhaps not even to the institute — in the first place.

The administrative mentality moves almost instinctively toward conciliation, consensus, *rapprochement.* The administrator perceives his position as medial, his function as mediatory. The art of the possible is his forte. His approach to empirical truth may become more "consensory" than objective. Unfortunately, that perspective is more suitable to the legislative process or the collective bargaining table than to scholarly research.

Even more valuable to the university and the institute than the administrator's skill in mediating controversy may be his skill in avoiding it. There are so many subjects to be investigated, so many ideas to be explored, so many hypotheses to be tested that all the institutes taken together could not exhaust them in the foreseeable future. Why, then, pick topics which might lead to trouble? The choice is not between controversial research and no research at all. Moreover, even in sensitive areas the inquiry often can be shaped to the general rather than to the specific.

There is a temptation to set up a contrast between moral men and amoral institutions; that formulation of the issue, however, would not give proper import to the fact that institutional decisions are made by men. The essential difference between the individual and the institution as research entities is that the institutional structure permits the ethical question to be masked. The author of a manuscript which is the property of the institute can accept no moral responsibility for its final form or disposition, because responsibility is commensurate with authority. If the final decision is made by an executive committee, responsibility is dispersed, and the weight of it felt by individual committee members may be fractional. Even when the ultimate decision rests solely on the director, the life processes of the institution may allow the issue to be reshaped, the values to be compromised, in such a way as to preserve the illusion of having salvaged and made consonant the best of two worlds which in reality are often incompatible.

The Sophisticated Researchee

Unlike materials under the scrutiny of the physicist or the astronomer, the researchee of the social scientist is alive — and may soon be kicking. And the toe of the boot is likely to be aimed at a vulnerable spot. A union leader about whom some midly unfavorable, fully documented remarks were made in a study initiated in the research center of a state university complained to the AFL-CIO headquarters in the capital, where the executive director had close relations with the governor, and also to a union official on the university's board of directors. The study was eventually shelved; whether the research center's action (or inaction) was prompted solely by pressure or not, the union leader considered it a victory.

Social science research encompasses close examination of the economic, political, and social institutions which are the substance of society. Those institutions have tended to become increasingly bureaucratized and sophisticated during the past twenty or thirty years. Sophistication often has heightened not only defensiveness but also defensibility regarding criticism.

Organizations give cooperation to the researcher for a variety of reasons: attention from the academic world may be flattering; there may be personal relationships between an organization official and the researcher or his superiors; the study may be perceived as useful to the organization as a whole or to some faction within it; the findings may be more valuable or less hazardous if the organization cooperates than they might be if it stands aloof; organization officials may wish to aid objective inquiry — or at least to avoid the appearance of frustrating it — in the public interest. Providing the subject matter for scholarly inquiry, however, is at most a subordinate objective of the organization. Cautious administrators are apt to take precautions against the possibility of injury. The unpolished administrator may bluntly demand control over the findings as the *quid pro quo* for opening the files to outsiders; he may even insist on a written agreement to that effect.

But there are subtler methods. The knowledgeable administrator knows how to handle the matter in a manner less offensive to academic sensibilities. Understandings can be informal, articulation oblique. The sophisticated administrator is aware of the kinds of values which his counterpart in the research institute must judge; he knows or makes it a point to learn the reputation of the institute for tact and practicality.

The product of academic research has become increasingly valuable to nonacademic institutions, both as an internal aid and as a potential weapon against rivals. In fact, it is now common for such institutions to initiate studies of their own by hiring academicians or letting contracts to academic research centers, although the focus in this paper is, of course, upon research which is initiated by scholars and to which the researchee is asked to contribute information rather than financial support.

The unease with which any organization, especially if it operates in sensitive or controversial fields, is likely to view research projects by outsiders is not hard to explain. Findings critical to the organization may cause it to lose face, force, friends, or funds. Critiques by noneducationists of school curricula and teaching methods, for example, particularly after Sputnik, roused public concern and drew a defensive reaction from the education establishment. A private social work agency lost contributions of volunteer services and money to a rival organization in a California community when the rival publicized a few critical comments contained in the report of an academic researcher who had received the cooperation of the first agency in making the study.

Another case concerns a political scientist associated with an academic research center in a southwestern city who studied the participation of labor organizations in municipal politics and found that in the previous two elections union support had gone overwhelmingly to the incumbent administration. His report, which discussed in considerable detail the money, precinct workers, amplifying equipment, and other aids contributed by unions or their members, was used effectively in anti-union segments of the electorate by the opposition party during the next campaign. Though the incumbent regime was returned to office, its leaders and irate union officials made their displeasure known to the director of the research center and vowed never to cooperate with it again.

A leader of a Negro protest organization, approached by a research team that wished to examine the composition of its membership and its relations with other civil rights groups, was friendly but hesitant. An educated, thoughtful man, he readily acknowledged the value of such inquiry; yet his first commitment, certainly in the immediate future, was to racial equality rather than to objective research.

"Sure, we have our differences with other civil rights organizations," he said, "and I think the questions about protest techniques are important. But the issues which separate us are as nothing compared to the need for unity, and I am reluctant to encourage a study which might play up our intergroup squabbles, perhaps giving ammunition to the racists."

A typical rationalization of such defensive reaction to criticism or unwanted revelation pivots on the importance of the organization to the welfare of the community as a whole or of the publics which the organization serves. Even if the value of research findings as a contribution to knowledge is granted by the organization under scrutiny, scholarly inquiry almost certainly will weigh short in the minds of particularist leaders when hung against the contribution which their institution, "unencumbered," can make to the common good.

It is no longer unusual for business enterprises, labor unions, farmers organizations, veterans associations, political parties, religious denominations, school administrations, protest movements and similar special interest groups to have, in addition to their own research programs, other specialized staff functions which require a professional corps. Frequently the professional staff have graduate degrees. Not only do the professionals set up internal research projects, supervise archives, service libraries, develop educational programs, and the like; they also provide defense in depth against critics.

The union or corporation research director with a Ph.D. knows what is going on in the academic world. He reads the technical journals; nothing printed about his organization is likely to escape him. And it is to him that academic researchers seeking information are likely to be referred. He speaks their language. He knows what they are up to. Sometimes he serves as a buffer between the probing researcher and the organization's line officials, who may be less discreet and knowledgeable than he is.

One doctoral candidate in a private university, seeking material for his dissertation, wrote the head of an organization to ask for an interview and received a reply from the research director, to whom the letter had been handed, suggesting that the student drop by and talk with him. After a lengthy conversation with the research director, the student, on his way out of the building, happened to run into the head of the organization, whom he recognized from newspaper photographs, and after introducing himself asked if he could have a few minutes for an interview. The organization leader, an outspoken and friendly person, talked frankly to the student for nearly two hours. A few days later the chairman of the student's academic department received a curt letter from the organization's research director; unless students were willing to proceed through "proper channels," he warned, the organization would discontinue all interviews and other research co-operation with members of the university community.

There was a time when organizations were not cautious, but it has become increasingly unlikely that the unannounced, uncredentialed researcher will be received with warmth. Arrangements, interpersonal or interinstitutional, must be made. The administrative official or the professional, preoccupied by organization affairs, has to be selective toward the growing number of investigators, casual and serious, who make demands upon his time. Naturally he tends to select those whose projects promise to be most useful and least risky.

Just as the line administrators of academic research institutes and of social organizations which may become the objects of research tend to develop mutual understanding and confidence, so do the staff men. They may attend the same professional society meetings; their social paths may cross. They have common areas of interest, similar problems in relating themselves to the nonprofessionals of their respective institutions. In addition, there are professional sensitivities, niceties, points of protocol which forge bonds of varying strength.

Of course, the accoutrements of professionalism can be manipulated to one's advantage. As personal relationships develop among the administrative and professional personnel of the researching and the researched institutions, criticism may take on the character of a breach of friendship. Perhaps most importantly, representatives of the research institute and the special interest groups may come to know each other's needs and vulnerabilities and to develop patterns of mutual accommodation.

The Research Apprenticeship

Many young academicians serve an important part of their apprenticeship in research institutes. For prestige, training, or financial aid, graduate students seek institute fellowships and appointments to work on projects of their own under the general supervision of the institute staff, or as junior members of a research team, or as research assistants to senior men. The publication-hungry young instructor or assistant professor gravitates toward the institute, particularly if the research he is interested in requires costly human or mechanical assistance.

Partly because it is easier for the foundations to give away millions of dollars in a few large grants to institutes than to split the money into many small grants to individuals, institutes serve increasingly as the middlemen of research. Even when a large grant is given to an individual scholar (and an important consideration in faculty or institute appointments these days is ability to attract research money), the research institute may perform medial functions, from routine administration upward. Institutes also perform an important acculturation function, for within their halls some of the folkways of academe are transmitted from one generation to another.

The unambitious and the unindustrious are not likely to subject themselves to the doctoral grind. Typically, the novice academician is an able young man eager to get ahead. If his origins are lower or lower-middle class, academic achievement, in addition to its intrinsic value, represents upward social mobility.

Like his professorial elders he is torn between the concept of the faculty as an academic guild, with a collective responsibility to protect free inquiry and other scholastic values, and the concept of the faculty as a group of individuals competing for recognition and reward. He feels the heft of many loyalties and responsibilities: to himself, to his wife and children, to a few individual professors, to the institute, to the university, to the profession, to truth, to society; and he learns to avoid, if he possibly can, situations which fractionate him by setting one loyalty or responsibility against another. He learns what questions to ask or not to ask, and of whom. The shelved manuscript, the taboo area of inquiry, and the other compromises, plus the institutional manner of defining issues, are part of his education. Rarely are the institutional mores bluffly articulated. He absorbs them not by formal indoctrination but by observation, by gossip, by the oblique reference and the cynical shrug. Or he may witness a revered professor cutting corners or recoiling from controversy. The chances are that his schooling in the facts of life began long before he reached the institute. Heroism is not the spirit of the times; righteous indignation is as outmoded as the Essex.

The apprentice's closest associations within a large institute are likely to be with other junior men moving up the ladder of academic progression or with the kind of marginal persons that institutes tend to collect as part of their staffs: the faculty wife (perhaps antinepotism rules prevent a regular appointment); the perennial graduate student or "all but"; the refugee from the world of commerce; the campus hanger-on and the geographically committed who would rather be peripheral to that university than to have full faculty status elsewhere; and so on. The insecurity of the marginal person tends to make him especially uneasy in controversy and therefore especially accommodative of pressure if, in spite of his precautions, it occurs. Certainly he does not wish to make trouble for his benefactors within the institute. From him, among others, the young intern learns the (perhaps magnified) hazards of offending certain groups.

A manuscript the apprentice produces is usually subjected to rigorous scrutiny by superiors, who may deal with it harshly on academic grounds. Perhaps the prose needs to be sobered, the excesses pruned, the glandular leakages stanched, the reasoning honed, even if the material is not "controversial." If the findings are likely to step upon sensitive toes, it is especially important to remember that there is more than one way of stating facts and conclusions. But it is not always easy to perceive where the canons of courtesy and scholastic probity leave off and undue regard for the sensitivities of special interest groups begins as a basis for amendment. The boundary between tempering and tampering is hard to fix.

The top men in the institute are frequently senior faculty members whose institute duties are added to a full teaching load. They sit on the committees which examine doctoral candidates and on the committees which make promotion and tenure decisions regarding junior faculty men. The relationship of the research apprentice to his supervisor may therefore extend beyond the institute.

Acknowledgment of the apprentice's research contribution ranges all the way from sole authorship to a mere mention in the preface. The fuller the credit the greater the boost to his career, but even the mention can be helpful in job hunting. Small wonder, then, academic emphasis on publication being what it is, that the apprentice does not jeopardize acknowledgment lightly. Especially would he be reluctant to invest months of effort in a study whose manuscript might be delayed or permanently put aside.

Even if he has reason to believe that the institute would stand firm under pressure, he must reckon with the possibility that as a consequence he may be associated in the director's mind with a discomfiting experience. The harassed administrator who has enough problems in the regular course of operations is apt to regard with something less than fervency the young man who adds to his troubles, especially if the administrator believes the institute's welfare to be contravened in the process. Forcing his seniors to confront the issue baldly is scarcely an endearing trait in the young academician.

A college president with a relatively good record on academic freedom once said to a faculty committee, after he had just been through a siege of abusive phone calls and other forms of pressure for affirming the right of a social science department to include a leftwing speaker in an open forum, "I figure that even the most discreet faculty member can run into public criticism, but if the same man gets me and the college into hot water a second time I begin to wonder if there isn't something wrong with either his politics or his judgment."

Codes of Ethics

The replacement of the ivied cloister by the multiversity, with its absorption in the world of commerce and power, has posed for the academician a wide range of moral questions. A few professional societies have attempted to deal with the issues by developing formal codes of ethics. In the social sciences the psychologists and the sociologists have taken that approach, and the codes in those cases deal more fully with client relationships — counseling, consulting and research contracting — than with the attempts of pressure groups to modify or suppress independent scholarly inquiry. "Ethical Standards of Psychologists," issued by the American Psychological Association in 1953, does not discuss specifically the central question raised here; yet the "incidents" it records illustrate the vitality of interest groups and the range of problems they pose for the academic community. For instance, in the section on "Issues Involving Social Values, Such As Racial Or Religious Prejudice, Freedom of Speech, Freedom of Research, Etc." the following illustration is given:

> A member of a special interest group wrote the chairman of a well-established committee of the APA suggesting that a representative of his group be appointed to the committee and clearly stating that if this appointment was not made the committee could expect no support for its recommendations from the members of the particular group.[2]

In the chapter on "Ethical Standards in Research" the following incident is related:

> In the development of a research project sponsored by a professional society, it was agreed by the social scientists involved that certain highly controversial areas would need to be explored in the interviews to be made. Before the

contract for the project was signed, there was full and frank discussion of the principle that the investigators must have complete freedom to include for investigation topics which they deemed essential with authority to formulate the relevant questions as they saw fit. Full cooperation was sought from representatives of the sponsoring organization, but their role was defined as consulting and advisory, rather than executive in any way. Subsequent developments seemed to underscore the desirability of threshing out this question in advance.[3]

In 1960 the American Sociological Association's new Committee on Professional Ethics decided to collect and consider "critical incidents which either directly or indirectly raise ethical problems involving the behavior of sociologists,"[4] as the first step in developing a code of ethics. The first draft of a code was submitted to the Association in 1964 in mimeographed form and was tabled. The preface reported that the Committee had become aware of

two rather opposite points of view among sociologists, both of which will lead those who hold them to be seriously critical of this Code. The first stands for the proposition that sociologists inevitably intervene in the situations that they study, that a research problem is always framed from a particular perspective and its results always reflect that perspective. This amounts to saying that there is no such thing as the role of an objective sociologist because our values enter into the manner in which we pose research problems. Holders of this view believe that any Code of Ethics, like this one, based upon the assumption that it is a sociologist's duty to be neutrally objective in his professional role is flying in the face of reality.

The other negative standpoint does not so much criticize the nature of the Code as hold it to be unnecessary. The partisans of this view believe that we are primarily scientists, that the American Sociological Association is a learned society, and that we have no ethical problems not shared by all scientists. This Committee is not persuaded that this is the case. We believe that to be a devotee of our discipline means to be brought into many situations where the pursuit of truth is complicated by relations to other people that are ethically problematic. It is in the hope that sociologists will welcome help in these situations that this Code is presented.[5]

With less than adequate precision and certainly not exhaustively, the proposed code for sociologists explores problems created by pressure groups. After observing that sociological research is often directed at collectivities whose representatives "may perceive sociological knowledge as potentially damaging or harmful to their welfare"[6] the Committee suggests that the sociologist "has an obligation to protect the identity of social groups or collectivities. Such protection, however, should be balanced against possible harm to social science coming from lack of communication within the scientific community."[7]

After noting that sociologists "often find it necessary to enter into consent agreements with representatives of social groups or collectivities to gain access to them" and that such agreements "raise ethical questions about what conditions can be made a matter of agreement and what comprises violation of them,"[8] the Committee suggests as the governing principle that the sociologist "is obligated to observe agreements made as a basis for entry into an organization even when it [reference unclear] interferes with scientific goals" but that at the same time "the sociologist should not enter into such agreements if he knows [or even suspects?] that they will infringe upon his scientific goals."[9]

Perhaps the most interesting part of the code for the central question of this paper is contained in a section called "Propriety of Censorship by Administrative Superiors." The Committee observes that in a research agency an administrative superior may wish to alter the research reports of professional investigators

> for a number of reasons, some of them ethically justifiable, others not. If it is to make the presentation more accurate or more readable, there can be no objection. If his agency is one that is subject to political pressures and he feels the manuscript goes beyond objective analysis to embarrassing advocacy of policy, he may require the elimination of such advocacy. But if, on the other hand, he is motivated by a desire to cover up methodological errors which the author has confessed, or to suppress conflicting evidence to make the research results appear "solid," the ethical lapse is clear.[10]

What cries out to be stated unequivocally at this point is that findings of fact and reasoned conclusions, if they are free of error and advocacy, shall not be tampered with as a concession to political pressures. If the omission was an oversight, the oversight is unfortunate.

The Committee goes on to state the principle that a "research administrator should not censor or suppress monographs and research papers produced by the sociological investigators in his program or agency except in the interest of scientific quality and objectivity, nor should the professional investigators tolerate such censorship." The force of that statement, however, is diminished by the sentence immediately following: "Any exceptions to these principles should be by written agreement in advance."[11] This last sentence is left to stand on its own, unless it is illuminated by the immediately preceding paragraph, which suggests that the "variety of possible conditions under which research agencies operate is so great" that "it may be occasionally justifiable to make exceptions to the principles specified."[12]

Even if code writers were omniscient and unequivocally frank, it would be difficult for them to handle adequately the complex ethical issues concerning special interest groups as those issues are evident (or camouflaged) and defined (or undefined) in the institutional setting. How, for example, might a code deal with the skillful avoidance of controversy at the expense of socially desirable scholarly inquiry? The code could scarcely assert that "every research institute shall issue in each biennium at least one report which objectively and without advocacy steps on the toes of some special interest group." Any professional society would shrink from the onus of telling individuals or institutions what they should investigate.

In like fashion, professional societies recoil from the enforcement of codes. In the final analysis the integrity of scholarly inquiry can be protected only by the courage of morally accountable individuals. The most that a code of ethics can do is to help make manifest their responsibilities.

Inquiry and the Public Interest

These words are written not in the spirit of *j'accuse* but from a persistent concern that mutual accommodation of institutional goals, needs, and vulnerabilities among foundations, centers of inquiry, and special interest groups may lead to Establishment Research, which would fall short of the public interest. The failure of Deep South academic researchers to examine with rigor the instruments of racial protest and resistance is an extreme case in point.

The ethical issues discussed here are far from simple. The imbrication of rights, equities, interests and proprieties which bound the relations of the researchers and the researched is not easy to dissect. Moreover, men are a variable in courage and integrity; the performance of individual investigators and investigative institutions under pressure has ranged from valiant to contemptible.

The locus of responsibility, authority, and initiative in research has tended to shift from the individual to the institution. But research is not alone; the general trend has been in that direction. Certainly the institutionalization of research has compelling assets. So complex and expensive has inquiry become in many fields that the explosion of knowledge in the past 20 years scarcely would have been possible without large-scale organization of inquiry.

Yet if research institutes are more sensitive to, and especially if they are more adaptive toward, pressures than an individual researcher would be, the institutionalization of scholarly investigation is at best a mixed blessing. The risks are great enough when the research center project is initiated and paid for by the university or a private foundation; when the inquiry is contracted for by a special interest group, government or private, the situation can become perilous for free inquiry.

The implicit question becomes whether the research institution can be made more responsible to the public interest in unfettered inquiry, or whether research can be restructured to reposit final responsibility for the shape and quality of the product in the individual, in an academic environment supportive of integrity.

Though giving away research money in small chunks is more troublesome and more expensive than making large grants, perhaps the added trouble and expense are a small penalty compared to the social costs of the giant research contract as it is now administered. If more money were available for the modest venture, neatly delimited, which the individual researcher through the abrasive application of shoe leather to pavement and pants seat to library chair could pursue on his own — and be held solely accountable for the results — there might be fewer grandiose schemes, some of which are writ large precisely because it is easier (or researchers think it is easier) to get funds for such projects.[11]

Where a project by the very nature of the inquiry must cover a large area, it often can be subdivided so as to locate authority and responsibility in one individual for each subdivision. If a large research task cannot be thus parceled, might it not be given to an ad hoc grouping of scholars, rather than to a permanent association such as an institute or center? Even so, final authority and responsibility concerning the quality and disposition of the findings should rest clearly in one member of the ad hoc team — in a man whose reputation for integrity as well as for academic competence make him a good ethical risk. Obviously the granting agency should have no particularist interest in the findings; furthermore, it should be as far removed as possible from the reach of particularist groups which might have such an interest.

The individual is not impregnable. But a distinguished scholar may be able to withstand the assaults of partisans better than a research institute can. Certainly he might be more likely to muster the will to do so. After all, if he is a top runner in his field, the university needs him more than he needs the university; he has the advantage of a seller's market, with demand far exceeding supply. Moreover, academic tenure might be recalled from its present drift toward "seniority" to serve its original function of shielding the scholar in his pursuit and dispense of knowledge. The point is that an individual who has authority over a research project must bear an awesome, unfractionated, unshiftable accountability for decisions about it.

These are but a few tentative proposals. The solution to this knotty problem must be hammered out painstakingly by an aroused scholarly community over the next few years if the quality of inquiry in prickly areas is to be protected. The importance of the challenge is difficult to exaggerate.

For although sensitive areas comprise only a small fraction of the territory still to be researched by social scientists, it is an important fraction. One of the functions of the university in an open society is to provide a critique of society. Unfortunately, although there is almost universal lip-service to that proposition as a general principle, its specific application is quite another matter. A particularistic interest group which readily concedes that academic criticism of society generally is in the public interest may resist, with vigorous indignation, scholarly scrutiny of its own policies and actions. The bishop or corporation executive or labor leader or school administrator who readily asserts that freedom of inquiry must be preserved as a social good too frequently is thinking of free inquiry in general or as it may relate to *other* organizations.

Democracy presupposes an enlightened electorate, but it requires a very high level of sophistication and commitment to the public interest indeed for the leader of a special interest group to take serious criticism of his organization philosophically, as necessary for the common good. One of the social products of a university ought to be social criticism, and the willingness of tax payers and donors to support higher education which openly declares social criticism as a *raison d'être* implies that the "product" is palatable to its "consumers" as a collectivity. Particular groups of consumers, however, may find the product highly distasteful in the specific case. So they raise questions not only about the necessity of the product but, more importantly, about the propriety of their having been forced or persuaded to help pay for a good they wish to reject.

The bigger and more powerful an interest group grows, the more significant its role in human affairs may become, and the urgency of subjecting its behavior to scholarly scrutiny increases accordingly. It is disquieting to ask whether the institutionalization of academic research may have weakened the will of the community of scholars to overcome that resistance.

NOTES TO THE CHAPTER

1. I have changed minor details in the case materials to protect the privacy of participants who shared their experience with me. For obvious reasons my thanks to them must be generalized, but I wish to acknowledge specifically the singular insightfulness and encouragement of my husband, Wilson Record.

2. American Psychological Association, *Ethical Standards of Psychologists* (Washington, D.C.: American Psychological Association, 1963), 9.

3. *Ibid.,* 114.

4. Committee on Professional Ethics, American Sociological Association, *Code of Ethics* (First Draft) (Washington, D.C.: American Sociological Association, 1964), 1.

5. *Ibid.,* 3.

6. *Ibid.,* 22.

7. *Ibid.,* 24.

8. *Ibid.*

9. *Ibid.,* 25.

10. *Ibid.,* 63–64.

11. *Ibid.,* 64. These remarks concern sensitive research areas. The quality of research in nonsensitive areas also is threatened by the institutionalization of research — but that is another article.

12. *Ibid.*

CHAPTER THREE

Governmental Intervention in Social Research: Political and Ethical Dimensions in the Wichita Jury Recordings

TED R. VAUGHAN

Given the nature of the material investigated by social researchers and the social setting in which such research occurs, ethical and political factors are inherent considerations in the research process. Ethical conflict is potentially present in all social research inasmuch as the values of science may conflict with the values of the social unit being studied. Proponents of the scientific ethic contend that the integrity of scientific knowledge is jeopardized when limitations are placed upon scientific inquiry. Others argue that certain social sectors are beyond the purview of science and any attempt to investigate these sectors violates the autonomy of the individuals and the sanctity of the institution involved. In addition to this potential controversy, social research is potentially threatening and disquieting to those in positions of power. A rather widespread distrust of social science research seems to exist.[1] In most cases, however, direct suppression of research on ideological grounds is not attempted. A principal contention of this chapter is that to accomplish ideological objectives censors interject themselves into the research process via controversy attending ethical conflicts.

Several cases document this thesis, but certainly one of the most dramatic was the University of Chicago Law School's study of the American jury system. Commonly referred to as the Wichita Jury Study, the project sought to further the understanding of jury operations through the recording of actual jury deliberations — without the knowledge or consent of the jurors — in a limited number of cases. In so doing, the study reflected in rather extreme form the conflict between the scientist's prerogatives and his social obligations. When news of the recordings became known, political authorities intervened to challenge the scientific canon of unrestricted inquiry. Indignant statements were issued by the U. S. Attorney General, public hearings were called, bills were introduced in both houses of Congress, and, subsequently, President Eisenhower signed into law a measure prohibiting, under penalty of $1,000 fine and/or one year in prison, the recording of jury deliberations of Federal petit or grand juries for any purpose whatsoever.[2]

This essay is a detailed examination of the ethical and political aspects of research recordings of the Wichita Jury's deliberations. The strategies by which political intervention was accomplished will receive special stress, but we shall also examine the nature of the ethical issue — a question largely ignored in the controversy surrounding the study.

First, however, it is important to review the background and operation of the research project itself. Although the ethical and political dilemmas involved in the recording of actual deliberations are of most interest here, these recordings were a minor, somewhat fortuitous part of a much larger research operation.

A natural history of the research project can be reconstructed from the records of the public hearings, and this approach has several supplemental advantages. It reveals, for example, the processual nature of even large-scale and initially well-planned research. It makes it possible to note necessary or accidental shifts in research emphasis. And it also indicates the emergent nature not only of political and ethical problems themselves, but also of the immediate responses of persons confronting them.

The Research Project

After several months of preparation, the University of Chicago — in June 1952 — submitted to the Ford Foundation a request for support of an ambitious program on law and the behavioral sciences. The introduction to that application embodies the philosophy and scope of the project.

> The subject of law is human behavior. The law deals with such behavior either in problem situations or where, for one reason or another, customary behavior without the added sanction of formal rules is deemed insufficient. The law builds on assumptions about human behavior. These assumptions are important in terms of the conduct to be regulated and in terms also of the effect of the regulation. Quite apart from all this, the institution of law is to

be understood and evaluated in terms of the techniques and knowledge of the behavioral sciences. Moreover, the law can furnish to the behavioral sciences a coherent set of problems which can be clearly defined and which can provide the basis for interdisciplinary research. The discipline of the law, its selection of problems and its insistence upon solutions thus can be helpful to the behavioral sciences, and anthropology, social psychology, sociology, and economic theory can aid in the realistic study of the legal system.[3]

As an initial approach to many aspects of the legal system, the application proposed five possible problem areas in three general categories from which three problems were to be selected for immediate investigation:[4]

  I. Law observance and infringement
      A. The youthful offender
      B. Obscenity
 II. Social institutions
      C. Correlation between beliefs about tax burdens and attitudes toward government spending
III. Administration of justice
      D. The jury system
      E. Arbitration

Of particular importance for the proper interpretation of subsequent developments is the description of the jury system problem contained in the original grant application.

> Although trial by jury in both criminal and civil cases is guaranteed by the Federal and most State constitutions, the jury system has long been under attack. The continuing criticism of an institution as basic as the jury underscores the desirability of studying the actual operation of the institution. The actual impact of many legal rules depends on their application by juries. The development of many procedural rules has been profoundly influenced by the existence of the jury system and by assumptions as to how juries operate. The appropriateness of both the substantive and procedural rules thus often depends on whether the assumptions made by the law concerning the jury system are warranted. Yet most of these assumptions have not been subjected to any empirical test. The justice of the legal system as a whole and justice or injustice in particular cases often depend on the successful operation of the jury system according to the assumptions made about it.[5]

Although there is the reference to "studying the actual operation of the institution," the suggested procedures for empirically assessing the operation of the jury systems do not include the recording of jury deliberations or any other form of direct observation during the deliberative stage. The proposal concluded in this respect that

> information can be obtained as to the actual operations of the system through systematic interviews with jury members after the close of a case . . . This is an area also where the trial and jury system can be closely simulated; that is, mock trials created with selected juries, and the behavior of such a simulated jury can be observed under controlled conditions. . . .[6]

On August 18, 1952, the Ford Foundation approved the application for the requested support of $400,000. Within a month the project was under way.

After additional planning and consultation, three immediate problem areas were agreed upon: (1) the nature and operation of the jury system, (2) the characteristics and performance of arbitration, and (3) the public's attitude concerning the distribution of the tax burden with special reference to the Federal income tax. Each project was placed under the direction of a member of the Chicago law faculty. The entire study was under the direction of Edward H. Levi, Dean of the Law School. While all three studies were considered an integral part of the program, the following discussion relates only to the jury study. In the course of the research, this problem area came to dominate the research endeavor in terms of financial and time consideration. Administratively, this portion of the research was successively directed by Bernard Meltzer, Phillip Kurland, Edward H. Levi, and Harry Kalven. Levi was the director at the time of the jury recordings.

By the spring of 1953, a prospectus for the study of the jury system had been prepared by Bernard Meltzer and was widely distributed to members of the legal profession. As Meltzer posed the problem:

> The jury has so often been called the palladium of our civil rights that this phrase has found a place in our dictionaries. At the same time, there has been continuous and lively criticism of the fitness of jury trial for some types of modern litigation. As a result, there have been significant reforms, both in this country and in England, and proposals for additional reforms. The discussion has often involved untested assumptions about the actual workings of the institution and community attitudes toward it. In addition to such matters, which can be illuminated by empirical investigation, the debate involves fundamental and pervasive issues, such as the proper role of the expert and the amateur, the proper distribution of power between the official and the citizen, and the extent to which particular values represented by basic institutions should override any operational inefficiencies which they may involve. Such issues cut too deeply into our social fabric to be resolved by even the

most comprehensive study. But a study could give us a store of reliable information about the actual workings of the jury in various contexts and the rules and usages which tend to promote or frustrate the various purposes ascribed to the jury. . . .[7]

In addition to the interviewing of jurors and the use of simulated trials and juries mentioned in the original grant application, the elaborated prospectus suggested several additional methods for obtaining information on the operation of the jury system. But again, these did not include any contact with actual jurors.

Even in the absence of any suggestion to impinge upon the privacy of jury deliberations, Meltzer foresaw the possibility of difficulty in studying the jury system. He concluded the prospectus by noting:

> It seems more appropriate to turn to some of the difficulties presented by the study which have general implications. Not the least of these is a more or less explicit feeling that ignorance about the jury may be bliss. This is a curious notion in a society which is based on free inquiry and yet which is relatively uninformed about the operations of its key institutions. There is a related notion, that the examination of an important legal institution is necessarily animated by hostility to the institution, which is completely inapplicable to the projected study.[8]

Paul Kitch, a Wichita lawyer and graduate of the University of Chicago Law School, subsequently replied to the prospectus with criticisms and suggestions for improvement. In a letter to Meltzer dated May 1, 1953, Kitch proposed recording actual jury deliberations.

> There is one conclusion which I long ago arrived at and from which I have never wavered and that is that jurors as a class are seldom accurate in their recollections as to actually what transpired in a jury room and many times intentionally deceive the interviewers in an effort to be all things to all men. In several instances we have actually examined jurors on post trial motions where there has been substantial conflict in the testimony as to what did and did not happen in the jury room. These are all matters covered by reported cases. Jurors are seldom conscious of the underlying psychological factors which have motivated their decisions.
>
> Your entire paper leaves me with the clear impression that all your faculty committee has outlined is a better coordinated and obviously more efficient use of the same testing techniques that have been used by the profession for generations.
>
> If the University would use the first allotment of funds for the purpose of first obtaining exact information as to what goes on in a jury room and then

organizing the next step of your project on the basis of interpreting such information I am sure that you would end up with something of considerably more value than what is presently indicated.

I am certain that you could get the cooperation of various courts in permitting you to install secret transcribing devices in jury rooms so that over a comparatively short period of time you could accumulate a substantial number of actual verbatim case histories. Adequate safeguards can be arranged with the courts for the protection of the identity of the individuals involved.[9]

Kitch had a previous interest in the study of the jury system, for as a member of a Wichita Bar committee, he had been involved in a survey study of juries and on another occasion had spent a year in England studying the jury system. He, along with another Wichita attorney, pursued the issue. In his testimony before the Subcommittee, he described the nature and effect of his eventual involvement in the jury recordings:

Mr. Stanley first took it up with some persons on the University staff — as to who, I do not know — at least the dean reported to me that he had taken up the idea and suggested that I come up and talk to him about it. And I came up and I talked to Mr. Levi.

He was a classmate of mine. And I told Mr. Levi that there was an opportunity to do some practical research where the definite advantage that would come from it could be pinpointed, in a practical utility to the profession, instead of dealing with my old criticism of law professors of getting unreal and theoretical, that here was a chance to sink their teeth into something.

He was reluctant. In fairness to Ed, I have to say that I sold Ed on the possibilities, and this public relations committee sold him on the possibilities.

To get out from under any commitment on it, he said, "Well, I can see that it has got merit," but he said, "how are you going to get permission to do this sort of thing."

He passed the buck on that. I was ready. I said, "The bar association will back me on it, and I will guarantee to you that we will find judges in Kansas who will give this kind of consent."

The next thing I knew one of the staff members wrote me and said that if we could get the consent, they would be interested.[10]

In November, 1953, over a year after the jury study was launched, Mr. Kitch — to demonstrate, as he testified, that he could get the desired consent — began negotiations with judges in the Tenth Judicial Circuit to gain consent for the project to record live jury deliberations. After obtaining preliminary approval from U.S. District Judge Delmas C. Hill, Kitch discussed the proposed research with Orie L. Phillips, Chief Judge, United

States Court of Appeals, Tenth Judicial District. In a letter dated November 23, 1953, to Judge Phillips, Kitch proposed a set of rules governing the procedures.

1. A recording microphone will be placed in each jury room. The recording instrument with a satisfactory locking device will be placed in the judge's office or at such other place as the trial judge may designate. The trial judge will be the sole custodian of the key. The operation of the instrument will be the responsibility of the court reporter or such other person as the trial judge may designate.

2. No recordings will be made in criminal cases. No recordings will be made in civil cases without the consent of counsel for each party.

3. When a recording is taken of a jury deliberation the record will be sealed and will remain in the custody of the trial judge or such other person as he may designate until final judgment has been entered and all appeals have been terminated. When this time arises the recording will be forwarded to a person to be designated by the research committee or to such person as the circuit court may prefer to designate. A single transcription of the record will then be made. Thereafter the original recording will be destroyed. Thereafter the research committee will supervise the editing of the transcript so that all personal names or geographical references and all other identifying statements will be edited in such a way as to avoid any identification of the persons or controversies involved. The edited transcript together with the original transcript will then be forwarded to the clerk of the circuit court of appeals or to such other person as your court may designate for review. If such officer is satisfied that the record has been appropriately edited he will then destroy the original transcript and will return to the research committee the edited transcript. If such officer feels that further editing is necessary he shall accomplish the same, destroying both the original transcription and the suggested edited transcription and will return to the committee the transcript as edited by such officer.

4. The entire project insofar as it involves the recording of jury deliberations will receive no publicity from any source until after the project is completed.

5. In the event that services of court reporters are required by designation of trial courts or in the event that any person is appointed by the circuit court to perform any of the duties called for hereunder such persons shall be compensated from the funds made available to the research committee in such amounts and at such times as the trial court or the circuit court may fix.[11]

Still Judge Phillips demurred stating that he had no objection to the research being carried out in the Tenth Circuit provided the jurors were informed. After subsequent conversations with Kitch and Hill, Judge Phillips agreed to waive the restriction in a limited number of cases. In early February, 1954, the University of Chicago Law School was informed that consent had been obtained for the recording of a limited number of cases without the knowledge of the jurors.

With the approval of the judges and in accordance with the safeguards proposed by Mr. Kitch, the research project dispatched representatives to supervise the installation of the recording devices in the Wichita jury room. Two microphones were concealed as part of the heating apparatus. These were connected to the recording machine locked in a cloak closet in Judge Hill's private chambers. The machine was not monitored while the deliberations were in process. This procedure was followed in the recording of six civil cases.

In July, 1954, Judge Hill advised Judge Phillips that the experimental recordings had been completed and that it was his conclusion that no further recordings should be made in his court. Thereupon, the recordings were returned to Chicago where they were edited by members of the research staff.

Some controversy exists as to the responsibility for the incident that led to public knowledge of the jury recordings. Mr. Levi testified that the court requested the return of the transcriptions for custody; Mr. Kitch testified that Judge Phillips wanted one of the edited versions to constitute part of the program for an annual judicial conference; Judge Phillips wrote that he simply asked Mr. Kitch to work up a section of the program, since he had done so very satisfactorily the previous year. Whatever the actual case, project officials dispatched Mr. Fred Strodtbeck, a sociologist and member of the research project, to Estes Park, Colorado, to present an edited version of one of the deliberations at the annual conference of the 10th judicial circuit. A public discussion session followed the presentation.

In the meantime the jury project had progressed along other lines summarized in these relevant sections of a project member's report:

1. Questionnaires have been given to some 500 state and federal trial judges. The judge is asked to record in cases which have gone to the jury how he would have decided the case had there been no jury. A brief description of the case, events at the trial, and when the jury differs, the judge's view on why the jury has differed is also requested. To date, responses covering some 3,000 civil and some 2,000 criminal cases have been received and are being analyzed. This study goes to the important question of the frequency and nature of judge-jury differences.

2. A public attitude study has been made in Peoria, Ill., among a sample

population of persons who have served on juries recently and a sample population made up of persons who have not had jury service. . . .

3. A companion study has been made of the jury selection system in Peoria in recent years. . . .

5. With the consent of the courts involved, relatively brief interviews immediately after service have been made with some 700 jurors who have served in criminal cases in Chicago and Brooklyn. . . .

6. With the cooperation of several liability companies which operate over the nation, a series of model personnel injury cases have been given to claim agents throughout the U.S. The agents who are particularly familiar with the jury verdicts in their locale are asked to give the top figure they would settle for rather than go to a jury trial. . . .

7. (omitted)

8. A detailed observation of some 18 jury trials has been made. The observer has been present throughout the trial, and has interviewed the judge and counsel in detail. With the consent of the court and the jurors, he has interviewed all members of the jury intensively after the trial. . . .

9. A major development in the work thus far has been the use of experimental trials with mock juries. With the consent of various courts, realistic recordings of mock trials based upon actual trials have been played to jurors which were assigned to this experimental deliberation by the court. These deliberations are recorded with the knowledge of the jurors and in addition by questionnaires which are given to the jurors at various stages of the proceedings. . . .[12]

Between the actual recording of the jury deliberations in the spring of 1954 and the playing of the edited version at the Estes Park conference in July, 1955, an additional request for funds for the study was submitted to the Ford Foundation. In the review of the jury study, this request, filed in December, 1954, no mention was made of the recordings. It was estimated in the request that none of the three original studies was as much as one-half completed, but the jury study was further along than the other two.[13] In August, 1955, the Ford Foundation had approved an extension of the grant and additional funds, although the grant had not yet been made public.

Political Intervention:
Public Hearings and Legislative Action

Although there was, as we shall subsequently note in detail, an ethical issue of major proportions in the research project with which political authorities with some legitimacy could have concerned themselves, the action of the political authorities was such as to subordinate this issue and thus involve the political machinery in the totally unwarranted role of social research censor. The initial phase of governmental intervention came with the calling of public hearings by the Internal Security Subcommittee of the Senate Committee on the Judiciary. This action represented one of the few times this potentially powerful mechanism of control has been used with respect to social research. A public hearing in itself need not pose a real threat to the integrity of scientific research; indeed, the Hearings might constructively have considered problems endemic in scientific-political relationships. That this possibility was not realized derived largely from the nature of the Subcommittee responsible for the particular hearings.

The Internal Security Subcommittee was, at the time, composed of nine members and chaired by Senator James O. Eastland, Democrat of Mississippi. The only other Subcommittee member in attendance at the Hearings was Senator William E. Jenner, Indiana Republican. In a controversy that was to become predominantly a political matter, it is significant that the only senators in attendance were political conservatives. More important, perhaps, was the fact that, in the years prior to the hearings, the same Subcommittee had been principally concerned with the communist subversive threat to national security.[14] The fact that the country was just emerging from the throes of the "McCarthy era" at the time of the Hearings made it more likely that the members would subordinate the ethical issue in the case to that of the political aspects of possible subversion.

Significantly, the expressed purpose of the Hearings actually stressed the ethical aspects of the case. Senator Jenner, for example, pointedly denied any "red-hunting" intentions.[15] And Senator Eastland's introductory remarks posed the purpose of the Hearings as that of determining *why* and *how* the recordings were made:

> We shall hear testimony today from persons who presumably have knowledge of the research project to which I have referred, and of what was done with regard to the recording of jury deliberations.
>
> I believe we shall be able today to establish on the record just what took place with respect to the recording of jury proceedings and deliberations; why this was undertaken, and how it was accomplished.[16]

Serious consideration of why the recordings were made would surely have involved some consideration of the scientific ethic, and of its relationship to other social ethics. But that important potential objective was not accomplished. The technical question of how the recordings were accomplished was somewhat more successfully answered, but neither the question nor the answer has much meaning apart from the ethical issues involved.

It is important to consider here *why* and *how* the Hearings were unsuccessful in accomplishing the stated objectives. Clearly, it was not because witnesses were unresponsive. A fair reading of the record reveals that there were no refusals to answer questions, no time consuming legal niceties or referral of questions to counsel, no evasiveness in responding to the questions, no resort to the right of taking the fifth amendment. In short, witnesses appeared anxious to explain their actions to the Subcommittee members. But they were not always able to do so, partly because of the limitations on dialogue imposed by the rules of legal examinations of witnesses, partly also because the Subcommittee members were apparently unwilling to hear what they had to say. On any number of occasions the Chairman interrupted witnesses demanding "yes" or "no" answers when such answers obviously added little to a record of what happened or why. Such practices hardly seem appropriate in any public hearings. They were especially inappropriate in this instance where the expressed intent was "putting the facts on the record."

The failure to accomplish satisfactorily the stated objectives of the Hearings seems to lie in the political and ethical orientations of the Subcommittee members themselves. A principal source of the discrepancy between the Hearings' objectives and its accomplishments was the initial failure to view the issue problematically. To the Subcommittee members, unaccustomed as they were to seeing things in the relative terms of science, the case presented no problem in the sense of an issue to be resolved. The only problem was that project members had violated a set of norms, and a set assumed by the senators to be superordinate to all others. And that problem could be satisfactorily solved through chastising the errant researchers and erecting obstacles to its recurrence.

This orientation was clearly demonstrated in the opening remarks offered by both senators. Eastland stated, "Legislation will, I am sure, result from this hearing."[17] And, in essence, Jenner agreed:

> I am inclined to think appropriate action in this instance necessarily means legislative action, but I have an open mind on the subject and I certainly want to hear the testimony of the witnesses who will come before us today, before attempting to reach any final conclusion either as to the need for legislation or as to the nature of legislation which may be necessary.[18]

Such introductory remarks pointed the Subcommittee away from its expressed purpose and toward a primarily political interpretation of testimony. The question of what the main issue would be and how it would be approached was settled before the Hearings got under way.

The task for the Hearings, then, was that of lecturing the participants on their misbehavior. Assuming that the constitutional guarantee of trial by jury includes secrecy of deliberations, Eastland reasoned that anything that poses a potential threat to the integrity of the jury system affects the internal security of the United States.[19] While the spirit of the seventh amendment has certainly included secrecy of juror deliberations, Eastland entirely disregarded the moot aspect of the technical points, and, more importantly, he also ignored the possibility of its irrelevance with respect to scientific investigation. His position is made clear in his questioning of one of the witnesses.

> THE CHAIRMAN. What is the seventh amendment to the Constitution of the United States?
>
> MR. KALVEN. It is the amendment providing for jury trial in civil cases.
>
> THE CHAIRMAN. Certainly.
>
> MR. KALVEN. In cases involving the Federal Government.
>
> THE CHAIRMAN. Certainly. That means secret deliberations?
>
> MR. KALVEN. I am not completely sure about that, sir.
>
> THE CHAIRMAN. You are not?
>
> MR. KALVEN. Not as a matter of technical constitutional law. As I understand it — and I do not profess to be an expert on this point — it was rather unclear at the time the Constitution was adopted just how much jury secrecy there was. And as I understand the constitutional test for the meaning of the seventh amendment, it goes back to the institution as of the time the amendment was adopted. I am not making that as a firm proposition of law, sir. It is just my impression on that point.[20]

Whatever the validity of the assumption that jury deliberation was meant to be secret, it does not necessarily follow that investigation of the jury system for scientific purposes constitutes a threat either to the system itself, or to the internal security of the United States. Nevertheless, Eastland presumed the answer to the problem, then proceeded to admonish the project participants:

> THE CHAIRMAN. Now, do you not realize that to snoop on a jury, and to record what they say, does violence to every reason for which we have secret deliberations of a jury?
>
> MR. LEVI. Senator, on that I think that reasonable men differ. I do not.
>
> THE CHAIRMAN. You do not think so?
>
> MR. LEVI. I do not.

THE CHAIRMAN. You do not think that a member of a jury would frankly express his opinion? Would he hesitate to frankly express his opinion if he thought there might be a microphone hidden, taking down what they said?

MR. LEVI. I think that if he were conscious of the fact that there was a microphone, while he was conscious of it, this might result in some inhibitions.

THE CHAIRMAN. Yes. But if those things secretly happen and then it is released and the records are played before people, how is he going to know whether there is a microphone there or not?[21]

And again to another witness:

THE CHAIRMAN. Where has there been an attack on the jury system?

MR. KALVEN. Sir, there has been an attack on the jury system for the last hundred years in America. I have a memorandum.

THE CHAIRMAN. Well, you know, there has been no real attack on the jury system —

MR. KALVEN. Sir, I have a —

THE CHAIRMAN (continuing). In civil cases, do you not?

MR. KALVEN. I do not know that, sir.

THE CHAIRMAN. How?

MR. KALVEN. I have a memorandum here which was prepared for another purpose, that I would be delighted to submit to the committee, which reviews the debate on the jury system which has been going on for at least a hundred years.

THE CHAIRMAN. Now, as a matter of fact, there has been no substantial attack, do you not realize that?

MR. KALVEN. I may be making the mistake an academician makes. I am talking about articles, literature of the kind of stuff that we read.

THE CHAIRMAN. I understand. There has been no substantial attack; you know that.

MR. KALVEN. What I meant, sir, was many criticisms, some of them extremely vigorous, have been voiced on the jury, and —

THE CHAIRMAN. It has not been attacked, has it?[22]

Continuing on the same presuppositions, Mr. Eastland clearly established his point with respect to future recordings:

MR. KALVEN. No. Over the next year, sir, if our plans had gone as projected, I think it is very doubtful we would have done any more cases. There were no concrete plans for doing any.

THE CHAIRMAN. I will guarantee you that you will not do any bugging after Congress passes some legislation.

MR. KALVEN. I admit, sir, the situation has changed somewhat.

THE CHAIRMAN. I will say it has.[23]

Not only were the project members chastised for their violation of the principle of secret deliberations, they were also instructed in the proper mechanics of research:

THE CHAIRMAN. Now, would not the proper way to handle that, Doctor, be to confer with the jury after the verdict is rendered?

MR. LEVI. We have done so.

THE CHAIRMAN. Before it has been discharged?

MR. LEVI. We have done so. One part —

THE CHAIRMAN. Answer my question.

MR. LEVI. I am sorry, sir.

THE CHAIRMAN. Is that not the proper way to handle it?

MR. LEVI. I think that is one proper way to handle it.

THE CHAIRMAN. That is the proper way to handle it; is it not?[24]

In addition, the Subcommittee counsel raised questions about the sampling procedure. His examination of witnesses implied that a probability sample of all jury cases would be necessary before any reliable data could be obtained.[25]

A second source of the Hearings' shift in purpose, closely related to the failure to see the issue as problematical, was the failure to differentiate between scientific inquiry directed toward the acquisition of knowledge and nonscientific investigation of or intervention in the jury process. Committed as the Subcommittee members were to the supremacy of one set of values and norms, they could see no need for making such a distinction. They failed to consider that science is itself a system of norms with the same claims to legitimacy as other normative systems. It is true that the norms of science are not always apparent to those engaged in scientific pursuits, much less to laymen. But to assume that scientific objectives are "naturally" subordinate to other normative systems and values is to beg the crucial question.

At various points in the Hearings, different project members tried to make the above distinction, as at least a partial justification of their operations. For example, one of the jury study directors raised the point in the following exchange:

THE CHAIRMAN. Mr. Kalven, do you believe in the American jury system?

MR. KALVEN. I do, very much, sir. That is the reason why I am interested in the study.

THE CHAIRMAN. Yes sir. Do you believe that juries should deliberate in secret?

MR. KALVEN. I think on the balance, it is better, sir, if they deliberate with an assurance of privacy.

THE CHAIRMAN. Do you believe that the American jury system is one of the greatest safeguards of human liberty?

MR. KALVEN. I think I would say, "Yes, sir," to that.

THE CHAIRMAN. Sir?

MR. KALVEN. Yes, sir.

THE CHAIRMAN. You agree to that?

MR. KALVEN. Yes.

THE CHAIRMAN. What would happen to that great safeguard if a jury's deliberations were "bugged"?

MR. KALVEN. Well, sir, I think it makes a good deal of difference who does the "bugging," under what circumstances. I agree that if all juries were conscious of the fact that their deliberations might be recorded, if you will permit the phrase, by anyone whomsoever and for any purpose —

THE CHAIRMAN. It would affect them?

MR. KALVEN. I think that is right. I think that is almost irrelevant.

THE CHAIRMAN. And yet you say for a jury, if they were conscious of the fact — well, do you not know that if it is done in some cases, that every juror is going to think, well, maybe there is a microphone in this room?

MR. KALVEN. I do not think so, sir. May I make one statement?

THE CHAIRMAN. You do not?

MR. KALVEN. The statement is this —

THE CHAIRMAN. Answer my question.

MR. KALVEN. The answer is, no, sir.

THE CHAIRMAN. You do not think that?

MR. KALVEN. No, sir. May I amplify my answer?

THE CHAIRMAN. Certainly.

MR. KALVEN. I think the only two points to be made here are these: The first point, it was not contemplated it would ever be having the degree of publicity there presently is about this. As Mr. Levi said this morning, it was not clear what final disposition would be made of these.

THE CHAIRMAN. Do you not realize that a procedure, so at variance with the American system of government, is bound to be widely known?

MR. KALVEN. I do not think so, sir. This procedure — this was done 15 months ago — it seems to me it has been kept a pretty good secret until recently.

THE CHAIRMAN. Everybody in the country knows it now, do they not?

MR. KALVEN. Not through our efforts.

THE CHAIRMAN. Sir?

MR. KALVEN. Not through our efforts.

THE CHAIRMAN. Regardless of whose efforts, it is known, is it not?

MR. KALVEN. In any event, I would like to get to my second point, which, I think, is more relevant. What is now known is that, with the consent of the attorneys and with the consent of the judge, and for scientific purposes, a few juries may from time to time be recorded. I see no reason why that should strike any fear in the heart of any juror in America. And that seems to me, at the maximum, the threat that has been created thus far.[26]

But such attempts had little effect, for Eastland's consistent position was that the recording of the deliberations was wrong regardless of who did it, for what purpose, under what auspices, or with what safeguards. Such an act was unconditionally a violation of the higher norm of jury secrecy:

THE CHAIRMAN. Well, now, what is the reason for secret deliberations of a jury?

MR. LEVI. The reason for secret deliberations of a jury is so that the jury shall not be disturbed in its discussions, so that the discussions can be orderly and that they can state their opinions. But, Senator —

THE CHAIRMAN. Now, that is it; so that they can frankly state their opinions. That is the reason, is it not?

MR. LEVI. I believe that is right, Senator. But —

THE CHAIRMAN. Certainly. Now, that is a principal reason, is it not?

MR. LEVI. It is certainly one of the major reasons.

THE CHAIRMAN. Yes. Now, you violated that, did you not?

MR. LEVI. Senator, I beg to differ. Our recording of these deliberations was under an arrangement with the consent of the trial judge and the chief judge of the circuit —

THE CHAIRMAN. Regardless, now, of who agreed to it; regardless of who agreed to it, you still violated it, did you not?

MR. LEVI. Senator, I was trying to answer that precise point.

THE CHAIRMAN. Well, I think you go off on a question of attempting to justify it by saying —

MR. LEVI. No, sir.

THE CHAIRMAN. By saying that a judge agreed to it.

MR. LEVI. No, sir. I was about to —

THE CHAIRMAN. The fact is that you violated the very reason that we have secret deliberations by juries.

MR. LEVI. What I was about to say, Senator, was that this was done under an arrangement which provided that there should be no publicity; that the recording, when transcribed, should be changed so as to remove all identifying statements, and that there shall be no release —[27]

The result of this failure to discriminate between scientific and nonscientific investigations of the jury system was that the scientific position did not receive a fair hearing. All the potential disadvantages and possible abuses of nonscientific intrusion on the deliberative process were assumed to hold for scientific research as well. If this position were consistently taken by political authorities, a considerable amount of current social science research would be terminated.

The third source of the Subcommittee's failure to achieve its stated objectives is a natural consequence of the preceding ones. The one possibly legitimate role representatives of the state could have in the research process would be that of mediating between conflicting systems of values and norms. Not only did the Subcommittee fail in this respect, the members did not even entertain such a role as a legitimate possibility. Although the entire Hearing operated behind the facade of concern for the privacy of jurors while deliberating a case, every indication was that this was not the major concern. The Subcommittee failed to treat the matter either as an ethical concern or as a political problem in institutional relations. Certainly, the matter was not fully anticipated in the ambiguous legal traditions the Senators apparently thought they were defending.

Additionally informative here is the government's general position with regard to the question of individual rights in the period just prior to the Hearings. The techniques used to investigate possible communist subversion in the "McCarthy era" are hardly compatible with a genuine concern for individual rights. The characteristic political feature of that period was the placing of the welfare and security of the nation above the rights of individuals. And the Subcommittee gave every indication of its adherence to that pattern. Senator Eastland, for example, attempted to link the scientists' invasion of the privacy of jury deliberations with a necessary threat to internal security:

> The jurisdiction of the Internal Security Subcommittee in this matter arises from the fact that anything which undermines or threatens the integrity of the jury system necessarily affects the internal security of the United States.[28]

The speciousness of the argument has already been demonstrated, if it is not patently clear from this statement.

At the time certain governmental officials were inveighing against the invasion of the privacy of jurors, the Justice Department was sponsoring a Congressional bill that would permit wiretapping under certain conditions. Yet, Attorney-General Brownell scored the research project particularly and the University of Chicago generally for "spying on panel's deliberations in sociological study." As quoted in the *New York Times,* "We in the Department of Justice," he said, "are unequivocally opposed to any recording or eavesdropping on the deliberations of a jury under any conditions regardless of purpose."[29]

The discrepancy between possibilities and actualities evident in the Hearings as an example of government intervention had several potentially serious consequences for social research aimed only at the acquisition of knowledge. For, frustrated in their attempt to make a case for scientific investigation of the jury system on nonutilitarian grounds, the witnesses fell back on a tested and tried procedure. They attempted to point to immediate practical consequences of the research. When asked by the Subcommittee counsel: "What was it hoped to learn through this project with respect to juries?", Dean Levi, for example, replied:

> It was hoped to learn how juries operate, to what extent they understand the instructions of the judges, to what extent they are able to handle difficult problems of evidence, to what extent it might be possible to speed up the jury system, so as to avoid the clogging of the courts in the urban centers and at the same time to preserve the jury system.[30]

And again:

> We hope to prove, and I believe we will be able to prove, that the jury is an efficient method of deciding cases, despite the clogging of the dockets, that it can be strengthened and preserved, and that the doubts that have arisen about the jury system in various parts of this country and in the world, as for example, in England, where the jury system has been much limited, are not well established.
>
> We wish to strengthen the jury system by this project.[31]

It is uncertain whether such an emphasis on the practical consequences set precedents which will hamper pure research. The Hearings were, however, official and had received wide publicity as well.

Another consequence of the Hearings was that, together with the publicity about them, they probably heightened public suspicion of the motives of scientists, especially social scientists. To the extent that the public shared or acquired the Subcommittee's nonproblematic view of the issue, all social research would be suspect. For from this absolutist perspective, the investigators were either ignorant of their actions or actually trying to subvert the system. And clearly at that time, it was much easier to believe the latter than the former about any college professor. The Subcommittee itself, despite members' denials, apparently seriously entertained the possibility that a communist plot was operating through the research. What else would explain that fully 40 percent of the space allotted to reporting the testimony of the principal witnesses — Levi and Kalven — covers materials relating to communists and communist organizations.[32] Not juror privacy but possible subversion of the system — and the society — was what was problematic for the Subcommittee, and probably also for many persons who read about the Hearings.

A third and more certain consequence is that the jury deliberations were effectively closed as an avenue of investigation, even before the proposed ban was submitted to Congress. The Hearings became a rallying point of public opposition to further recordings, sufficient to render such research virtually impossible even if Congress had failed to pass the regulation. With few exceptions, communication media supported the position of the Subcommittee.[33] And against this public furor, no scientific group or organization raised a voice of protest or argued for freedom of scientific inquiry.[34]

In view of the conduct of the Hearings, the witnesses' testimony had little impact in the actual drafting of the bill. Its content would probably have been the same had no public hearings been conducted. The members had apparently made up their minds before meetings were held, and this seems to suggest still other motives for having the Hearings in the first place.

We have already observed that the Hearings served as a forum for the public chastisement of the project members. Others suggested at the time that the Hearings and the related news coverage were designed to harass and publicly embarrass the institutions involved — The University of Chicago and the Ford Foundation.

> The great editorial and Congressional hue and cry that has been raised over the disclosure that microphones were concealed in a Wichita jury room is directly related not to the merits of the issue, which are important and worthy of comment, but to the current campaign to "smear" the Ford Foundation and the Fund for the Republic. The case is ideally adapted to these purposes. It involves legal scholars at the University of Chicago, an institution which must be punished because its former president has been identified with the

Ford Foundation and the Fund. The Ford Foundation, of course, financed the research on the jury system out of which the incident arose.[35]

An argument that the project provided an opportunity for conservatives to excoriate social research seems well founded. The extent of their opposition is clear in the Internal Security Subcommittee's report which cited "the incident as possible grounds for restricting the exemption from federal taxes of such organizations as the Ford Foundation which financed the undertaking."[36] Senator Eastland's colleague from Mississippi, Senator Stennis, "also attacked the Fund for the Republic for financing a research project in which jury proceedings were recorded,"[37] although the Fund had no connection whatsoever with the project.[38] An attempt to punish and seriously weaken institutions in the forefront of social research is understandable in terms of the conservative's fear that such research will lead to social change and the belief that all research of this nature is motivated by hostility toward the object of investigation. The jury recording case provided an excellent opportunity to register such conservative opposition, because it could be done in defense of the commonly held sentiment that such deliberations unquestionably should be secret.

In the course of events, Senators Eastland and Jenner introduced a bill proscribing any form of invasion of the jury's deliberation for any purpose. There being no opposition on principle, the bill passed both Houses of Congress. Approval by President Eisenhower was a foregone conclusion inasmuch as he was already on record as favoring such a ban. And in August, 1956, the bill was signed into law.

To be sure, not everyone who opposed the research approved the activities of the Subcommittee or the actual legislation either. Nevertheless, although the legislative action preserved the historic principle of secret jury deliberations, it also imposed restrictions upon freedom of scientific inquiry, and only compounded the ethical issue the Hearings had ignored.

The Ethical Problem

The fact that political intervention in social research is a paramount issue here should not obscure the significance of the ethical dimension of the case. In this particular case, as is true of much research, political and ethical questions are intertwined in a very complex manner. The one, however, is not the necessary concomitant of the other. Because ethical problems are especially endemic to social research, their resolution must be given the most careful and serious consideration. Through such a procedure, political involvement in the research process can be opposed in principle and in practice. Because the Subcommittee members missed a vital opportunity to deal with the issue of ethical conduct in research, a chance to contribute to research procedure by clarifying the ethical conflicts in the case was lost.

Despite the fact that the issue was largely ignored, there is an advantage in pursuing the ethical question in a case in which the issues are so clearly joined. On the one hand, there is the norm prescribing unrestricted freedom of scientific inquiry. On the other, there is the normative proscription against intruding upon the privacy of jury deliberations. Under most circumstances these norms can be simultaneously subscribed to by the same person. On occasions such as the scientific study of the jury system they are posed as conflicting norms. When a person is thus placed in the position of making a decision as to what to do in such a situation, the ethical issue is established. Decisions of this nature, though ordinarily not of such magnitude, are encountered daily. But what is the scientist to do in a seemingly impossible situation? We neither posit simple solutions nor attempt to establish a code of ethics for scientists. We do, however, question some of the solutions that have been utilized in similar circumstances. To posit a hierarchy of values, for example, and then operate exclusively on that basis is to be unrealistic about the issue. To argue that in the final analysis one's conscience should be his guide is hardly any better, because one's decision is inevitably based on a pre-existing value system. By presenting the arguments we feel should have occurred during the Hearings, we shall offer some other possible guidelines for dealing with ethical problems of the sort posed in the jury study.

The arguments in defense of unrestricted freedom of scientific inquiry are fairly well known to the social scientist, if only because they receive some prominence in textbooks on methodology.[39] The following abbreviated review is intended primarily to indicate the linkage between the immediate issue and more fundamental assumptions and to provide a contrast for the judicial argument.

The immediate issue, of course, is the freedom of the scientist to investigate on-going activities of an operating jury without pressure, constraint, or control by nonscientific agencies. Justification of this action is usually predicated on the broader norm that there should be unrestricted freedom of scientific inquiry, a norm which, in turn, rests on the value premise that men have the inherent right to know, i.e., that knowledge is always superior to ignorance and that nothing external to the object of investigation itself should influence the acquisition of knowledge. If knowledge is a value, any other circumstance which endangers its achievement, or influences its outcome in any way, is undesirable. The scientific enterprise cannot make significant advances without maximal freedom from external control. The pernicious effects of the intrusion of the special interests of political, religious, or other groups into the research process are well documented in the literature. Scientists could and should oppose actual or potential attempts by nonscientific interests to control or influence social research.

More specifically, the conventional textbook view would have it that investigation of the actual operations of the jury system, or any other basic social institution, is justified by the value of knowledge itself. It is better to know about the workings of the jury system than not to know. The same legitimacy that attaches to knowledge in a general sense legitimates the quest for knowledge in the particular case. From this perspective, the jury system has no special claim to inviolability from scientific investigation. More pragmatically, the investigation can also be legitimated on the grounds that any decision to alter or revise an institution such as the jury system should be based on the most accurate, precise information available. Such information would be available only through direct inquiry into the mechanisms of jury operations. If, as claimed by many reputable critics, the jury system is in need of revision, the process should not be willy-nilly but carefully planned. And scientific investigation poses no real threat to the integrity of the jury system because the scientist is not concerned with the action of individual jurors, only with patterns of behavior. Data obtained are treated as classes, not as individual attributes. As a professional scientist, furthermore, the social investigator is already bound to a long-standing set of rules that proscribe the revelation of anything that might identify a person and thereby possibly embarrass, harass, or otherwise do him injury or harm.

What such textbook methodology usually ignores is that the scientific ethic (values and norms) is only one in a system of many conflicting, competing ethics making up the social fabric. It tends, instead, to assume there is a hierarchy of ethics with the scientific ethic at the pinnacle. But in actual practice, especially in field research, as the Wichita case reveals, ethical issues are much more problematic. There is no natural law to which the scientist can appeal. Like others, he bases his decisions on personal predilections and particular values. But one person's predilections — be he scientist or saint — are not perforce more natural than another's. The proclivity among scientists to minimize, if not ignore, competing social ethics, and to define science in some independent sense, is quite widespread. In short, the scientist typically subscribes to the notion that the end of knowledge justifies the scientific means.

Counterposed to the scientific ethic are the values and norms of the judicial process.[40] Advocates of this position contend that no circumstances justify the invasion of the traditional privacy and confidence of jury deliberations, for, normatively, there should be inviolable privacy of such deliberations. This norm, in turn, also derives from a more basic value assumption in a democratic society: that there is an inalienable right to trial by an impartial jury. Anything that undermines in any way the impartial nature of the jury should not be permitted. And, the argument continues, the jurors' impartiality is influenced by the actual or possible invasion of the jury room irrespective of the purpose. Any actual or potential surveillance undermines impartiality because it raises the possibility of considerations extraneous to the merits of the case itself. Obviously, impartiality is threatened if there are attempts to influence the verdict. Even if scientific investigation is not directed toward influencing verdicts, it still threatens impartiality to the extent that it introduces any question of possible embarrassment, coercion, or other such considerations into the minds of actual jurors. A jury is impartial to the extent that nothing but the consciences of the individual jurors influence its decision. Even if anonymity is assured or the members are unaware of immediate surveillance, impartiality is threatened unless the norm of inviolable privacy prevails. In terms of this principle, the matter of safeguards in scientific research is largely irrelevant. To protect the opportunity for an impartial and just verdict, secret deliberations must be preserved regardless of the ultimate value that might result from the scientific investigation of the jury system. In short, the integrity of the jury system demands privacy of deliberations. Supreme Court Justice William O. Douglas has summarized this general judicial view:

> A jury reflects the attitudes and mores of the community from which it is drawn. It lives only for the day and it does justice according to its light. The groups of 12 who are drawn to hear a case make the decision and melt away. It is not present the next day to be criticized. It is the one governmental agency that has no ambition. To preserve this kind of status for our jury system, it is essential that we keep completely private what transpires in a jury room during the deliberative stage.[41]

The countervailing ethical arguments are summarized paradigmatically below:

THE ISSUES

Freedom to study the activities of operating juries.	Freedom to prohibit investigations of the jury system.

BASIC VALUE ASSUMPTIONS

There is an inherent right to know — i.e., knowledge is superior to ignorance.

There is an inalienable right to trial by an impartial jury.

NORMATIVE ORIENTATIONS

There should be unrestricted freedom of scientific inquiry.

There should be inviolable privacy of jury deliberations.

ARGUMENTS FOR

General:

1. If knowledge is a value, then all factors which endanger its achievement are undesirable.
2. Science cannot make significant advances without freedom from external control.

Specific:

1. The jury system, and any other social institution, should be understood, and some of this understanding can come only from careful, direct investigation.
2. Scientific investigation poses no threat to the integrity of the jury system because the scientist is not concerned with the action of individual jurors, only with patterns of behavior.

General:

1. Anything that undermines in any way the impartial nature of the jury should not be permitted.
2. The actual or potential invasion of the jury room for any purpose whatsoever affects the impartial nature of the jurors' deliberations.

Specific:

1. Any actual or potential surveillance undermines impartiality because it raises questions extraneous to the merits of the case itself.
2. In order that the opportunity for an impartial and just verdict not be compromised, secret deliberations must be preserved regardless of the ultimate value that might result from scientific investigation of the jury system.

The conflict of issues delineated above seems to place the social scientist in a most difficult position. If similar conflicts characterize much social research, then the situation is problematic indeed. Inasmuch as the discussion of science and ethics has been largely nonpublic, we can only attempt to reconstruct the patterns of adjustment that the resolution of conflict has assumed.

These patterns include the attempts to avoid, ignore, or suppress the conflict issue. None, however, is satisfactory, because each fails to seriously address the reality of conflict. The avoidance pattern has especially severe repercussions for social research. To avoid problems in which ethics contrary to science are vigorously justified is to avoid issues that are central to a given society or group. Emotional commitment to an ideal is often a sensitive indicator of its meaningfulness to social life. To avoid such problem areas is to permit the social climate to dictate the legitimate problems for research. Another reaction pattern that fails to meet the issues is the frequently used resort of largely ignoring the condition of conflict — if not the conflict itself, at least the consequences of it for the conduct of research. But to ignore the conditions of conflict is, from one perspective, to be intellectually dishonest. Such a failure to acknowledge external influences upon the research design, operation, and subsequent findings is but another way of asserting the independent nature of the research process — a view of the nature of science increasingly held to be invalid. Still another reaction of scientific practitioners is that of asserting the supremacy of the scientific ethic regardless of the circumstances. If the scientific ethic does not prevail, this position argues, the integrity of science is compromised. But such an argument epitomizes the lack of concern for ethical problems in social research.

Our own present position is that if certain general principles are accepted, the conflict of ethics neither poses a hopeless dilemma nor restricts action to the alternative responses already reviewed. These basic premises include the denial of a natural ordering of ethics and the affirmation that the merits of the individual case determine the ascendancy of particular ethics for that particular case. If the assumption is granted that science is a part of the social system, an institution with values and norms not inherently superior to others, then ethical conflicts are inevitable. And they cannot satisfactorily be ignored, avoided, or suppressed.

To re-emphasize the need for a self-conscious sense of ethical responsibility in social research, we can conclude by very briefly indicating two general procedures which should be included in decision-making by social science researchers. First, a self-conscious and serious sense of reflection is needed, including detailed awareness and consideration of the points of view of respondents or other participants. Genuine understanding of another's point of view, including the basic values upon which his argument rests, may, of course, convince one completely of the merits of one's own position. But the decision is made on the basis of comparison not abstraction. Simply to assert scientific prerogatives as abstractions is to attempt an easy solution to a difficult problem. When contradictory positions are thoroughly understood, a decision can be based on the merits of the case. Such understanding need not necessarily alter research objectives, although this may well be the case, but it may force a reconsideration of means. Such a reassessment may necessitate more creative, innovative research procedure.

A commitment to a serious and specific understanding of subjects, for example, leads to a second commitment. Not only does the social scientist need to see the problem from the perspective of others, he needs to cultivate such counter perspectives quite consciously. At one level, scientists must take a position favoring unrestricted research, not as some absolute right that has been bestowed upon them, but — as the Chicago researchers attempted to establish in the Hearings — as an ideal to be pursued. At another level, as the scientist actually approaches the ideal in a particular case, he must protect against the despotic implications of absolutism through the encouragement of his own opposition — whether it be that of Senator Eastland or someone else.

Conclusion

The Wichita jury recording study exemplifies a state of affairs probably present to some extent in virtually all social science research. An ethical question of important scope and magnitude was involved in the conduct of the research operation — a question worthy of the most serious and exhaustive consideration. Although much attention was focused upon the case, the ethical problem was largely ignored. In the Congressional Hearings officially convened to consider the issues relating to the research project, the failure to view the matter in problematic terms, the failure to differentiate between scientific inquiry and other attempts to intervene in the judicial process, and the concern with subversion and national security so characteristic of the period all combined to divert attention away from the resolution of contradictory principles in the research. They produced, instead, the political censorship of a significant project in social research.

When the values of science conflict with those of other value systems, reflective judgment is imperative. To be sure, the particular conflict of values discussed in this paper would not necessarily occasion difficulty for researchers in some other society. Nevertheless, social researchers need especially to be self-conscious with respect to possible ethical conflicts in their research irrespective of the specific values involved. Such self-consciousness protects against scientific activity becoming totalitarian in character. If the individual scholar cannot satisfactorily resolve the ethical issues in his own investigations, he cannot constructively protect social research from political censorship.

NOTES TO THE CHAPTER

1. Irving Louis Horowitz notes a pervasive anti-social science bias among political and military officials in 1965 with respect to "Project Camelot." Such a climate was even more characteristic during the "McCarthy era" of the early 1950's. See Horowitz's "The Life and Death of Project Camelot," *Trans-action,* 3 (November, 1965), pp. 3–7.

2. For the full text of the law, see Public Law 919, *United States Statutes at Large,* 84th Congress, 2nd Session, 70 (1956), 935–36.

3. "Recording of Jury Deliberations," *Hearings before the Subcommittee to Investigate the Administration of the Internal Security Act and Other Internal Security Laws of the Committee on the Judiciary, United States Senate* (Washington, D.C.: United States Government Printing Office, 1955), 225. (Hereinafter this document will be referred to as *Hearings.*)

4. *Ibid.,* 225–26.

5. *Ibid.,* 229.

6. *Ibid.*

7. *Ibid.,* 160.

8. *Ibid.,* 163.

9. *Ibid.,* 164.

10. *Ibid.,* 153.

11. *Ibid.,* 178.

12. *Ibid.,* 41–42.

13. *Ibid.,* 237. In a letter dated November 14, 1955, to the Senate Subcommittee, Professor Harry Kalven estimated that as of September 30, 1955, $390,500.00 of the original $400,000 grant had been expended. Of this amount $201,036.47 had been spent on the jury project. *Ibid.,* 38.

14. See Eastland's introductory comments on criticisms of the Subcommittee, *ibid.,* 1–2.

15. *Ibid.,* 3.

16. *Ibid.,* 2.

17. *Ibid.*

18. *Ibid.*

19. In justifying the legitimacy of the Internal Security Subcommittee to conduct the Hearings, Eastland made this argument. See his introductory comments, *ibid.,* 1–2.

20. *Ibid.,* 46.

21. *Ibid.,* 5.

22. *Ibid.,* 62–63.

23. *Ibid.,* 62.

24. *Ibid.,* 5.

25. See his questioning of one witness, *ibid.,* 169–73.

26. *Ibid.,* 45–46.

27. *Ibid.,* 6.

28. *Ibid.,* 1.

29. *The New York Times,* October 6, 1955, sec. 3, p. 15. This motivation is seriously questioned in an editorial comment in *The Nation,* 181 (October 22, 1955), p. 335. "It was Mr. Brownell, wasn't it, who sponsored a wiretap bill before Congress which would have allowed him to designate those whose telephone lines were to be tapped, for purposes which can hardly be described as scientific, and in whose homes and offices secret microphones were to be planted? Is the jury room more sacred than a man's home? Should it be made a criminal offense to eavesdrop on the deliberations of a jury weighing the issues in a personal injury suit while eavesdropping on private conversations is regarded as perfectly proper? Mr. Brownell should make another speech and let us all know just where he stands on wiretapping."

30. *Hearings, op. cit.,* 5.

31. *Ibid.,* 8.

32. In the 105 pages covering the testimony of Levi and Kalven, well over 40 pages are devoted to subversion-related topics.

33. *Newsweek,* 46 (October 24, 1955), p. 32. This source noted that "Most officials and newspapers denounced the experiment."

34. Although one study reported that there was rather strong support for the practice of recording jury deliberations among lawyers, political scientists, and sociologists, no organized group protested the conduct of the Hearings. See Waldo Burchard, "A Study of Attitudes Toward the Use of Concealed Devices in Social Research," *Social Forces,* 36 (December, 1957), pp. 111–16.

35. *The Nation, op. cit.,* p. 335.

36. *The New York Times,* July 13, 1956, sec. 1, p. 41.

37. *The New York Times,* July 28, 1956, sec. 2, p. 17.

38. *The New York Times,* August 7, 1956, sec. 5, p. 8.

39. For a representative example, see William Goode and Paul Hatt, *Methods in Social Research* (New York: McGraw-Hill Book Co., 1952), esp. Chap. 3.

40. See, for example, a speech delivered by Warren E. Berger, Assistant Attorney General of the United States, before the Northwest Regional Meeting of the American Bar Association in St. Paul, Minn., October 12, 1955. *Vital Speeches,* 22 (November 15, 1955), pp. 78–80.

41. Quoted in the testimony of Irving Ferman, Washington Office Director of the American Civil Liberties Union, *Hearings, op. cit.,* 187.

CHAPTER FOUR

The AMA and the Gerontologists: Uses and Abuses of "A Profile of the Aging: USA"

LEONARD D CAIN, JR.

Gerontology has displayed phenomenal growth in recent years, both in its research endeavors and in its political influence. Of major concern to gerontology has been the health status of the aged. Political controversy over how best to maintain the health of the aged has on occasion erupted, especially during periods in which the United States has had under consideration various plans to provide medical and other health services to the aged. One of the most dramatic controversies in recent years directly involved sociologists. This is the dispute resulting from the research project, "A Profile of the Aging: USA," conducted by Professors James W. Wiggins and Helmut Schoeck, and the use of the study by the American Medical Association and other agencies to discredit plans to expand governmental support of medical care for the aged.

The Research Project

A 1963 report of the United States Senate's Subcommittee on Problems of the Aged and Aging included these observations on recent gerontological research:

> During the period 1959 through 1962, the fruits of an enormous amount of research into the health status and needs of the elderly were offered for consumption and digestion. In instances some of the fruit was slightly rotten,

as in the case, for example, of a supposedly objective, scientific, academic study, the ill-famed Wiggins-Schoeck survey, which appeared in reputable disguise but which, fortunately, was quickly unmasked and revealed as pseudo-scientific half-effort.[1]

A footnote in the Subcommittee's report elaborated on the allegedly "slightly rotten," "ill-famed," "pseudoscientific half-effort" of Wiggins and Shoeck:

> This [Wiggins-Schoeck study] was a glowing report released in 1960, on the health status of the elderly which was widely publicized and promoted by the American Medical Association. . . . The report's errors — both in technique and conclusions — were so glaring that it was immediately repudiated, in letters to the Subcommittee on Problems of the Aged and Aging, by the majority of the sociologists who had supervised the interviewing. These men had not been afforded an opportunity to assist in drafting the questionnaire employed, determine the population sample, nor participate in evaluation of the findings.[2]

Who are Wiggins and Schoeck? Who are these "sociologists who supervised the interviewing" for the Wiggins-Schoeck study? On what grounds and in what manner did some of these sociologists "repudiate" the study, and how was it that they did not "participate in evaluation of the findings?"

Dr. James W. Wiggins, Professor of Sociology and Chairman of the Department of Sociology, Emory University, during the period of the research project, earned a PhD degree from Duke University in 1956. He had served on the faculty at Emory since 1946. Dr. Helmut Schoeck, Associate Professor of Sociology at Emory, earned his PhD degree from the University of Tübingen in 1948 and had taught at Emory since 1954. Neither is any longer at Emory. In 1959 they jointly received a $20,000 research grant from the William Volker Foundation through its subsidiary, the Foundation for Voluntary Welfare, of Burlingame, California, to conduct a nationwide survey of the aged in America, called from its inception, "A Profile of the Aging: USA."

In an invitational letter to prospective research associates for the "Profile" study, Wiggins announced that he and Professor Schoeck were initiating a foundation-supported study of a sample of the aging population of the United States — a project which would focus on the characteristics of the non-institutionalized aged and on the estimated 90 percent of the population over 65 not living on public charity. They argued that the present image of the aged has been derived mainly from studies of captive or destitute groups.

The letter also referred to the use of an "area probability sample." In addition it detailed the functions of the co-operating research associates. The associates were to find and. supervise local interviewers, check the schedules, and initiate follow-up calls to correct interviewers' errors. The assignment was to end when the completed interviews were accepted by the director. The research associates were to be paid a minimum honorarium of $100.00 above the cost of the interviews. And Wiggins and Schoeck explicitly announced that they themselves would design the schedule, draw the samples, tabulate and analyze the materials, and write the report.

By November, 1959, the recruitment of research associates had apparently been completed. The so-called area probability sample would include the following 15 communities: New York City; Santa Barbara, California; Columbia, Missouri; College Park, Maryland (two interview supervisors); State College, Pennsylvania; Cleveland, Ohio; Buffalo, New York; State College, Mississippi; Memphis, Tennessee; Lewiston, Maine; Denver, Colorado; Carlinville, Illinois; Omaha, Nebraska; Corvallis, Oregon; and Medford, Massachusetts.

By December, 1959, rather explicit instructions regarding the choice of interviewees had been forwarded, presumably to all participants. Those to be interviewed, the instructions announced, must meet these requirements:

1. All respondents are to be white (U. S. Census definition).
2. All respondents are to be over 65 years of age, without specific requirements of age distribution.

Additionally, an undated sheet called "Instructions to Interviewers," advised that "An occasional respondent may be senile, and impossible to interview. If such cases are found . . . the interviewer should terminate the interview as promptly and gently as possible, and move to another respondent."

But there were further restrictions imposed by Wiggins and Schoeck. Quotas, based on social class, sex, and rural-urban differences, were announced. Assigned social class percentages apparently varied slightly among the various communities, but *an obvious overweighting of the sample toward the upper classes is evidenced* by the instructions to the three sociologist-participants from whom this information is available.

One research associate received this quota: upper- and upper-middle class — 24 percent (7 males, 9 females); middle class — 67 percent (20 males 25 females); and lower class — 6 percent (3 males, 3 females). The research associate with this quota reported that, to obtain the interviews from those in the upper classes, he sent his interviewers into a neighborhood of

$65,000–$75,000 homes. Another associate reported his social class quota as follows: upper- and upper-middle class — 23 percent (9 males, 11 females); middle class — 65.5 percent (25 males, 32 females); and lower class — 11.5 percent (4 males, 6 females). A third associate reported that she was assigned 14 interviews with the upper class (32 percent), 23 with the middle class (52 percent), and 7 with the lower class (16 percent).

The invitational letter made no mention of the fact that minority racial groups would be excluded from the sample nor that the directors would impose a quota based on social class. Note, however, that the research associates were made aware of the severe pinching of the "Profile" sample *before* any interviews were conducted, and therefore before they had invested any appreciable time in the study.

Correspondence from Wiggins to an associate mentioned "suggestions for finding respondents and general areal assignments." Although I have not been able to examine a copy of these suggestions, it is my understanding that the associates were instructed to use their own discretion in distinguishing among upper-, middle-, and lower-class respondents; and that after one old person in a neighborhood was located and interviewed, referral by this initial interviewee to other older persons in the neighborhood was the recommended technique for filling the quota.

Full accounts of the methods used in selecting the areas from which the interviewees were to be drawn, of the procedures for establishing the quotas in each class, or of the instructions to the research associates are not available, but evidence reviewed above suggests rather strongly that the directors of "Profile" made a deliberate effort to delete from the sample those older Americans most likely to be ill and to have few resources to pay for medical treatment. Whether a so-called "normal" population ought to exclude such people is another issue. To the best of my knowledge, none of the sixteen participating sociologists protested the sampling procedures before issuance of the results; rather, they apparently assumed that the directors, both bona fide sociologists, would fully report the deleted categories in their announced results.

However, the participants had at least two additional reasons to question the research design: the composition of the interview schedule itself, and the difficulties encountered in administering the schedule. There were at least two versions of the schedule. At least one, probably more, of the research associates raised questions and sought clarification upon examination of the first version. One associate had fourteen distinct questions. A statement from the directors, titled "The Interview Schedule," undated but obviously a response to the inquiries, rationalized that clarification of the purpose of various schedule items was necessary, because it had been impossible, even with pre-testing, to anticipate every situation that might arise. Included were 19 explanatory statements which sought to clarify points on 27 of the 97 questions in the schedule. It is not known how many of the interviews were conducted using the first issue of the schedule or before the clarifications were distributed.

Although charges such as "loaded questions" and "poor questions and instructions" were leveled against the schedule *after* the announcement of the results of the study, the associates, at least the sociologists, apparently submitted only requests for clarification, not protests of bias, to the directors, during the conduct of the study. It is of course difficult to second guess a composer of questions for a schedule; it is also risky to remove questions from context; however, selected questions which may be interpreted as "loaded" or "slanted" are hereby reproduced.

#9. As you know, some people had not enrolled in a medical insurance plan, such as Blue Cross or Blue Shield, before they became 65 years old. What do you think would help such a person most?

Let people over 65 enroll _____

Establish new private medical insurance plan for people over 65 _____

Federal Government to set up medical insurance plan for people over 65 who want it _____

Federal Government to set up medical insurance plan which everybody over 65 must buy _____

Although the sociologists selected as associates were not necessarily gerontologists, widespread publicity had been given to various "medicare" plans, some of which (including the version eventually adopted by the Congress in 1965) were not even dimly represented as alternatives in #9. The "must buy" option has not, to my knowledge, ever been seriously proposed anywhere.

#15. You certainly agree that all welfare programs have to be paid for, that medicines, hospitals, food, and so on, cost somebody money. Since you are experienced and mature, would you tell me which of these welfare agencies, in your opinion, gives the best service with the least waste? (Check column A.) Which one gives the best service with the most waste? (Check column B.) Which one gives the worst service with the most waste? (Check column C.)

	A	B	C
Local Welfare Departments			
Churches			
Salvation Army			
State Welfare Departments			
Private Welfare Agencies			
Individual Charity			
Federal Government			
Red Cross			
Labor Unions			
Former Employers			

With no one currently on welfare rolls eligible for interview, and with a sample of only one in eight or ten in the lower class, this question, catering to the "experience" of the interviewee, is patently absurd.

A final methodological point is found in a letter from the social scientist who supervised the tabulations of the responses to the questions of the "Profile" schedule.

> . . . I want to emphasize that precautions were taken to prevent carelessness and especially that there was not, to my knowledge, any intentional bias in designing the categories under which the answers were grouped or in fitting individual responses to the alternative categories. As I recall, most of the alternatives were rather obvious. There were some open-ended questions which were difficult to code within a set number of alternative categories. It was in regard to these that I tried to exercise the greatest degree of supervision and consulted most frequently with Dr. Wiggins. I am satisfied that the coding categories which were developed were quite adequate to our task. In order to prevent technical errors or errors of judgment, I rechecked several hundred of the coded questionnaires. My impression was that the coders had done well. The punching of the IBM cards was done by a commercial agency, so I have no knowledge of what happened from this point forward. . . .
>
> I was quite surprised to learn that the motives of [Dr. Wiggins'] research had been questioned. That portion of the project with which I am directly acquainted was conducted with complete integrity and open-mindedness.[3]

Although the record of the actual conduct of the "Profile" research is incomplete, enough letters and other documents have become available so that a clear picture of the information in the hands of the research associates can be evaluated. Professors Wiggins and Schoeck made it abundantly clear that the associates' roles were to be limited and that certain categories of the aged were not to be included in the study. It is my personal opinion that, although the research plans and their execution reflect inexperience and naiveté, and although there are hints of conservative ideological attachments by the directors, there is no substantial evidence that the directors sought to deceive the research associates or to distort their data.

Formal Release of the Results

Apparently during the Spring of 1960, with the 1,500 or so schedules completed, Wiggins and Schoeck were able to begin analysis of their data. Also about this time one of the research associates wrote to Professor Leonard Z. Breen, sociologist at Purdue University and organizer for one of the sections of the forthcoming meeting of the International Congress of Gerontology, asking him if she could prepare a paper for the Congress, using substantially those data collected for the "Profile" study in one of the communities. Later that year in a letter to Senator McNamara Breen noted:

> . . . I wrote back to her suggesting that for an international meeting, such a paper might be inappropriate, but that the report of the total study might be of some interest to us, and I then wrote Professor Wiggins to that effect. On March 11, 1960, Professor Wiggins wrote me that they were "attempting to get an accurate picture of several aspects of the lives of 'normal' persons past 65, through the use of a national sample of this population." On March 29, 1960, I wrote Professor Wiggins inviting him to present a paper on his study at the International Congress of Gerontology, . . .
>
> On June 30, 1960, I wrote Professor Wiggins acknowledging receipt of an abstract of his paper for inclusion in our printed program of the congress. In that abstract, he said his paper would be "a preliminary report of some conclusions from a national area sample (United States of America) of 1,500 noninstitutionalized persons 65 years of age and over." I did not see a copy of the final paper until August 10, 1960, the day before it was read at the meeting of the congress.[4]

During the Summer of 1960, both the Republicans and the Democrats had written "medicare" planks in their quadrennial party platforms. The House of Representatives passed a rather mild version of a medicare bill. As the International Congress of Gerontology convened in San Francisco in August, the United States Senate's Finance Committee began formal consideration of the House of Representatives' bill which would provide medical benefits for the aged.

August 11, 1960, was, for purposes of this report, the first dramatic day. Before Wiggins read "A Profile of the Aging: USA" to members of the gerontological congress, he, together with, apparently, a representative of the Foundation for Voluntary Welfare (which had supplied the research grant), held a news conference and released a statement to the press. The release, prepared for the August 12 morning editions, stated:

Nine of every ten older persons report they have no unfilled medical needs, and the remainder list lack of money as one of the least important reasons for failure to relieve the needs.

This revealing picture of the aged, upsetting many conventional stereotypes, was part of a wide-ranging report made yesterday at the Fifth Congress of the International Association of Gerontology by an Emory University sociologist.

Dr. James W. Wiggins, co-director of a national survey focusing on the "normal" person 65 years and over, was assisted by 25 highly qualified research associates, most of whom are college professors of sociology and psychology. [Only the 16 participating sociologists have been identified by name.]

Of the older persons contacted, 90 per cent said they enjoyed good or fair health; 68 per cent said they could pay for a medical emergency costing at least $1,000 out of their own means. Wiggins concluded that most older persons can cope with a large medical bill by conventional or personal means.

The economic picture of older persons presented by Wiggins' study is encouraging. Half of his respondents reported incomes in excess of $2,000 a year, and one out of twenty reported more than $10,000. More persons received $2,000–$3,000 cash income than any other income bracket. Most of the aged reported a net worth in excess of $10,000.

80 per cent of the respondents were members of a church. Two-thirds were in retired status, although a number in this category were still gainfully employed. 60 per cent did not think a new department in the federal government could do something for them personally. . . .

Wiggins explained much of what has been reported about the health and welfare of older persons is based upon inaccurate data derived from the experience of a generation ago or from studies of the hospitalized or chronically dependent.

The study, Wiggins reported, "Shows that the aging, like others in our population, are not characteristically dependent, inadequate, ill, or senile."

He concluded: "Since all resources are limited, whether of family, kin, private or public agencies, the recognition that the dependent and helpless in our aging population are limited in number, will allow available resources to be applied with discrimination, with far greater hope of return to the society and to its people."[5]

Shortly before the reading of the paper, a wire service reporter, who had attended the press conference, received a request from the *Indianapolis Star* for information on the Wiggins paper to be forwarded in time for the afternoon edition. A letter dated May 27, 1963, from the sociologist, Harold Orbach, recounts the role of the reporter in the "Profile" affair:

> . . . [Leonard Breen] and the critic of the paper [Wayne Thompson] received the copies [from Wiggins and Schoeck] about two days before it was to be read, it having been accepted on the basis of a short general abstract saying reports would be given on a national sample of the aged.
>
> Neither paid much attention to it until about an hour before it was due to be presented when the AP reporter came upon myself and [another sociologist] in the lobby of the meeting asking us if we knew anything about the paper. He had been to a press conference where it had been presented and was dubious about many of the claims which seemed so much at variance with the great majority of other recent, well-conducted studies. There were also a number of curious side-remarks (omitted in the reading and in the printed version in *Geriatrics*) about "shock reaction to mention of public housing" and "FDR being the most numerous response when asked who was to blame for inflation" . . . But the thing that got him most curious was how the *Indianapolis Star* — probably the most reactionary newspaper in the east — knew about the paper in advance so that they had wired San Francisco AP to send them the story in a hurry to meet their deadline that day. We looked [the paper] over, noted the tendencies to conceal aspects of the study in generalities and the results in dubious statistics, and also noted the press release put out in San Francisco by the Foundation for Voluntary Welfare in advance of the paper, which exaggerated further the contentment and happiness of the average aged. The result was the story did not go out over either AP or UP wire service. The *Indianapolis Star* did not get its story that day. A large number of people showed up to hear the paper, alerted to its nature, and it was soundly criticized and not answered properly. Examples: only floor questions revealed the "profile of the aged" was a quota sample not a probability one; that in addition to omitting all non-whites, all persons living in public housing and on OAA were omitted (not mentioned when published 1½ years later); . . .[6]

But what did Wiggins say in the paper he read in San Francisco?[7] He made many of the same points that appeared in the news release. However, he observed that the paper was preliminary and partial. There was a rather straightforward effort to announce that the study was to deal with the "normal" aged population, in contrast to a "captive," much studied, population to be found in hospitals and on dependency rolls. He criticized previous gerontological studies for generalizing from a biased sample, and he stated that his available data were organized upon modal characteristics, with other forms of organizing his data to be presented in subsequent writings.

Wiggins reported an area probability sampling procedure and observed that each aged person had an "equal chance to be included." But he did not make it clear that a high percentage of the respondents were, through assignment of social-class quotas, from upper social classes, although Wiggins did mention "occupational distribution." The "equal chance to be included" statement was clearly gratuitous.

Wiggins, finally, provided two explanations for the higher percentage of the aged who are healthy and satisfied than reported in previous studies: first, the abnormality of previous samples, and second, the conclusion that a new type of old person, more healthy, and apparently more vigorous and affluent than a decade or more earlier when previous studies were conducted, had emerged on the American scene. In the paper Wiggins mentioned explicitly the deletion of the "institutionalized" from his sample, and implicitly the deletion of the chronically dependent. In a footnote he apologized for the deletion of non-whites from the sample.

I was present during the reading of the paper in San Francisco by Wiggins; I heard the criticisms by the discussant, Wayne Thompson, and the harsh and sustained protest of the paper from several in the audience, an audience of perhaps over one hundred.

I was confused and puzzled by the unexpected reactions by many gerontologists. During the reading of the paper I became vaguely aware that its conclusions would surely provide solace to those who may be politically conservative on welfare matters, but I frankly did not grasp immediately the ethical and political ramifications of the study.

Shortly after the session adjourned, I accosted Wiggins in the hallway. With him was a man introduced as Mr. "Baldy" Harper (who, as I learned later, was an official of the Foundation for Voluntary Welfare). No one else seemed willing even to speak to Wiggins. The two men appeared to be dazed but not angered by the criticism to which Wiggins had been subjected. I recall having mentioned to Wiggins and Harper that I had recently completed annotating a bibliography of seven hundred references on gerontology, and that in my textual analysis I had suggested that the publications in gerontology reflected, along with a scientific orientation, many characteristics of a social movement.[8] At the time it appeared to me that the actions of the protesters of the Wiggins paper somewhat confirmed my diagnosis.

Public Reaction: AMA, the Press, and Congress

AMA Appropriation of the "Profile" Data. The San Francisco press gave top billing to the Wiggins-Schoeck report in the August 12 editions,[9] although it was not until the following Monday morning, August 14, that an American Medical Association press conference (held in Chicago) and news release introduced "Profile" to much of the nation.

I have not been able to determine how long in advance the AMA planned the press conference, or whether the decision followed the apparent failure of the national press to give emphasis to the original San Francisco press conference on August 11 and to the delivery of the paper itself. But the August 14 conference certainly did focus national attention on the study. Unfortunately, I have been unable to obtain a copy of the full text of the AMA release. Nonetheless, *The New York Times* of August 15, 1960, incorporated some of its text, added information supplied by the AMA President, Dr. Leonard W. Larson, and also shared results of the reporter's further sleuthing:

> The president-elect of the American Medical Association said today [August 14, 1960, in Chicago] that most persons over the age of 65 did not want a Government program of health care.
>
> Dr. Leonard W. Larson . . . said in a statement issued by the A.M.A. that this conclusion had stemmed from a study that showed that the "vast majority" of the elderly wanted voluntary health programs and that only 10 per cent supported "compulsory plans."
>
> Congress should take note, he said.
>
> Dr. Larson's statement was preceded by one attributed to the Medical Association that said:
>
> "An independent national survey just completed by university sociologists [Wiggins and Schoeck] emphatically proves that the great majority of Americans over 65 are capably financing their own health care and prefer to do it on their own, without Federal Government intervention."
>
> . . . Dr. Larson said the study "disproves some dangerous misconceptions about the aged." . . .
>
> "The A.M.A. is vigorously supporting voluntary legislation to help those of our aged citizens who really need help. We are opposed irrevocably to compulsory legislation that seeks to cover everyone regardless of whether they want help or need it."[10]

The *Times'* story also included information obtained from Professor Schoeck:

> When reached by telephone in Atlanta, Professor Schoeck said that the survey had cost $20,000. This was furnished by the Foundation for Voluntary Welfare of Burlingame, California, a subsidiary of the William Volker Fund.
>
> Civic sources in Kansas City said today that the fund was a charitable and educational foundation set up in the nineteen-forties by the late William Volker, an industrialist and philanthropist . . .

An A.M.A. spokesman described the Volker Fund's outlook as "conservative."[11]

The *Times'* story included one other bit of information crucial to our interpretation of the reactions to this study:

> Professor Wiggins, who approved the medical association's statement and ordered fifty copies for his own use, is a consultant to the association's medical economics department. He was said to receive expenses when he came to Chicago, but no other compensation.[12]

Note that the *Times'* story did not report that minority racial groups, the institutionalized aged, and certain other categories were excluded from the so-called "random sample." I presume that the AMA news release and Dr. Larson failed to include this relevant information.

From this story and from other limited information I have deduced that the AMA news release listed the names and academic affiliations of the 16 participating sociologists, but not of the additional nine or more participating social scientists. Why this was done I cannot imagine and have not been able to determine. But it is clear that the listing of the 16 was a major tactical blunder by the AMA, because local reporting of the names of participants alerted them to how the study was being used. The list also was available for quick use by the Senate Subcommittee on Problems of the Aged and Aging.

A search through the veritable "catacombs" of the *Journal of the American Medical Association* in the issues published during the period of the "Profile" controversy brought forth no references whatever either to "Profile" or to the attacks on the AMA for its news release on the study.

However, the *Journal* of August 13, 1960, published during the week of the Wiggins paper and the AMA news release, reprinted testimony of AMA President-elect Larson before the Senate Finance Committee on HR 12580. He contended that, contrary to popular misconception, the majority of our aged are in good health and that such a program as medicare would compel the non-needy to accept federal medicine rather than buy medical care voluntarily through their own resources.[13]

This and other fragmentary evidence, however, do not support a charge of conspiracy, or even complicity, between the AMA and the directors of "Profile," although the "tone" and the "emphasis" of the AMA's orientation and the types of questions designed by Wiggins and Schoeck, as well as their conclusions, are similar. Yet, I must ask, isn't the "tone" of the remarks of certain liberal officials and gerontologists somewhat similar to the questions posed and the conclusions drawn by "scientific" researchers in gerontology? At least, this is what AMA witnesses charged.

Press Treatment of "Profile." The AMA news conference led to stories in newspapers throughout the country. Although the reported results prompted numerous editorials, it has not been feasible to attempt a survey of the national press. Rather, I have reviewed the handling of the issue in two major newspapers with nationwide circulation, *The Wall Street Journal* and *The New York Times.* Their coverage reflects rather divergent orientations toward the Wiggins-Schoeck study.

One week after the delivery of "Profile" in San Francisco, *The Wall Street Journal*[14] published a condensed version of the paper and added an editorial which used the paper's data to repudiate medicare proposals. Actually almost 50 per cent of the original paper's text was reproduced under the heading: " 'The Aging': Neither Indigent Nor Childlike, They Want Government Aid As Very Last, Not First, Resort." In this condensation there is not even a hint that any segment of the aged was purposefully deleted from eligibility for interviewing. The prefatory remark mentions "probability sampling." The concluding paragraph begins: "It is hoped that further research into the normal can be carried out." The "normal" is nowhere defined. This *Wall Street Journal* version, just as the original paper and the version subsequently published in *Geriatrics,*[15] claims that "The study . . . shows that the aging, like others in our population, are not characteristically dependent, inadequate, ill, or senile." But, after all, the "dependent," "ill," "senile," and, I suppose, the "inadequate," were purposefully (along with non-whites) left out of the sample.

In columns adjacent to the condensation of the Wiggins paper in the *Journal* was an editorial entitled "Limited Problem, Collectivist Remedy." The editors argued that

> [The] problem of medical care of the aged has been inexcusably exaggerated by the politicians and commentators. Indeed, the whole picture of the over-65 group in this country that is usually drawn is nothing more than a caricature. That is the word used by Professors Wiggins and Schoeck . . . in their revealing report on the aging — a report based on a careful interview-survey of a large cross-section of people outside of hospitals or institutions. . . .[16]

Although, as shall be presented shortly, a number of the participating sociologists renounced the Wiggins report and its appropriation by AMA, and although the study was repudiated on the floor of the U.S. Senate, *The*

Wall Street Journal seems to have produced only three subsequent references to the issue — two letters to the editor which were sharply critical of the report[17] and one reference in a news story.[18] In the story the battle techniques of the AMA and the AFL-CIO in the medicare fight were viewed as similar, since the one was plugging the Wiggins-Schoeck study before Congress and the other was denouncing the study as rigged.

Although *The Wall Street Journal* paid little heed to the continuing uproar over the Wiggins paper and its use, the issue was kept alive in *The New York Times*. Both letters to the editor and news reports followed in the wake of the story of August 15 (cited above).

The first letter, drafted by a Columbia University professor on August 16 and published on August 22, stated that ". . . neither Congress nor any one else should take note of the [Wiggins-Schoeck] report until there has been sufficient time to subject it to scientific review."[19] (Parenthetically, the *Times* failed to report the speech of August 22, 1960, by Senator Eugene McCarthy on the floor of the U. S. Senate, in which the Wiggins study and its use by the AMA were repudiated.)

Professor Wayne Thompson of Cornell University, the discussant of the "Profile" paper in San Francisco, wrote a letter on August 17 which was published on August 25 in the *Times*. His criticisms, much like those of other participants we discuss below, were directed against the sampling techniques, but he also raised the question of Professor Wiggins' role as consultant to the AMA's medical economics department.[20]

On September 1 there appeared a letter submitted on August 22 by Professor Joseph P. Fitzpatrick, a Fordham University sociologist and one of the 16 participating sociologists. Fitzpatrick objected to the *Times'* news story which had listed him as an assistant in the Wiggins-Schoeck study, and he defined his role as only that of engaging interviewers and supervising "the interviewing of eighty-seven persons in the New York area, according to a prepared schedule, and on the basis of a sample which had been drawn by the directors of the study."[21]

On September 18, the *Times* presented information collected by Dr. Harold Sheppard of Senator McCarthy's Subcommittee on Problems of the Aged and Aging.[22] Sheppard had collected critical replies from nine of the sociologists who participated in the Wiggins-Schoeck study, and the *Times* account listed four criticisms of "Profile" that were gleaned from the responses of these sociologists. All four criticisms, three of which were related to sampling procedures and one to a question in the interview schedule, were of a methodological nature.

On September 23 Wiggins and Schoeck responded to the coverage of the whole story by the *Times* with a 2,500-word letter, including a request that it "be published in full in an early edition . . ."[23] This request was not granted. Rather, on October 2, the *Times* published a story under the headline, "Directors Defend Study of Elderly: Attitude Survey on Health Plan is Called Up to Date in Letter To the Times." Although few of the phrases placed in quotation marks in the news story are to be found in precisely the same form as those in the original letter, it would appear that the October 2 story accurately reflects, as far as it goes, the points of the letter. The *Times* story read, in part:

> . . . Professors Wiggins and Schoeck said that their study was the first national one to cover its wide range of characteristics of the aging. They asserted that other studies of the aging were generally out of date. . . .
>
> They said census estimates proved their sample was representative of the aged population of the United States. . . .
>
> "The exclusion of certain classes from a survey sample is quite common," they [Wiggins and Schoeck] went on. "Persons in institutions are usually excluded. The often-cited social security study [reported in *Social Security Bulletin,* especially October, 1959, November, 1959, and January, 1959 (1960?)] excluded about 55 per cent of persons over 65, and did not include persons receiving Old Age Assistance unless they were also drawing Social Security payments. Another study excluded the hard of hearing and persons whose English was not adequate. One recent study excluded 'individuals in certain occupational groups and those living in institutions' " . . .
>
> "The U.S. Bureau of the Census reported recently that from 1951 to 1958 the income of aged males increased at a rate twice as fast as that for all adult males. Health status of the aged has also improved, since death rates for persons over 65 have declined faster than those for any age group except children under five. The old stereotypes of the aging are not supported by the present facts."[24]

Although the reporter's paraphrasing of the contents of the letter apparently did not distort the original meaning, of considerable significance is the deletion altogether from the news item of some of the points in the letter, which I have examined. Wiggins and Schoeck felt that many of the previous reports in the *Times* represented the viewpoint of, and were gathered by a staff member of, the Senate Subcommittee on the Aged and Aging. They also argued that the critics did not cite current figures to question their findings; instead they charged that the critics speculated about their research techniques and motives. Wiggins and Schoeck also presented more details than did the *Times* story on surveys that excluded certain groups — e.g., the NORC study, which did not include those who were sick, hard-of-hearing, or those who did not speak English. Of course, it is a bit difficult to reconcile this defense by Wiggins and Schoeck of their "Profile" methodology with their remarks in the invitational letter to the research associates: "the present image of the aging is derived largely from studies of captive (institutionalized) and destitute groups."

Reaction in Congress. Shortly after the AMA news release on August 14, 1960, had listed the names and addresses of the 16 participating sociologists, Dr. Harold L. Sheppard, research director for the Senate Subcommittee on Problems of the Aged and Aging, solicited their reactions to the Wiggins paper and its use by the AMA. The responses from at least nine of the sociologists provided material not only for the *Times'* story on September 18 (discussed above) but for Senator Eugene McCarthy's speech on August 22. The Senator said not only that the Wiggins-Schoeck study did a disservice to older people and to the medical profession but that it hurt the reputation of American social science. The study, according to Senator McCarthy, was "completely inaccurate":

> By their own admission and despite the American Medical Association propaganda, Wiggins and Schoeck actually did not conduct a survey of a true cross section of the 16 million people over 65 in the United States. . . . For example:
>
> 1. They deliberately did not interview anyone over 65 who was receiving old age assistance. Yet, this group represents 16 per cent of all the aged.
>
> 2. They deliberately — because, they said, they lacked funds — omitted non-white people over 65 who represent about 7 per cent of the aged.
>
> 3. [They] deliberately left out of their survey aged persons in hospitals, homes for the aged, nursing homes and other institutions. This group represents about 4 per cent of the people over 65.
>
> 4. Dr. Wiggins admitted — but only after persistent questioning by other sociologists attending the International Gerontological Congress in San Francisco, where he first gave his findings — that this study had about a 20 per cent "refused to be interviewed and not available category." . . .
>
> . . . in the final analysis between 25 to 35 per cent of the aged in this country were not covered by the AMA-publicized so-called "scientific" survey of America's older citizens. . . .

> Two claims of the . . . study, by themselves, are conclusive proof that the sample reported on is not representative of the aged of the United States:
>
> 1. The authors assert that 64% of their sample report some form of health insurance. Why, even the insurance lobby doesn't claim any more than 49%, and [HEW] estimates only 42%. . . .

2. The authors assert that nearly 34% (33.6) of the aged in their sample are in the labor force, but the Bureau of Labor Statistics . . . reports only 20% of the 65 and over population as being in the labor force today. . . .

Contrary to Professor Wiggins' own statement in his San Francisco report, his sample was not based on an "area probability" selection. Instead it was based on what is called the quota method, [a] much discredited technique . . .

Apart from the matter of the distorted sample covered in the report, there is still the highly important question about the ability of an individual in an interview with sociologists to determine the actual state of his physical (or mental) condition, or whether he has or does not have any unmet health needs. For the AMA to accept the statement that 90 per cent of the aged have no unfilled medical needs is to fly in the face of the day-to-day clinical experience of the doctors who are members of the AMA. . . .

. . . what we have here is another attempt by the American Medical Association to dissuade the Congress from taking effective action on the issue that cries out for solution — now. It is regrettable that the AMA has rejected its stethoscope and chosen instead the horoscope . . .[25]

Apart from a few questions on the floor of the Senate, and the insertion by some conservative Senators of anti-medicare newspaper editorials inspired by "Profile," there was no effort to rebut Senator McCarthy's repudiation of the AMA's use of "Profile."[26]

Professional Reaction

Reactions of Professional Participants. Although I have, in the context of the previous discussion, noted some of the reactions of those who participated in the Wiggins-Schoeck study, it is essential that we consider these at greater length.

Of the 16 sociologists listed as participants, as research associates, in the "Profile" study, 10 have kindly responded to my letter requesting information and their personal views on the issue: Glenn Bakkum, Jack R. Conrad, Ross Ensminger, Joseph E. Faulkner, Joseph P. Fitzpatrick, Kent Geiger, Noel Gist, Millard Jordan, Bruce Melvin, and Edith Sherman. I have personally interviewed some of the above as well as three other participants: Margaret Cussler, Clovis R. Shepherd, and Constantine Yeracaris. Two others, Anders Myrhman and T. Earl Sullenger had letters published in the Congressional Record.[27] I have had no word at all from only one of the listed participants, Dorris Rivers.

Professor Gist was apparently the first participant to protest the announced results of "Profile," in letters to his hometown newspaper, the AMA, and the Senate Subcommittee.[28] In a letter to me on April 26, 1965, he recounted his protestations:

> In the spring of 1960 I had a letter from Dr. Wiggins saying that he had received a grant from an unnamed foundation for a national sample study of the aged. He said in his letter that the area in which I live fell within the sample, and wondered if I would be willing to participate . . .
>
> When the interview schedules were received it was quite apparent that they were the work of research amateurs, since the instructions were vague or incomplete, and the questions badly framed. The instructions were to interview only white persons over 65 who were rural residents and who were not receiving old age pensions or other forms of public support. Obviously, this eliminated a lot of people, especially those from the lowest income brackets. This procedure is quite acceptable, of course, providing it is made explicit that such a group is *not* a representative sample of all people in the higher age brackets. I did not question this, however, because I assumed that Wiggins knew what he was doing and that he was conducting the survey in an ethical manner.
>
> Some weeks later I was shocked to read in the local newspaper a news story saying that a national survey showed a very small percentage of older persons in financial straits. The story emanated from the headquarters of the American Medical Association. My name as a professional participant, along with the names of a number of other sociologists who had agreed to partici-pate, was mentioned in the story. It became immediately apparent that the whole thing was a propaganda device with political implications. The story was written with the slant that the participating sociologists endorsed the findings of the survey, . . . Of course, the survey itself was rigged by the nature in which the sample was selected.
>
> I publicly repudiated the whole business . . . I also sent a strong letter to the American Medical Association, but was not given the courtesy of a reply or a defense. It was quite clear that the AMA was caught red-handed in an attempt to foist a phony research on the public. Whether Wiggins was knowingly and willingly involved, or whether he was so naive that he did not see through the whole dirty business, I do not know. . . .
>
> . . . I think the AMA rather got their fill of the adverse publicity the project attracted. I was personally embarrassed, as were some of the other sociologists who participated.
>
> Subsequently, I heard that the outfit putting up the money was the Volker Foundation, which has a record of opposition to such programs as old age assistance and public medical care for older persons. But no mention was ever made of the identity of the foundation in Wiggins' correspondence with me. If such mention had been made, or if I had known the AMA was in-volved, I certainly would not have agreed to participate. And I had no reason

to suspect the motives or competence of a fellow-sociologist, though I did not know Wiggins personally.[29]

Professor Edith Sherman was another participant who promptly protested the misuse of the data contributed by her to "Profile."   In a letter to Harold Sheppard, August 23, 1960, she wrote:

I was profoundly shocked and appalled at the conclusions which had been drawn from the [Profile] research, as well as the uses to which it is evidently being put. . . . I would like . . . to list the following comments or criticisms . . .

I. *Sampling*

The issue of the sampling procedure and breakdown cannot I believe be called the "normal" aging population.

a. All so-called indigent people were excluded; all OAP were excluded; all Negroes were excluded; although Spanish-Americans or Mexicans were included — in our area where they represent at least 10 to 15% of the population . . . , none appeared on the sample for the very good reason that social class breakdown (see below) included 4 urban cases of lower-class and that this group represents in our city the lowest socio-economic group and by chance did not show up in those four cases.

b. The breakdown of socio-economic level in my sample of 44 cases was . . . 16% . . . lower class, 52% . . . middle class, [and] 32% upper class. I know of no other sociological study in the United States which would use a sample in which the upper class number would be twice the size of the lower class . . .

c. Because it was impossible for the interviewers in the Denver area to get into apartment houses (locked doors and no-solicitor signs and refusal of people to allow strangers into apartments), none of the sample lived in apartment houses. I feel very strongly that a sample of people who maintain their own homes, yards, etc., would most probably be in better health in order to be able to do so, . . .

II. *Interpretation of responses to questions*

. . . It is very difficult to understand from my area sample the interpretation of these questions [specifically #9 and #15] as a reflection or a rejection of government programs of welfare or insurance and a desire to use "conventional and personal means" to cope with medical problems. The only interpretation it would seem to me is that the aging population shows a high incidence of unawareness and lack of acquaintance with any sort of plan — private, public, voluntary, or compulsory — but are individually deeply concerned that they not face a serious or excessively costly illness. . . . As the preliminary report stands today, I can only say that the conclusions seem highly misleading according to my own local experience.[30]

Mrs. Sherman elaborated her concerns in a letter, dated September 6, 1960, addressed to Wiggins himself:

> . . . I cannot, of course, quarrel with you about the "results" of the study since I have no access to the total findings. I am really surprised, however, and somewhat disturbed by the interpretation of these results and the uses to which they are being put. I had no idea when we started to work on this study that the "hypothesis" was "that modern life is not as complicated and frustrating for the aged as it is pictured in the current social science literature." (p. 14, your report). I knew of no hypothesis, except that we wanted to get an accurate profile of the aging population. Likewise, the fact that my sample in the Denver area was approximately 16% lower class, 52% middle class, and 32% upper class could not be presumed to indicate a so-called "norm" of the aging population. I think the study had every right to select a sample which left out certain portions of the population, but then the findings could not be used to generalize about the "total aging population." In Denver, which I understand has from 50,000 to 75,000 Spanish-Americans, none appeared on our sample and probably because of the class bias of the sample. Also, because of the difficulty of gaining access to the people living in rooms and apartments, these people were eliminated from our interviews, although I feel that the fact of living in apartments correlates clearly with poor health and a lack of independent status. . . .
>
> Most disturbing, however, to me were the interpretations of the answers to questions No. 5, No. 9, and No. 15. First of all, these questions were ones to which we found the greatest confusion. These elderly people just did not understand the economics of medical care, it seems to me. The responses, if anything, reflected great ignorance and unawareness of any kind of insurance programs — public, private, voluntary, or compulsory. The use of the term "must buy" in question No. 9 was highly loaded. . . .
>
> From the local sample in which, as you know, I participated to a large extent [as interviewer], I find it difficult to believe the interpretations which have emerged from the study and the seizure by the AMA, the *Wall Street Journal,* etc., of these findings as "proof" of their positions regarding medical care for the aged.[31]

We have already mentioned that Professor Fitzpatrick wrote to *The New York Times* on August 22, 1960, regarding his limited role in the "Profile" study. The following day he sent a copy of the letter to Wiggins, stating, "I sincerely regret the fact that the use of the partial report by the American Medical Association made it necessary for me to write this letter.[32] Wiggins later responded and apologized for this situation. In the meantime, Fitzpatrick had been busy with answering other inquiries about his participation. He responded on August 20 to an inquiry from a Harvard graduate student:

> . . . my part in the survey was not very accurately described. I had nothing to do with the design of the study, with the drawing of the sample, with the collation or interpretation of the data. . . .
>
> I agreed to take care of the interviewing . . . I returned the completed interviews . . . , and the next I know is the story in the *New York Times,* in which I appear to have a major role . . .
>
> What annoyed me about the story in the *Times* is the implication that public policy can (or should) be set on the basis of public opinion polls or opinion surveys. . . . You determine this by hard study and analysis and then, in legislative halls, by serious debate, consideration and, in the end, inevitable negotiation and compromise.[33]

Of course, Fitzpatrick received a letter from Harold Sheppard of the Senate Subcommittee, dated August 19, which requested that the participating sociologists react to the AMA release. Fitzpatrick, on August 23, dutifully responded:

> . . . Some of the statements used in the American Medical Association release omitted extremely important qualifications. . . . I do not think the study can be considered seriously in relation to public policy until the complete report is available and has been scientifically analyzed for validity.[34]

Fitzpatrick was called upon to review his role in and submit his interpretation of the "Profile" study on at least one additional occasion. Wiggins had accepted an invitation to review his study at a seminar to be conducted in New York on October 21, 1960; Fitzpatrick was invited to participate. Since he could not, he submitted a rather lengthy written statement to a Columbia University professor who was to participate. In this he reiterated his previous objections. His complaint was not with the study itself but with the fact that publicity was given to a partial report:

> . . . Thus, unqualified "findings" were used to support public positions, and, what should have been a careful scientific inquiry became a heated public controversy.[35]

Fitzpatrick's further comments were organized around two main issues: 1. An upper class bias in the distribution of the sample; and 2. methodological problems related to so-called area probability sampling. After reporting that he had been instructed by Wiggins to interview twice as many in the upper and upper-middle class as in the lower class, he added:

I realized this was not representative of the New York City population. I presumed that the sample had been selected on the basis of the total population of the Nation, and New York was not typical.[36]

It seems clear from the exchange of correspondence between Fitzpatrick and Wiggins that the latter was never explicit about his definition of "area probability sample." The first instruction was to circle an area of a few blocks which were upper, middle, and lower class and locate respondents in these areas. Later, when questions were raised about determining who was a lower-class person or a middle-class person, regardless of where he lived, Wiggins resolved the problem by indicating class membership should be made on the basis of common-sense judgment.

Another of the associates recounted that he assigned interviewing tasks to students in a research methods class, and that he severely criticized the "Profile" schedule as an example of a poorly constructed instrument. Yet, the students conducted the interviews using the schedule, and the sociologist forwarded the completed forms to Wiggins. The associate also recalled that the assignment was rather lucrative for the amount of time he spent on it.

A number of other participating sociologists have criticized the Wiggins-Schoeck study, either in letters to Dr. Sheppard or to me. These criticisms, by and large, repeat those reviewed above. They center upon weaknesses in the methodology and the related problems of the interpretation and presentation of results. In my judgment Wiggins and Schoeck did not analyze their data with care, nor did they report adequately the limited universe from which their sample was drawn. The intense reactions to these asserted deficiencies, especially in the political context engendered by the appropriation of the study by the AMA, indicate that ethical and political problems can indeed arise not merely in the collection of data but in their analysis and presentation as well.

Although the critics of Wiggins and Schoeck have been numerous, and often harsh, there are those who have supported their endeavors. One of the associates, in a letter dated August 17, 1965, wrote as follows:

> . . . I thought the survey accurately reflected the opinion of those approached, but . . . two critically important (in my estimation) groups were ignored: (1) Negroes and (2) the indigent nursing home ("poor house") population.
>
> Yet I have never had anything but the highest respect for the professional competence and ethical standards of Dr. Wiggins. Any researcher is free to restrict his sample in any way he chooses so long as he makes this known. At no time to my knowledge did the "Profile of the Aging" project attempt to conceal the fact that these groups were excluded from the survey.

I recall that some sociologists who participated in the survey repudiated it on what to me were incredibly flimsy grounds. Dr. Wiggins was criticized for not allowing participants to examine the entire mass of collected data. This was apparently meant to indicate that he had something to hide. . . . I should add that on several occasion's Dr. Wiggins encouraged me to begin some intensive analysis of the . . . data and assured me that the larger files in Atlanta were open to me.

Personally I have always believed that some of the criticism of Dr. Wiggins was rooted in the fact that he paid a very low amount of money to the interviewer. . . .

. . . from the first I have believed that the "Profile of the Aging" study, although having the basic weakness of restricted sampling, was of exceptional value.

A somewhat different stand was taken by another participant in a letter to me dated September 7, 1965:

. . . I could not agree with the so-called statistical method that was used in selecting the aged and aging as typical for [my region]. I protested on several counts with Dr. Wiggins . . .

I believe that it was at the Chicago meeting where the Society of Sociology Professors [Society for the Study of Social Problems?] was ready to condemn Jim for what he had done. At that time I strongly opposed condemning him. He was not at the dinner where the proposal was made but he was attending meetings. I believe a committee was appointed to make further investigation and reports. I never heard anymore about the committee.

My own feeling was that someone who had provided the money for the study had dictated the method and preconceived results. . . .

Reactions of Other Professionals. The reactions discussed above were to a large extent the product of Wiggins' speech in San Francisco and the resultant controversy in Congress and in the press. However, there is some overlap with the issues raised by the Wiggins-Schoeck article in *Geriatrics,* published in 1961. As Professor Orbach notes below, in a letter to the editor of *Geriatrics* on September 14, 1961, this article raised other issues, because Wiggins and Schoeck apparently had not qualified their position, even in face of the extended public controversy. Orbach wrote to the editor as follows:

Your publication of the article by Wiggins and Schoeck, "A Profile of the Aging: USA," astonished me. This paper was . . . immediately roundly scored by the gerontologists who heard it presented, and then exposed when it became a national incident through the columns of the *New York Times.* . . .

As one of those present when the paper was given — I have the original copy — it is even more astounding that the authors now publish it with no changes or emendations to alter the completely erroneous impression that this was based on a representative sample. They have completely ignored the criticisms made of it and deign to act as though they never existed.[37]

Although Orbach had not been directly involved in the Wiggins-Schoeck project, he had written the McNamara committee (the Subcommittee on the Aged and Aging) an evaluation of Wiggins' "Profile" paper. In this he had attacked the sampling procedure, had raised questions about Wiggins and Schoeck's acquaintance with the literature in the field of aging, and had raised questions about the reporting of the data. Specifically he argued that modal categories are rather useless as an indicator of responses unless a full and complete description of the entire range of responses is provided, and that *not a single tabular presentation* accompanied the Wiggins report.[38]

Geriatrics twice wrote Orbach. In the second letter the journal's representative requested permission to publish (with some editing) the September 14 letter. Although Orbach did not wish to have the letter published, he said that "... if you are interested in publishing my *comments* on the paper, I might agree to this dependent on what editing you want to do and if I had the opportunity to revise it."[39] This seems to have ended the exchange.

But the Wiggins-Schoeck issue lived on. In my book review of Donahue and Tibbitts, *Social and Psychological Aspects of Aging* (a book that reproduced papers from the San Francisco conference), I raised a question concerning the deletion of the Wiggins-Schoeck study.[40] Orbach took me somewhat to task:

> ... I cannot agree with your comments on the Wiggins and Schoeck affair because of my own intimate connection with this from the moment of exposure on. Not that I might not agree that it should have been included — as an example of conceived and presented political propaganda — but that it did an effective job of criticizing gerontological research. Far from it — the critique was a slip-shod restatement of other competent gerontologists own self-criticism rather loosely spaced in time of origin designed only to introduce their own biased materials.
>
> ... The paper was omitted on ... the grounds of lack of scientific merit and also because of the clear evidence that the authors had arranged to use their presentation for a political campaign.[41]

Orbach advanced other criticisms, including the reminder "that Wiggins had neglected to make clear that at the same time he conducted the study and gave the paper he was a paid consultant to the AMA." Then he asked me what I would have done as an editor in similar circumstances. I replied in a letter dated June 10, 1963:

> I appreciate very much . . . your detailed report on l'affaire Wiggins. . . .
> . . . I was at the presentation of the paper in San Francisco. I observed Ethel Shanas and Lenore Epstein, among others, running around like wounded birds. I talked with Wiggins afterward (about the only one present who would!) and have corresponded with him and . . . "Baldy" Harper of Wabash a couple of times since. I have talked with Breen (last November in Los Angeles). I have read Senator McCarthy's speech on the subject. I have explored the situation a bit with an Emory graduate student, . . . I have learned, from sociologists in Southern universities, of Wiggins' repudiation by Emory; I have read the *Geriatrics* version [of the paper]. . . .[42]

I then agreed that the study was biased and also that there might be ethical issues involved in the Wiggins-Schoeck study, as Orbach had suggested:

> . . . I simply contend, first, that a number of gerontological studies have been biased "the other way"; in my trend report [*Current Sociology*] I suggested gerontology was a social movement, partly because I spotted over and over again indications that data were being used to promote a "cause," a good one, but a cause. And, I contend, secondly, that there are more proper ways to direct charges of unethical behavior than were done by some of my colleagues. That is, I say either let an unbiased study correct the Wiggins' distortions, or inaugurate procedures through the professional society to declare Wiggins unethical. . . .[43]

Reactions of Professional Associations

Early in my investigation I gained the impression that both the Society for the Study of Social Problems (SSSP) and the Committee on Ethics of the American Sociological Association had conducted investigations of "Profile" and its use by the AMA, with focus on ethical considerations. My original information, it turns out, was in both instances inaccurate. However, the information gleaned in following up the inaccurate leads is vital to a thorough review of the affair.

SSSP, which convened its annual meeting in 1960 less than three weeks after the San Francisco reading of "Profile," passed a resolution repudiating the misuse of sociological data provided by the study and authorized the establishment of a special committee to investigate. On September 16, 1960, Professor Marvin Sussman, a sociologist from Western Reserve University, Vice-President of SSSP, and chairman of the special committee, sent a letter to Wiggins at Emory. Sussman informed Wiggins that SSSP had discussed the "Profile" issue and that he, Sussman, had been appointed chairman of a committee to examine the study's reliability and validity and its use by the AMA. The letter informed Wiggins that SSSP had, before the committee was formed, passed a resolution which condemned the misuse of sociological data in "Profile," but that some members persevered to insist that a careful review of the study and its use by lay organizations be undertaken. With this recapitulation as context, Sussman asked Wiggins to cooperate by forwarding the research design, the questionnaire, codes, a description of the sampling procedure, sets of tables, and the paper itself. A less than cordial response from Wiggins followed.

Although, as mentioned above, informants indicated to me that they thought SSSP had actually conducted an investigation, the failure of the special study committee to complete its assignment has been reviewed and explained in a letter to me from Professor Sussman, dated October 6, 1965:

Dear Professor Cain:

. . . In the year the [Profile] incident occurred, the matter was discussed by the Executive Committee of SSSP as well as by the membership. The recommendation was that a committee of outstanding persons be formed to make an impartial investigation into the matter, and I suspect that the outcome of such an investigation would be some action, at that time unspecified, which would express censure or support for those involved in this case, namely Wiggins and Schoeck. In being given this assignment, it was my understanding that in the event these distinguished and impeccable sociologists would not undertake responsibility for such an investigation, I give serious consideration to dropping the investigation so that the outcome would not resemble the work of witch hunters. This may be somewhat unclear, but the Executive Committee clearly stipulated that if top-flight people would not undertake such an investigation for any number of reasons, I discontinue the appointment of a committee because the end result of such an investigation would suggest persecution rather than objective study and recommendation. The committee selected by an elimination procedure would obviously be biased against those being investigated.

The first three top-flight sociologists expressed some concern but disinterest in participating in such an investigation. About that time I learned that Robert Angell was chairman of a new committee of ASA and that this committee, which I believe was the Committee on Ethics, was going to investigate the matter. It was at this time that I decided to discontinue my efforts to form a committee, and at a subsequent meeting of the Executive Committee and the membership I notified them of this action. . . .[44]

Clearly neither SSSP nor its representatives charged Wiggins and Schoeck with unethical behavior, but it is less clear that members of SSSP were so restrained. Rather, the very fact of a resolution to begin with, combined with the reported fears by the Executive Committee of SSSP and Sussman of "bias," "persecution," and "witch hunt," suggests that charges of unethical conduct were in the air.

The reference by Sussman to the ASA Committee on Ethics is undoubtedly related to an effort which took material form as a report by one of the Committee members of Wiggins' defense of "Profile" at the previously mentioned seminar in New York on October 21, 1960. This report, which was originally distributed to the members of the Committee, is now in the files at the national office of the ASA. I have made an unsuccessful appeal to the Executive Officer of the ASA for permission to examine the document. I have suffered frustration over my failure, especially because I have received conflicting interpretations of the conclusions of the report.

Although the contents of the report have not been made public, the fact that there is a report and that it remains classified are significant for this study. In 1960 the Executive Committee of the ASA had favorably considered the establishment of a special committee to explore the prospects of development of a Code of Ethics for Association members. The Committee on Professional Ethics, with Professor Robert Angell as chairman, was appointed. The Committee had not yet convened when the "Profile" issue erupted. Although the charge presented by the Executive Committee was broad and apparently poorly delineated, the tasks of the Committee on Professional Ethics did not necessarily include judicatory functions related to charges of unethical conduct by fellow sociologists. Nonetheless, when Professor Wiggins appeared before the seminar at Columbia University, ostensibly to defend his research and to review the appropriation of his interpretation of the results, one of the members of the Committee on Professional Ethics was in attendance.

On the basis of several interviews and lengthy correspondence, I believe I have been able to reconstruct this incident rather accurately, although some details remain obscure and the significance to be attached to the various decisions remains unclear. One of the members of the not yet organized Committee heard about Wiggins' forthcoming visit to New York and telephoned the chairman to inquire whether he might attend the seminar as a Committee representative. The Chairman agreed that he should do so. However, shortly before the meeting was to begin, a professor of law, during a chance meeting in an elevator, advised the Committee member that participation as an official representative of the Committee may make the ASA vulnerable to legal charges by Wiggins. It is my understanding that the previously designated representative presented himself at the seminar as an "unofficial observer." However, he drafted a report of the seminar and shared it with members of the Committee.

The Committee subsequently solicited the membership of the ASA for cases in which professional ethical issues were believed to be involved, for the purpose of drafting a relevant Code of Ethics. The chairman has indicated that the report of Wiggins' performance at the seminar, although admittedly acquired in an unorthodox manner, was utilized by the Committee in the same way as those cases submitted as a result of solicitation of the membership. Both the report on the seminar and the several cases submitted by members are currently considered classified documents.

It may be legally prudent for the ASA and also protective of Wiggins that the report not be made public. However, with benefit of hindsight, the Chairman has indicated to me that he may not have recognized at the time the full import of problems associated with this distinctive means of gaining information for his Committee. This admission does not cast aspersions on the chairman, but it does reveal the lack of confrontation by sociologists of the complex issues the Committee faced and the paucity of guidelines in these matters. The ambiguous role of the Committee suggests that the profession ought to examine closely procedures of investigating the professional behavior of its members and to ponder deeply the function of secrecy. It may be added that I have encountered an ethical thicket as I have sought to exercise propriety in reporting names and interpretations of the consultants who provided the information reviewed above.

The Committee on Professional Ethics has since been discharged. The proposals submitted by the Committee to ASA members did not eventuate in a Code of Ethics for the profession. The Chairman told me that the Committee's solicitation of cases calling for ethical judgment resulted in a relatively limited response from sociologists. But at least one participant in the "Profile" research informed me that he submitted a statement which raised ethical issues about the Wiggins-Schoeck case. Among the stands he took was that in research requiring consultantships from fellow sociologists there must be an explicit statement of the general purpose of the study and a report of the sponsorship of the research.

Reactions of Wiggins and Schoeck

Although the recorded reactions of Wiggins and Schoeck are limited, their perspective is vital for this study. We already have mentioned the Wiggins and Schoeck letter to *The New York Times*, which, though not published, was discussed at length in a news story that the *Times* printed. Wiggins and Schoeck also published a rebuttal to their critics in *Science*. This journal had published an article, "Science and Politics: AMA Attacked for Use of Disputed Survey in 'Medicare Lobbying',"[45] which reflected somewhat unfavorably upon the "Profile" study and its use.

In May, 1961, the published rebuttal[46] began by pointing out that within seven weeks after the first report Wiggins and Schoeck had sent a response to *Science*, via registered mail. *Science*, after a delay of several months, informed Wiggins and Schoeck that their correspondence had been received but misplaced; an apology accompanied the admission. Eventually their comments were published.

In the article in *Science*, Wiggins and Schoeck again noted that they had indeed excluded certain groups, especially the recipients of old age assistance grants. They felt justified because the Social Security Administration had in 1956 conducted a study which excluded recipients of old age assistance unless these persons also received social security payments. It has been estimated, according to Wiggins and Schoeck, that this widely cited study excluded 55 percent or more of those persons 65 and over.

Still a very serious question can be raised about Wiggins' and Schoeck's defense both in their letter to the editor of *The New York Times* and in their letter to *Science*: Why did they not attempt to deal more directly with the sampling problem, and with some of the other problems their critics had raised?

Yet, we are here concerned with the defense by Wiggins and Schoeck. From correspondence I have had with Professor Wiggins I judge that he believes that gerontologists have reacted to him largely in political and ideological terms — that they have not been oriented towards the search for truth. Thus, in his judgment, they continue to ignore the basic findings of "Profile." And although some of the associates did not like the findings reported in the study, Wiggins has observed that none of them returned the money he paid them for collecting the data.

Schoeck wrote me first on April 28, 1965, and again on September 22, 1965. In the first letter he observed:

> One hunch of mine has been that in addition to whatever social action goals our findings about the aging population may have appeared to question, one of the motives for the incredibly ferocious and unethical attacks on us was simply professional jealousy. Because of an unusual set of circumstances, our study received such instant nationwide attention that it threatened to dwarf various studies, published or about to be published. . . .

It may also interest you that not a single letter or comment of any kind, and certainly no rejoinder, has appeared in *Science* in response to our letter. Apparently, by the summer of 1961, our critics had realized that they could not win on the grounds of numbers and statistics. They chose to proceed with more McCarthyite methods from then on.[47]

In the second letter, in response to some specific questions, he answered:

The AMA had nothing whatever to do with "Profile." I was never a consultant to them. Wiggins, together with other professors from U. of Chicago, U. of California, and others, joined an advisory panel for the AMA in January of 1960; all in all I think he attended two or three meetings.

Mimeograph copies of the San Francisco paper were sent by the Foundation for Voluntary Welfare to several newspapers. Presumably, the *Indianapolis Star* ignored the release date.

I have never heard directly either from the American Sociological Association or the SSSP anything relating to their investigations. I doubt that the ASA ever had one.[48]

Also, Schoeck, in a rebuttal to the many criticisms leveled at him and Wiggins, rewrote an essay, "Truth in the Social Sciences":

Establishing truth in the areas of discourse conventionally of interest to the social sciences resembles establishing truth in the courtroom: it is subject to the adversary system. . . .[49]

The more sophisticated layman might think that among scientists and scholars there is some kind of self-policing that makes fraud and self-deception impossible because of the nature and organization of scientific work. This is questionable. . . .[50]

Next, Schoeck poses a question important for contemporary sociology:

What if the potential findings of a particular line of research threaten to be so unpopular politically, religiously, or emotionally, that no one except a single researcher and his associates are willing to go through the necessary procedures to research the question?[51]

And he continues:

Indeed, there is a strong assumption that as a particular field or science in general progresses and becomes more and more institutionalized, the less likely are unorthodox and potentially embarrassing investigations in it. . . . The more science becomes big business, the more is at stake, the greater the effective pressures for orthodoxy. The more anxiously the social scientist vies for status with the mighty policy makers in his society, and the more he tries to gain assurance by emphasizing the methods of the natural sciences, the more elusive he may find the problem of "truth."[52]

Conclusions

In my original letter of inquiry on April 15, 1965, to "those who may have relevant information on the 'Wiggins Case'," I sought to assure those from whom I was soliciting aid:

> It shall not be my purpose at all to expose anyone, to embarrass anyone, or to conduct any type of kangaroo court. Rather, it will be simply to develop a case study of a research project which acquired nationwide notoriety and which has raised some basic questions about research and the use of the results thereof.

Frankly, the fulfillment of my goal became considerably more complicated than I had initially anticipated. Persons, rather than data and their interpretation, were often the target of attack. Although the guidelines for discretion in matters ethical are blurred, especially when emotional factors have been intense, I trust I have fulfilled my pledge.

My personal concerns have been not so much with the goals of the gerontologists as with the possible abuses of science. I sense a sharp distinction between lack of skill in methodology and a purposive abuse of methodology.

I consider myself a political liberal. I have been an activist in civil rights, peace, and related issues. I support medicare fully, and probably would do so if ninety per cent of the "total," not just of Wiggins' "normal," American population over sixty-five reported they were currently in good health and able to pay for minor medical expenses themselves. However, I am disturbed that a Congressional Committee report, in providing arguments supportive of medicare, can make scurrilous attacks on sociologists with apparent immunity and impunity, although the information on "Profile" available to the Committee was only partial and was collected under circumstances fraught with tension.

Study after study of the aged has suggested that the older person in the United States is financially deprived and dependent. To my knowledge the methodology of most of these studies has not been scrutinized. Wiggins and Schoeck produced contrary data. Surely few research ventures in American sociology have been subjected to such thorough review as that experienced by "Profile" in the weeks following the AMA press conference in August, 1960. One of "Profile's" participating sociologists who, incidentally, refused to respond to Sheppard's request for a response to the study's results for use by the Senate Subcommittee, told me in an interview that "at least fifty percent of the research projects that produce articles for the major sociology journals are at least as poor in design and execution as the Wiggins-Schoeck study. I chose not to single out their study for exposure." How should suspicions of methodological inadequacies be aired? How should improvements be attempted? By replication? By remonstration?

I have experienced shifting responses to questions raised by "Profile." My initial sympathies were with Wiggins. The attacks on his paper in San Francisco appeared to me then to be more "gerontological" than "scientific." Again, I was disappointed when I discovered that "Profile" had been deleted from *Social and Psychological Aspects of Aging*. To exclude a paper from a publication of the proceedings of the gerontological congress, without even mentioning reasons for the exclusion, I considered questionable. Also, to make charges of "propaganda," to imply that unethical conduct was involved, I thought of doubtful propriety. But now, as I have accumulated and pored over the vast array of interpretation and opinion on "Profile," I am more ambivalent.

Clearly, no institutionalized mechanism to handle "ethics" cases in the sociology profession now exists. Are the risks too great to take in setting up the machinery to receive complaints and to judge on disputes about ethics? Will efforts to make our research less fallible make ourselves as persons more fallible? Is an investigatory apparatus the answer? Or a renewal of confidence in colleagues, and a recognition that in our fallibility misuses of data and reputations are likely? Under which circumstances ought a sociologist seek to censor, and under which ought he to seek to censure, a colleague for interpretations believed to be inadequate or inaccurate?

Under what circumstances is it the responsibility of professional researchers — the sixteen sociologists in the present instance — to sense that a sample or schedule or set of instructions is methodologically weak or "loaded"? And, more importantly, when is it his responsibility to demand not only clarification but correction, and, in the absence of a satisfactory response, to refuse to participate in the study or to expose what are believed to be weaknesses in the study? Or, do ethical considerations in sociological research call upon a colleague to trust implicitly and fully the research efforts of those whom one may be assisting?

In the case at hand, the information on the sampling techniques which led to the selection of certain communities for study and of certain types of interviewees is limited. The reasons for designing the schedule and wording the questions in the ways done can only be surmised. But at best there are great risks in imputing ulterior motives to others. Rather clearly, the sampling methods raise many questions of reliability, and some of the questions quite likely elicited biased responses, but how are methodological inadequacies, or believed inadequacies, to be properly handled by social scientists? By restudy? By charges of incompetency? By charges of unethical behavior?

It is true that some of the participating sociologists made inquiries about method to the directors of "Profile." But I discovered no evidence of protest (although, of course, there may have been sociologists who refused to participate because of objections to the sampling procedures, or to the questionnaire). Most of Fitzpatrick's inquiries, for example, appear on the surface to have methodological roots, but at the periphery, occasionally at the heart of his questions, are several vitally important ethical issues. Our evidence suggests that Fitzpatrick, along with the others whose names were released, was made vulnerable to embarrassment and harassment. But, let us remember, Wiggins and Schoeck were also subject to embarrassment and harassment. To what extent, however, were those responsible for collecting the data to begin with also responsible for the results quoted by the AMA? Several of the participants disavowed responsibility for the results. Wiggins has suggested that the participants, in providing the raw data, were indeed responsible.

The involvement of professional associations in the controversy contributed nothing to the resolution, or even the clarification, of the impasse. Surely the inability of the SSSP special committee to pursue its charge to conduct an impartial investigation of "Profile" ought to lead sociologists to pause and ponder the context of their research efforts and their obligations to colleagues and to truth. The secrecy surrounding the content of the report to the Committee on Ethics of the ASA, although knowledge of such a report is apparently rather widespread, is disturbing. A semi-public investigation secretly reported can victimize the innocent. If there is evidence of malfeasance, doesn't the profession have the right to be informed?

The Wiggins-Schoeck case not only reveals that sociological research has developed with little attention to ethical issues relating to the collection of data and the reporting of findings, but it also raises vital questions regarding the proper role of sociology in formation of public policy. In the particular issue of health needs of the aging, the scientific test may be whether or not sociology can sever itself from gerontology as a social movement; the humanistic test may be whether or not sociology can properly refrain from contributing to the success of gerontology as a social movement.

Possibly no summary or analysis of the ill-fated "Profile" study is needed. In some ways the documents and the diagnoses and the rationalizations speak for themselves. Surely the responses to the Wiggins-Schoeck study and its appropriation by the AMA underline the fact that the sociology profession in America has no effective means of handling charges of unethical behavior by its members. The Wiggins-Schoeck case cannot provide the profession with an answer to the question of whether or not sociologists ought to establish a code of ethics and a machinery to investigate charges of code violations. But the case does suggest that sociologists ought to be considering more diligently than in the past the question of whether there ought to be a code.

I conclude with three questions: What is the current and prospective health status of the aged in America? If "Profile" had produced data more supportive of "liberal" political causes, or if Wiggins had at least given "liberal" interpretations to his data, or if Wiggins had been a consultant for a "liberal" organization instead of the AMA, would sociologists have created a furor over biased sampling and misleading interpretations? Finally, what are the prospects for a sociology of sociology?

Notes to the Chapter

1. United States Senate, *Developments in Aging: 1959 to 1963*. A Report of the Special Committee on Aging, United States Senate. Report #8, 88th Congress, First Session (Washington, D.C.: U. S. Government Printing Office, February 11, 1963), 2.

2. *Ibid.*

3. Letter from Eugene F. Miller, Assistant Professor of Political Science, Furman University, June 23, 1965.

4. Letter from Leonard Z. Breen, Purdue University, to Senator McNamara, August 19, 1960, reprinted in the *Congressional Record,* August 22, 1960, 17001.

5. James W. Wiggins, Professor of Sociology, Emory University, News Release, San Francisco, August 11, 1960.

6. Letter from Harold Orbach, Research Associate, Division of Gerontology, University of Michigan, to Leonard D Cain, Jr., May 27, 1963.

7. The three paragraphs following are based on the manuscript read at the International Congress of Gerontology, San Francisco, August 11, 1960. Essentially the same version was subsequently published as J. W. Wiggins and H.

Schoeck, "A Profile of the Aging: USA," *Geriatrics,* 16 (July, 1961), pp. 330–42.

8. Leonard D Cain, Jr., "The Sociology of Ageing: A Trend Report and Bibliography," *Current Sociology,* 8 (1959), pp. 57–133. "It is apparent that social gerontology, as a social movement and as a source of sociological data, is rather far advanced and continuing to enrich a sociological perspective." (p. 65). Again, in my chapter, "Life Course and Social Structure," in R. E. L. Faris (ed.), *Handbook of Modern Sociology* (Chicago: Rand McNally, 1964), 272–309, I wrote: ". . . the development of gerontology heralds a social movement whose dimensions and directions are not yet understood. Although gerontology regularly associates itself with scientific endeavors, the gerontological literature, gerontological organizations and conferences, and the proclaimed commitments of many gerontologists display the characteristics typically associated with a social movement. . . . A major task confronting sociology is the study of gerontology as a social movement." (p. 304).

9. For example, the *San Francisco Chronicle,* August 12, 1960, presented a page 2 headline, "Surprise Nationwide Poll: Typically Aged Are Fit, Don't Need Medical Funds."

10. *The New York Times,* August 15, 1960, p. 11.

11. *Ibid.*

12. *Ibid.*

13. Leonard Larson, "Statement before the Senate Finance Committee on HR 12580, 86th Congress (June 30, 1960)," *Journal of the American Medical Association,* 173 (August 13, 1960), pp. 1738–39.

14. *The Wall Street Journal,* August 18, 1960, p. 10.

15. Wiggins and Schoeck, *op. cit.*

16. *The Wall Street Journal,* August 18, 1960, p. 10.

17. *The Wall Street Journal,* September 12, 1960, p. 12.

18. *The Wall Street Journal,* August 24, 1960, p. 1.

19. *The New York Times,* August 22, 1960, p. 24.

20. *The New York Times,* August 25, 1960, p. 28.

21. *The New York Times,* September 1, 1960, p. 16.

22. *The New York Times,* September 18, 1960, p. 60.

23. From copy of a letter to *The New York Times,* September 23, 1960, supplied by Professor Schoeck.

24. *The New York Times,* October 2, 1960, p. 78.

25. Eugene J. McCarthy, "Public Policy and Poor Public Opinion Polls on America's Aged," prepared for delivery on the floor of the United States Senate, August 22, 1960. The version quoted was released from Senator McCarthy's office. A

modified version appeared in the *Congressional Record,* August 22, 1960, 16990–93. Included in the speech are excerpts of letters from Professors Noel Gist, Gordon Streib and Wayne Thompson, and Leonard Breen.

26. See the *Congressional Record,* August 24, 1960, 16987–17002, and Appendix, A6309.

27. *Congressional Record,* August 24, 1960, Appendix A6309.

28. *Congressional Record,* August 22, 1960, 16999–17000.

29. Letter from Noel Gist, University of Missouri, to Leonard D Cain, Jr., April 26, 1965.

30. Letter from Edith Sherman, University of Denver, to Harold Sheppard, August 23, 1960. (Copy supplied by Professor Sherman.)

31. Letter from Edith Sherman to James W. Wiggins, September 6, 1960. (Copy supplied by Professor Sherman.)

32. Letter from Joseph P. Fitzpatrick to James W. Wiggins, August 23, 1960. (Copy supplied by Professor Fitzpatrick.)

33. Letter from Joseph P. Fitzpatrick, August 20, 1960. (Copy supplied by Professor Fitzpatrick.)

34. Letter from Joseph P. Fitzpatrick to Harold Sheppard, August 23, 1960. (Copy supplied by Professor Fitzpatrick.)

35. Statement by Joseph P. Fitzpatrick, undated. (Copy supplied by Professor Fitzpatrick.)

36. *Ibid.*

37. Letter from Harold Orbach to the Editor of *Geriatrics,* September 14, 1961. (Copy supplied by Professor Orbach.)

38. Letter from Harold Orbach to the Senate Committee on Problems of the Aged and Aging, undated. (Copy supplied by Professor Orbach.)

39. Letter from Harold Orbach to the Editor of *Geriatrics,* October 27, 1961. (Copy supplied by Professor Orbach.)

40. Leonard D Cain, Jr., review of Clark Tibbitts and Wilma Donahue (eds.), *Social and Psychological Aspects of Aging* (New York: Columbia University Press, 1962) in *American Sociological Review,* 28 (June, 1963), pp. 496–97. "Although the editors report that 'virtually all' the papers presented at the [International Gerontological] Congress are included, notable by its absence is the controversial study of Wiggins and Schoeck, 'A Profile of the Aging: USA.' This deletion is unfortunate, since both the sampling techniques and the types of questions posed by gerontologists are proper targets for criticism; Wiggins and Schoeck criticized thoroughly — maybe too well." (p. 497).

41. Letter from Harold Orbach to Leonard D Cain, Jr., May 27, 1963.

42. Letter from Leonard D Cain, Jr., to Harold Orbach, June 10, 1963.

43. *Ibid.*

44. Letter from Marvin Sussman to Leonard D Cain, Jr., October 6, 1965.

45. "Science and Politics: AMA Attacked for Use of Disputed Survey in 'Medicare' Lobbying," *Science,* 132 (September 2, 1960), pp. 604–05.

46. "Data on Aging," *Science,* 133 (May 19, 1961), pp. 1625–26.

47. Letter from Helmut Schoeck to Leonard D Cain, Jr., April 28, 1965.

48. Letter from Helmut Schoeck to Leonard D Cain, Jr., September 22, 1965.

49. Helmut Schoeck, "Truth in the Social Sciences," in Thomas J. J. Altizer, William A. Beardslee, and J. Harvey Young (eds.), *Truth, Myth, and Symbol* (Englewood Cliffs, N. J.: Prentice-Hall, 1962), 19.

50. *Ibid.,* 30.

51. *Ibid.,* 33.

52. *Ibid.*

CHAPTER FIVE

The Harvard Drug Controversy: A Case Study of Subject Manipulation and Social Structure

J. KENNETH BENSON AND JAMES OTIS SMITH

Research in the behavioral sciences often involves the manipulation of human subjects. Manipulation consists of the exposure of human subjects to conditions or treatments which are designed to alter their mental state or overt behavior. Experimenters have sought to induce or vary frustration, inter-group conflict, embarrassment, dissonance, anger, hostility and other types of psychological and social responses in subjects. Although subject manipulation is used for research purposes, the ethical and social limits upon its employment remain obscure. There is no verbalized consensus regarding the type or the degree of manipulation that is ethically permissible. Nor is there a general understanding of the social controls which may be brought to bear when the ethical limits of experimental subject manipulation are thought to have been traversed. Thus, we are confronted with two basic questions. What are the practical limits to subject manipulation? And in actuality who establishes and upholds those limits?

Our thesis is that the practical limits to experimental subject manipulation lie in the interests of the social groups, organizations, and professions involved in or impinged upon by the research in question. Of crucial importance in this connection is the network of changing, at times competitive, at times contradictory, *mandates* of professional groups and organizations involved in, supporting, or responding to research in the behavioral sciences, as well as the manner in which these mandates are articulated by individuals representing professional groups and organizations.[1] To a large extent, these mandates and their interrelations determine the ethical issues which are raised and the practical limits or social controls which are ultimately instituted in a particular case of subject manipulation. And further, the likelihood that a given case of manipulation will become the object of controversy is to a large extent determined by the network of mandates.

The ethical issues potentially involved in a particular research project employing subject manipulation may be numerous and complex, allowing a wide range of alternatives among which the responding organizations, professions, and individuals may choose. Correspondingly, a large repertory of motives is generally available to justify — both privately and publicly — the actions of an organization, profession, or individual.[2] This being the case, an organization, profession, or individual may adapt its response to particular needs at hand and yet present motives suitably justifying the response.

To elaborate upon our thesis, we employ a case study approach wherein we analyze one research project: the investigation of the effects of psilocybin conducted originally at Harvard University by Drs. Timothy Leary and Richard Alpert. The selection of this case is based on the following considerations. First, subject manipulation is clearly involved in the case. That exposure to psilocybin altered the mental state and overt behavior of subjects, at least temporarily, is disputed neither by the critics nor by the directors of the research. Second, in this instance subject manipulation became the object of an extensive controversy involving reactions from a wide variety of persons and organizations. Thus, it is possible to analyze the limits of acceptable subject manipulation through a study of this case. Third, much information concerning the research project and the reactions to it is available in the public domain. Thus, we can analyze the controversy by reference to published accounts and opinions and thereby avoid engaging in an exposé.

Our analysis of the so-called Harvard Drug Controversy is based on data drawn almost entirely from materials already a matter of public record. Much of our information concerning events in the case has come from articles appearing in the popular press and in professional journals. In addition, public statements issued by organizations and individuals have been utilized. Certain other data were drawn from materials which were printed or mimeographed and distributed in the vicinity of Harvard but have not yet been published. We deviated from our policy of using only information in the public domain in one instance; i.e., we corresponded with some of the persons involved in order to verify the reports in question and gain additional background information against which we could interpret the published accounts.[3]

Given the nature of the data, the ensuing analysis must be treated as tentative and suggestive. It is conceivable that interviews with persons directly involved in the case would alter the analysis considerably. However, a wealth of information has been obtained and to some extent validated by the procedures outlined above. Therefore, cautious confidence in the data seems justified.

A Chronicle of Events

In 1960 Dr. Leary and Dr. Alpert obtained a supply of psilocybin from Sandoz Pharmaceuticals, Inc., and began research on the "consciousness-expanding" properties of the drug. The research began as a thoroughly respectable inquiry in a burgeoning field of research. Alpert was an assistant professor of Clinical Psychology and of Education and Leary a lecturer on Clinical Psychology at Harvard. Both were associated with the Center for Research in Personality, a research arm of Harvard's Department of Social Relations. Both men were respected members of their profession. Leary had previously published an influential book on personality diagnosis.[4]

In initiating the research, Leary and Alpert entered a rapidly developing field of investigation. Research on the effects of peyote, mescaline, psilocybin, d-lysergic acid diethylamide (LSD-25) and other materials with similar effects has been greatly accelerated within the last twenty years. Psychiatrists and others have been interested in the psychotomimetic properties of the materials. Some have believed that the substances produced a temporary psychosis which might be studied in search of a pharmacological explanation and treatment for psychosis.[5] Although enthusiasm for this view has waned,[6] it is still the basis for some research.[7] In addition, the military has been interested also in the psychotomimetic properties of the substances. Some persons have argued that these materials might be used to produce a temporary state of insanity in an enemy which would permit conquest without death and destruction.[8]

Numerous investigators have been concerned with the mystical, insightful experiences reported to follow from the ingestion of psilocybin, LSD-25, and related materials. A variety of reports of mystical insight, consciousness-expansion, and increased understanding of self as a consequence of exposure to the drugs have appeared in the literature.[9] Some psychiatrists and clinical psychologists have been interested in the therapeutic potential of such experiences. It has been suggested that mind-altering substances might be profitably employed as an adjunct to psychotherapy or even as a therapy in itself.[10] Other reports support the idea that these materials can be helpful in the rehabilitation of criminals, alcoholics, and narcotics addicts.[11] It has also been suggested that the pain and anxiety of dying patients can be somewhat relieved by chemically induced insight and understanding.[12]

Leary and Alpert were interested in the study of the mystical insight and understanding produced by LSD and related drugs. However, their interest extended beyond the strictly therapeutic potential of the drugs. They argued that exposure to the substances could provide an expansion of consciousness which would enhance one's creativity, intelligence, understanding of life, and social adjustment.[13] While some of their research involved a rehabilitation program for criminals,[14] the bulk of their efforts were expended in studies of "normal" subjects.[15]

As the research progressed, the activities of Leary and Alpert reportedly became more promotional and less restrained. Concerned for the welfare of students, Harvard University officials reached an agreement with Leary and Alpert in the Fall of 1961 that undergraduates would not be used as research subjects. In March, 1962, the misgivings of some colleagues in the Department of Social Relations led to a meeting of the Center for Research in Personality, at which the Leary-Alpert research was roundly criticized. Published accounts of the meeting stimulated a widespread controversy culminating in an investigation of the project by the Massachusetts Public Health Department. The decision of the investigators to permit the research to continue, with minor changes, seemed to signal a reduction in the level of public controversy, although the efforts of Harvard officials and the Department of Social Relations to establish satisfactory arrangements for the control of the drugs were unsuccessful.[16]

The controversy bloomed anew in the Fall of 1962 when Leary and Alpert returned to Harvard after a summer of drug research in Mexico. In October they formed an organization called the International Federation for Internal Freedom (IFIF) which was to sponsor and encourage research with hallucinogenic drugs.

University officials became alarmed by reports of extensive illicit use of hallucinogens by Harvard undergraduates. Although responsibility for this development could not be readily assigned to the psilocybin researchers, two university officials — Dean John U. Monro and Health Services Director Dana Farnsworth — issued public statements warning students of possible harm and decrying the sophisticated, intellectual promotion of the hallucinogens. Leary and Alpert responded with a defense of their research and of the hallucinogens in the pages of the student newspaper, *The Harvard Crimson*. An exchange of charges and countercharges ensued in the letters-to-the-editor columns of *The Crimson* and elsewhere.

During the Winter of 1962–63 the activities of IFIF continued to be a center of controversy. Though Leary and Alpert had officially separated their research from Harvard and attached it to IFIF in the Fall, they remained on the Harvard faculty. In April, Leary allegedly left Harvard and his teaching responsibilities without permission; he was dismissed by the Harvard Corporation in May for failure to perform his teaching duties. Alpert was dismissed later the same month after University authorities learned that he had given a drug to an undergraduate in the Spring of 1962, in violation of his earlier agreement not to involve undergraduates.

Social Controls

The Harvard psilocybin project was the object of widespread public and private criticism and of numerous more tangible social control measures. The normative issues raised by critics and the reform measures proposed or instituted varied with the mandates of the reacting organizations and groups.

In the following pages, we examine some of the normative issues that arose and analyze the sources of social control. As employed here, the term "social control" incorporates criticism and direct action intended to limit or alter human behavior. The agents of social control treated here include the Harvard University administration, the medical profession, behavioral scientists, and governmental departments and bureaus. Each is treated in detail at that point which seems most appropriate in view of the normative issues under discussion. For example, members of the medical profession frequently raised the issue of medical control over drugs; therefore, their responses are analyzed in detail in connection with that issue, even though other issues were also involved in their responses.

The Health of the Research Subject. Perhaps the most frequent complaint lodged against the Leary-Alpert psilocybin research project concerns the alleged failure of the researchers to provide adequate safeguards for the health of their research subjects. Such a complaint was voiced by behavioral scientists at a meeting of the faculty and students of Harvard's Center for Research in Personality.[17] Some public reactions to the research by individual members of the medical profession have included expressions of concern for the welfare of research subjects.[18] During the controversy, some editorials (one written by Harvard's Farnsworth) appearing in medical journals warned of possible harm from hallucinogenic materials without naming the Harvard research project specifically.[19]

The concern of critics seems to have been based on the following presumed dangers of exposure to psilocybin and other hallucinogenic drugs:[20]

(1) short-term psychosis-like experiences are reported by some subjects;
(2) long-term mental disorders are precipitated in some cases;
(3) suicide attempts occur in a few instances;
(4) psychological dependence sometimes develops, even though physiological addiction apparently does not;
(5) the use of other, more dangerous, drugs may be encouraged;
(6) long-term changes in the personality of the subject may take place.

For their part, Leary and Alpert denied that the health of their research subjects was in jeopardy. They argued that the deleterious effects of the hallucinogens reported in earlier studies were accounted for by the variables of "set" and "setting." If research subjects expect a psychosis-mimicking experience and are exposed to the drugs in a clinic-like setting appropriate to psychosis, then a terrifying, potentially harmful experience will ensue, they contended. By contrast, exposure to the drugs in a friendly, relaxed, supportive atmosphere in which subjects have been led to expect beneficial, insightful, educational experiences is productive of such experiences.[21] In Leary's words,

> Set and suggestive contexts account for ninety-nine per cent of the specific response to the drug. Thus, you cannot sensibly talk about the effects of psilocybin. It's always the set and suggestive context triggered off by the drug. A fascinating tension between these two factors — set and context — inevitably develops. If both are positive and holy, then a shatteringly sacred experience results. If both are negative then a hellish encounter ensues.[22]

There is considerable agreement among psychopharmacologists that the suggestive context of the drug experience largely determines the psychological effects of the hallucinogens.[23]

Leary and Alpert did not deny that personality changes were occurring among their research subjects. They argued, however, that the changes were for the better, providing the subject with a better understanding of himself and of others and enhancing his capacity for self-improvement, for creativity, and for love of others.[24]

Concern for the physical and mental well-being of subjects, then, was expressed frequently by critics. That subjects were being harmed was denied repeatedly by the investigators. However, other issues were closely interwoven with that of subject health and should therefore be examined in association with it.

Drug Control. Another prominent issue in the controversy concerned responsibility for the administration of drugs. To many critics, the Harvard psilocybin project was objectionable because drugs were administered in nonmedical settings by persons other than medical doctors; moreover, it was alleged that there was relatively little participation by physicians in the selection of research subjects and the supervision of drug sessions.

The question of medical screening and participation was one of the issues raised by members of the faculty of the Department of Social Relations.[25] The lack of medical participation stimulated an investigation by the Massachusetts Public Health Department which concluded with the stipulation that the research could legally continue provided a physician be in attendance at each administration of the drug.[26] After the Harvard controversy broke, both Harvard[27] and the American Psychological Association[28] issued research guidelines calling for medical participation and the use of medical facilities in drug research, though in neither case has it been possible to establish that the Leary-Alpert research was responsible for their issuance.

The objections of Leary and Alpert to extensive medical participation in their research were based on their hypotheses concerning set and setting. They believed such participation would impose a medical model on their investigations and thus induce unfavorable responses to the drugs.[29] In a letter to prospective members of IFIF dated April, 1963, Leary asserted:

> When these materials are administered by psychiatrists or researchers to unprepared subjects, the results are psychotic-like terror. If well prepared, however, and in settings which the subjects themselves have planned and arranged, the results are positive and educational.[30]

Resistance to medical control stemmed also from concern that future utilization of consciousness-expanding materials should not be restricted to medical-therapeutic purposes. It was argued that in addition to their strictly therapeutic uses, the consciousness-expanding drugs promise educational-theological benefits which should be developed. In order to utilize the materials for the latter purposes, they should be dispensed with a minimum of control by "managerial or professional elites."[31]

On the basis of information available to us, it is difficult to ascertain the extent or the type of control actually exercised by the researchers. Some reports indicate that volunteers were screened by medical and psychological tests and that many volunteers were rejected.[32] However, other reports indicate that while control was exercised at times, for various reasons it was not employed at other times. Rather early in the psilocybin project, David C. McClelland, Chairman of Harvard's Department of Social Relations, expressed concern about the matter in these words.[33]

> One of the most difficult parts of the research has been to introduce any order into who takes psilocybin under what conditions. Any controls have either been rejected as interfering with the warmth necessary to have a valuable experience or accepted as desirable but then not applied because somehow an occasion arises when it seems "right" to have a psilocybin session.

The critical reactions of physicians included expressions of concern for the health of research subjects, pleas that medical controls be instituted in order to protect subjects, and warnings that a solution should not be sought in legislation. This point of view is clearly expressed in the following statement by Dr. Walter E. Barton, then Medical Director of the American Psychiatric Association.[34]

> There is, of course, a place for medical research with these drugs, but only when it is carried out under extremely careful controls and in the pattern of rigid traditional models of medical research. We in medicine are strongly of the conviction that the administration of any agent that will alter the psychophysiology of a human being must be considered a medical procedure and done under medical control. Unfortunately, the controls in many instances are very difficult to work out without defeating the research goal itself, particularly when the answer is sought in legislation. But that does not gainsay the principle involved.
>
> Our association has not made any official policy statement on the hallucinogenic drugs, but I am confident that Dr. Farnsworth's sentiment would be shared overwhelmingly by our fourteen thousand members and by physicians everywhere, for that matter.

The opposition of some segments of the medical profession to the extension of federal authority over drug research is well expressed in comments and recommendations of the American Medical Association on recent revisions of Federal drug regulations. The representatives of the AMA strongly opposed any attempt to circumscribe the freedom of the physician and of the medical research worker to employ drugs as they see fit. Safeguards against misuse of drugs, from this perspective, should be left to the medical profession with a minimum of outside interference.[35]

Thus, physician-critics seem to have responded to the Harvard psilocybin project in a manner understandable on the basis of their professional mandate to define, to prevent, and to treat physical and mental illness. Included within that mandate is the notion that physicians alone should have the "license" to administer potentially harmful materials to human subjects. Apparently, the drug control question was the catalyst which brought the research to the attention of medical authorities. Had the research not involved the use of drugs, it seems unlikely that members of the medical profession would have been so concerned with it. And, had the research involved the extensive participation of physicians in selecting subjects, in administering drugs, and in observing reactions, it seems likely that physicians would have been much less concerned with the project, even though the level of threat to the health of subjects might not have been materially reduced by such participation. The physician-critics of the psilocybin project were not simply defending their vested interests and ignoring the problem of subject welfare. Rather, they apparently saw a close connection between their mandate to safeguard health and their "license" to administer drugs.

It is of interest that the investigation conducted by the Massachusetts Public Health Department began and ended with concern over the issue of drug control.[36] Reportedly, the rationale for the investigation was based on legislation requiring that potentially harmful drugs be administered only by medical doctors. The investigation concluded with the stipulation that in future research a medical doctor be present at the time the drug is actually administered, although he need not remain for the entire session. Thus, the regulatory agency appears to have defended the mandate of the medical profession along with taking steps to protect the health of research subjects.

The Goals and Methods of Science. Some critics, especially behavioral scientists, attacked the psilocybin research for what they regarded as a departure from the proper goals and methods of science. The overlap between research and application within the project runs counter to the view that research activity should be insulated from problems of practical application.

The psilocybin investigators were impressed with the potential benefits of the consciousness-expanding drugs. In a paper presented in 1961, Leary argued as follows:

> The basic aim of physical science is to reduce human helplessness in the face of the physical environment. Physical science has other goals, of course: to understand, to explain, to control, to measure, to predict. . . . Why explain? Why predict? To lessen fearful ignorance. The technologies which have grown up around the physical sciences, engineering, medicine, also

take as their goal the reducing of human helpessness. . . . and the social technologies — psychiatry, social work, applied psychology — is not their goal the reduction of confusion and the increase in human freedom?[37]

When people come to us and ask us to change their behavior, why can't we do it? Why can't we teach them to see the game structure of human society?[38]

Change in behavior can occur with dramatic spontaneity once the game structure of behavior is seen. The visionary experience is the key to behavior change.[39]

The most efficient way to cut through the game structure of Western life is the use of drugs, consciousness-expanding drugs.[40]

Leary and Alpert contended that consciousness-expanding drugs would eventually produce extensive changes both in individuals and in social systems. They sometimes interpreted opposition to their research as an attempt to defend the status quo. For example, in a paper entitled "The Politics of Consciousness-Expansion" they argued that because LSD can change the functioning of the nervous system it proves a threat to the established social order and therefore challenges "every branch of the Establishment."[41] They characterized the fear consciousness-expansion caused among the Establishment as "more frightening than the Bomb!" They argued that this fear was the result of potential socio-political change rather than of physical or physiological change occurring in individual subjects. "Man" they state "is about to be changed . . ." and the ". . . present social establishments had better be prepared for the . . . floodtide, two billion years building up. The verbal dam is collapsing. Head for the hills, or prepare your intellectual craft to flow with the current."[42]

It is, of course, not necessarily unscientific to believe that one's research is of practical value. As clinical psychologists, Leary and Alpert were members of a profession highly committed to the practical application of research findings. Researchers in other areas, e.g., the sociology of deviant behavior, have been much concerned with the utilization of research findings in prevention and rehabilitation. However, Leary and Alpert went even further, attempting to engage in research and in practical application concurrently.

The goal of the research sessions run by the Harvard-IFIF group was not to produce and study frightening disturbances of consciousness (which was the goal of most psychiatric investigations of model psychoses), but to produce the ecstatic experience, to expand consciousness, to provide the subject with the most memorable, revelatory, life-changing experience of his life. . . .

From the beginning of our research, our attention was directed to the engineering of ecstasy, the preparation for, the setting for, the architecture of ecstasy.[43]

Apparently, the production of ecstatic experiences was both a means to the discovery of the causes of such experiences and a desired end product of the research. Such a combination of theoretical and practical interests is, of course, not unique to the psilocybin project. Frequently, in drug experimentation the investigator hopes that his research will cure or prevent illness among research subjects while at the same time providing valuable knowledge. In studies of delinquency control and prevention one may hope not only to discover causes and cures but also to reduce delinquency within the population studied.

The combination of research and application becomes objectionable to many when the applied concerns of the investigator interfere with his search for valid knowledge. Such interference was alleged by critics of the Harvard psilocybin project. Some contended that the scientific goals of the psilocybin investigation were eventually obscured in the attempt to produce mystic ecstasy as an end in itself. Consider, for example, the comments of Brendan A. Maher, chairman of the Center for Research in Personality at the time of the controversy:

Taking a drug, sitting in a fox-hole, falling in love, or falling out of an airplane all provide experiences. To the extent that we engage in any of these activities because the experience is an end in itself, then we are doing it — to speak colloquially — for "kicks." A university is an institution intended to provide a rather special set of experiences; experiences that lead to increased competencies, capacities for intellectual self-discipline, interest in examining all of the evidence and an understanding of the intellectual history of man. Experience *per se* is not part of a University's commissariat. . . .

Among the members of the faculty at the Center there was serious concern when it became apparent that not only were students being indoctrinated in the belief that communicable knowledge was the end-product of some kind of pointless "game," but that the drug experience was being held out to them as a kind of redemption from the rigors of rationality.[44]

Similar concern was reportedly voiced by Dr. Herbert C. Kelman (then a lecturer in Social Psychology at Harvard) at a meeting of the faculty and students of the Center for Research in Personality. He contended that "the

program has an anti-intellectual atmosphere. Its emphasis is on pure experience, not on verbalizing findings."[45]

The methods as well as the aims of the psilocybin research were criticized.
The setting in which drugs were administered and the participation of
research workers in the drug sessions led to considerable opposition.

Drug sessions were often held in private homes and apartments. Research
subjects were led to expect and to prepare for pleasant, insight-provoking
experiences. The research setting was pleasant, relaxed, and supportive. Music,
paintings, books, and drinks were sometimes provided. Research workers
often took the drug with the subjects.[46]

The careful arrangement of the research setting was based on several
considerations. First, the investigators believed the expectations of research
subjects and the social context of the drug sessions to be important determinants of reaction to psilocybin. They argued that many of the negative
reactions reported by some other investigators were consequences of negative
pre-exposure attitudes and of threatening research settings.[47] Second, the
investigators felt that the participation of research workers in the drug
sessions facilitated favorable reactions by eliminating the social distance
between the subject and the observer.[48] Third, the investigators thought that
reactions to psilocybin were properly understood only by persons who had
themselves been exposed to the drug.[49]

The procedures intended by Leary and Alpert to be provocative of
desirable psilocybin reactions and of valid scientific data were seen by
some critics as conducive to a party-like atmosphere inappropriate to scientific research.[50] The critics charged that the participation of research workers
in the drug sessions precluded rather than facilitated the collection of
reliable information.[51]

The negative reactions of behavioral scientists to the psilocybin project
included criticism of goals and methods in conjunction with concern for
the well-being of research subjects and the control of drugs. The matter of
subject health was not dealt with separately as an ethical issue apart from
other issues. Instead, behavioral scientists reacted to the combination of
potentially harmful operations and questionable purposes and methods. If
the research had been regarded as both worthy in its aims and rigorous in its
methodology, there might have been far less furor over subject health.
Similarly, if the research had not involved a potential threat to subject
health, there probably would have been far less controversy over its methods
and purposes.

The reactions of behavioral scientists appear consistent, for the most part, with the American Psychological Association's ethical standards regarding the welfare of research subjects. The standards, which were published in 1963, include the following statements:[52]

a. Only when a problem is of scientific significance and it is not practicable to investigate it in any other way is the psychologist justified in exposing research subjects, whether children or adults, to physical or emotional stress as part of an investigation.

b. When a reasonable possibility of injurious aftereffects exists, research is conducted only when the subjects or their responsible agents are fully informed of this possibility and agree to participate nevertheless.

c. The psychologist seriously considers the possibility of harmful aftereffects and avoids them, or removes them as soon as permitted by the design of the experiment.

Here, as in the Harvard Drug Controversy, consideration of the scientific value of a study enters into the determination of whether or not a potentially stressful research operation is justified.

The involvement of behavioral scientists in the issue of drug control seems also to have been qualified by other considerations. While some behavioral scientists apparently felt that there should have been more adequate provisions for medical participation in the psilocybin project, their positions on this matter were often articulated so as to preserve the right of the behavioral scientist to conduct research on subjects, and via methods of his own choosing.

Concern for the integrity of the profession's "license" to conduct research with drugs seems evident in a letter to *The Reporter* by Joseph B. Margolin, an official of the American Psychological Association.[53] In this letter Margolin acknowledged that psychologists are generally expected to collaborate with physicians on drug research, but he defended the right of psychologists to conduct such research. Similar concern was more directly expressed by Maher in a paper appearing in the *Newsletter of the Massachusetts Psychological Association*.

The membership of the Massachusetts Psychological Association has, perhaps, a particular stake in the problems that were raised [in the psilocybin affair at Harvard] insofar as they were related to the laws of the Commonwealth regarding the use of drugs by non-medical researchers. In the long run, however, we have an even greater stake in the more serious questions that have been asked about the possibility of an erosion of the freedom of researchers to do research on topics and in a manner of their own choosing.[54]

Maher argued that freedom to carry out research is sometimes threatened by irresponsible researchers. It sometimes becomes necessary, he contended, to exert control over such researchers in order to preserve academic freedom. The irresponsible investigator was said to forfeit his right to the protection of his colleagues and institution. In addition, he argued that one of the obligations incumbent upon a researcher is to supplement his own competences by collaborating with other professionals, especially where failure to do so might occasion an unnecessary risk to the health of research subjects.

It seems that the concern of behavioral scientists with the welfare of research subjects and with drug control was not separable from their involvement in other mandate-related issues. Questions concerning subject health were inextricably intertwined with problems regarding research methods and purposes. The contention that medical control over drugs should be maintained was qualified by the insistence that such control can be provided through medical collaboration in projects directed by psychologists. Furthermore, the willingness of some behavioral scientists to accept restrictions on the activities of Leary and Alpert was related to their concern that the misuse of academic freedom might lead to its eventual suspension. The issue of academic freedom is addressed more directly in the following pages.

Academic Freedom. Another issue in the Harvard controversy concerns the limits of academic freedom. It is clear that the activities of Leary and Alpert were restricted to some extent by social control measures. Early in the research, the Harvard administration reached an agreement with the psilocybin investigators that undergraduates would not be used as research subjects. Later, at the insistence of the Massachusetts Public Health Department, the presence of a medical doctor at each drug administration became mandatory. At several junctures, Harvard officials issued public statements which were construed as criticism of the promotional activities of the psilocybin investigators. Still later, the psilocybin research was separated from Harvard because of the failure to devise control measures satisfactory both to the research workers and to representatives of the Laboratory of Social Relations. Finally, both Leary and Alpert were dismissed from their appointments on the Harvard faculty.[55]

Despite the restrictions described above, it has been argued in some quarters that the principle of academic freedom was not violated. Obviously, the argument hinges upon one's concepts of academic freedom. In fact, much of the Harvard psilocybin controversy consists of a protracted, though muted, debate over the meaning of academic freedom.

The debate concerns two major issues. First, what kinds of activities are protected by the guarantees of academic freedom? Second, what types of control may be exercised over research activities without violating academic freedom?

The controversy can be partly understood as a debate concerning the scope of the term "research." Psilocybin investigators were given occasionally to very broad usage of that term. For example, in a mimeographed form letter of April, 1963, and appearing under an IFIF letterhead, Leary argued in effect that these substances are powerful agents for developing human potentialities.[56] Because they are fundamentally educational rather than medical instruments, their use and availability should follow the educational model. Leary also stated that anyone who could benefit from the experience and who had some training in the area should be able to undertake *research* into the expansion of his consciousness.

By contrast, various social control agents seem to have been intent upon utilizing a narrower concept of "research." A distinction between research and nonresearch activities seems implicit in the responses of Harvard officials. To our knowledge, administrative officials never publicly criticized the formal research activities of Leary and Alpert. They did, however, on several occasions criticize the intellectual promotion of the hallucinogens.[57] Although the criticism was not aimed unequivocally at Leary and Alpert, they saw fit to reply to it.[58]

A clear attempt to delimit the concept of research was apparent in the negotiations within the Laboratory of Social Relations intended to establish acceptable conditions for the control of the drug. Robert F. Bales, Director of the Laboratory, and others, felt that the Laboratory could not continue to assist the psilocybin investigators in any way unless promotional uses of the project's psilocybin supply (e.g., to impress prospective financial supporters) were eliminated. The "nonresearch" uses of psilocybin led to severance of the connection between the psilocybin project and the Laboratory of Social Relations.[59]

Leary and Alpert lost their positions at Harvard, but the official reasons for their suspensions do not suggest any objections to their "research." Leary was dismissed for failure to meet his classes, Alpert for giving hallucinogens to an undergraduate. In a statement released to newsmen on May 27, 1963, Nathan M. Pusey, President, Harvard University, asserted that Alpert's appointments (both his current one and a prospective one-year appointment in the School of Education) had been terminated by the Harvard Corporation because:

(1) it has recently been determined that in the spring of 1962 Dr. Alpert violated an agreement which he had entered into in November, 1961, not to involve undergraduates in his work with drugs (it was an additional part of this agreement that no students would be used before they had been cleared for such activity by a member of the medical staff of the University Health Services); and (2), because subsequently, in November, 1962, he assured an officer of administration of the University that he had not given drugs to any undergraduate.[60]

The statement issued in regard to Leary read:

On May 6, 1963, the Harvard Corporation: VOTED, because Timothy F. Leary, Lecturer on Clinical Psychology, has failed to keep his classroom appointments and has absented himself from Cambridge during term time without permission, to relieve him from further teaching duty and to terminate his salary as of April 30, 1963.[61]

Thus, Harvard officials were able to extricate themselves from the affair without a frontal assault upon the freedom of the research worker.

In reacting to the controversy, some observers have accepted the view that no violation of the principles of academic freedom occurred. After the dismissal of Alpert, *The Harvard Crimson* editorialized as follows:

Dr. Alpert's dismissal should not be construed as an abridgment of academic freedom. The University has supported his researches and has been more than reasonable in the precautions it has asked him to take. In dismissing him, it reacted to wilful repudiation of these safeguards.[62]

Notice the suggestion that since the university had supported the "research," and the dismissals resulted from extra-research activities, academic freedom was not affected.

In a similar vein, Brendan A. Maher argued that academic freedom should not be construed to mean that incompetence is approved. As Maher put it in a general statement preceding his description of the Harvard controversy,

It is difficult to see how academic freedom is threatened by the expectation that a scholar demonstrate his competences, especially where there is the slightest possibility that harm may be caused to others by an unskilled performance. . . . Academic freedom does not include a license to be incompetent where it is possible for competence to be provided.[63]

Later in the same article in a discussion of the Harvard research, he asserted,

No infringement of academic freedom seems to have been involved; indeed the University continued to offer protection for these activities long past a point at which tolerance might well have been exhausted.[64]

Thus, in many quarters there seems to have been an attempt to define the guarantees of academic freedom so as to exclude some of the activities of Leary and Alpert from their protection.

In addition, those dealing with the psilocybin research came to grips with the problem of research control. Does the principle of academic freedom mean that the investigator should be free to investigate any and all topics without interference? In the case at hand, the attempt to establish control led to severance of the connection between Harvard and the psilocybin project. Efforts were made to establish a committee within the behavioral science faculty which would oversee the psilocybin research, at least to the point of determining the conditions under which the drug was to be administered. Since an agreement satisfactory to all parties could not be reached, the proposed committee was not established. However, the effort to establish such a committee indicates an apparent preference on the part of some persons involved for controls from within the behavioral science discipline rather than from administrative officers of the university. Intra-professional controls were apparently perceived as more palatable than extra-professional ones.

The administrators of Harvard University were placed in a difficult position as a result of the psilocybin controversy. Having a broad mandate to satisfy diverse publics — the Harvard faculty, the broader academic community, the students, the parents of students, the general public — they were caught in a dilemma. Their mandate required them to protect students, to defend the principle of academic freedom, and to uphold the reputation of Harvard, among other things. Should they have failed in regard to any of these responsibilities, a dissident public would certainly have arisen to challenge them. The complexity of the mandate may account for the careful, measured response of Harvard officials. They took steps to insulate the research from the most impressionable segment of the student body, the undergraduates; they warned students against the unsupervised use of hallucinogenic materials; and they implemented measures to screen research volunteers and to supervise drug sessions. Since they did not openly and directly attack the research project itself, they were able to avoid, for the most part, the accusation that academic freedom had been infringed upon.

The commitment of the Harvard administration to the protection of research subjects was apparently less than complete. They took measures designed to reduce the risk to undergraduate students, but they avoided more severe steps, e.g., insistence that the research proceed in accordance with the conservative, medical model for drug research, a model involving small numbers of carefully selected subjects in closely controlled medical settings. They attempted to invoke collegial rather than bureaucratic control measures in an apparent effort to preserve the form, if not the substance, of professional autonomy. The health of research subjects might have been most efficiently protected by bureaucratic fiat terminating or narrowly restricting the project. However, the other issues in the controversy, especially the matter of academic freedom, made such a simple solution impossible.

Indicative of the complexity of the University's mandate was a new set of rules governing research with healthy human subjects, which was promulgated by the President and the Fellows of Harvard on April 1, 1963. The new regulations appear to be the result of a concerted effort to protect both the health and well-being of human subjects and the autonomy of researchers. The rules did not abolish the responsibility of the research worker to judge the ethical implications of his research. However, certain types of research were said to require the approval and participation of the University Health Services. Furthermore, departments were encouraged to form committees which would serve as the first line of defense against an irresponsible investigator. Although the promulgation of these rules cannot be regarded simply as a response to the psilocybin controversy, it seems likely that the controversy had some effect upon their formulation.

In summary, concern with the principle of academic freedom added to the complexity of reactions to the Harvard psilocybin project; some social control agents, especially officials of Harvard, were apparently constrained by that principle from responding exclusively to the issue of subject manipulation as it related to subject health.

Conclusions

On the basis of the foregoing analysis, several conclusions regarding the limits of acceptable subject manipulation are possible. First, it is clear that those limits are in part determined by a network of professional and organizational mandates. Mandates determine in large measure whether or not the members of a profession or organization will become involved in a particular case of subject manipulation. Moreover, many of the issues debated in a particular controversy are likely to be mandate-related.

The Harvard Drug Controversy involved several complex normative issues, i.e., the goals and methods of science, academic freedom, drug control, and the health of research subjects. Critics of the research responded in diverse ways, varying with the mandates of their professions or organizations.

Although the issue of subject health was frequently raised, it was often clouded or hidden by other mandate-related issues.

Second, the varied, somewhat conflicting, responses to the Leary-Alpert research are indicative of a lack of normative consensus which is characteristic of mass society. No generally accepted standards were invoked to evaluate the research by weighing its potential value against its risks. Behavioral scientists perceived that the accumulation of scientific findings is, at least in the long run, a significant contribution to the general good. Physicians assumed that the maintenance of medical control over drugs is good not only for the medical profession but also for the general public. Educators assumed that the protection of the investigator's freedom from extra-professional interference is a contribution to the general welfare. In the absence of normative consensus, the interests of society at large are protected only to the extent of their congruence with the mandates of powerful interest groups or organizations. Yet, there are some circumstances under which the vested interests of any group diverge from the general welfare. Some may agree with Malcolm Taylor's assertion that the point of divergence comes later for the medical profession than for most other groups.[65] Others may claim a similar status for scientists or educators.

The interests of the research subject are, like those of society in general, defended only to the extent that they coincide with the mandates of powerful interest groups or organizations. As a research subject, as in other roles, the individual in a mass society is at the mercy of powerful interest groups. He lacks the knowledge to decide intelligently whether or not to participate in a research project. He must depend upon the researcher to provide accurate information, to take proper precautions, and to judge the value of the research. In all of these matters the investigator is theoretically subject to the scrutiny of colleagues, other professionals, and organizations; but the judgment offered by them may be highly particularistic and may reflect an exclusive concern neither with the welfare of the subject nor with the welfare of society.

Third, although participants in the controversy invoked somewhat conflicting and competitive mandates as bases for action, the mandate which enjoyed the widest acceptance was that of the medical profession. The fact that drugs were used rather than some more subtle form of manipulation, e.g., deception, brought the case to the attention of medical authorities at Harvard, of the medical profession generally, and of drug regulatory agencies.[66] Many behavioral scientists took the position that, although psychologists have a right to conduct research with drugs, they should also collaborate with physicians in such research whenever feasible. Harvard authorities insisted that the University Health Services play a role in screening research subjects, though they were obviously concerned with other issues as well. The Massachusetts Department of Public Health was drawn into the controversy on the basis of a legal version of the medical mandate; and the agency terminated its investigation of the psilocybin research with the stipulation that the medical mandate be respected in the future through the presence of medical doctors at research sessions. Furthermore, the issue of medical control was prominently raised in many of the published accounts of the controversy.

Fourth, some types of subject manipulation are more likely than others to encounter opposition. Other things being equal, the manipulation of hospitalized, institutionalized, or otherwise disenfranchised subjects is less likely to occasion extensive controversy than is the manipulation of "normals." For example, drug researchers often employ drug addicts or prisoners as subjects without precipitating widespread controversy. Moreover, the Leary-Alpert research on the rehabilitation of prisoners apparently received less criticism than their research with non-institutionalized populations.

When healthy human subjects are exposed to manipulation, it is generally expected that they be fully informed, mature volunteers or that their participation be approved by persons responsible for them. Thus, the Harvard administration's exclusion of undergraduates from the psilocybin research was apparently intended to protect emotionally immature "normals." In effect, Harvard acted in place of parents as the responsible agent of the undergraduates.

Regardless of the type of subjects, certain means of manipulation seem to be more acceptable than others. Manipulation resulting in permanent, irreversible change in the subject appears to be ethically questionable except where the changes are generally considered to be desirable. The Leary-Alpert research stimulated controversy partly because the changes allegedly induced were considered by critics to be not only permanent but also undesirable, e.g., leading to drug dependence, a stigmatized condition in our society, and to detachment in role behavior, exemplified in the notion of game-playing.

Given that permanent effects are likely, manipulation with the intent of producing change in the direction of generally accepted norms probably enjoys wider acceptability than that aimed at the assessment of theory alone. The least acceptable manipulation appears to be that with revolutionary intent, i.e., with the purpose of producing changes in opposition to generally accepted norms.

Notes to the Chapter

1. The term "mandate" is used here in the sense suggested by Everett C. Hughes. The following statement is indicative of Hughes' usage: "An occupation consists, in part, of a successful claim of some people to *license* to carry out certain activities which others may not, and to do so in exchange for money, goods or services. Those who have such license will, if they have any sense of self-consciousness and solidarity, also claim a *mandate* to define what is proper conduct of others toward the matters concerned with their work." See Everett C. Hughes, "Licence and Mandate," in *Men and Their Work* (Glencoe, Ill.: The Free Press, 1958), 78.

2. For this perspective on the motivational content of communications we are indebted to Gerth and Mills. See Hans Gerth and C. Wright Mills, *Character and Social Structure* (New York: Harcourt, Brace, and World, 1964), 114–19; C. Wright Mills, "Situated Actions and Vocabularies of Motive," *American Sociological Review,* 5 (October, 1940), pp. 904–13.

3. We have received assistance of various kinds from the following persons and organizations: Robert F. Bales, who was director of the Laboratory of Social Relations at the time of the controversy; William Bentinck-Smith, Assistant to the President of Harvard University, who replied to our queries directed to President Nathan M. Pusey; Richard Doctor, Secretary of the Committee on Scientific and Professional Ethics and Conduct, American Psychological Association; C. Henzl, Senior Vice President, Sandoz Pharmaceuticals, A Division of Sandoz, Inc.; Hugh H. Hussey, Director, Division of Scientific Activities, American Medical Association; Herbert C. Kelman, who was a member of the faculty of the Center for Research in Personality, Harvard University, at the time of the controversy; David C. McClelland, who was Chairman of the Department of Social Relations, Harvard University, at the time of the controversy; Brendan A. Maher, who was chairman of the Center for Research in Personality, Harvard University, at the time of the controversy; W. B. Rankin, Acting Commissioner, Food and Drug Administration, Department of Health, Education, and Welfare at the time of this writing; Andrew T. Weil, who wrote the account of the controversy which appeared in *Look* magazine and edited an issue of the *Harvard Review* relating to hallucinogenic drugs.

Obviously, none of these men bears responsibility for the content of the present paper, but their assistance in making it possible is greatly appreciated. Unfortunately, repeated inquiries addressed to Dr. Leary and Dr. Alpert failed to bring a reply. However, their views have been widely circulated in research reports, newspaper and magazine articles, letters to the editors, etc. We have depended upon such sources for a knowledge of their positions.

4. Timothy Leary, *Interpersonal Diagnosis of Personality* (New York: Ronald Press Co., 1957).

5. Sidney Cohen, *The Beyond Within, The LSD Story* (New York: Atheneum, 1964), 12.

6. Sanford M. Unger, "Mescaline, LSD, Psilocybin, and Personality Change," *Journal of Psychiatry,* 26 (May, 1963), pp. 115–16.

7. For a recent example see: Abraham Wikler, Charles A. Haertzen, Richard D. Chessick, Harris E. Hill, and Frank T. Pescar, "Reaction Time ('Mental Set') in Control and Chronic Schizophrenic Subjects and in Postaddicts under Placebo, LSD-25, Morphine, Pentobarbital, and Amphetamine," *Psychopharmacologia,* 7 (May, 1965), pp. 423–43.

8. For a discussion and critique of this view see: E. James Lieberman, "Psycho-chemicals as Weapons," *Bulletin of the Atomic Scientists* (January, 1962), pp. 11–14.

9. For examples, see: Aldous Huxley, "Culture and the Individual," in David Solomon (ed.), *LSD — The Consciousness Expanding Drug* (New York: G. P. Putnam's Sons, 1964), 29–39, and Richard Jones, " 'Up' on Psilocybin," *The Harvard Review,* 1 (Summer, 1963), pp. 38–43.

10. For a more detailed discussion and bibliography of this issue see: Unger, *op. cit.,* 116–19.

11. *Ibid.,* 121–23.

12. Sidney Cohen, "LSD and the Anguish of Dying," *Harper's Magazine,* 231 (September, 1965), pp. 69–78.

13. This point of view has been expressed in many places but particularly in the following: Timothy Leary, "How to Change Behavior," in Solomon (ed.), *op. cit.,* 97–113, and Timothy Leary and Richard Alpert, "The Politics of Consciousness Expansion," *The Harvard Review,* 1 (Summer, 1963), pp. 33–37.

14. Descriptions of the prisoner rehabilitation project are included in: Timothy Leary and Walter Houston Clark, "Religious Implications of Consciousness Expanding Drugs," *Religious Education,* 58 (May-June, 1963), pp. 251–56, and Timothy Leary, "How to Change Behavior," *op. cit.,* 110–12.

15. *Ibid.,* 109–10; Leary and Clark, *op. cit.,* 251; Timothy Leary, George H. Litwin, and Ralph Metzner, "Reactions to Psilocybin Administered in a Supportive Environment," *Journal of Nervous and Mental Diseases,* 137 (December, 1963), pp. 561–73.

16. Information in this and the immediately following paragraphs has been drawn from published accounts of the events. These accounts have been supplemented and verified via correspondence with the principals. With the knowl-

edge so gained we have relied most heavily upon the following accounts: Noah Gordon, "The Hallucinogenic Drug Cult," *The Reporter,* 29 (August 15, 1963), pp. 35–43, and Andrew T. Weil, "The Strange Case of the Harvard Drug Scandal," *Look,* 27 (November 4, 1963), pp. 38–48.

17. Robert E. Smith, "Psychologists Disagree on Psilocybin Research," *The Harvard Crimson,* March 15, 1962; Gordon, *op. cit.,* p. 37; and Weil, *op. cit.,* p. 44.

18. Efrem Sigel, "Psilocybin Expert Raps Leary, Alpert on Drugs," *The Harvard Crimson,* December 12, 1962, p. 1. For additional examples of this view see letters to the editor in *The Reporter,* 29 (September 12, 1963, and September 26, 1963).

19. For example, see: Dana L. Farnsworth, "Hallucinogenic Agents," *Journal of the American Medical Association,* 185 (September 14, 1963), p. 165, and Roy R. Grinker, "Lysergic Acid Diethylamide," *General Psychiatry,* 8 (May, 1963), p. 425.

20. For documentation of the possible deleterious effects, see: Frank Barron, Murray E. Jarvik, and Sterling Bunnell, Jr., "The Hallucinogenic Drugs," *Scientific American,* 201 (April, 1964), pp. 29–37; Sidney Cohen, "Lysergic Acid Diethylamide: Side Effects and Complications," *Journal of Nervous and Mental Diseases,* 130 (January, 1960), pp. 30–40; Grinker, *op. cit.,* 425; Arnold M. Ludwig and Jerome Levine, "Patterns of Hallucinogenic Drug Abuse," *Journal of the American Medical Association,* 192 (January, 1965), pp. 104–18; Unger, *op. cit.,* 111–25; Farnsworth, *op. cit.;* Richard Blum, Eva Blum, and Mary Lou Funkhouser, "The Natural History of LSD Use," in Richard Blum and Associates, *Utopiates: The Use and Users of LSD-25* (New York: Atherton Press, 1964), 22–68; Cohen, *op. cit.,* 208–28.

21. Richard Alpert and Timothy Leary, "Letter to the Editor," *The Harvard Crimson,* December 13, 1962, p. 3.

22. Timothy Leary, "How to Change Behavior," *op. cit.,* 109. (Reprinted by permission of G. P. Putnam's Sons from *LSD — The Consciousness Expanding Drug,* Ed. by David Solomon; © 1964 by David Solomon.) For other expressions of this point of view see: Timothy Leary, George H. Litwin, and Ralph Metzner, "Reactions to Psilocybin Administered in a Supportive Environment," *Journal of Nervous and Mental Diseases,* 137 (December, 1963), pp. 561–73; and Ralph Metzner, George Litwin, and Gunther M. Weil, "The Relation of Expectation and Mood in Psilocybin Reactions: A Questionnaire Study," *Psychedelic Review,* No. 5 (1965), pp. 3–39.

23. Unger, *op. cit.,* 118.

24. Gordon, *op. cit.,* 41; Leary, "How to Change Behavior," *op. cit.*

25. Smith, *op. cit.;* Weil, *op. cit.,* 44; Maher, *op. cit.,* 4.

26. "State Will Investigate Research on Psilocybin," *The Harvard Crimson,* March 21, 1962, p. 1; Gordon, *op. cit.,* 37.

27. Harvard University Health Service, "Rules Governing the Participation of Healthy Human Beings as Subjects in Research," April 1, 1963.

28. The American Psychological Association added to its Code of Ethics the following statement in regard to drug research: ". . . investigations of human subjects using experimental drugs (for example, hallucinogenic, psychotomimetic, psychedelic, or similar substances) should be conducted only in such settings as clinics, hospitals, or research facilities maintaining appropriate safeguards for the subjects." See: *American Psychologist,* 20 (December, 1965), p. 1034.

29. Richard Alpert and Timothy Leary, "Letter to the Editor," *The Harvard Crimson,* December 13, 1962.

30. Timothy Leary, letter distributed to prospective members and supporters of the International Federation for Internal Freedom April, 1963.

31. *Ibid.*

32. Richard Alpert and Timothy Leary, "Letter to the Editor," *The Harvard Crimson,* February 21, 1962.

33. Gordon, *op. cit.,* 37. (Reprinted by permission of *The Reporter.*)

34. Walter E. Barton, "Letter to the Editor," *The Reporter,* 29 (September 26, 1963), p. 8. (Reprinted by permission of *The Reporter.*)

35. F. J. L. Blasingame, "Comments of American Medical Association, Proposal to Amend Regulations Pertaining to New Drugs for Investigational Use." *Journal of the American Medical Association,* 182 (December 1, 1962), pp. 134–38. A similar view was expressed by Farnsworth, "Hallucinogenic Agents," *op. cit.,* 165.

36. Gordon, *op. cit.,* 37.

37. Leary, "How to Change Behavior," *op. cit.,* 101. (Reprinted by permission of G. P. Putnam's Sons from *LSD — The Consciousness Expanding Drug,* Ed. by David Solomon; © 1964 by David Solomon).

38. *Ibid.,* 102.

39. *Ibid.,* 104.

40. *Ibid.,* 105.

41. Leary and Alpert, "The Politics of Consciousness Expansion," *op. cit.,* 34.

42. *Ibid.,* 34–35.

43. Timothy Leary, Richard Alpert, and Ralph Metzner, "Rationale of the Mexican Psychedelic Training Center," in Blum, *op. cit.,* 180. (Reprinted by permission of the Publishers, Atherton Press. Copyright © 1964, Atherton Press, New York. All rights reserved.) It is not entirely clear from the context of the statements whether they were intended to apply only to the Zihuatanejo center set up in the summer of 1963 or to that and prior research as well. In either

case, the statements are indicative of a point of view that seems to have extended throughout much of the research both at Harvard and in Mexico. For earlier statements in this vein, see: "Statement of the Purpose of the International Federation for Internal Freedom," January 24, 1963.

44. Brenden A. Maher, "Drugs and Academic Freedom," *Massachusetts Psychological Association Newsletter,* 7 (October, 1963), p. 4. (Reprinted by permission of the *Massachusetts Psychological Association Newsletter* and Brenden A. Maher.)

45. Quoted by Weil, *op. cit.,* 44.

46. For more detailed discussions of this aspect of the research, see: Leary, "How to Change Behavior," *op. cit.,* 109–10; Leary, "Introduction," in Solomon, *op. cit.,* 13–14; Leary, Litwin, and Metzner, *op. cit.,* 562; and Metzner, Litwin, and Weil, *op. cit.,* 3–6.

47. Leary, "How to Change Behavior," *op. cit.,* 109; Alpert and Leary, "Letter to the Editor," *The Harvard Crimson,* December 13, 1962.

48. Leary, "How to Change Behavior," *op. cit.,* 107–13; Gordon, *op. cit.,* 36.

49. Alpert and Leary, "Letter to the Editor," *The Harvard Crimson,* December 13, 1962, *op. cit.*

50. Gordon, *op. cit.,* 37; Sigel, *op. cit.*

51. For example, David C. McClelland, Chairman of the Department of Social Relations, reported that repeated exposure to the drugs lessened the interest of the investigators in science. See Gordon, *op. cit.,* 37; Sigel, *op. cit.*

52. Joseph B. Margolin, "Ethical Standards of Psychologists," *American Psychologist,* 18 (January, 1963), pp. 56–60.

53. *The Reporter,* 29 (September 12, 1963), pp. 6–8.

54. Maher, *op. cit.,* 3. (Reprinted by permission of the *Massachusetts Psychological Association Newsletter* and Brenden A. Maher.)

55. See: Gordon, *op. cit.,* and Weil, *op. cit.*

56. Timothy Leary, letter distributed to prospective members and supporters of the International Federation for Internal Freedom, *op. cit.*

57. Fred Hechinger, "Use of Mind-Distorting Drugs Rising at Harvard, Dean Says," *New York Times,* December 11, 1962, p. 1; Bruce L. Paisner, "Monro Repeats Psilocybin Warning, Identifies Drug Promotion Here," *The Harvard Crimson,* December 6, 1962, p. 1; Joseph M. Russin, "Monro, Farnsworth Warn Students About Drug Use," *The Harvard Crimson,* November 27, 1962, p. 1.

58. Alpert and Leary, "Letter to the Editor," *The Harvard Crimson,* December 13, 1962, *op. cit.*

59. Andrew T. Weil, "Corporation Fires Richard Alpert for Giving Undergraduates Drugs," *The Harvard Crimson,* May 28, 1963, p. 1; Maher, *op. cit.,* 5.

60. Nathan M. Pusey, "Statements Given to Newspapers in Response to Queries," *University News Office,* May 27, 1963.

61. *Ibid.*

62. Editorial, *The Harvard Crimson,* May 28, 1963, p. 1.

63. Maher, *op. cit.,* 4. (Reprinted by permission of the *Massachusetts Psychological Association Newsletter* and Brenden A. Maher.)

64. *Ibid.,* 5.

65. Malcolm Taylor, "The Role of the Medical Profession in the Formulation and Execution of Public Policy," *Canadian Journal of Economics and Political Science,* 26 (February, 1960), p. 127.

66. The ethical and methodological problems of deception in social-psychological experiments have been addressed in the following recent papers: Diana Baumrind, "Some Thoughts on Ethics of Research: After Reading Milgram's Behavior Study of Obedience," *American Psychologist,* 19 (June, 1964), pp. 421–23; Herbert C. Kelman, "The Human Use of Human Subjects: The Problem of Deception in Social-Psychological Experiments," unpublished paper presented at the meetings of the American Psychological Association in Chicago, Ill., September, 1965.

CHAPTER SIX

Project Camelot: Selected Reactions and Personal Reflections

GIDEON SJOBERG

Project Camelot has been one of the most controversial of research studies in recent years. It has inspired numerous commentaries, and others will no doubt continue to appear.

This chapter does not examine the events that led to the rise and fall of Project Camelot. Rather it is concerned with the reactions — both political and ethical — to the cancellation of the Project. Any effort by a social science association to draft a code of ethics must take account of the sharply differing views that social scientists hold; these are dramatized in the discussions of the Camelot venture. I shall use these reactions as a take-off point for analyzing what I personally consider to be the central political and ethical issues not only in Project Camelot but in many other research efforts as well.

This is not the place to elaborate upon the events that resulted in the cancellation of the Project, but some background data are essential. The reader may wish to consult Irving Louis Horowitz' extended essay for a detailed account of Project Camelot.[1] My own ideas about the social structure of research, which I presented in a public lecture several years ago, came into sharper focus in the course of reviewing this material along with an even lengthier manuscript of Professor Horowitz which he kindly permitted me to read.

The Evolution of Project Camelot

The concept of Camelot originated in the Office of the Chief of Research and Development, Department of the Army, and the Project was subsequently carried out by the Special Operations Research Office (SORO) of the American University, Washington, D.C. SORO, which operates under contract with the Department of the Army, ". . . conducts research in the social and behavioral science fields (nonmaterial research) in support of the Army's mission."[2]

Project Camelot, as indicated in one of the Army's fact sheets, was a "basic social science research project on preconditions of internal conflict, and on effects of indigenous governmental actions — easing, exacerbating or resolving — on these preconditions."[3] It seems fair to conclude that this Project was concerned with the problem of counterinsurgency and was predicated on the assumption that with increased knowledge of this problem the Army could more effectively cope with internal revolutions in other nations.

Operating with a budget of upwards of $6,000,000, Project Camelot was to involve surveys and other field studies in various countries in Latin America and ultimately elsewhere in the world as well. At the time of the Project's demise, the actual field work within these nations had not yet been initiated. However, plans for such were well advanced. Rex Hopper had been appointed project Director in December, 1964, and he and his staff had recruited a large number of social scientists to serve as consultants. Most of the consultants provided only technical support and their association with the Project was in general limited to a period of a few days. Among those who served were the sociologists Jessie Bernard, James Coleman, Lewis Coser, S. N. Eisenstadt, William Gamson, Gino Germani, W. J. Goode, William Kornhauser, Jiri Nehnevajsa and Neil Smelser; the political scientists Frank Bonilla, Harry Eckstein, and Frederick Frey; the economists Thomas C. Schelling and Gordon Tullock; and a psychologist, Robert Hefner. Bernard, Coleman, Nehnevajsa and Hefner were associated with the Project on a more continuing basis and were responsible for aspects of the technical design.[4]

The Project was cancelled on June 8, 1965, by Secretary of Defense Robert McNamara as a result of adverse reactions to the Project in Chile. Although the details of this incident are the subject of some debate, certain events seem clear. Johan Galtung, a Norwegian sociologist then in Chile, apparently called the nature of this Project to the attention of Chilean intellectuals and ultimately also certain members of the Chilean Senate and various left-wing elements in that country. Galtung's actions followed certain informal efforts by Project Camelot (through the anthropologist Hugo Nuttini) to establish working relationships with Chilean social scientists.

The Chilean Left sharply scored the Project and hurled charges against American researchers and the United States. This controversy led the American Ambassador to Chile, who apparently had not been informed by the Army of its activities, to call for cancellation of the Project. Actually, the situation reflected long-standing tensions between the Departments of State and of Defense concerning research in other societies. In the end, the controversy led to a Presidential communication giving the Department of State authority to review all federally-financed research projects involving research activities in other nations and potentially affecting foreign policy.

The Reactions of Social Scientists

Project Camelot has been both praised and (perhaps to a greater extent) condemned by politicians, editors, newsmen, and social scientists. Here I am concerned with the reactions of the last-mentioned group. One of the staunchest defenders has been Alfred de Grazia, Editor of the *American Behavioral Scientist:*

> Recently another unhappy episode in the history of relations between science and government has been enacted. A Norwegian pacifist named Johan Galtung egged on a Chilean communist paper to agitate South American anti-yanqui jingoism among a few professors to perturb the American ambassador to declaim to the State Department against unauthorized and damaging projects going on in his domain with Army support, and the State Department suffered one of its convenient leaks that let the world know the communist side of the story, which helped Senator Eugene McCarthy (no relation) denounce the research, with all the more righteous indignation since the State Department's research chief had teared all eyes with a story of research poverty in State and illegitimate research largesse in the Army, whereupon Generalissimo McNamara himself decreed that the army had no right to do research on insurgency (the situation in Viet Nam to the contrary notwithstanding) and, within a few days from the first communist yelp, project Camelot, a six-million dollar world-wide empirical-theoretical study of the roots of civil violence, staffed by such fine behavioral scientists as Rex Hopper, James Coleman, Jiri Nehnevajsa, and Robert Boguslaw, plus excellent foreign scholars and qualified young Americans, was D-E-A-D. It is all so matter-of-fact that it even makes sense when it's all stuffed into

a long sentence. And some think that physicists have worrisome problems of politics!

We should like our readers to consider the following questions:

1. Is it not true that since 1940, the Army, Navy, and Air Force have contributed incomparably more to the development of the pure and applied human sciences than the Department of State?

2. Is it not true that the State Department might on dozens of occasions have sought much more extensive research and intelligence facilities than it has actually sought or employed?

3. Is it not reasonable that the Armed Forces' mission in respect to insurgency should include research on areas where revolution might occur?

4. Are Cuba and Santo Domingo, Lebanon and Vietnam, and other cases too, going to stand as historical proof that the Army can send men in to be killed but cannot help anyone go in to forestall by preventive understanding the occasions of killing?

5. Is "clearance" so vital to an Ambassador that a large, important activity should be destroyed for want of it?

6. Is it wise for any agency to seek to get a few more research funds by invidious comparisons with the worthy research efforts of another department of government?

7. Are leaks, false assertions, quotations from Anti-American sources, and other tactics to be condoned in treating with problems of scientific research?

8. Should the Social Science Research Council, the American Political Science Association, the American Psychological Association, the American Association of University Professors, the American Sociological Association, the American Historical Association and the American Anthropological Association, in conjunction with various international counterparts, have acted promptly to investigate the situation, inquiring, among other matters, whether issues of freedom of inquiry were not present? And, while they are at it, might they not investigate the ugly and distorted articles carried in the Washington Press, particularly the *Washington Star,* against Project Camelot and social science research? . . .

There is absolutely nothing an American can do in any country of the world to avoid all criticism from all quarters of the country. Should American companies surrender a billion dollars of French investments because General De Gaulle makes menacing noises toward them? Why then should American professors surrender? The task of the American ambassador is to defend American rights, not to surrender them, and certainly not to surrender them out of pique.

Project Camelot was an open project, conducted by the American University, with Army funds, to solve problems of pressing and universal interest in the present day. It was skillfully manned, well-planned, and supported by some of the best foreign scholars in Latin America. Certain State Department officials have little to be proud of in the incident. They may have harmed the national defense effort and impeded social science.[5]

A more modest justification of Project Camelot has been offered by David Riesman.[6] He suggests that if "liberal" social scientists, who have been vociferous in their condemnation of Project Camelot, do not co-operate with the Army's research efforts, then data collection and analysis will by default be left to more conservative researchers and the more liberal elements of the Army will not receive support.

Another kind of reaction to the abandonment of Project Camelot has been that by Jessie Bernard, a rather active participant in this research effort. Although she grants the legitimacy of the Project's goal — i.e., to help reduce revolutions — she does raise for public discussion a number of crucial questions:

The major issues of concern to social scientists resulting from the cancellation of the project appear to be: 1) the responsibility of social scientists for the use made of their findings; 2) the ethical problems involved in funding; and 3) censorship.

1) What are the moral or social responsibilities of the social-scientist researcher with respect to the uses of the results of his work? This question was raised with reference to Project CAMELOT, as it has also been raised with atomic research. Some argued that the findings could be used to foment revolutions (e.g., John Chamberlain, *Washington Post,* August 14, 1965); others, that they could be used to repress them (e.g., *El Siglo* (Chile), June 15, 1965: see also Richard Dudman, *St. Louis Post Dispatch,* June 30, 1965). Project CAMELOT was especially "vulnerable" because findings were to be unclassified, hence available to "bad guys" as well as "good guys."

Since all scientific findings can be used by "bad guys" as well as by "good guys," the question arises as to whether the problems set for Project CAMELOT should be researched at all. Or, if researched, should they be classified, "undercover," and available only to the sponsor?

2) . . . the second question is, By whom should the research be done? A number of people believed that the problems should be researched (see Howard Margolis, *Washington Post,* July 3, 1965) but that the research should not be funded by Department of Defense. Perhaps by the United Nations or by foundations. Even, however, if funded by a peace research organization, the findings could still be used by both "good" and "bad guys." The first issue raised remains unresolved.

Since such research requires a large staff and a great deal of money, it may be that the major problem is how it should be organized. Perhaps a totally new concept is needed in the field of the organization of science in politically sensitive areas. A concept which would make the findings non-suspect.

3) On August 5, an Executive Order was issued requiring all research in foreign countries which use federal funds to be cleared by the Department of State. The censorship implications of this Order constitute a fundamental issue for social scientists. The implementation of this Order is, therefore, a major concern for them. They will certainly wish to be consulted in the setting up of guidelines.[7]

We come now to more critical judgments on Project Camelot — those offered by Silvert and Horowitz. Silvert takes a stand (implicitly at least) on one of Bernard's questions — that relating to the structure that supports research. Horowitz, dealing with a wide range of issues, considers her other two questions — those relating to the scientist's responsibilities regarding the use of his data and to the matter of censorship.

Silvert comments as follows:

> The academic problems sharpened, but not invented, by Project Camelot can be expressed in three relationships: the first, between social science and the government; the second, between professional competence and integrity; and the third, between Latin American studies as such and the general performance of the American academic community.
>
> The least difficult to discuss is the nature of the proper ties between the political and academic worlds. The trail has already been blazed by the physical scientists, and formalized procedures and institutions exist in all fields clearly defining the relationship of the scientist to his task, to the public, and to his profession. Legitimate differences of opinion exist, of course, concerning whether a scientist working on The Bomb has a special citizenship duty, for example. But the public identification of interest is plain, and the set relationships to the policy process into which any physical scientist may wish to place himself are also evident.
>
> No such clarity exists in the social sciences. We have no National Science Foundation discharging a brokerage function between the two worlds. We have had no such consistent public debates on academic objectivity and public commitment as have, say, the atomic physicists. No broadly accepted statement of ethics has come from our professional associations, and very few university administrations have concerned themselves with the problem. The result has been that social scientists have generally crossed and recrossed the lines separating their functions from governmental policymaking, the only inhibitions being their personally held standards of conduct.

No problem of integrity exists for two polar groups of social scientists: those who work inside government on a long-term basis, and those who because of their disciplines, research interests, or convictions stay entirely inside the university world. (A third group, the commercial contract scholar, sells his services where he wishes. His product is sometimes of very high quality. In any event, he does not concern us here because he has neither the pretensions nor the security of the academic scholar.) It is the social scientist working both fields who is in danger of betraying both of his masters through the loss of his powers of independent analysis. And he adds to his other academic difficulties a partial silence imposed by his access to classified materials, so that paradoxically he is often able to muster fewer data for his students than his uncompromised colleagues.

A serious question exists whether social scientists under certain kinds of government contract should continue to have the protection of academic tenure. As is well known, the purpose of tenure provisions is to assure academic freedom. But sometimes the exercise of such freedom is in conflict with necessary security provisions. More subtly, how does a scholar under contract know that he is adopting one hypothesis instead of another for truly scientific reasons, rather than because of a particular applied interest or even political prejudice? How can the persons reading the published work of this scholar know that he may have a personal, nonacademic involvement in the research? . . .

By no means am I suggesting that social scientists should turn their backs on policy questions, that government should refrain from employing social scientists or using social science materials. What I am suggesting is that the peculiar attribute and unique scientific virtue of the university-affiliated social scientist is his freedom. Once abridged, for whatever reason, then the people relying on his objectivity are in serious danger of accepting a misrepresented product, as many government agencies have learned.

I am fully aware that individual personality factors may prevent a professor from benefiting from the security given him by tenure. I suggest, however, that institutionalized temptation to the voluntary relinquishment of freedom be avoided, in the expectation that personal idiosyncrasy will be cancelled out of the final product by the numbers of persons engaged in the social sciences, as well as by the free exchanges in our increasingly numerous journals.

Let me add too, that I do not believe that our present state of ethical disarray has created a Frankenstein's monster rapidly conducing us to the socially engineered society. It is this possibility which has frightened some Chileans inordinately . . .

Latin Americans can relax on the issue of the magical effectiveness of the social scientists. But when they say they can no longer accept individual

American social scientists at face value, they are correct. The solution for Latin America, however, is not to close the doors to all foreign conducted or sponsored research and teaching. It is rather to insist upon clean credentials and academic competence — just as should we.[8]

In turn, Horowitz writes:

It is clear that some of the most critical problems presented by Project Camelot are scientific. Although for an extensive analysis of Camelot, the reader would, in fairness, have to be familiar with all of its documents, salient general criticisms can be made without a full reading.

The research design of Camelot was from the outset plagued by ambiguities. It was never quite settled whether the purpose was to study counter-insurgency possibilities, or the revolutionary process. Similarly, it was difficult to determine whether it was to be a study of comparative social structures, a set of case studies of single nations "in depth," or a study of social structure with particular emphasis on the military. In addition, there was a lack of treatment of what indicators were to be used, and whether a given social system in Nation A could be as stable in Nation B.

In one Camelot document there is a general critique of social science for failing to deal with social conflict and social control. While this in itself is admirable, the tenor and context of Camelot's documents make it plain that a "stable society" is considered the norm no less than the desired outcome. The "breakdown of social order" is spoken of accusatively. Stabilizing agencies in developing areas are presumed to be absent. There is no critique of US Army policy in developing areas because the Army is presumed to be a stabilizing agency. The research formulations always assume the legitimacy of Army tasks "if the US Army is to perform effectively its parts in the US mission of counter-insurgency it must recognize that insurgency represents a breakdown of social order. . . ." But such a proposition has never been doubted — by Army officials or anyone else. The issue is whether such breakdowns are in the nature of the existing system or a product of conspiratorial movements.

The use of hygienic language disguises the anti-revolutionary assumptions under a cloud of powder puff declarations. . . . To have used clearly political rather than military language would not "justify" governmental support. Furthermore, shabby assumptions of academic conventionalism replaced innovative orientations. By adopting a systems approach, the problematic, open-ended aspects of the study of revolutions were largely omitted; and the design of the study became an oppressive curb on the study of the problems inspected.

This points up a critical implication for Camelot (as well as other projects). The importance of the subject being researched does not *per se* determine the importance of the project. A sociology of large-scale relevance and reference is all to the good. It is important that scholars be willing to risk something of their shaky reputations in helping resolve major world social problems. But it is no less urgent that in the process of addressing major problems, the autonomous character of the social science disciplines — their own criteria of worthwhile scholarship — should not be abandoned. Project Camelot lost sight of this "autonomous" social science character.

It never seemed to occur to its personnel to inquire into the desirability for successful revolution. This is just as solid a line of inquiry as the one stressed — the conditions under which revolutionary movements will be able to overthrow a government. Furthermore, they seem not to have thought about inquiring into the role of the United States in these countries. This points up the lack of symmetry. The problem should have been phrased to include the study of "us" as well as "them." . . .

THE ETHICS OF POLICY RESEARCH

The issue of "scientific rights" versus "social myths" is perennial. Some maintain that the scientist ought not penetrate beyond legally or morally sanctioned limits and others argue that such limits cannot exist for science. In treading on the sensitive issue of national sovereignty, Project Camelot reflects the generalized dilemma. In deference to intelligent researchers, in recognition of them as scholars, they should have been invited by Camelot to air their misgivings and qualms about government (and especially Army sponsored) research — to declare their moral conscience. Instead they were mistakenly approached as skillful, useful potential employees of a higher body, subject to an authority higher than their scientific calling.

What is central is not the political motives of the sponsor. For social scientists were not being enlisted in an intelligence system for "spying" purposes. But given their professional standing, their great sense of intellectual honor and pride, they could not be "employed" without proper deference for their stature. Professional authority should have prevailed from beginning to end with complete command of the right to thrash out the moral and political dilemmas as researchers saw them. The Army, however respectful and protective of free expressions, was "hiring help" and not openly and honestly submitting a problem to the higher professional and scientific authority of social science.

The propriety of the Army to define and delimit all questions, which Camelot should have had a right to examine, was never placed in doubt. This is a tragic precedent; it reflects the arrogance of a consumer of intellectual merchandise. And this relationship of inequality corrupted the lines of authority, and profoundly limited the autonomy of the social scientists involved. It became clear that the social scientist savant was not so much functioning as an applied social scientist as he was supplying information to a powerful client.

The question of who sponsors research is not nearly so decisive as the question of ultimate use of such information. The sponsorship of a project, whether by the United States Army or the Boy Scouts of America, is by itself neither good nor bad. Sponsorship is good or bad only insofar as the intended outcomes can be pre-determined and the parameters of those intended outcomes tailored to the sponsor's expectations. Those social scientists critical of the project never really defined its freedom and independence, but questioned instead the purpose and character of its intended results.

It would be a gross oversimplification, if not an outright error, to assume that the theoretical problems of Project Camelot derive from any reactionary character of the project designers. The director went far and wide to select a group of men for the advisory board, the core planning group, the summer study group, and the various conference groupings, who in fact were more liberal in their orientations than any random sampling of the sociological profession would likely turn up.

However, in nearly every page of the various working papers, there are assertions which clearly derive from American military policy objectives rather than scientific method. The steady assumption that internal warfare is damaging disregards the possibility that a government may not be in a position to take actions either to relieve or improve mass conditions, or that such actions as are contemplated may be more concerned with reducing conflict than with improving conditions. The added statements about the United States Army and its "important mission in the positive and constructive aspects of nation building . . ." assumes the reality of such a function in an utterly unquestioning and unconvincing form. The first rule of the scientific game is not to make assumptions about friends and enemies in such a way as to promote the use of different criteria for the former and the latter. . . .

In conclusion, two important points must be clearly kept in mind and clearly apart. First, Project Camelot was intellectually, and from my own perspective, ideologically unsound. However, and more significantly, Camelot was not cancelled because of its faulty intellectual approaches. Instead, its cancellation came as an act of government censorship, and an expression of the contempt for social science so prevalent among those who need it most. Thus it was political expedience, rather than its lack of scientific merit, that led to the demise of Camelot because it threatened to rock State Department relations with Latin America.

Second, giving the State Department the right to screen and approve government-funded social science research projects on other countries, as the President has ordered, is a supreme act of censorship. . . .

We must be careful not to allow social science projects with which we may vociferously disagree on political and ideological grounds to be decimated or dismantled by government fiat. Across the ideological divide is a common social science understanding that the contemporary expression of reason in politics today is applied social science, and that the cancellation of Camelot, however pleasing it may be on political grounds to advocates of a civilian solution to Latin American affairs, represents a decisive setback for social science research.[9]

More severe criticisms have been leveled at Project Camelot from other quarters. Marshall Sahlins, an anthropologist, is particularly concerned with the impact of the Cold War upon social research and intimates that research conducted for military ends may undermine the scientist's primary goal — the search for "objective truth."[10]

Sahlins is supported in this position by the objections of some Latin American sociologists who argue as follows in a letter to the Editor of *Revista Latinoamericana de Sociología* (translated from the Spanish):

> . . . In the project under discussion the ideological orientation will be the basis not for the creation of hypotheses but for something quite external to this: the data will be collected and analyzed for their direct utilization for politico-military ends that are foreign to the theoretical and empirical interests of contemporary sociology. . . .
>
> The formulation of a project of this kind very seriously affects the aims of many sociologists who are desirous of institutionalizing in Latin America a serious, rigorous, and professionally responsible scientific tradition . . . It also raises serious doubts concerning the objectivity and scientific worth of such co-operation. . . .[11]

The words of Ober and Corradi, the former an historian at Connecticut College, are even harsher.[12] Their position is more in line with left-wing thought in Latin America — views which most American scholars regard as radical. From this perspective, Project Camelot was an instrument of American foreign policy and military power. This reasoning cannot be disregarded if one hopes to understand how a significant body of foreign scholars view our research efforts.

In sum, the responses to Project Camelot by social scientists reflect a wide range of intellectual and ideological themes. For example, de Grazia has apparently accepted the goals of the American government and the military as legitimate, and he does not question the aims of Project Camelot.[13] Riesman, too, grants considerable legitimacy to the Army and its goals as well as to its research efforts. Silvert's criticisms regarding American nationalism and military power are more oblique. But Horowitz clearly challenges the goals of the Project — its failure to consider the positive aspects of revolutions and its asymmetric study of "them" but not "us."

When we move to the arguments of Sahlins, the Latin American sociologists, and particularly Ober and Corradi, we find the legitimacy of America's political and military orientations not only questioned but challenged — as is also the research pursued in line with these orientations.

Personal Reflections[14]

Because so many aspects of Project Camelot have been explored by other writers, we can use this Project as a basis for examining some broader theoretical issues. Here I am especially concerned with one of the questions raised by Bernard and considered in part by Silvert: What kind of structure is essential for the effective conduct of social research? Or, more generally, what are the necessary conditions enabling the scientist to acquire "objective knowledge" and at the same time maintain a "sense of responsibility"?

I shall argue that the major problem social scientists faced in Project Camelot, and encounter in many other research projects as well, is the inability to achieve a sufficient degree of autonomy vis-à-vis the administrative-control sector of the social system that supports these research efforts. The problem has been intensified as social scientists have gained added power and authority in modern society; they are playing an increasingly larger role in the administrative-control sectors of the federal, state, and local governmental units as well as other large-scale organizations. And when scientists take on administrative tasks they tend to give up their scientific allegiance.

These trends are related to the expansion of the industrial-urban order, wherein, if planning is to be effective, the system must acquire information about itself and its external environment. But the data that researchers provide about formal organizations and how they operate may threaten the system by exposing it to criticism. To avoid this, administrators frequently attempt to control the course of research and the manner in which findings are disseminated.

This situation is the basis for my main thesis herein: that where social scientists seek to exercise freedom of choice regarding their research projects and wish to analyze and publish their data in an objective manner, tensions and conflicts between the research function and the administrative-control function of social systems inevitably arise. Moreover, if social scientists are to protect their informants from administrative sanctions, and thus to sustain their own legitimacy as scientists, they must avoid becoming integrated into, or overidentified with, the administrative-control sector of social systems, especially that of government. The failure to maintain autonomy in this respect accounts in large part for the political and ethical issues engendered by Project Camelot.

Social science researchers seem to hold a position analogous to that of newsmen in modern democratic societies. Cohen, in his book, *The Press and Foreign Policy*,[15] elaborates upon the built-in "love-hate" relationship that typifies the interaction between executive policy-makers and the working press, a tension that is heightened by the pressures upon reporters to "get a story." Indeed, many government administrators nurse considerable resentment of newsmen — and with good reason, especially during periods of social crisis. Administrative functionaries, therefore, often attempt to control the writings of newsmen; this tendency has been especially well documented for the war in Vietnam. At the same time, newsmen are protected by the value of freedom of the press and by the legal structure of American society. Moreover, reporters are often strategic sources of information for the very policy-makers who view them as a threat.

To the extent that a conflict exists between administrative-control and social research operations, researchers have a vested interest in institutionalizing a "private" sector in modern society. I am using the term "private" in a special manner — namely, in contrast to the administrative-control sector of any system. Therefore, even in the so-called "private" sector in American society — e.g., within a privately supported university — the researcher must be able to seal off his role to a considerable degree from the administrative-control sector if he is to carry out certain kinds of research.

While the major political and ethical issues in Project Camelot stemmed from the researcher's particular relationship to the administrative-control system of the Army, this case is far from unique, even on the international plane. Moreover, sociologists are constantly confronted by the need to work out satisfactory relationships with the administrative-control arm of the government or other organizations within a nation.

The National Scene. Within a nation such as the United States, the researcher's identification with an organization may well result in loss of freedom to select and develop his own research. But an even more pressing danger is the researcher's possible use of administrative controls to ensure the co-operation of, or to otherwise manipulate, informants. Opportunities for these practices exist whenever one has a "captive audience" — such as students, prisoners, or members of the military. Academic researchers often face such an ethical problem when they utilize students in their classes as respondents. The former may employ administrative controls in such a manner that the latter are forced to co-operate.

Of greater import to the analysis of Project Camelot is the situation wherein administrators support research as a means for gaining access to knowledge about their clients in order to "manipulate" the latter more effectively.

The problem first came to my attention when I conducted a survey of day care centers for the Austin (Texas) Community Council. This project was financed by the State Department of Public Welfare, which exercises police power over day care facilities through licensing procedures. I therefore had to take steps to ensure that no information on violations of regulations by directors of the centers would drift back to the Welfare Department; and in this the Department fully acceded. As the study progressed, it became clear that the center directors would not have provided us with certain information had the interviewers been employed by the Welfare Department. The Community Council, however, being removed from the administrative controls of the Welfare Department, could execute this study without the possibility of harm to the respondents. Even so, certain tables in the final report had to be constructed in such a manner that violations were "covered up."

A more significant case was a struggle on the national governmental level: the case of *The St. Regis Paper Company v. the United States*. In December, 1961,[16] the Supreme Court ruled that copies of reports filed with the Bureau of the Census could be subpoenaed by the Federal Trade Commission and the information thus obtained used in legal proceedings against alleged violators of FTC regulations. Up to that time, it had been assumed that copies of census reports had confidential status — similar to that accorded the original reports filed with the Bureau of the Census. Indeed, a confidential relationship had developed over the years between the Bureau and millions of business firms which furnished statistical information on request. More than half of the materials were furnished voluntarily, and it was common practice for a company to keep one copy of each statement for itself. Until the St. Regis case, it was assumed that the copy retained by a company for its files was vested with the same confidentiality as reports filed with the Bureau of the Census — reports, incidentally, that contained approximations and estimates which were not always available from an examination of the company books. In the end, remedial legislation gave businessmen the right to claim confidentiality for copies of reports they retained in their files. In other words, a special rule or norm was developed to separate research activity from administrative-control functions.

The point is that sociologists, too, must recognize that they are dependent upon institutional (especially legal) norms in the pursuance of their research; these not only enable them to protect their informants but make it possible for them to discuss freely certain kinds of social events. In a case involving Commissioner Sullivan of Montgomery, Alabama, and *The New York Times*, the Supreme Court ruled that newsmen may, unless malicious intent is demonstrated, write as they please about public officials. This norm offers sociologists more protection than they commonly recognize.

But to bring our argument into sharper perspective, let us examine selected patterns in other nations. In Nazi Germany, for example, many social researchers, as well as natural scientists, were incorporated into the administrative-control apparatus of the State. Scientists thus found their research activities channelled toward the goals defined by administrators. And they were expected to employ administrative controls to secure data about the citizenry in order that the State might more effectively manipulate the latter.

Of considerable theoretical significance also is the emerging situation in the Soviet Union. Considerable evidence indicates that Soviet researchers are struggling to legitimize and institutionalize their activities. This is, however, proving difficult, because the administrative-control functions of the Party (and the State) are given clear priority. In fact, except for certain present-day intellectuals, Marxist theoreticians in the U.S.S.R. have denied the existence of a "private sector" for either persons or organizations apart from the Party or State.

Given the relative absence of a private sector, the Soviet social researcher is confronted by at least two problems. As a scientist, he must seek to attain some degree of autonomy in the formulation of his scientific objectives and research design. And he must develop a means for ensuring that the responses of his informants will not leak back to the administrative-control sector and thereby lead to the manipulation of these informants. In the long run this protection for respondents is essential if they are to trust the scientist to the point that they will provide him with reliable and valid information.

Even in a democratic, pluralistic society such as the United States where researchers may exercise considerable control over their research design, the problem of protecting respondents has by no means been resolved. Personality or attitude tests, as well as other questionnaire data, can (and have been) employed by administrators — be these heads of government bureaus or universities or others — to manipulate or control respondents in their roles as citizens, employees, students, or whatever. At least some of the current debate in America concerning privacy for the citizenry deals with this very issue. The practical solution seems to be to develop rules or layers of norms concerning the relationships between researchers and respondents and administrative officialdom. These rules must somehow limit the latter's access to, and use of, confidential information so that these data cannot be readily employed for social control purposes.

The International Scene. The problems relating to the manipulation of respondents do not end at the national shoreline. Indeed, the difficulties of attaining objectivity are greatly intensified in research on a cross-national plane. For, as Project Camelot suggests, many social scientists working in foreign cultures tend to equate the interests of their own nation (and its administrative functions) with those of science.

But Project Camelot is only one case among many. We now know that the Central Intelligence Agency has supported a number of research projects in other societies. Michigan State University's research and action program in South Vietnam — which was partially staffed by CIA personnel — has received wide publicity.[17] Moreover, the Center for International Studies at Massachusetts Institute of Technology was, from the time of its founding until very recently (1966), financed in part by CIA funds.[18] And many prominent social scientists have been connected with this Institute without objecting to this arrangement. Yet this *sub rosa* sponsorship of research violates the principle of "openness" within science. In addition, the CIA's funding of projects may well leave a subtle impact upon the research process itself, especially where researchers are interested in attracting continued support from this agency. For example, some projects may have been selected over others because they are congruent with the goals of the funding agency.

I am not suggesting that the researchers at MIT were engaged in any kind of "conspiracy." However, we know that social scientists do respond (and at times rightly so) to the expectations of funding agencies. Certainly they are likely to ask themselves: What statements in my reports might adversely affect the agency or the continued funding of this study?

Sponsorship by an organization such as the Central Intelligence Agency may also undermine the "legitimacy" of American social science research in other societies. Intellectuals and the general public in other nations have had cause to wonder whether American social scientists are more intent upon "manipulating them" than upon attaining "scientific truth." Wesley Fishel,[19] the political scientist in charge of Michigan State University's research efforts in South Vietnam (mentioned above), has given no indication in his published defense of his activities that he recognizes the possibility that CIA support of social research might lead peoples in other nations to question the goals of American social scientists and ultimately undermine the legitimacy of American social research on the international scene.

With respect to Project Camelot, we must recognize that the Army, like the CIA, has a vested interest in control — such is its very reason for existence. And it was because of the identification of the Army with administrative-control functions that social scientists and intellectuals in Latin American nations reacted so adversely to Project Camelot. The American social scientists who participated in the Project apparently failed to recognize the "image" they were conveying to scientists in other societies — viz., that American social researchers are part and parcel of an administrative-control apparatus designed to collect information with the express purpose of controlling the course of social change in the underdeveloped world.

Because of the mission with which the Army was charged, there was also a question of whether the researchers felt free to criticize Project Camelot's goals and research design. Apparently there was tacit acceptance of the Army's right — i.e., moral obligation — to engage in activities that would further its ability to manipulate other nations, a viewpoint that seems inherent in de Grazia's argument. Conversely, the participation of social researchers served to legitimize the Army's role at home and abroad, including its efforts to engage in diplomatic as well as military maneuvers.

But we need to explain why so many eminent and conscientious social scientists agreed to participate in Project Camelot without apparently questioning its basic goals. A number of writers have observed that the participants apparently did not ask themselves: How would American intellectuals, or the American public in general, have responded if the Soviet military, or the French military, or whatever, had sent a group of researchers to investigate the Watts riots or the Vietnam peace demonstrations? Nor did most co-operating social scientists reflect upon the fact that it was their alignment with a major power structure that would enable them to carry out the research in the first instance.

In answer to the question of why so many social scientists accepted the Project so readily, I would like to offer two tentative hypotheses: First, American social scientists (including sociologists) have been socialized, both as citizens and scholars, to an almost unquestioning acceptance of the authority and power wielded by their own nation-state system and consequently the administrative controls of the national government. (Nationalism is perhaps the most pervasive, yet the least explored, of the influences that shape the research carried out by American social scientists in other nations.) Second, the increasing stress in social science upon achieving professional (as opposed to scientific) status serves to rationalize the acceptance of administrative controls emanating from the national level. The professional organizations of social scientists in fact encourage their members to maintain a position of "respectability" in the eyes of the broader society. And one means of achieving this image is to forge links with the major institutional systems in the society, notably those that exert administrative controls over citizen and scientist alike. Here the actual norm stands in marked contrast to the ideal norm calling upon the scientist to engage in the search for truth without regard to the needs and orientations of any particular organization.

Conclusions

Project Camelot, as a case study, suggests that overidentification with an administrative-control structure can undermine objectivity as well as generate political and ethical dilemmas with respect to the handling of respondents. These dimensions are interrelated in complex ways, not only in research efforts on the international scene but also in those carried out within a given society.

It is in fact exceedingly difficult to gain an objective evaluation of controversial issues — e.g., the great revolution now under way in the "third world." It is well-nigh impossible if one is handicapped by over-identification with the goals of any particular administrative-control system. In light of this, we must ask: What strategies can be employed to increase the researcher's autonomy, which today seems less than adequate for many purposes?

One strategy has already been suggested — that of building layers of norms between the scientist (and his respondent) and the administrative-control sector of large organizations, especially the nation-state. Such a course of action means that the researcher must sacrifice immediate control over the administrative apparatus (and social power) in order to attain long-range goals. At the same time, this separation of research activities from administrative controls can be advantageous for administrators as well. It ensures them against being co-opted by any one group of social scientists who, unwittingly or no, may impose their views upon them. The insulation of researchers from the administrative-control sector of systems also means that administrators are not directly threatened by heretical or radical ideas, though they must face up to the impact of these over the long haul.

We have a situation where administrators and social scientists seem to need one another but their overall objectives lead to fundamental tensions and conflicts. Administrators are committed to organizations, scientists ideally to broader issues and ideas. Consequently, scientists — as "loners" or as loosely organized groups — must struggle to maintain their autonomy, whereas administrators, given their commitments, will (and must) criticize the scientists. Indeed, the idea of autonomy for the researcher should never be equated with freedom from criticism. Quite the contrary. The greater the autonomy the sharper should be the criticism from the administrative-control sector and the broader public, if the social scientist is to shoulder his broader social responsibilities.

This brings us back to the comments of Silvert, who, it appears, views the university as an ideal setting for sustaining the autonomy of the scientist. His argument is not without merit. Had Camelot been sponsored by an American university, the reactions in Latin America might have been quite different. However, Silvert ignores certain realities. Universities exert administrative controls of their own, and their respect to governmental (and other external) controls makes them less than adequate bases for studying highly sensitive topics, not only those that deal with questions transcending nationalistic considerations but those that may lead to conflicts with major power groups within a society. Paradoxically, while academicians tend to avoid highly controversial areas, they also fail to undertake certain types of relatively noncontroversial policy-oriented research for large-scale organizations. Although social scientists must attain greater autonomy if they are to carry out their "calling" more effectively, this ideal is difficult to realize when organizations want (and need) information on specific issues. For these organizations can purchase this information on their own terms. However, Project Camelot demonstrates the drawbacks to the sponsorship of research by organizations whose primary function is that of control. The Army, for instance, is not an agency that persons in other nations will long accept as a legitimate sponsor of social science research.

In addition to modifying the existing institutional order, an effort must be made to create new types of research structures — those uncommitted to the specific goals of any one nation-state. But these new forms will prove ineffective if social scientists persist in stressing order and neglect to create norms maximizing freedom to do research.

Ultimately I suspect the relative lack of autonomy for social scientists in certain realms will, for some time to come, force us to rely upon "alienated" scholars — i.e., free-floating intellectuals such as C. Wright Mills — to provide us with a perspective and a conscience regarding large-scale research efforts. Mills, incidentally, was apparently able to maintain his marginal role not only because he was connected with a private university but also because he was marginal to that system. And he gained financial and social rewards from the society he criticized.

Then, too, sociologists in smaller nations may provide us with a perspective on our efforts. Social scientists in, for example, Sweden or Poland are likely to achieve somewhat more autonomy from administrative controls (and certain ideological commitments) than are researchers in America or the U.S.S.R. Their autonomy will never be complete, but it should permit them to reflect critically upon the work being carried out in the major power blocs.

Overall, sociologists have the obligation, insofar as they strive to attain objective truth, to avoid overidentification with any particular administrative-control system. Their long-run interests lie not with a particular group but with the broader concerns of mankind. However, major ethical and political dilemmas arise as social scientists seek to define these broader concerns and orient their research in these directions, while at the same time accepting support from specific social organizations. It is in this context that Project Camelot must be viewed.

Notes to the Chapter

1. Irving Louis Horowitz, "The Life and Death of Project Camelot," *Transaction*, 3 (November-December, 1965), pp. 3–7, 44–47. Professor Horowitz is currently writing a book on this subject.

2. *Behavioral Sciences and the National Security,* Report No. 4, and Part IX of the Hearings on *Winning the Cold War: The U.S. Ideological Offensive,* by the Subcommittee on International Organizations and Movements of the Committee on Foreign Affairs, House of Representatives (Washington, D.C.: U.S. Government Printing Office, 1965), 192.

3. "Statement by Senator J. W. Fulbright on Department of Defense Research in Foreign Policy Matters," *Congressional Record,* August 25, 1965, 20906.

4. *Behavioral Sciences and the National Security, op. cit.,* 62.

5. Alfred de Grazia, "Government and Science . . . An Editorial," *American Behavioral Scientist,* 9 (September, 1965), p. 40.

6. David Riesman, "Letter to the Editor," *Trans-action,* 3 (January-February, 1966), p. 2.

7. Jessie Bernard, "Letter to the Editor," *American Sociologist,* 1 (November, 1965), pp. 24–25.

8. Kalman H. Silvert, *The Conflict Society: Reaction and Revolution in Latin America* (rev. ed.; New York: American Universities Field Staff, Inc., 1966), 150–52.

9. Horowitz, *op. cit.,* 45–47.

10. Marshall Sahlins, "The Established Order: Do Not Fold, Spindle, or Mutilate," Unpublished paper presented at the annual meeting of the American Anthropological Association, November, 1965.

11. *Revista Latinoamericana de Sociología* (Buenos Aires), 1 (July, 1965), p. 253.

12. John David Ober and Juan Eugenio Corradi, "Pax Americana and Pax Sociologica: Remarks on the Politics of Sociology," *Catalyst* (Buffalo), No. 2 (Summer, 1966), pp. 41–54.

13. De Grazia fails, for instance, to recognize that the Army could have ultimately put a secret classification on the materials collected in Project Camelot, even though it was listed as an "open project."

14. I first set forth some of these ideas in a public address sponsored by the Department of Sociology, The State University of New York at Buffalo, April, 1964. Revised versions of that paper were presented at Washington University (St. Louis), January, 1966, and at the Graduate Center, The City University of New York, April, 1966.

15. Bernard C. Cohen, *The Press and Foreign Policy* (Princeton: Princeton University Press, 1963).

16. Thomas Corcoran, "On the Confidential Status of Census Reports," *American Statistician,* 17 (June, 1963), pp. 33–40.

17. "MSU: The University on the Make," *Ramparts,* 4 (April, 1966), pp. 11–22. One must evaluate this report with care. There have been many charges and countercharges with respect to this case. See "School-C.I.A. Link Denied at Inquiry," *The New York Times,* May 17, 1966, p. 6, and Wesley Fishel, "CIA Men Used but They Weren't Secret Agents," *The Evening Bulletin* (Philadelphia), May 10, 1966, p. 33. Also Robert Scigliano and Guy H. Fox, *Technical Assistance in Vietnam: The Michigan State University Experience* (New York: Frederick A. Praeger, 1965).

18. "M.I.T. Cuts Agency Ties," *The New York Times,* April 27, 1966, pp. 1, 28.

19. Fishel, *op. cit.*

CHAPTER SEVEN

Political Pressures and Ethical Constraints Upon Indian Sociologists

T. N. MADAN

In response to the task assigned me by the Editor, I shall survey the political and ethical problems that emerge in the study of villages in India by Indian sociologists and anthropologists. In the first section, on the development of village studies in India, I attempt to show that administrative and ameliorative motives, rather than scientific curiosity for its own sake, have in the past provided the dominant impetus for these studies, and continue to do so now in the case of Indian researchers. In the next section are outlined the severe limitations of inadequate teaching and research facilities which blight rural studies by Indian scholars. This section is followed by a discussion of some political pressures and administrative controls, a section on ethical constraints, and some concluding remarks.

The data on which this paper is based are, besides the author's own experience, written communications from the following Indian sociologists or social anthropologists: Mr. Imtiaz Ahmad, Miss Lakshmi Iyer, and Drs. André Béteille, G. Chattopadhyay, B. R. Chauhan, S. C. Dube, R. S. Khare, L. K. Mahapatra, K. S. Mathur, Ramkrishna Mukherjee, M. C. Pradhan, M. S. A. Rao, Sachchidananda, A. M. Shah, Indera P. Singh, D. P. Sinha, Surajit Sinha, and L. P. Vidyarthi. I am grateful to all these friends for their courtesy in writing me and to Dr. M. N. Srinivas for his comments on the paper.

Development of Village Studies in India

The formal beginnings of ethnographical and Indological studies in India go back to the founding of the Asiatic Societies of Bengal and Bombay in the 1780's. The academic activities of these Societies were soon supplemented by the exertions of civil servants who produced a special and by now famous genre, namely the district gazetteers and the series of volumes on the tribes and castes of the various Provinces. The first such ethnographic survey was ordered by the Court of Directors of the East India Company in 1807.[1] The fruits of such surveys were not analytical studies of villages or communities but merely compendia of information on ethnic groups and social usage "intended primarily to acquaint the administrator with the diversity of custom in the different segments of the country's population."[2]

Commenting on the sociological significance of these scholarly activities, Mukerji writes:[3]

> . . . the social drive behind the search for knowledge of oriental history and culture was the urgency felt by commercial interests suddenly called upon to combine trading with ruling to carry on both the enterprises with the minimum disturbance to the onerous undertaking. People had to be governed well in order that commerce might flourish. Good government in those days of Bentham and Smith meant noninterference with the habits and customs of the people. So those customs and habits had to be studied. They could be studied in two ways: a) by reading the texts, which meant translation by the pundits of the Fort, and also hunting them out; b) by observation. The first led to oriental scholarship and Indology, the second to ethnology.

Monographic accounts of tribes and an interest in village studies took much longer to get established in the country. The former got involved in unfortunate misunderstandings and controversies. Thus, there was a widespread feeling among educated Indians that those whom anthropologists study are savages. Similarly the stress on caste and religion in census ethnography, and the official policy of creating separate administrative pockets out of predominantly tribal areas, gave rise to suspicions against ethnographical inquiries.

The first analytical studies concerned with the village in India were those by Maine and Baden-Powell,[4] and both of these scholars wrote of the Indian village in general rather than of particular villages. Maine with his evolutionary bias had given much prominence to the alleged antiquity and widespread distribution of *joint* villages in India, and Baden-Powell endeavored in his books to correct this false impression.[5]

By the beginning of the twentieth century Indian agriculture, and consequently the Indian village, had acquired a new importance because of recurrent famines and the general unsettlement and disintegration of rural economy in the face of commercialization.[6] After World War I the poverty and disorganization of village life came to the attention of officialdom and the educated public. Consequently the Government appointed the first Royal Commission on Agriculture in 1926. At the same time, the Indian national movement did much to stimulate interest in the study of village life. It was during the 1920's that "village studies" in the sense the term is employed today took form.[7]

As may have been expected in these circumstances, the academics who engaged in village studies were economists. Sociologists and social anthropologists were negligible in numbers and their orthodox interests lay in other fields.

Majumdar complains that

> Sociologists and anthropologists have been preoccupied in India with their special interests, the former with urban life, city planning . . . [etc.]; and the latter with tribal cultures. . . . This has given a sort of monopoly, as it were, to the economists who have . . . perfected their techniques and begun to use quantitative data to understand and interpret the socio-economic problems of rural life. *But these problems have been studied without any relevance to the cultural background so that the interrelations that exist between different sets of social phenomena have to a large extent been ignored.* (Italics mine.)[8]

The genuineness of the concluding part of Majumdar's complaint will be apparent if one looks into well-known books by Indian economists such as *The Indian Rural Problem* by Nanavati and Anjaria.[9]

The solitary exception to the lack of sociological or social anthropological writings on India's rural life was the classic work, *Behind Mud Walls,* by the American missionaries William and Charlotte Wiser, published in 1930, containing a rounded account of life in a north Indian village.[10] It is, however, significant that the book did not really attract much attention among sociologists and social anthropologists till the 1950's.

A break with the traditional preoccupations occurred towards the middle of the century when village studies by sociologists and social anthropologists, particularly the latter, burst upon the Indian academic scene with the suddenness and profusion of the monsoon. The reasons for this development were notably the following:

1. The century-old concern of social (and cultural) anthropology with tribal (preliterate) peoples was already on the wane at the beginning of

World War II; the break became pronounced after the end of the War when social anthropologists all over the world turned in increasing numbers to the study of peasant communities.[11]

2. A large increase in the number of colleges and universities, as well as rural sociology courses at the graduate and undergraduate levels, resulted in a greater number of students wanting to take up research assignments.[12]

3. The contacts, on the personal as well as the institutional levels, between these students and an increasing number of foreign (mainly American and British) scholars who were visiting India for field work in peasant villages, and the influence of these contacts.

4. The widespread concern with rural development in India, reflected most prominently in governmental policy and action (the Five-Year Plans, Rural Credit Surveys of the Reserve Bank of India, Land Reforms, Community Development and *Panchayati Raj* Programmes, and so forth) and in socio-economic movements (most prominently the *Bhoodan* March of Vinoba Bhave and the *Sarvodaya* Movement of Jaya Prakash Narayan).[13]

It should be clear from the foregoing account of the growth of village studies in India that, for the *Indian* sociologist or social anthropologist, such studies are of more than academic interest; they are, in fact, inextricably bound, historically as well as contemporaneously, with the socio-economic problems facing the Indian village and the efforts to find suitable solutions to them.[14]

Teaching and Research Facilities

Studies of villages or rural communities by Indian sociologists and social anthropologists have been and continue to be severely handicapped by the relatively small number of trained scholars available and the appalling paucity of funds for research.

According to the *Handbook of Universities in India,* 14 of the 55 Indian universities had only a department of sociology during 1962–63; five had departments of sociology as well as of anthropology; and six had only departments of anthropology.[15] In other words, more than half of the number of universities did not provide courses or research facilities in these two subjects. It is also worth noting that 1) in 1950 there was provision for teaching anthropology and/or sociology at only seven universities out of 19, and 2) of the three oldest universities in the country (founded in 1857), Bombay has only a department of sociology and Calcutta and Madras only departments of anthropology.

Although I have been unable to obtain official figures, it seems from such reports as I have been able to obtain (mainly in the form of personal communications from teachers) that not more than 10 per cent of the students who obtain the master's degree in sociology or anthropology register for doctoral work; and a much smaller percentage is able to complete the work and obtain the doctorate. The main reasons for this lack of interest or inability to complete work are careless selection (of students by supervisors and of topics of research by the former) and/or financial stringency, as well as overburdened teachers.

Scholarships available from governmental or nongovernmental sources and of the value of 300 rupees per month, which amount may be regarded as the least needed by a single research worker to maintain himself,[16] are negligible in number. Thus the awards mentioned in the middle of 1965 by the University Grants Commission for *the whole country* were 57 junior fellowships of 300 rupees per month and 19 senior (post-doctoral) fellowships of 500 rupees per month.

So far as university teachers of sociology and social anthropology are concerned, personal field work by them is well-nigh impossible for a number of reasons, notably the following:

1. The teaching load is heavy throughout the session — six to twelve lectures a week is not uncommon — precluding even short absences in the field.

2. A system of periodical leave, such as the "sabbatical" year, is absent.

3. Study leave is granted to permanent teachers only, on full or half pay, provided that they engage themselves in "improving their professional competence through higher studies." Further, anyone who obtains such leave usually has to undertake to serve his university for twice the period of absence on his return from leave.

4. There are no "foundations" or "trusts" which finance sociological research. Governmental or semi-autonomous bodies such as the Research Programmes Committee (of the National Planning Commission) give large grants for *research projects* involving the employment of several research workers, and for research in problems in which these groups are interested. The University Grants Commission has, however, introduced a scheme of field-work grants for university teachers. A few individuals are also able to get grants from foreign countries, but the great majority of teachers are unable to engage in research for want of time and money. It may also be added here that the idea that research by college and university teachers is as much a part of their work as teaching, and valuable to the community at large, has yet to establish itself.

This bleak situation is somewhat relieved by the fact that the Government itself conducts sociological and anthropological research through such central agencies as the Anthropological Survey of India and the Department of Social Security, and through the Tribal Research Institutes and Social Welfare Departments in the various States. But since such research is divorced from teaching it fails to make a notable impact. Further, the stranglehold of bureaucracy over research is undoubtedly inimical to its growth, so that some of the major government departments have produced work which is unimpressive both in terms of quantity as well as quality.

Political Pressures and Administrative Controls

I will now discuss some of the political pressures and administrative controls that affect Indian sociologists and social anthropologists in the study of rural communities.

"Political pressures" are exerted upon a researcher when organized or semi-organized groups prevent, or seek to prevent, him from following his own judgment (where the latter would be approved by his professional colleagues) in 1) the choice of a problem for study and of a place for field work, 2) the scope and manner of his inquiries, and 3) the context and place of publication of the results of his research.[17] "Administrative controls" stem from the rules or norms of the government department or private research institution that supports or employs the researcher.

The main characteristic common to political pressures and administrative controls is that if the researcher disregards them, it may become impossible for him to pursue his inquiries because of official directives to abandon them, excessive interference by his superiors, withdrawal of financial support, or lack of co-operation (which may develop into hostility) on the part of some or all of the people being studied.

The Impact of Politicians and the Sponsoring Agency. The simplest and most extreme form which governmental pressures upon the independent worker may take is the withholding of permission to do field work in a certain area. One of the earliest and better-known instances of this was in 1923 when the late K. P. Chattopadhyay, later Professor of Anthropology at Calcutta University, was refused permission by the Government of India to enter Nepal for field work as an Anthony Wilkins student, apparently because of his radical (left-wing) political opinions.

Even now (i.e., after 1947) the Government is very particular about keeping a close watch on scholars who want to engage in social studies in areas of strategic importance. Thus, the Research Programmes Committee of the National Planning Commission formed a special subcommittee some time ago to scrutinize research projects involving field work in international border areas. Besides academic experts, representatives of the Ministries of Defence and Home Affairs of the Government of India and the State Governments concerned sat on this subcommittee, and in 1965 they gave approval to only one of five proposals submitted.

Similarly, in 1957–59 some pressure was exerted by the local civil administration upon a social anthropologist working in Central India not to get too close to a former ruler of an Indian principality who was trying to whip up political discontent.

Governmental pressure or control is more often exercised indirectly. Most of the money available for social research is distributed by such Union Government or Central agencies as the University Grants Commission, the Research Programmes Committee, the National Council of Educational Research and Training, the National Institute of Community Development, and the Department of Social Security. All these bodies have definite research objectives, and it is widely known to Indian social scientists that the kinds of research projects that are likely to be approved by the former are those dealing with socio-economic problems, sponsored change, and social welfare activities. The result is that, in the absence of other sources of financial support, scholars intending to engage in social research are compelled to choose only such topics as are likely to find favor with the sponsors. None of these bodies would be interested in supporting a study of, say, cross-cousin marriage (a *cause célèbre* in contemporary social anthropology) or the rituals of kinship, not to speak of purely theoretical research devoted to the fundamental task of conceptual clarification.

The same holds true of research funds available from the State Governments and their specialized agencies like Tribal Research Institutes and Social Welfare Boards.

Several scholars have also complained of the obstructionist attitude of government departments and civil and revenue officials because of suspicion of the outsider, which may well be a legacy of the days of colonial rule. Thus an historian was, after prolonged correspondence, refused access to certain documents though these were not concerned with security matters. Similarly, a social anthropologist encountered persistent hostility from a Block Development Officer because the latter thought that the former had reported unfavorably on his work.

Inter-state and inter-departmental conflicts also may adversely affect the inquiries of a research worker. Thus a social anthropologist belonging to a certain State found the officials of a neighboring State, where he was doing field work, unco-operative because they feared that he might be secretly working for a "merger movement" which had earlier been launched by some political parties of his home State to seek the transfer of certain border areas of the neighboring State concerned.

Inter-departmental rivalries are reported to have adversely affected research by a government anthropologist. He writes that in his State the head of the Department of Welfare was very anxious that the activities of the Department should not be made the subject of evaluation studies by the Tribal Research Institute.

Research studies by government employees are subject to a number of controls. Thus, there is the research program of the department into which each individual has to fit; and the lower the rank of a research worker in the bureaucracy, the less freedom of choice he has in this respect. Another important mode of control is the requirement that no officer shall publish the results of his inquiries without the prior scrutiny of his paper, report, or book by a superior officer. This results in much subservience among the younger research workers who try to please their superiors and change even the contents of research reports at the latter's suggestion.

Control over the publication of research studies is exercised not only by government departments with regard to government employees but also by the specialized agencies with regard to independent research workers. Thus, I am currently engaged in making a study of the role which various religious communities (viz., Brahmans, Christians, Lingayats, and Muslims) have played in providing educational facilities (through schools, hostels, scholarships, etc.) in Mysore State. The required financial assistance has been made available by the National Council of Educational Research and Training, New Delhi, and one of its conditions is that I or my research assistant shall not publish any part of our findings but shall first submit them in the form of a report to the Council.

Private sponsoring bodies, such as the Sri Ram Centre of Industrial Relations of New Delhi, impose similar conditions. In fact, even where no more help is given than permission to make studies inside a factory or workshop, the management may insist that a copy of the report should be shown to it before publication.

Political pressures may also emanate from the clearly political sector of society. At times it is a government research officer himself who has to face pressures from politicians outside or inside the government. Thus, popularly elected ministers of two States tried to exert pressure on the head of a Central research institute to drop some of his inquiries into the political process of *Panchayati Raj.* That they failed in this because of the high academic and bureaucratic status and the tenacity of the social scientist involved is not important; what is so is the fact that such pressure was applied.

Several other social scientists have complained of the pressure which ministers, members of Parliament, members of the State legislative assemblies have exerted on them to give a particular slant to their findings and recommendations. In one case pressure was exerted to have a particular community declared as a scheduled tribe. When the government anthropologist refused to alter his findings to the contrary, a campaign was started by the disgruntled politicians against the research institute of which he is the head.

In another case, a university teacher, on deputation with a research institute and in charge of a socio-economic survey of tribal communities in a particular State, was asked by some tribal members of Parliament and of the State Legislative Assembly to show his report to them before he submitted it to the sponsors. When he refused to do so, one M. P. argued with him that since the researcher was not himself a tribesman, he was likely to misrepresent their socio-economic condition and needs and thus defeat the very purpose of his survey. Whereas such interference is fairly common, ministers, M.P.'s, and high officials on the other hand often cold shoulder Indian sociologists, though they seem eager to be interviewed by foreigners.

National and international politics also may impinge upon the social scientist. The rather uneasy Hindu-Muslim relationship in the Indo-Pakistan subcontinent affords a good example of this. One of my correspondents writes:

> In a study of Indian Muslims I found that there were marked separatist tendencies among them which found expression in their apathy and indifference to the political and social issues facing the country. I, however, soon realized that though the conclusions were valid, it was not politically desirable to publish them.

My own feeling about the data I have collected on Kashmiri Muslim villagers has been similar: I have so far hesitated to publish the results of my inquiries though for somewhat different reasons. The Kashmiri Muslim is far from being orthodox, mainly owing to past and present Hindu influence. Many of the customs of these Muslims, and their beliefs also, are contrary to the teachings of Islam. I have hesitated to publish my findings because of the fear that, in view of the present political situation in Kashmir, many readers may mistake my sociological conclusions for political propaganda. More importantly, the villagers themselves may become hostile and refuse to co-operate in any future inquiry that I may want to undertake among them.

This leads us to the people being studied by an ethnographer and the pressures they exert upon him.

The Impact of the People Being Studied. It is the peculiar experience of the Indian field worker that as soon as he takes up residence in a village, the villagers try to "locate" him in the caste hierarchy. This may be done either directly by inquiring about his social background, or indirectly by taking note of his choice of residence within a particular street or neighborhood and of the commensal relations (particularly the groups from whom he accepts food) he establishes in the village. Once he is thus "located" in the social life of the village he is under pressure to observe the norms of the group with which he is identified. A nonvegetarian anthropologist had to stick to vegetarianism in the Brahman street of the Tanjore village in which he did field work. The visit of an untouchable boy to his rooms caused enough displeasure among his hosts for him to take care that such a mistake did not occur again. Another sociologist reports that his belonging to a high caste of the cultural region in which he did field work prevented him from making participant observations among the untouchable castes. Although as an outsider the researcher is allowed some latitude, there is no compromise on basic issues.

More important is the involvement of the field worker in village politics, as I can vouch for from my own experience. To begin with, everybody was pleasant to me in the village of Utrassu-Umanagri in South Kashmir where I spent a year in 1957–58. Within a few weeks, however, I was able to anticipate who would be the most useful informants because of their knowledge, friendly disposition, communicative nature, and relative freedom from work. I tried to cultivate the friendship of these persons, only to discover later on that they had strained relations with some very influential members of the village community. The latter developed a deep suspicion that their own misdoings would find their way into my book and were not happy about my presence in the village, causing me quite some worry. At the same time they also tried to win me over to their side.

A sociologist reports of a similar involvement in village factions in a western Indian village, as does also an anthropologist in a village in the State of Uttar Pradesh. Still another researcher describes how his friendship with certain individuals in the village he studied obliged him to render them help when one of them was involved in a case of elopement, and how this caused some jesting at his expense as well as critical comment about himself.

Usually villagers also try to influence the social scientist to present his findings in such a way that only the good things will become known; "the name of the village must remain unsullied" is how an informant of mine put it. And if there is any possibility of benefits following upon the submission of the report or the publication of the book, then they try their best to get their demands and grievances recorded. This results in numerous man-hours of work lost for the field worker, but he must be patient or else he may not find the villagers co-operative when he makes the inquiries he is interested in.

Since the field worker cannot afford to be indifferent to what is said about him and how people in the village feel about him — lest his work be put in jeopardy — these sayings and feelings constitute a genuine restraint upon him.

The Impact of the Scientific Community. Regarding pressures from the academic community, three types have been mentioned by my correspondents. First, there is the complaint that the few sociological and social anthropological journals that exist in the country are in the hands of a few individuals, and therefore the acceptance or rejection of an article is dependent more upon the editor's discretion than upon an assessment of the worth of the contribution through consultation with referees.

Second, the personal research interests of teachers often result in the imposition of research topics upon students. Third, complaints have been voiced about project research. Whereas an anthropologist who has directed several research projects writes of how difficult it often is to keep his team under administrative and academic control, another complains of the un-necessary interference in his project by the head of his department.

It may here be mentioned that two of my correspondents (including one of the senior social scientists in the country) feel that insufficient pressure is exercised in India by the academic community upon its members, with the result that a lot of unsatisfactory and shoddy research continues to appear year after year in journals as well as in the form of books. One of the reasons for this is the appointment of academically wrong men to teaching posts on the grounds of region, language, religion, or caste. Concrete examples of such bad appointments have been reported from several educational institu-tions. Another reason may well be the absence of professional bodies (like the American Sociological Association, the American Anthropological Association, and the Association of Social Anthropologists in Britain) with their annual meetings and seminars at which unsatisfactory work could be subjected to severe public criticism.

Ethical Constraints

Ethical constraints may be said to be *felt* by the individual research worker whenever there is a conflict between what he thinks he ought to do as a social scientist and what he believes he ought to do as a kinsman, friend, guest, host, follower of a certain religion, citizen, or human being.[18] Sometimes pressure may be exerted upon a research worker by appealing to his "moral sense," but this kind of pressure does not involve the sort of sanctions associated with political and administrative pressures.

To say that ethical constraints are *felt* by the individual researcher does not, however, imply that ethical decisions are divorced from "broader values and belief systems." What ideally should be sought is that the force of an ethical constraint be on the conscious level and voluntarily acknowledged by the individual concerned.

An Indian social scientist shares, or is *expected* to share, with the villagers he studies many of the basic values and attitudes that have a pan-Indian validity. Avoidance of certain types of food and drink is one such value. A sociologist has written of his inability to engage in participant observations among certain communities because of their "unhygienic living conditions and habits" and also because of his "personal reservations" regarding the consumption of liquor. The conflict here is between the ethnographer's needs to mix freely with the people he studies and his personal ethics.

That women too have a place in public life and may engage in many of the tasks that men do, is still not widely recognized in rural India. The proper place for a woman is the home and the proper roles those of daughter, wife, and mother. A woman anthropologist, who has just completed a year of field work in a rural area, had to take her mother with her to the village as a chaperon to satisfy those persons who refused to believe that there could be any valid reasons for a young woman in her twenties to stay unmarried and make "idle" inquiries in the villages.

Yet another widespread attitude in rural India is that men and women shall not discuss sexual matters or marital problems — their own or those of other people. During the early phase of my field work, no women communicated with me. Later on only young girls (below the age of about fifteen) or elderly women engaged in conversation with me. But the ethical notions of the people under study ruled out any talk about husband-wife relations. Even men became reticent when conversation turned to sex or wealth.[19]

Of more serious consequence is the loyalty the researcher develops towards his hosts and informants as it may come into conflict with the primary commitment to his discipline. Barnes puts it succinctly:

> Historians may be safe in saying what they like about the dead, but social scientists who write about the living have special responsibilities not to betray the confidence of the people they study.[20]

This was my own principal problem in the course of writing a book on Kashmiri peasants.[21] A good deal of very significant information was given me by several villagers, not because I was an interested ethnographer, but because they had come to regard me as a friend with whom they could afford to be frank. Some of this information was vital to the adequate explanation of certain events or social changes. For example, the first case of widow remarriage in a particular village had taken place when a widow became pregnant and her rich lover persuaded a man of limited means, by offering him monetary inducement, to marry her. I must not mention this if I ever write a book on the said village because the villagers will see the book, and this will cause hurt feelings as well as resentment.

Similarly, I came to know of several fictitious partitions of land in the course of my inquiries in half a dozen villages in Kashmir. These partitions had been registered with the appropriate revenue officials although they had not in fact taken place. The motive for doing so was to retain more than the 22 acres of land permitted to a householder under a law that came into being in 1950. If I were to mention the details of these cases, the result might well be prosecution of the concerned households by the revenue authorities of the State Government.

An anthropologist who worked in a Tanjore village gives expression to the same dilemma:

> Many facts were revealed to me in confidence; I would not think of disclosing such facts without concealing the identities of the parties involved, because, among other things, their publication may have legal consequences.

One practice has become established in Indian studies through which the ethnographer seeks to rescue himself from this quandary: this is to disguise the name of the village by giving it a pseudonym and/or to change the names of particular individuals to prevent their identification. It seems, however, that often villagers dislike the fact that the true name of their village is concealed,[22] and the changing of the names of individuals may be of no avail in the case of certain happenings because of the importance of the latter. The only way out in such cases is a decision to either publish the information or withold it. My own decision has been that, in the case of certain information I have (excluding, for example, knowledge about the whereabouts of thieves, murderers, and the like), it is morally right for me to suppress it rather than hurt my informants or get them into trouble with the administration.

Ethical considerations have also been invoked to suppress other types of information. One social anthropologist writes of how it was suggested that he not publish his critical views of the Community Development Programme because these would damage the "image" of the country abroad. Another anthropologist writes that when he showed a draft of his doctoral thesis on some aspects of rural Hinduism to his Indian teacher, the latter advised him to consult a particular member of the faculty who is an authority on Hindu philosophy:

> I explained to him that my interpretations were based on folk belief rather than on scriptures. He told me not to behave like a 'kid,' and that more than an anthropologist I was a Hindu and an Indian . . .

Finally, I would like to raise an ethical problem that has bothered me a great deal, namely that of co-authorship. Some papers and books have been published by Indian social scientists the basic data for which have been collected either by students or by paid research investigators. The final publication has, however, denied more than a mere mention of their names to those who did the actual field work. This is particularly applicable to large research projects. The names of investigators, research supervisors, etc. are usually mentioned in the preface, but even this courtesy is denied if the data have been taken from field-work reports or students' M.A. theses. The only proper procedure seems to me to acknowledge the contribution of one's colleagues (be they students, investigators, or research assistants) by clearly and truthfully stating what it has been. If help has been received even in the writing of the report, the only proper course seems to be to accord them the status of co-author.[23]

Concluding Remarks

I have only briefly outlined, because of limitations of space, some of the political pressures, administrative controls, and ethical constraints that affect Indian social scientists in the course of field work among Indian rural communities. I now want to conclude by offering a few observations which should help the reader to gain a balanced view of the Indian scene and which recapitulate the main points of the above discussion.

1. Analytical rural studies in India by Indian sociologists and anthropologists have only recently begun and are as yet severely limited by the inadequacy of trained personnel and research funds. However, the improvement in the situation which has been recorded since Independence (in 1947) has been indeed impressive. To appreciate the progress that has been made in India during the last two decades one has only to compare the situation here with that obtaining in other South and Southeast Asian countries. Even in Britain, the current spurt of academic interest in sociology is of recent origin; as late as in 1948 there was only one university (London) which had sociologists on its staff,[24] and even today (1966) Oxford and Cambridge Universities do not have Chairs in the subject. The neglect of sociology in Britain must be taken into account when we survey the Indian scene, because before Independence the academic fashions in India reflected those in vogue in British universities. American influence in Indian academic life is a post-Independence development, and it has helped the expansion of social science research in several ways.

2. For historical and contemporary reasons there is an almost overwhelming stress on applied research much to the neglect of conceptual clarification. Whereas I bemoan this neglect, I do not deny that the preoccupation with development has led to the acceptance and expansion of social science research in India. One may also hope that out of the interest in the applied aspect of sociology will emerge an interest in fundamental research. I may here add that several Indian sociologists attribute the preoccupation with applied research to, *inter alia,* the influence of American universities and foundations.

3. A variety of political pressures are exerted upon the Indian sociologist, but the most important of these seem to stem from the government, from specialized semi-autonomous agencies which derive their own finances from governmental grants, and from political opinion groups such as ministers, M.P.'s, and M.L.A.'s.

4. Ethical constraints are broad in their scope, involve an appeal to abstract principles, and are, therefore, also rather vague and difficult to define. Further, the elements of subjective reaction and individual decision are of considerable importance.

5. The distinction between political pressures and ethical constraints is not always clear-cut. For example, how is one to characterize the force of opinions of one's professional colleagues? It is obviously as much ethical

as it is political, in the broad but permissible sense in which I have used the latter term.

6. Since the main concern of this paper has been a description of pressures and constraints, I hope the reader has not got the *wrong* impression that sociological research is carried on in India under highly restrictive conditions and that researchers always yield to external pressures. There is, in fact, considerable freedom in the conduct of social research. Further, the government is not over-sensitive to the criticism of its policies. Thus, there has been much unfavorable comment of its Community Development Programme and often by sociologists whose inquiries have been financed by governmental agencies.

7. The different ways in which various sociologists react to the external pressures is an interesting and relevant area of inquiry, but limitations of space have prevented my going into it, as also into the wider and basic problem, "Should social research be completely free of restrictions by the sponsor and the state?"

Notes to the Chapter

1. D. N. Majumdar, *The Matrix of Indian Culture* (Lucknow: Universal Publishers, 1947), 40.

2. S. C. Dube, "Social Anthropology in India," in T. N. Madan and Gopala Sarana (eds.), *Indian Anthropology: Essays in Memory of D. N. Majumdar* (Bombay: Asia Publishing House, 1962), 237.

3. D. P. Mukerji, *Diversities* (New Delhi: People's Publishing House, 1958), 120.

4. See e.g., H. S. Maine, *Lectures on the Early History of Institutions* (London: J. Murray, 1875) and B. H. Baden-Powell, *The Indian Village Community* (London: Longmans, Green & Co., 1896).

5. See e.g. Baden-Powell, *op. cit.,* vif., 4f., *passim.*

6. R. C. Dutt, *Economic History of India in the Victorian Age 1837–1900* (London: Routledge & Kegan Paul, 1956).

7. Ramkrishna Mukherjee, *The Sociologist and Social Change in India Today* (New Delhi: Prentice-Hall of India, 1965), 169–70.

8. D. N. Majumdar, "Introduction," in D. N. Majumdar (ed.), *Rural Profiles* (Lucknow: Ethnographic and Folk Culture Society, 1955), v.

9. M. D. Nanavati and J. J. Anjaria, *The Indian Rural Problem* (3d ed., Bombay: Indian Society of Agricultural Economics, 1947).

10. William Wiser and Charlotte Wiser, *Behind Mud Walls* (New York: Agricultural Missions, 1930).

11. See e.g., Raymond Firth, *Elements of Social Organization* (London: Watts, 1951); Robert Redfield, *Peasant Society and Culture* (Chicago: University of Chicago Press, 1956); Dube, *op. cit.,* 239f.; and F. G. Bailey, "The Scope of Social Anthropology in the Study of Indian Society," in Madan and Sarana, *op. cit.,* 255f.

12. T. B. Bottomore, *Sociology* (Englewood Cliffs, N. J.: Prentice-Hall, 1963), 21.

13. Carl C. Taylor, Douglas Ensminger, Helen W. Johnson, and Jean Joyce, *India's Roots of Democracy* (Bombay: Orient Longmans, 1965); Gyan Chand, *Socialist Transformation of Indian Economy* (Bombay: Allied Publishers, 1965).

14. M. N. Srinivas, *Caste in Modern India and Other Essays* (Bombay: Asia Publishing House, 1962), 120ff.

15. Before 1950 the following Universities had Departments of Sociology and/or Anthropology: Bombay (Sociology, established 1919), Calcutta (Anthropology, 1921?), Delhi (Anthropology, 1947), Gauhati (Anthropology, 1948), Lucknow (Sociology, 1949), Madras (Anthropology, 1944), and Osmania (Sociology,?).

The Departments that have started functioning since 1950 are Agra (Sociology, 1956), Andhra (Anthropology,?; Sociology,?), Annamalai (Sociology, 1953), Baroda (Sociology, 1951), Bhagalpur (Sociology, 1956), Delhi (Sociology, 1959), Gorakhpur (Sociology, 1958), Gujarat (Sociology, 1954), Jabalpur (Sociology, 1960), Jodhpur (Sociology, 1962), Kalyani (Sociology, 1962), Karnatak (Sociology, 1957; Social Anthropology, 1959), Lucknow (Anthropology, 1952), Mysore (Sociology, 1962), Punjab (Anthropology, 1960; Sociology, 1960), Patna (Sociology, 1951), Rajasthan (Sociology, 1961), Ranchi (Anthropology, 1952), Saugor (Anthropology, 1954), and Utkal (Anthropology, 1958).

16. One dollar is equal to seven rupees and 50 paise.

17. "Politics is about policy, first and foremost; and policy is a matter of either the desire for change or the desire to protect something against change." J. D. B. Miller, *The Nature of Politics* (Harmondsworth: Penguin Books, 1965), 14.

18. S. F. Nadel, *Anthropology and Modern Life* (Canberra: Australian National University, 1953); A. M. Rose, *Theory and Method in the Social Sciences* (Minneapolis: University of Minnesota Press, 1954), 179ff.; J. A. Barnes, "Some Ethical Problems in Modern Fieldwork," *British Journal of Sociology,* 14 (June, 1963), pp. 118–34.

19. See Raymond Firth, "Social Organization and Social Change," *Journal of the Royal Anthropological Institute,* 84 (January–December, 1954), p. 2f. on the lack of social freedom which an investigator faces in the study of his own society. Also T. N. Madan, *Family and Kinship: A Study of the Pandits of Rural Kashmir* (New York: Asia Publishing House, 1966), 11–12.

20. J. A. Barnes, "Foreword," in Madan, *op. cit.,* ix.

21. Madan, *op. cit.*

22. Dr. A. C. Mayer tells me that the people of the Malwa village he has described in *Caste and Kinship in Central India* (London: Routledge & Kegan Paul, 1960) were disappointed to find that he used a pseudonym for it. Dr. André Béteille reports a similar reaction to the fictitious name given by him to the village he discussed in his doctoral dissertation. As for my own informants, they insisted that I should not conceal the identity of the village. Madan, *op. cit.,* ix, 12.

23. A statement on Professional Ethics has recently been circulated on behalf of some Indian anthropologists who formed an Association in 1964. Nothing is known of the activities of this Association. However, one of the points in their statement was: "While publishing the research findings the role of each worker in the team should be clearly indicated." The principle that in supervised research schemes both the investigator and the supervisor should be shown as co-authors is also enunciated.

24. Alan Little, "Sociology in Britain since 1945," *Social Sciences Information,* 2 (July, 1963), p. 64.

CHAPTER EIGHT

Research in South Africa: The Story of My Experiences with Tyranny*

PIERRE L. VAN DEN BERGHE

That the social scientist (or, for that matter, any scientist) can achieve olympian detachment and objectivity is a myth which is fortunately not as widespread as it was thirty or more years ago when the behavioral sciences, except in Germany, were still largely under the sway of positivism. An increasing number of autobiographies, mainly of anthropologists, have been published, highlighting, often in moving terms, the human drama of social research.[1] Social scientists have even become characters in works of fiction, and the ambiguities of their roles have been a rewarding subject for novelists and for social scientists analyzing their own profession.[2] Here I want to relate my experiences as a sociologist working in a highly explosive situation ridden with racial conflict, namely in South Africa, during the period February, 1960, to December, 1961.[3] While South Africa probably represents an extreme case, many of the incidents and feelings mentioned here have, of course, been reported by other social scientists, notably anthropologists doing field work in a colonial context.

South Africa was not my first exposure to tyranny. As a child, I had experienced subjugation under German military occupation in Belgium and France. As an adolescent, I learned what it meant to belong to the *Herrenvolk* when I returned to the land of my birth, the then Belgian Congo. I am ashamed to confess that I rather relished this feeling of racial superiority which, as a white colonial, I rapidly shared with my fellow

183

Europeans. At that time, I completely failed to make a parallel between the tyranny I had suffered under in Europe and that from which I benefited in Africa. So much does one's class position blind one to social realities that superficial dissimilarities can hide profound resemblances. Only by repeating this cycle of being alternatively on the subordinate and on the dominant side of the fence did I reach my present position. A few years after my Congo interlude I found myself again in the position of the underdog, as a private in the United States Army. When I finally went to South Africa, I once more became a member of the *Herrenvolk* by virtue of my skin pigmentation, but this time it was despite my militant rejection of such a role. During my two years' stay in the country, my political opinions continued to evolve from a rather old-fashioned nineteenth-century liberalism towards a nonmaterialistic Gandhian socialism.

I should perhaps spell out my present position somewhat more fully. I have become increasingly convinced that parliamentarianism in a Western type of bourgeois democracy, even under conditions of universal adult suffrage and legal equality, is not capable of solving the most fundamental problems faced by modern societies (e.g., land distribution, the optimum use of human labor and leisure, medical care, city planning, etc.). The liberal laissez-faire model, which is increasingly being abandoned in "developed" countries, is even more blatantly inadequate in the Third World. At the same time, I believe that, while the work of Marx was a great contribution to sociology and to the analysis of nineteenth-century European capitalism, Marxian socialism is hardly more relevant than liberalism to the problems of the still largely agrarian countries of the twentieth century. This is particularly true of tropical Africa, where Marxian class analysis bears little relationship to social reality, a fact recognized by the proponents of African Socialism.

In addition to these and many other problems of substance, I disagree with the classical Marxian ethos on two major ideological grounds. First, I am a non-materialist in the dual sense that, as a pantheist, I cannot deny the existence of the "supernatural," and in that I do not accept the primacy of material over non-material goals and determinants of social action. For all its wealth, I regard the United States as farther removed from the ideal society than many poorer social orders. Similarly, South Africa, the continent's richest country, also has the most ethically bankrupt social order. Nor is the problem simply one of *distribution* of wealth, for gross inequities can exist in societies with a relatively equal distribution of material rewards, a problem long recognized by Marxian and other socialists. Second, I regard physical violence against persons as morally reprehensible, and I consider Gandhian techniques of opposition to be both ethical and efficacious. Nevertheless, I regard myself as a socialist insofar as I believe that private property should be limited to consumer goods, and, in developing economies where still relevant, to small-scale land and tool ownership by self-employed farmers and artisans.

The present account is an attempt to retrace the impact of the South African brand of racial tyranny on myself as a sociologist and as a person, and on my scientific methodology and findings. I shall try to deal with the problem from four main points of view:

1) relations with the government
2) relations with private persons, both whites and non-whites
3) subjective feelings and attitudes
4) problems of scientific objectivity

Defining my relationship with the South African government seemed at first a fairly simple matter, dictated mostly by expediency. From the outset, I decided that I should have no scruples in deceiving the government and that the paramount consideration in my dealings with the state would be to minimize obstacles to my research without compromising my principles. When applying for a South African visa, I decided that it would be unwise to reveal the real purpose of my stay (namely to study race relations), and I declared that I was a social scientist interested in "the spectacular economic development of South Africa." Once in the country, however, the problem became much more difficult. Generally, my strategy was to avoid attracting the attention of the authorities without letting undue caution interfere with my research, and without sacrificing my integrity. If caught in a violation of law or custom, I was determined to "play it dumb." Such a broad line of conduct, while it proved workable in most instances, nevertheless required constant decisions as new contingencies arose. I quickly became aware that, try as I may, there was no escape from the color bar, and that I must, however reluctantly, comply with segregation much of the time. Inviting arrest for violation for apartheid regulations would have defeated the purpose of my stay, and besides, jails also are segregated, so that even in prison I should have enjoyed against my will countless special privileges.

Probably to save my self-respect and allay my feelings of guilt, I decided that I would engage in some symbolic protest actions, that I would refuse certain "customary" white privileges, and that I would break some laws which I considered iniquitous or which exposed my non-white friends to embarrassment. For example, I refused to be served before non-white customers in shops or in government offices; similarly, I filled in the item labeled "race" on official questionnaires with the term "human" or "American," often to see it changed surreptitiously to "white" by a state official who must have wondered at the stupidity of foreigners who do not even know that they belong to the master race. When I invited Africans to my house, I offered them alcoholic beverages, a criminal offense until 1962, and when in the company of non-whites I always tried to avoid using segregated facilities, or, when I did, I used the non-white ones.

In addition, I broke other laws and regulations not so much on grounds of principle, but because compliance with them would have jeopardized my research more than their evasion. For example, whites are required to carry special permits to enter most African "locations" and "reserves." I entered such places countless times without ever asking for a permit. To state candidly the purpose of my visits (either research or simply social intercourse with African friends) would have appeared both incredible and suspicious to the authorities. Violation of the law, on the other hand, made me more inconspicuous, inasmuch as I was rarely detected. When caught, my skin color ironically protected me from adverse consequences, and I always got away with a warning. Most of the time I pretended to have lost my way, and the police gave me elaborate road directions, while commenting on the danger of traveling unarmed in "Native areas." Had I had a black skin, of course, I would have been repeatedly arrested and convicted for "pass" offenses. Even in my defiance of the law, I was given preferential and often deferential treatment, simply because of my lack of pigmentation.

On one occasion, however, I narrowly escaped arrest for breaking a racial taboo. When I offered a female colleague of mine a lift home in my motorcar, she accepted but suggested that my wife accompany us. As my colleague was a Muslim of Indian origin, I assumed at first that her request was motivated by reasons of propriety, although, emancipated as she was, I was somewhat surprised. I soon discovered that her prudent foresight spared both of us arrest for "immorality." Under the Immorality Act, it is a criminal offense punishable with up to seven years of prison for whites and non-whites of opposite sex to engage in "immoral or indecent acts." (Oddly, homosexual intercourse across the color bar is licit, perhaps because it does not lead to "bastardization" of the *Herrenvolk*.) My colleague sat next to me on the front seat of the car and my wife in the back. As we reached an intersection a policeman, shocked by the sight, was about to pursue us on his motorcycle and only desisted when he noticed my wife in the back of the car. Had my wife not accompanied us, we would undoubtedly have been arrested and our presence alone in an automobile would have been accepted in court as incriminating evidence of intention to have "illicit carnal relations."

In one respect at least, my role vis-à-vis the state was simplified. As a naturalized American citizen, I was debarred from taking part in any political activity in South Africa on penalty of losing my United States passport. This proved a useful conscience-saving device to justify my political inaction, although this reason seemed to wear thinner as time went on.

As part of my efforts to avoid attracting official attention, I had recourse to the authorities for information only as a last resort. While this course of action may have debarred me from certain sources of data, I am convinced that the loss has been smaller than the gain. On the few occasions when I did approach government agencies for information, I encountered such secrecy and lack of co-operation that my attempts proved fruitless.

There were many occasions, however, when my policy of inconspicuousness proved impracticable. These included attendance as an observer at non-white political meetings and demonstrations, participation in interracial gatherings, and delivering public lectures. All these activities gave me insights and entrées into groups that would otherwise have been closed to me, but they also exposed me to observation and, on one occasion, to interrogation by the secret police. However, as these actions were all perfectly legal, I decided that the advantages outweighed the drawbacks and that the dangers involved were minimal. In public lectures, I was often asked to talk on some racial topic, and I generally obliged by talking about the United States, the Congo, Mexico or some other foreign countries, but I never tried to evade questions dealing specifically with South Africa.

Generally speaking, I encountered many fewer hindrances to my research on the part of the State than I had anticipated. This reflects, I believe, the inefficiency of South African officialdom rather than its tolerance. I am reasonably certain that the State was unaware of the nature of my activities. In one respect only did racial restrictions interfere with my research. When I was doing a community study of a sugar town, I found it impossible to reside there, as the town had been zoned for Indians or Africans; whatever "white" housing existed was reserved for civil servants or sugar company employees. Except when invited overnight by friends, I had to commute from near-by Durban. There were, to be sure, two hotels for whites in town, but, inasmuch as I could not have received non-whites on the premises, there would have been little point in staying at either of them; the one non-white hotel was not licensed to accept me.

As my stay in South Africa lengthened, my aversion to the entire State machinery became more intense, to the point where, like most Africans, I reacted with faint nausea at the mere sight of any police or army uniform. This seemingly hysterical reaction built up as a consequence of observing police brutality and shooting at first hand, and of having many people recount their arrests, searches, beatings and periods of imprisonment.

My relations with individual South Africans as private citizens are much more difficult to describe, for they involve several dimensions, among which the most important are skin color, political opinions, the definition of my role, and the degree of intimacy. Normal, uninhibited relationships across the color line are practically impossible in South Africa. This is true in part because the range of places and activities which can be attended or engaged in by persons of different races is extremely limited, and because the legal sanctions and social pressures against breaking apartheid taboos are severe. But, more importantly, there is a climate of mutual distrust and conflict which poisons most attempts to bridge the racial chasm.

Naturally, this state of affairs substantially affects, and interferes with, data collection, and raises important questions of factual validity. In my own work, the most extreme example of interference with data gathering arose from my attempt to conduct interviews among migrant agricultural workers. These nonliterate peasants belonged to the Pondo subgroup of the Xhosa and were at the time (early 1961) in open revolt against the South African government. With few exceptions, they spoke only Xhosa and Zulu. On both linguistic and political grounds I decided to train an African assistant to conduct the interviews. The latter were anonymous and quite short (taking from ten to fifteen minutes to administer). They consisted largely of non-sensitive questions on family composition, work history and the like, with, however, two sensitive items tacked on at the end concerning attitudes toward whites and Indians. A trial run in a geographically isolated workers' compound was made, during which the African assistant conducted the interviews under my supervision. The workers responded, though slowly and sullenly, as they would have in most situations involving a white man giving orders.

The replies to the census-type questions seemed trustworthy enough, but the responses to the items concerning attitudes toward whites were highly uniform, stereotyped, and evasive. Almost invariably, the workers cautiously replied: "I have nothing against them," or "They don't bother me." Intuitively I knew better than to attribute much validity to these answers, but, as I felt reasonably satisfied with the conduct of the interviews, I left my assistant on his own. On the same day, he conducted another thirty-five interviews, and as soon as I had left the scene, answers to the attitude questions revealed, as I had expected, intensely negative feelings toward whites: "They are my worst enemies," "I hate them," "I will feel much better when I am dead than being ruled by the Europeans," etc.

On the following day, my assistant again attempted to interview workers in three other compounds up to twelve miles away from the first one, and met with complete failure. Overnight a non-cooperation order had spread over the entire area, and my assistant returned with a none-too-common 100 percent refusal rate. It turned out that the interview schedule was thought to be a government census. A few weeks earlier the government had conducted its decennial population census and had met with an effective boycott in Pondoland. The workers now plausibly assumed that the government was making a fresh attempt to collect the information, and they consequently boycotted my study.

To a degree, one can determine the nature of one's relationships through one's own behavior. Here the basic alternative in my case was either to behave as most white South Africans did, or to act in a "color-blind" fashion as I would in Europe or America. The first approach would have meant ignoring the most elementary rules of courtesy towards non-whites. Not only would I have found such a role highly uncongenial, but such an approach would have seriously jeopardized my research. For a white person living permanently in South Africa, the rigid master-servant model of interracial behavior is undoubtedly the easiest to adopt, but for my purposes it would never have worked, assuming that I should have been willing to compromise my principles. The other possibility, i.e., to act in a way which made it clear that I considered race as of no consequence, was obviously the one I adopted, not as a result of long deliberation but, rather, "naturally." The simple fact of treating non-Europeans with elementary courtesy, I quickly discovered, was enough to arouse the hostility of many whites. This animosity was, however, a relatively small price to pay. Nevertheless, "color-blind" behavior, because of its highly unusual character in South Africa, entails many other complications, including frequent suspicion among non-whites.

On both sides of the color bar, attempts were made to explain or rather re-interpret my unconventional behavior in terms of existing roles. For whites I was a Communist agitator, or more frequently an odd foreigner who had not yet learned how to "handle the Natives." Amusement at my social "ineptness" was a more common reaction than anger or even annoyance.

Often whites predicted that I would soon become converted to their way of thinking and acting. It was probably on the part of westernized Indians that my role was most readily accepted at face value, and that initial suspicion, amusement, or hostility was most completely absent. Among Africans distrust was common. Politically militant and educated Africans often tried to fit me into the role either of a police informer or an *agent provocateur*, or of a missionary-type "do-gooder" or paternalist. Traditional or older Africans, on the other hand, whether through caution or through inability to shed suddenly the force of habit, often continued to behave in the submissive manner that most whites expected. Needless to say, this imbalance in the relationship made for much awkwardness.

My experience thus confirms a common observation of social scientists doing field work: Due to the unusual nature of their role, they can only partially determine its definition. A note of humor might be interjected here. Lest the suspicion that I belonged to the secret police appear far-fetched, I should add that it was not entirely unfounded. I discovered, rather late in my field work, that the car I had purchased, a beige Volkswagen, happened to be of the model and color used by the "Special Branch" of the police. My Afrikaans-sounding surname, a common one in South Africa, was an added liability, not only among non-whites but also among Afrikaners who considered that our ethnic affinity made my lack of color discrimination an even more heinous crime. To make matters even worse, a high-ranking police officer was named Colonel van den Berg, another bit of "evidence" which linked me, however vicariously, with the forces of repression in the minds of Africans. In fact, I myself developed such an aversion to my surname that, when I learned that a namesake was to become my next-door neighbor, I feared the worst. Actually, he turned out to be one of the country's hundred-odd Afrikaner liberals, and we became close friends.

Except in small intellectual circles, regular association with non-whites on the basis of equality entails nearly total ostracism from the white community. But the small *avant-garde* interracial cliques that form in the large cities and to whom my social contacts became gradually more restricted constitute by no means "normal," unstrained islands of sanity in a sea of racialism. They too are poisoned, however subtly, by the larger environment. Africans associating with such groups open themselves up to accusations that they are tame "mission boys" curtseying for the favor of white paternalists who condescend to "drink tea with clean Natives." Parties can be held only in private homes, usually of whites, and non-whites are mostly in no economic position to reciprocate the hospitality. Interracial parties are frequently raided by the police, spontaneously or on the complaints of white neighbors, and African guests are subjected to humiliations such as smelling their breath to check whether they have been drinking. Recent white converts to non-racialism behave unnaturally under the strain of trying to be "natural" and remain conscious of their unconventionality — which they display with the self-complacency and titillation of one who has entered a daring, reckless bohemia. At the same time, a white person must be constantly on guard lest an innocent remark be given a racial twist, or lest he mention an activity or place from which non-whites are debarred. Many topics of conversation, such as the cinema or the theater, thus become taboo, and consequently the only safe topic becomes, paradoxically, politics. However, as political opinions tend to be homogeneous in these small self-contained groups, disagreement is rare except on minor tactical issues, and discussions soon become dull. Once in a great while, a relationship across the color bar becomes intimate enough that one's racial caste can be forgotten or at least laughed away, but this is exceptional.

My role as a lecturer at the University of Natal, at that time still an "interracial" though internally segregated institution, was also greatly complicated by the racial situation. As with most of my colleagues, I faced the dilemma of whether I should grade the work of all my students strictly on the basis of their objective performance, or whether I should make allowances in the case of my non-white students. The temptation was, of course, to do the latter. To most non-whites, the language of instruction was a foreign idiom; furthermore, as a consequence of school segregation, non-white students had received an inferior primary and secondary education. Even within the university they did not have equal opportunities with whites, for they were denied access to the main library, to all the best dormitories, dining halls and lounges, to all sports grounds, to laboratories, and to many other facilities. Yet how could I justify discrimination in reverse? I adopted the attitude that my judgment was to be based solely on objective performance, while at the same time I tried to redress some of the most glaring aspects of academic inequality (such as differential access to books), but I felt quite uncomfortable about it all the same. I should add that several of my best students were Africans and Indians, though a disproportionate number of students with inadequate backgrounds also were.

As employers of African labor, my wife and I have had a completely unsuccessful experience, largely again because of the racial situation. For a short period of about three months we employed a part-time maid. The master-servant relationship quickly proved untenable, however. On the one hand, we felt unbearably guilty for being exploiters; although we paid her more than current wages we could not afford to compensate her on a scale which we would have considered equitable. On the other hand, our domestic, unused to being treated as a human being, rapidly became more of a liability than a help. As we failed to fulfill her role expectation of white bosses, she became unable to play her role of servant and neglected her most elementary duties. We decided to terminate her services, but she continued to visit us, and our relationship became a friendly one when it ceased to be on a master-and-servant basis. Henceforth, we did not employ any domestics, an almost unprecedented fact among white South Africans.

However much environmental contingencies aggravate one's difficulties in a country like South Africa, the greatest source of strain in my case and in that of most white liberals and socialists is internal, not external. To maintain one's intellectual and emotional balance becomes an extremely difficult task. Oppressed non-whites carry a heavy burden of frustration, but white liberals carry, besides ostracism and punishment, the millstone of their own guilt for enjoying privileges which they abhor. There is no escape from apartheid, not even in suicide, for even hearses and cemeteries are segregated. One may, of course, leave South Africa, but then one feels guilty for abandoning the sinking ship. I could not escape a nagging feeling of guilt for doing the simplest things such as going to the cinema, driving my car or swimming, all things from which my non-white friends were debarred by law, custom, or poverty. Even the freedom to take a leisurely stroll becomes a white caste privilege in a country where Africans have to carry "passes" in order to have the right to be anywhere at all.

One may seek, of course, to escape the guilt by identifying completely with Africans, assuming that those around you will let you forget your skin color. But then, one can easily became anti-white, a danger of which my wife had to keep reminding me, oftentimes to my considerable annoyance. All things considered, the surprising fact is not that there are so few white liberals in South Africa, but rather that there should be any at all, at any rate outside psychiatric hospitals.

Fear of physical violence was never a source of strain as far as I was concerned, although in periods of particularly acute crisis many whites became panic-stricken, stocked food, and bought large quantities of firearms. If I stress this point, it is not to brag about my courage but to dispel the myth that individual white civilians in South Africa are under constant threat of violence. Non-whites are the victims of considerably more violence, both on the part of police and from thugs and criminals, than are whites. Even at the height of the abortive revolt of 1960 I never was personally threatened, although I frequently went to African areas at night and was sometimes in the midst of crowds of African demonstrators.

So far I have dealt mostly with personal relations and attitudes. From a scientific viewpoint, the effect of these on my research is of far greater importance than my personal tribulations. Some of my writings about South Africa have been attacked as biased and their language has been described as intemperate. Thus, a recent book of mine which was reviewed in American periodicals as "objective," "remarkably clear" and "meeting the highest standards of scholarship," was described in the Johannesburg *Sunday Express* in the following terms: "Dr. van den Berghe . . . gives a confused picture of South Africa, and his book, which is a strange mixture of the sensational and the sociological, contains several contradictions." On another occasion, one of the prominent members of the small community I studied (who was one of my main informants, and was by no means a virulent racist) accused me of anti-white and anti-South African feelings. He seemingly regarded the two charges as synonymous with one another and with a rejection of racial discrimination and segregation.

Far from denying the charge of bias, I have tried to make my ideological position explicit. I have always claimed that the attainment of objectivity is an illusion, although its approximation may be an ideal. I feel reasonably confident that the selection of my facts has not been influenced by my views and experiences. Likewise, I think that I am familiar with every argument advanced by each of the major South African political groups to defend a given ideology. My interpretation of facts has, of course, inevitably been colored by my own position. For instance, many persons who are not racists make value judgments and use double standards in comparing different cultures. Such people often accept discrimination and segregation based on cultural differences or the standard of Western education (as distinguished from "race") as inevitable, natural, and "in the nature of things." Differential treatment is justified by the premise that some people are civilized and responsible, while others are in a state of permanent cultural infantilism and dependence. Now, I am not an extreme cultural relativist, and I accept that there is such a thing as cultural evolution from the simple to the complex (at least in material culture). However, I regard the concept of "primitivism" as misleading and invidious insofar as it often connotes inferiority or incapacity in the moral, intellectual, and political spheres, and I reject the postulate of cultural infantilism. Hence, I interpret invidious distinctions between people of different cultures, not as being dictated by the nature of social "reality," but rather as the product of ethnocentrism. Since very few white South Africans, including even "liberal" ones, share my premises, my interpretation of the facts must necessarily and rightly appear biased to them.

Some South African and American scholars have also taken exception to my choice of vocabulary. Terminology is, of course, highly debatable and, in last analysis, largely arbitrary. However, in a situation such as that of South Africa ordinary words become inadequate. For example, to use "conservative" as a euphemism for "reactionary" distorts reality. Terms like "oppression," "exploitation," "racialism," "tyranny" and "reaction," although they have acquired derogatory connotations, are the only appropriate ones, intemperate though they may sound to scholarly ears.

The problem of objectivity plagues all the sciences, but our present concern is with South Africa, or, more broadly, African scholarship. Much, if not most, of the African literature is accepted as "objective" because it uses the accepted vocabulary of Western European academics and refrains from making *overt* value judgments. Yet, until the last few years, most publications on Africa were written from a predominantly European viewpoint and contained a great number of unstated value judgments and double standards. Until Africans regained their independence, African historiography, for example, was almost entirely the monopoly of European scholars and consequently became the historiography of colonialism, with its elaborate mythology of African "primitivism" and the European "civilizing mission." African nations and states became "tribes"; African religions were dubbed "heathen" or "pagan"; European military conquests were termed "punitive expeditions" or "pacification"; white persons travelling through areas known for centuries to the outside world became heroic explorers by virtue of their skin color; Christian missionaries were held to be selfless dispensers of all of civilization's blessings. The history of the slave trade was rewritten to make it sound like an Arab undertaking to which great humanitarians like Léopold II of Belgium (whose agents killed and maimed Congolese by the tens of thousands) put an end.

Anthropologists have generally been more sensitive to the distortions of ethnocentrism, at least during the last three or four decades; nevertheless, they often became tools of the colonial administration and tended to advocate policies which favored the status quo under the guise of not disturbing traditional African societies. Though they often served colonial regimes, many anthropologists strangely seemed to ignore the colonial situation in their descriptive monographs, thereby also slanting African reality.

All these criticisms of the old "colonial" school of African scholarship applies to much of the literature on South Africa. Even attacks against apartheid have been mostly couched in the restrained terms of an obsolete, nineteenth-century, British-style, humanitarian paternalism, and until recently the "Natives" were viewed as the passive objects of white administration. Only in the past decade is the African point of view becoming heard.

It is far from my intention to plead for a re-writing of African history from the point of view of Pan-Africanism or any other form of fashionable orthodoxy. For South Africa, I have simply tried to show that it is not a "white man's country" with a few "Native" and game reserves as a colorful backdrop, but a conflict-ridden country where a non-white majority is exploited and oppressed by a racialist "albinocracy." I have done so in universalistic terms, i.e., in terms which reject the particularistic creed of apartheid. Apartheid is not only a set of laws and regulations but also a deeply ingrained ideology shared by most whites and a frustrating, crippling way of life for its non-white victims. Any account of apartheid must include not only "objective" realities but also the subjective feelings of the participants in the system.

I readily confess that writing on South Africa has often had cathartic value for me; every revision of my manuscripts has raised anew the nagging problem of objectivity, and has resulted in a deletion of gratuitous sarcasm or of misplaced emotionality, a toning down of adjectives and an elimination of value judgments. If the end result still conveys a repellent picture of apartheid, could I suggest that the fault lies perhaps with the South African government rather than with my lack of objectivity? Some pictures are *not* two-sided, and an attempt to make them so does not lead to objectivity but to distortion.

There is, of course, one facile way to escape emotional involvement — namely, to adopt an attitude of detached, urbane amusement at the insanity of apartheid. Before going to South Africa this outlook was easy to maintain, but on the spot the humor of the situation wore thin. To be sure, humor remained a useful tension-release mechanism, and particularly incongruous twists of apartheid occasionally excited a grim kind of hilarity on my part. On the whole, however, apartheid is not very funny if you are on the receiving end of it.

The title of the present collection of essays indicates that ethics and politics are the twin foci of the contributors' remarks. The one salient conclusion which the South African scene confirms is that the distinction between ethics and politics in an actual research situation is analytical rather than empirical.

Once more, the South African case is extreme in that the fundamental tenets of the ideology and practice of apartheid conflict with virtually all religious or secular systems of ethics evolved over the last three thousand years of human history. In that context, the injunction to be apolitical thus becomes a precept of amorality. These remarks are not exclusive to South Africa, of course; they apply with nearly equal strength to such other places as Mississippi and Alabama, or indeed California and Ohio. The last centuries of Western history, and most especially the nineteenth, have been tainted by the nearly ubiquitous aberration of racism.

My last dealings with the South African government took place in December, 1961, at the customs office of the Johannesburg airport. A bored official routinely inspected my luggage, which contained many irreplaceable and incriminating documents. I greeted his lack of zeal (to which the ungodly hour of four A.M. probably contributed) with a subliminal sigh of relief. I had successfully passed the last test of my *rite de passage* as an Africanist. Invaluable as my two years in South Africa had been, I knew that they would leave a profound and durable impact on me; I also knew that I would badly need the six-months European vacation ahead of me in order to regain some intellectual balance.

NOTES TO THE CHAPTER

* The title of this essay paraphrases Mahatma Gandhi, who spent two trying but highly formative decades of his life in South Africa. See Mohandas Gandhi, *Autobiography or the Story of My Experiences with Truth* (Ahmedabad: Navagivan, 1927).

1. See, among others, Claude Lévi-Strauss, *Tristes Tropiques* (Paris: Plon, 1955); Elenore Smith Bowen, *Return to Laughter* (New York: Harper & Bros., 1954); and J. F. Holleman, *African Interlude* (Cape Town: Nasionale Boekhandel, 1959).

2. E.g., a brilliantly satirized and thinly disguised Lloyd Warner appears under a pseudonym in John P. Marquand, *Point of No Return* (Boston: Little, Brown & Co., 1949). Dennison Nash analyzes the function of field work in anthropology in "The Ethnologist as Stranger: An Essay in the Sociology of Knowledge," *Southwestern Journal of Anthropology*, 19 (1963), pp. 149–67. A number of issues germane to this paper are discussed in two recent collections by sociologists: Arthur J. Vidich, Joseph Bensman, and Maurice R. Stein (eds.), *Reflections on Community Studies* (New York: John Wiley & Sons, 1964),

and Phillip E. Hammond (ed.), *Sociologists at Work* (New York: Basic Books, 1964).

3. I have reported the bulk of my findings in a community study entitled *Caneville, The Social Structure of a South African Town* (Middletown: Wesleyan University Press, 1964), and in a more general work, *South Africa, A Study in Conflict* (Middletown: Wesleyan University Press, 1965).

CHAPTER NINE

The Natural History of Revolution in Brazil: A Biography of a Book

IRVING LOUIS HOROWITZ

To write on the background of one's own work, in this case on how *Revolution in Brazil*[1] came into existence, is in effect to write on the psychology of sociological performance. This is a neglected area for at least two big reasons.

First, scholars are notoriously self-conscious about their motives since they often feel, sometimes rightly, that such motives are irrelevant to the actual product yielded. Although this is not the place to pry into the question of the relationship between psychological motivation and sociological perform-ance, I think in all fairness I must admit that from my particular vantage point, the two are closely interrelated. Therefore the psychology of sociolog-ical performance is not at all separated from the final product. In other words, the biography of this book reflects an intellectual autobiography, however fragmentary, of the author.

Second, there is more than a hint of ostentation and vanity in a clinical and diagnostic recording of a social scientific product. It may be acceptable behavior for a novelist or a painter to record even his trivial impressions; but for the scholar to engage in a blatant literary activity seems like needless tempting of the gods — and of the critics; akin to a physician describing his reasons for specializing in plastic surgery over internal medicine before the Ladies' Aid Society. Yet, upon reflection, it should be perfectly plain that the social scientist is in a unique position, and has a special frame of reference, to record the social as well as the personal motivational bases for writing a book.

Personal and Social Motivations

I came to an appreciation of the importance of Brazil indirectly: microscopically, through a steady focus on the social structure of Argentina, that Latin American nation with which I have the deepest and most familiar — indeed family — acquaintance; and macroscopically, through a continuing study of the processes of social development in the Third World. By means of this double focus, I began to realize the special characteristics of Brazil with respect to Hispanic America and the Third World. Brazil is that South American nation which has the widest range of differences from other South American nations and the largest number of attributes in common with the emergent nations of Africa and Asia. It was no accident that Brazil, especially during the period when I was producing the book (the era of "Jan-Jan" — of Jânio Quadros and João Goulart), developed the closest relationships with other sections of the emergent world.

In effect, Brazil saw itself in terms of this double vision: it was different from the rest of Latin America, although being within it, and it also had a general link with the whole process of development in the Afro-Asian bloc. From both an intellectual and a personal point of view, the study of Brazil intrigued and excited me. Its proximity to Argentina made it a logical nation to study insofar as comparative studies of nations are valid. At the same time it offered the kind of concrete and directly observable terrain which hopefully would be broadly incorporated in a general study of the Third World bloc.[2] In other words, the Brazil book, far from being a work in macro-sociology, was to serve as a limited pilot study for the Third World.

There are genuine contrasts between Brazil and the rest of Latin America in terms of such ephemeral qualities as *esprit* and *élan* no less than the modernization process or the level of industrial production. In the world of art, Brazil has produced a neat blend of technical sophistication and folk appreciation which is very rarely found in the rest of Latin America, with the possible exception of Mexico. There is less imitation of the styles of New York or Paris, a more profound desire to be individual and unique in forms of life, in forms of art, in styles of architecture, in music, in the way Cariocan women walk, and in all of the creative aspects of life which in some sense transform a *nation* into an authentic *people*. There is a powerful ethnographic attraction that Brazil exercises upon me. This factor certainly contributed to my decision to produce a volume on Brazil.

I started out with a problem and an assumption. The problem is why the developmental processes in Brazil have been different than in the rest of South America; and the assumption being that it has to do with what economists call the difference between monetarist and structuralist solutions to economic development. Gino Germani introduced these concepts into the sociology of Latin America, and it was from him that I learned to employ this language in a personally meaningful way. In Brazil, from Vargas to Goulart, there was a powerful impetus given to the solution of economic problems not so much in terms of monetary pump priming, of desperation loans, but rather in terms of agricultural reforms in the Northeast, the growth of an articulate if somewhat satellitic labor movement in the cities, the modernization of the interior through forced urbanization, and the nationalization of basic mineral wealth and natural resources. From attempted solutions have arisen the problems of land reform in the North and nationalization in the South, which are rather striking illustrations of "creeping socialism" from above rather than "galloping radicalism" from below. This would distinguish Brazil from the rest of Latin America again, with the exception of Mexico.

At the same time, a relative emotional detachment from Brazil made it possible to conduct my inquiries in a way which was free of the romanticist bias often found in young scholars from North America who "fall in love" with the object of their study. If I have a "love object" in terms of a nation, it would certainly not be Brazil. It would be Argentina. In the latter, I have family associations and university affiliations. In part, therefore, to understand Argentina better meant to get to know Brazil. Even though this may seem to be a reintroduction of the *verstehen* doctrine through a side door, there is one justification for my so doing. An emotional connection, if heaped on an ideological commitment to Latin American revolutionary movements, could easily have distorted the views presented in *Revolution in Brazil.* But because of a foreknowledge of fragmentary Argentine efforts to break free of North American tutelage, I could appreciate the attempt and the shortcomings in the Brazilian efforts along the same lines. In effect I was able to approach the object of study comparatively and also compassionately — through the eyes of an Argentine (rather than a North American) looking at a sister Latin American nation, Brazil. At the same time this allowed for a retention of a certain objectivity and detachment which in effect stood me in good stead as the regime of Quadros toppled, and as the Caesaristic idea of national liberation from the top down also collapsed.

Along the same lines, although I have a deep regard for a sociological approach to big political issues, for a meaningful macroscopic approach to problems of social change, *Revolution in Brazil* is not a work of personal reportage, but rather a social scientific examination of a major nation and culture. It remains my hope that this book can offer a basic introduction to specific data on the people, politics, and population of Brazil, and at the same time detailed information about intellectual and ideological disputes which are currently taking place in Brazil. From this double perspective of providing a primer in the English language containing the minimal data necessary to the understanding of this huge nation, and at the same time a volume which offers a sociological ethnography of the social problems and social forces which divide Brazilians from each other, I undertook to write and to edit *Revolution in Brazil*.

An important "ego-drive" for me has been the conduct of certain North American scholars working in the field of Brazilian studies. Even with good men doing their best work we find an emphasis on "policy issues" at the expense of political honesty. One scholar whose book appeared at the same time as my own found it necessary to terminate his book with a chapter outlining how, if he were a Brazilian, he would feel toward the world, and especially the world of the North Americans.[3] My concluding chapter deals with Brazil and the clash of world systems, with special focus on the problem of the economic mix between capitalism and socialism that would have to be responsive both to internal Brazilian needs and to world needs. This was a very different kind of ending and one that I believe is more genuine, since it avoids the *ersatz* liberalism of suppressing one's true identity. It does not ask, "If I were a Brazilian, how would I feel?" The important thing is not to ask, "If I were a Brazilian," but to state first: "I am a North American." Second, "I am not an 'ugly North American,'" and third, "I am really a good North American because I believe in the validity and in the worth of the Brazilian Revolution and in the Brazilians' right to self-determination free of foreign intrigue." Even if this is only an embellished way of saying "Let the Brazilians make their own mistakes," it says more than cloying phrases about inter-American togetherness. The paternalism underlying customary State Department-approved stances arouses animosity and misunderstanding, even when well-intentioned policy recommendations are forthcoming. The consequence of this is telling others how to behave politically, while at the same time failing to stand for anything political in the "home country."

One of the great problems in Latin American studies, especially in the past few years, is that they have become so highly professionalized that it is no longer particularly important to take a stand on major issues. Indeed, I sometimes feel that expertise is misanthropically mistaken for pure truth by some Latin Americanists. Latin America becomes a field of study, like urban sociology. The field of study is erected, operationalized, isolated from the human sources of such study. The reader of such literature is left with a Zombie effect: an objectivity which depersonalizes the observer, who becomes capable of accepting anything: e.g., a prison house is called a low-income housing project, or, in the case of area studies, manipulative bureaucracies are labeled developmental incentives. This total separation of fact and value is exactly what is least appreciated about the conduct of social science in the United States. It creates a lack of trust that cannot help but lead to an increase of suspicion on the part of Latin American scholars.

In the production of *Revolution in Brazil* I early determined that the book would adopt a direct and uncompromising tone with respect to its beliefs in the ultimate worth of the Brazilian Revolution. I mean by this emotive phrase the felt need for industrialism, the rise of urbanism as a way of life, the increase in the economy, the growth of public-sector mass political consciousness, things which enable Brazilians to grapple effectively with the larger world. There is a world not only outside of Brazil but external to the United States orbit. The need for Brazil to penetrate world markets if it is to become a world power is self-evident. This form of identification with Brazil on my part was clear and unequivocating. It enabled me to be critical of Brazil without at the same time arousing fears that I was yet another North American professional Latin Americanist writing *on* Brazil but *for* the United States ruling directorate.

Rarely absent from my thoughts were various kinds of works and writings on Brazil that I had become acquainted with in the process of becoming abreast of Latin American affairs. They left me with a deep feeling of dissatisfaction. I tried to picture exactly the kinds of American professionals who generally work and live in Brazil. These types of persons were certainly a motivational force in the way I wrote the book. I wanted to avoid making the mistakes I felt that they had made. The book was in part my settlement of accounts with "ugly Americans."

Myths in the Study of Brazil

Too many studies of Brazil suffered from at least one of the four major myths: (a) From a public-relations bias more concerned with touristic images and a leisure-class *ethos* than with unpleasant reality intrusions. (b) From the anthropological bias in favor of "primitive man" over and against the social realities of "developing man." (c) From the ideological bias rooted in the imagined requirements of United States foreign policy and in the supposed needs of American private investors. (d) From a Hispanic bias resting upon an acceptance of judgments about Brazil made by the Spanish-speaking nations of the Hemisphere for reasons having little or nothing to do with scientific comparison.

First and foremost were public relations experts, professional slick magazine writers who have taken on the heavy responsibility of resolving American ambivalence with respect to Brazil: the need to assuage United States guilt with respect to a history of gunboat colonialism in Latin America, and the equal desire to minimize any real challenge to North American proprietorship over a country like Brazil. From the point of view of the public relations mind, Brazil had acquired an enigmatic quality that served to dull the consciousness of the American nation which public relations gimmicks ostensibly sought to explain. What we get is a confused and confusing picture of fun-loving people and Yankee-hating people, militaristic and democratic people, lazy and philosophical people, ignorant and ideological people. The picture is so confusing that the urge is strong to be careless about a country like Brazil; to accept, on the basis of articles in *Look, Holiday,* or the *National Geographic,* the nonviolent good-time image of the proper Brazilian.

Public relations experts have a penchant for viewing any development in another society as an opportunity to exaggerate: to embroider myths about intrinsic libertarianism or equally fantastic tales of Communist subversion. For the mid-cult crowd, the key word is *happiness,* while for the mass-cult crowd, the magic word is *horror.* Those who travel, who live in terms of jet carriers, must be encouraged to fall in love with Brazil, while masses, who do not travel, or who rarely have the opportunity of meeting people from Brazil, must be reinforced in their fears by stories of subversion and cries of treason. The public relations "experts" have done their job well. The false images about Brazil remain intact. The image-makers have earned their fees. It is certainly the case that I wanted *Revolution in Brazil* to stimulate a therapeutic reaction to this, preserving the more thoughtful from the programmed distortions that a public relations image of Brazil has sought to foster.

The second source of error in professional American writings on Brazil has been the legacy provided by tradition-bound cultural anthropologists. Until now, serious writings on Brazilian society have been basically in their hands. As a result, the public vision of Brazil has been that of a vast quaintness, or better, of a quaint vastness. Kinship relations in Brazil have been described in great detail. The "exotic" tribes of the Amazon have been enshrined in Hollywood films and jungle-adventure tales. And such other features of Brazil as its tropical climate, speculative surges of boom and bust, pottery-making, and vast geographical expanses have all been well described. A Brazil which, according to one recent book, "rekindles boyhood dreams of treks through unexplored jungles," is substituted for some much-needed exploration of the unexplored jungles of militarism and militancy in Brazil.

It must be stated bluntly that whereas Brazil has entered the modern world, American social science in relation to Brazil remains in its pristine anthropological-archaeological form. Even where American anthropologists have attempted to make adjustments to the new reality, these have been unsatisfactory and incomplete — reflecting anthropological nostalgia rather than the sociological realities of modern Brazil. Anthropologists are, after all, not simply dedicated men of science. They are also men who study "primitive culture" from the vantage point of "advanced culture." The relativism is only one-way and decidedly asymmetrical. Brazilians do not come to the United States to study our "race problem," but Americans go to Brazil to study its "race problem" — although I leave it to the reader to guess which is the nation with higher racial tensions. Brazilians do not examine our "overdeveloped society"; but we examine their "underdeveloped society." Nostalgic attitudes toward Brazil abound — as if sectionalism, nationalism, socialism could not possibly pertain to a charming world of big plantation houses and stable self-contained little coffee-producing communities.

The situation would not be tragic if it represented only the nostalgia of anthropologists. Here we come upon the third big source of academic misanthropy — the "policy-making" area approach. Brazil is said to represent a "field," an "area." Yet, until my book appeared, no significant attempt was made by any North American scholar to connect the revolutionary tides sweeping Brazil with the general movement of events in other parts of Latin America, Asia, and Africa. A kind of Brazilian "exceptionalism" was allowed to set in, to further advertise the unique value of "the area." This is not to deny special features to Brazilian development. But its unique features are special aspects of phenomena and expectations common to all underdeveloped or, better, developing societies. And the counter-revolution which took place in Brazil in April, 1964, makes it painfully clear that Brazil is very much a part of Latin America — its palace *golpes* and street *manifestações* no less than its chronic economic and organizational instability.[4]

The policy orientation in relation to Brazil has tended to concentrate on perennial social factors in a state of equilibrium. There is an attempt to speak in terms of eternal verities rather than in terms of historical variables. In this way, even when sociological studies are carried out, little is done to explain the variance between facts and findings. They are criticisms made from the viewpoint of Brazilian structural features and at the expense of developmental features; of systems of group norms instead of processes of class, caste, and status relations. When factors of social change are treated, they are usually confined to showing how changes in Brazilian social structure affect United States interests in the area. Invariably, policy-science examinations of Brazil conclude with judgments on how this or that class, or this or that ruler, has reacted to United States interests. Even those social scientists managing to escape the anthropological bias are still tied up in knots by a "policy-science" bias; that is, by a need to evaluate any given Brazilian development by its positive or negative effects on United States foreign policy.

Brazil's social scientists, as well as its political statesmen and social thinkers, have created a perceptive, indigenous literature. Before we can instruct, we must learn from Brazilians themselves. By giving over many of the pages of the book to Brazilian commentators and policy-makers, to radical and conservative points of view, I wanted to show that even the terms "radical" and "conservative" have quite different meanings than the American or European definitions of such terms. The fact must be faced that Brazilian development is no longer uniquely determined by official sentiment in the Pan American Union, or by the size of loans issued by the International Monetary Fund. Brazil has its own political and economic logic, its own framework for discussing development, its own national interests. As such, it must be studied on its own terms and not in terms of inherited ideologies.

In a stable economy, balanced budgets may be significant; but not in Brazil, which maintained an annual economic growth rate equal to that of the United States while in the midst of a massive inflation. In an industrial community the population size may uniquely determine problems of under-employment; but not in a country which needs all the manpower it can train. In an old European nation, parliamentarianism may define the limits of democracy, but not in a newly conscious nation like Brazil, which moves inexorably toward the creation of a bureaucratic and technological elite. What Brazilians are worried about, what they talk about, is how to achieve economic independence from both capitalist and communist powers; how to navigate a political course between the Eagle and the Bear; how to get an agrarian reform under way which would wipe out the latifundists; how to get a public economy uniquely suited to the needs of Brazilians.

A fourth and final widely held misconception about Brazil is the Hispanic myth. This myth asserts that Brazil is a *big* nation, but that it is not a *great* nation. Although Brazil is said to be a land with many problems it is also considered a land of passive, samba-dancing people. The reason for the propagation of this myth in South America has to do with the exaggerated "European consciousness" of Argentines, Uruguayans, and Chileans. *Pensadores,* the "thinkers" of former times, were caught in the grip of this chauvinistic view of their Luzo-Brazilian neighbor. Inferiority complexes rationalize themselves and harden into defense mechanisms — even on a national scale. One white European immigrant was supposed to be worth ten to a hundred (it depends on whom you read) Brazilian Indians, and God alone knows how many Africans. In the nineteenth century, the tropical region was elevated to a climatic-geographical view of history in an effort to prove the impossibility of Brazilian development.

Thus it was that *Revolution in Brazil* sought to move beyond previous studies — at least in political sophistication, if not necessarily in data processing. No doubt my own work suffers the infirmities of its own perspective. But it at least raises the problem of perspective as a legitimate and powerful concern of the "area specialist."

Development of the Book

Revolution in Brazil started modestly enough, with a translation of the three speeches of Francisco Julião, and a brief set of introductory remarks about rural problems in the Northeast. But it soon became evident that Julião's Peasant Leagues did not even define the situation of the agrarian sector, much less the social structure of the Brazilian complex. The book slowly broadened out to include an analysis of the contrasting ideologies and institutions of the Brazilian Northeast — including Catholic and Communist organizational efforts among the peasantry. But even this defined only one region and one class in the Brazilian Northeast. What I was after was a total picture, a general framework, and, no less, a set of interviews on select variables or an ethnographic set of impressions. Indeed both types of work were included in the final version of the English language edition of *Revolution in Brazil.* What I wanted was a worldly perspective of a national revolution, whether such perspectives derived from journalistic reports or from survey data. Only in such a setting could the developmental process be meaningfully discussed. Thus, a book which started as a limited effort to understand a revolutionist and his personal movement ended as a study of a social revolution and a social movement.

This does not completely cover the subject of the genesis of *Revolution in Brazil*. There are all kinds of variables in the production of a commodity offered for public sale: accidental, irrational, and technical components.

The accidental component was the fortuitous publication of the book during the same week that the April Counter-Revolution took place. At the time I undertook the actual writing of *Revolution in Brazil* there were many convergencies moving in that direction. Some of my graduate students were Brazilian in origin and extraction. They provided a constant stimulus. At critical junctures they offered reassurance that the work was important and that it had to be done, and, more important, they expressed confidence in my capacity to do it. In addition to reinforcements from the world of graduate students and professional colleagues, it might be added that the book was a function of a personal time-table. I did not feel ready to tackle the Third World *per se*. I first needed to have much more concrete comparative data for any complete study of the Third World. Brazil from Vargas to Goulart represented an exciting and interesting developmental syndrome in the Western hemisphere — and one which had not been presented within a sociological framework, even though the data were, in the main, available.

In addition to these components of locale, and of having intelligent and mature students at the right place and the right time, my travels tended to make me increasingly curious about Brazil. On one of my trips I became acquainted with a young couple who functioned as the private secretary and personal escort of Francisco Julião, the peasant leader of the Peasant Leagues and also a Senator (now an ex-Senator) from the Northeast of Brazil. These people who worked for and with Julião presented such an exciting, interesting picture of the efforts of the Peasant Leagues that it deepened my belief that a work on Brazil would be valuable in its own right and also as a base line for my study of the Third World. It became important for me to know more about Brazil in order to know more about Latin America and about the Third World. At the same time it kindled a desire to know about Brazil with greater intimacy and precision.

My initial vision of a work on Brazil was quite theory-bound. It was to provide an indication of the points of parallelism and difference between the ideology of a man like Julião and someone like Castro. This was, hopefully, to have the effect of arousing interest on the part of American citizens in the plight of the Brazilian Northeast and in the revolutionary efforts to overcome these problems. Initially, the book was an attempt to explain Francisco Julião to a North American public in terms they had come to understand — in terms of the Cuban Revolution. The traces of the origin of the book can be found even in the final version. There is a fairly heavy wading through the problem of agricultural reform and peasant revolution, which is perhaps inordinate in the light of my present understanding of the problems of Brazil as being basically problems of industrialization and urbanization rather than problems of agrarian reallocation and confiscation.

As a matter of fact, it was a discontent with Julião's approach, a feeling that he was really not going to be the savior of Brazil, that led me to look at the issues of land tenure and occupancy more deeply. Brazil's history did not lend itself to the kind of analyses that Julião was offering, which were basically concerned with problems of a pastoral society rather than of a rapidly industrializing and urbanizing society. I also had the feeling that Julião, quite unlike Fidel Castro, had far more of the religious zealot and messianic savior in him, and far less of the organizational shrewdness that one associates with peasant revolution, to allow him to conduct a successful revolution. This discontent with my original motivations, the dissatisfaction with the line of reasoning of Francisco Julião, and a desire to work out alternative routes and solutions,[5] led me to be sharply critical of apocalyptic visions and solutions of the Brazilian problem — even though I retained, throughout the book, a healthy respect for this element as a practical myth for promoting revolution.

It is interesting that a work of macro-sociology can actually have started out as a work of micro-sociology: How does one man view the revolution in Brazil? In retrospect, I find this a strange unfolding in that the book underwent a transition from a concern with peasants and the life and times of Francisco Julião to a general picture of Brazil and its revolution. Once the magnitude of my approach became settled, the pattern of the book took shape. Only when I knew this would be a book about a nation instead of a national hero did I really begin to frame it in terms of a more rational and a more sociological variety. In other words, although there was a psychological thrust to my originating questions — the attractiveness of the person and personality of Francisco Julião — in order for the book to be truly "universalistic" it had to shed, in great measure, these originating motivations and concern with charismatic personalities.

Problem Areas in Retrospect

On a number of occasions I have been asked whether my use of the phrase "revolution in Brazil" was not a misnomer or simply mistaken.

More precisely, did I allow myself to be swayed by the passions of the heady years between 1960–64? Had I not taken a "revolution of words" on the part of the secondary echelon of Brazilian leadership as equivalent to a "revolution of deeds?" Had I not relied too exclusively on elite interview techniques, and not enough on objective circumstances? This represents a serious criticism that deserves vigorous analysis. But at the outset, let me say that my use of the term "revolution" in the book is sociologically legitimate. The tremendous acceleration of primary industrialization and the parallel emergence of an urban "mass society" which began in 1930 shows no signs of slowing up. It was furthermore dignified by everyone from Church dignitaries to Government officials. At the time of the *coup d'état* of 1964, as a matter of fact, a special issue on the Brazilian Revolution was being prepared by the *Revista Brasileira de Sociologia*.

The Revolution in Brazil *politically* was and is still a complicated affair. It was basically elitist in character and administrative in form. It elicited a network of support from the middle sectors on the impulse of Jânio Quadros, from the working urban sectors under the impulse of Goulart and Brizola, and from marginal elements in the educated world of engineers, priests, doctors, university professors, especially from the leadership of these expanding marginal groups. To be sure, the Revolution that began in 1930 with Vargas and was suspended in 1964 by the ouster of Goulart was a revolution from above. It is no accident therefore that the military regime of Castelo Branco has continued these bureaucratic and elitist characteristics. Nonetheless, the present military counter-revolution terminated the middle-class-democratic stage of the Revolution. Its repressive qualities have opened up wider possibilities of revolution — this time a revolution from below. The case of the Castelo Branco regime's severance of the General Workers Council (C.G.T.) from the Brazilian Labor Party (P.T.B) — of labor organization from its traditional sources of political patronage — has revitalized possibilities of a more vigorous and classical working-class movement. This demonstrates an adage of mine: only a stupid and corrupt bourgeoisie can in this day and age bring about a Marxist political solution.

One thing writing *Revolution in Brazil* taught me is that revolutions from above, like those concluded in Brazil, can undergo a quick and ready collapse as a result of a single mistake. The conventional enemies of the revolution, the landholders, military, etc., are left intact. Revolutions from below, like those in Mexico and Cuba, can involve a great number of mistakes without suffering collapse or contraction, since the traditional enemies of revolution are eliminated as serious contenders of power. Thus, while I would reaffirm my belief in the title no less than in the contents of the book, I would add that the actual course of events in Brazil necessitates a deeper understanding of the different styles and stages of social revolution. We need something more dynamic than a conventional "natural history of revolution" model, and something less tautological than the "unilinear theories of revolution" based on extrapolating an economic or political factor from all of the rest.

Social science is comparative. In large measure the materials we deal with have to do with the relationship of one nation to another no less than of one person to another. What I had in mind throughout the actual production of the book was a set of dialectical hypotheses both about Brazil and about its "generalized other" — the Latin American area. The first paired concept was that Latin America is a unified whole, yet an uncoordinated agglomeration of distinct nations and cultures. The concept of Latin America was made plausible by the rise of foreign colonial domination and a history of that domination which the whole of Central and South America have in common. The irony is that the concept of Latin America should also serve as a rallying cry against such domination. It is also the case that the contrary hypothesis, that of Luzo-Brazilian exceptionalism, states in effect that Latin America does not exist, and that Brazil is different from Latin America, even if it does exist. This is supposedly proven by differences between Portuguese and Spanish linguistic formations and cultural traditions, by the racial and ethnic hegemonies in Brazil, and by the Brazilian monarchical background in contrast to the republican origins of most other Latin American countries.

Thinking about the problem of definitions in such a study entails the necessity of thinking in terms of polarities. There is the "holistic" frame of reference — i.e., Latin America as a unity — in contrast to the "atomic" frame — i.e., Brazil as its own unity in contradistinction to Latin America. In the production of the book, what I emphasized were methods to better understand these contrasting hypotheses. I wanted to explain in what ways Brazil is like the rest of Latin America and in what ways it differs. Most important of all, this approach made it possible to indicate in what respects Brazil wants to be different from the rest of Latin America, and in what respect it wants to be more like Latin America.

When this polarity is linked to the problem of class mobility and class stratification, a deeper appreciation of the significance of economic and political variables can be established. Here lies the crux of the issues.

Is the middle class the agency of social revolution, or is it the corruption of that revolution, the prevention of that revolution? There is among Latin Americanists in various disciplines a profound schism between those who think the middle classes are the prime agencies of change, and those who (like myself) see the middle sectors as historically unable to perform a constructive and revolutionary role, as basically parasitical. In the study of Brazil, in the study of the problems of mobility and stratification, this problem of class vitality became of special concern for me. The results that I managed to piece together, from the technical literature on stratification, the popular press, and personal observation, all tended to confirm my belief that the middle classes of Brazil are if anything, more *Latin* than other strata in the society. They tend to be low in national concern and high in nationalistic rhetoric. They are profoundly oriented toward consumer goods, with a low threshold to delay personal gratification in order to gain the *social* benefits of development. They want to fight inflation, but keep their own fortunes in Swiss banks. There are exceptions to these middle-class characteristics. Particularly among professionals, such as physicians, engineers, and physicists, there are men who tend to behave in terms of standards of personal sacrifice. But, as with the Brazilian commercial, trading, and entrepreneurial sectors, even the most enlightened middle-class sectors tend in their behavior to confirm my skepticism as to the possibility of their assisting the revolutionary process. Their capacity to help secure mass democracy for the disenfranchised of the rural regions and the disaffiliated of the cities is limited as much by a lack of consciousness as by any congenital disinterest. If anything, the behavior of the middle classes during the counter-revolution of April Fool's Day, 1964, and the strength of that *coup* in such middle-class centers as São Paulo and Santos, confirms the rightist and centrist character of the middle sectors — especially their parochialism with respect to problems of national development.

Another major area for testing the "Latin" versus the "Exceptional" character of Brazil concerns the role of the military. Nowhere is military determinism more interesting than in Brazil. There is a great amount of unexplained variance in the structure of the military apparatus. This in part is due to an absence of any basic literature on the subject, which in turn stems from a considerable reluctance of military officers to permit any study of their institutions or personnel. As a result, in conjunction with several advanced graduate students, I am engaged in a project to amass authentic and comparable data on 120 nations, with 20 Latin American nations as the controlling focal point.

Certain quite significant characteristics could be explained on a comparative basis. For example, in contrast to the classic Latin American military establishments, such as those which obtain in Argentina, Peru, and Colombia, the military of Brazil are far more heterodox in their social origins and in their political orientations. The Brazilian military establishment, for a variety of historical and sociological reasons discussed in the book, tends to be more responsive to the actual division of social classes in the nation. Noncommissioned officers have a considerably greater policy role than elsewhere. Low-echelon officers tend to be more conservative than their superiors, in that they are drawn from a stratum of the lower middle classes rather than from the established bourgeoisie. The history of the Brazilian military, or at least that portion linked with the Tenentismo movement, has been linked to the reform and revolution aspirations of the liberal bourgeoisie. The lieutenants of yesteryear, in some degree, became the generals of the present. This fact caused both Vargas and Goulart to seriously overestimate the radicalization of the military elite. This mistake, based as it was on solid interferences from past performances concerning nationalization of basic industries, and military support for such activities, pointed up how little is yet known about the military of Brazil, even by its civilian leaders — although it must be added that American scholars such as Edwin Lieuwen, John J. Johnson, and Lyle N. McAlister have done a great deal to fill the gap.[6]

Yet a third major area for a comparative analysis of Brazil with the rest of the hemisphere is that of urbanization. In the main, the continent shows a very heavy concentration of people in a large, cosmopolitan center, with relatively little growth of middle-sized cities or agricultural sectors. Brazil has sharp divergencies from this "city-State" pattern — although whether such divergencies are unique enough to warrant being called qualitative remains to be studied. The attempt to foster the development of such cities as Recife and Santos, no less than internal centers like Brasilia, is a response to the rapid urbanization of the nation. It is an effort to break the structural imbalance so characteristic of Latin American "city-States." Even the competition between Rio de Janeiro and São Paulo serves to give Brazil some genuine ecological vitality absent elsewhere in the Hemisphere. For example, there is no rival for greatness to the capital cities of even such relatively well-developed nations as Argentina, Uruguay, and Chile. Yet, for all of that, the powerful magnet of big coastal cities in relatively mild climatic regions is a factor preventing any rational diaspora. Brazil remains a nation where 80 percent of the population inhabits less than 15 percent of the land. In a country which is reputed to be unlike Latin America in urban structure, where people are easygoing, relaxed of mores and manners, one finds an intense desire to live and work in the big cities rather than in the big plantation houses.

I raise matters of continuities and discontinuities, commonalities and contradictions — not to open for discussion matters dealt with at length in the book, but to show how ethnographic statements must be cast in a meaningful systematic framework if they are to yield sociological information. It makes little sense for an American sociologist to apply open-ended interviews to Mexican businessmen or projective tests to Argentine students if he does not at the same time understand enough of the language and culture to know when he is being "turned on." Similarly, field observations can become easily transformed into travelogues unless the full force of comparative social history and intensive involvement is brought to bear on the subject of analysis.

Appropriate methods of work either suggest themselves or the researcher can hardly cope satisfactorily with studies on a national or an international level. At this level, thinking in pairs, in opposites, thinking dialectically, becomes more than a choice; it is a downright necessity — imposed by the nature of comparative research in which nations are transformed into manageable units of investigation.

One begins to appreciate the fact that the study of dyadic and triadic relations applies not simply to two- or three-person groups, but to two or three nations, and even area clusters. Organizational analysis suddenly poses new interesting insights: Why, for example, should underdeveloped countries such as Brazil possess such overdeveloped bureaucratic structures? Even studies in marriage and family become more meaningful. How are divorce rates in Brazil held in check? Why is a Catholic culture so "strict" in its application of marriage vows in the United States and so loosely interpreted in a Brazilian context? Preparation in basic sociology is not superfluous in area studies. The study of Brazil is not simply a matter of knowing its history, culture, and language. It is a matter of coming to this area with a sociological style and a sociological imagination.

Traditional distinctions between the journalistic and the scholarly, between what is newsworthy and what is academic, also tend to dissolve in field researches. There are no departmental barriers or administrative confusions to contend with while dodging police in downtown Rio. There is a job to be done and information to be gathered. There is the task of understanding people behaving in different circumstances. In the heat of a *golpe* the fields of social structure and collective dynamics melt into each other. In conditions of conflict, sociology is fused to political life.

What takes place is an awareness of the essential oneness of the concept of society and the binding value that sociological categories such as role, status, power, force, and coercion have in the performance of national units as they do in personality units. The most important methodological lesson that I derived from *Revolution in Brazil* is that the magnitude of an investigation does not uniquely determine its difficulty. Also, to write a book such as this is in some measure to prepare a legal brief, to prepare a strong set of arguments *for one side*. This can only be done with a full *knowledge* of *the other side*. What is required is a passionate conviction that one's own "client" is correct and not just fodder for the analysis.

The Book and its Audience

The strategy of *Revolution in Brazil* was to create a mix between research papers and my own writing. This provided me with an opportunity to be free in my style and flexible in my handling of various themes. Weaving my materials into those of others had the effect of creating mutual legitimation and reinforcement by fusing data and generalizations.

These papers are of several varieties and produced by several different types of people. First, there are those written by sociologists. They are concerned with the analysis of data on voting patterns in the Northeast (Soares); class mobility and the middle classes (Pereira); and the organization and ideology of labor unions (Aguiar-Walker). This last paper emerged from a seminar of mine on Latin American social development. The author imaginatively wove a pattern of working-class organization in Brazil based on such widely known sources as Arthur Schlesinger on the New Deal, S.M. Lipset's studies on union democracy, and the significant work by Gino Germani on mobilization and integration of class formations in Latin America.[7]

Second, there are papers on the social history of Brazil which attempt to provide a knowledge of Brazilian society in a comparative historical context. In this category one can place the paper on the historical foundations of Brazilian foreign policy (Rodrigues) and the comparison of Brazil with modern China (Freyre).

Then there was a third group of papers which can be classified under the rubric of policy analyses. These are statements not about political first principles, but rather about how modern Brazil came to be what it is. In this category I was particularly fortunate to have the use of the work of Hélio Jaguaribe on Quadros' Bonapartist democracy, and Suarez' paper on the relationship of industrialization and undercapitalization.

Finally, there was a group of papers which were directly concerned with the entire spectrum of Brazilian political thought and action, and here use was made of statements from the right wing, and from the present economic advisor to the Castelo Branco regime, to the leaders of the two communist parties of Brazil.

It would have been just as simple, if not simpler, to integrate these materials into my own commentary. However, by employing primary resources and prime personnel in the way that I did, it becomes much clearer where "mine" leaves off and "thine" begins. The fact of comparative authorship, of providing nearly half the space of the book to these primary source materials, had a liberating effect on me. It made the book more unconventional than it might otherwise have been. Such an approach undercuts the kind of infallibilistic assumptions too often made in social science writing without at the same time leading to a political default on my part.

In addition to this formal use made of the work of other scholars, I took the opportunity on a number of occasions to interview experts on Brazil, to share my ideas with them, and to encourage their critical appraisals of what I had done. At the same time discussions of a similar nature have taken place at a more advanced level since the book has appeared. But confining myself to the pre-publication period, I must say that on a number of significant points my controversial posture grew out of these discussions. For example, Luis Costa Pinto convinced me that the benefits of migration from the rural to the urban regions far outweighed the horrors of living in *favelas*. It was Celso Furtado who pointed out to me that the role of inflation was the taxation of the middle and upper classes of Brazil, and hence that inflation was functional with respect to the structural development of the nation. Neuma Aguiar-Walker proved to my satisfaction that the weakness of unions in Brazil stemmed in large part from the dependent role labor had with respect to the State in all disputes with management. Even where I was not convinced, such as in Glaucio Soares' argument concerning the traditionalism of the rural peasantry of Northeast Brazil, I became sensitized and attuned to the problems at stake in the urban-rural imbalance with respect to Brazilian politics. In other words, my framework in writing this book was broad-based and not limited to a formalistic or ethnographic account of the problem.

Doing a book like *Revolution in Brazil* distinguishes itself from the performance of a research project in another extremely important way: the question of audience. The problem of audience does not really arise in a research project because the purchaser is often a granting or contracting agency, who judges projects in advance of their actual realization. The granting agency has only a vague and prayerful notion of what the pay-off is going to be on its investment. The problem of audience for a book author is of a different sort. Here the audience may become quite large. And the larger it gets, the more amorphous it gets. There is no clear idea either of what the audience wants or what it expects for its payment. There is a public-aesthetic dimension. The language of a book, the contents of a book, the drama of a book — all of this places it at a commodity level, into a world of competition with other commodities.

The research project is a unique single occurrence, generally speaking. The book, on the other hand, is a publicly sold commodity. From that point of view it imposes a unique set of demands upon an author. Its special demands stem, in part, from the desire to have an audience. The task of a writer of a book is not fulfilled with the realization of the book. It is fulfilled only with size and the kind of audience an author has. In this sense, the kind of book that *Revolution in Brazil* represents distinguishes itself not only from the research project but also from the kinds of specialized books where the audience is highly limited and known in advance. The audience for *Revolution in Brazil* is in part determined by its sheer size. Nor is this a consideration which is resolved with the completion of the research or write-up activities.

Considerations of audience potential insinuate themselves into the production and manufacture of a book. They determine what portion of a book will be given over to popular thematic material. They determine the structure of chapters. They even determine chapter headings. They determine the kind of language used, especially the permissible degree of technicality of a professional language. The existence of a large amorphous audience also means in part that an author has to have a differential set of multiple responses to a differentiated and multiplied audience. In this kind of relationship, the product one makes, the commodity that is put on the market for sale, is undoubtedly affected. Let me try to show how this works its way out specifically and concretely in relation to my book, particularly the decisions which have to be made about such a work.

The first thing about *Revolution in Brazil* which was determined by the potential audience was a painful decision arrived at between my friend and editor at Dutton, Peter S. Prescott, and myself not to have footnotes. It was a decision to have a casual and informal set of listings of other works in the body of the text. When there were citations and references, they were inset in the body of the text. The detailed references all appeared in the bibliographical bank at the end of the book. Quite unlike conventional scholarly procedures, page numbers and specific references were omitted, at least to the maximum degree that this was feasible. The second decision we worked out was to have a bibliographical bank at the end of the book which could be used for scholarly purposes by anyone, and for whatever purposes might be deemed necessary; but again, not to allow this to encumber or affect the specific contents of the book. The third decision, which was determined by market problems, was to have as wide a variety of material as possible. In other words, not to develop an exclusively sociological book, but rather to use sociological analysis as the basis and to employ political, historical, and economic materials insofar as these could be illustrative of the main problems and themes. A fourth important determination was to develop at great length the international ramifications of Brazilian foreign policy, that is, how the Goulart, Quadros, Kubitschek, and Vargas regimes affected foreign policy, how this foreign policy affected the United States in the first instance, and how it also affected the Soviet Union and the Eastern bloc. This popular approach was alternately what determined the inclusion of a chapter on the Sino-Soviet split and its effects on a nation such as Brazil. The likelihood is that from a scholarly point of view the Sino-Soviet split could have been included in an earlier chapter on Brazilian foreign policy. But the magnitude of the split and its potential for audience participation and audience appreciation determined that it be given a separate chapter.

The potential service of the book for a large audience also determined the polemical style no less than the actual selection of materials. In some measure the tone of the book, or at any rate the polemical aspect of the tone, was determined by a profound belief in the Brazilian Revolution and a conviction that these commitments must be stated as explicitly and as thoroughly as possible if they were to be, first, plausible, and, second, accepted as bona fide by the audience I hoped to reach with such a book. But at the same time it must be said that a knowledge that this was a mass book with a mass potential determined its partisan quality; at least the opening section was dedicated to a serious critique of previous works on the subject of the Brazilian society. For the style, form, and the appeal to popular misconceptions are at the same time a hope for a new popular conception. These, I would say, are in the main the points at which the problem audience determined the form and substance of *Revolution in Brazil*. Of course it must be said that in some measure this is a metaphysical predisposition on the part of the sociological writers, since there is no real guarantee — no real certainty — that this or that book will actually sell well or that this or that book will ever really reach even a small slice of the envisioned mass audience. And from that point of view, the kind of audience appeal may in fact be a form of self-hypnosis and it may in effect weaken the scholarly aspects of the book in the name of the mythology of the mass audience. This is only a risk. One can build as many safeguards as possible into a book and yet walk away with the feeling that one has not completely warded off the dangers of the appeal to a large audience.

Nonetheless, it is my opinion, and one based on experience, that it is possible to walk a straight line, even considering the vicissitudes of the demands of a mass audience as a factor in a book. We ought not to view the existence of a mass audience as simply a negative factor coloring a book, or merely as something which impedes the production of scholarship. The appeal to a mass audience can also be said to be, possibly and hopefully, an appeal for clarity, an appeal for minimizing the use of jargon except where necessary, an appeal to the widest possible range of public opinion, and therefore for minimizing the assumptions that one so often takes for granted in scholarly writing. In short, the existence or the metaphysics of appeals to a large audience are not uniformly negative in their effects on scholarship.

But although it is the mythology of a large audience that the writer appeals to, it is through the pragmatics of the review process that this quest for audience is gauged, and hopefully in the case of *Revolution in Brazil,* the appeal to a mass audience was in effect a means for the strengthening of the contents of the book.

Reactions Toward the Book

Ironically enough, in Brazil — two months after the *coup d'état* that deposed Goulart on March 31, 1964 — a comment, appearing in *Diario de Noticias,* said in part that: *"Revolution in Brazil* is a book neither of the Left nor of the Right, but rather a work of scholarship, serious, documented, revealing a deep sensitivity to the sociology of Brazil and the psychology of the Brazilians." This is revealing in that even at this late date the political aims of the Castelo Branco regime were cloudy; and the repression of press reports only fragmentarily enforced.[8]

From this point on, commentaries flowed: the book was praised as "by far the best book on modern Brazil" by the knowing journalist of *The New York Times,* Tad Szulc.[9] It was termed "the first major American study of the social changes taking place in Brazil which is free from ideological bias or misinformation" by Louis Wiznitzer in *The Nation.*[10] Writing in *The Christian Science Monitor* James Nelson Goodsell noted that "Horowitz is convincing in his arguments," and "this book is particularly useful for North Americans trying to understand the Brazilian reality."[11] Nor has the book lacked severe critics. The young Harvard historian, Thomas E. Skidmore, writing in *The New York Review of Books,* said that "Comparing Professor Horowitz' book on Brazil with other recent essays, one cannot help concluding that he has come off badly in his self-declared war with his scholarly colleagues."[12] For R. H. Miller, writing in *The National Review,* the theme of the book is only a ruse to inculcate the innocent with Marxism. "The study of Brazilian politics and society is only incidental to the author's restatement of the major tenet of Marxist dogma, the inevitability of socialism."[13] Perhaps the most fantastic response of all to the book was that offered by the military attaché of Castelo Branco. He either saw a reference to the book, or read the dust jacket. In any event, he convinced himself that *Revolution in Brazil* was an account of the April 1st take-over, and so sent me an exultant note with an enclosure which consisted of Castelo Branco being "interviewed" in the popular journal *Machete,* and declaiming against corruption in administration, extremism in politics, and decadence in social welfare. And, of course, the "solutions" proffered amounted to a call for dedicated attention to the cause of national renovation. This then was the bizarre acceptance of the book as a vindication of events it neither forecasted nor desired.

It should be noted that scholarly reviews followed the script set by the popular media. John D. Martz said that "*Revolution in Brazil* is thought-provoking and clearly among the best available studies."[14] Karl M. Schmitt, while valiantly granting that "there is much of value in the work," was upset with my "looseness" over the use of socialism. A public sector-private sector "dichotomy is misleading since obviously the United States has socialistic features . . ."[15] Finally, there is a review by Peter G. Snow which sees *Revolution in Brazil* "except for the first and last chapters as largely in the form of rehashing what has already been said in the parts written by Brazilians." How this is possible, given the conflicting opinions of the Brazilian contributions, or even whether such views are right or wrong independently of who can claim priority, is ignored in the review.[16]

That *Revolution in Brazil* has been in the main positively received is a consequence of the general liberal and undogmatic spirit of most English-speaking reviewers. But under present circumstances, with Brazil undergoing a revolution and a counter-revolution of major proportions — changes that have produced three Presidents in three years — to ask whether sociological scholarship bears political relevance to the matter is akin to asking whether Christianity has any linkage to Judaism. The important question is the character of this linkage between Brazilian politics and the sociology of Brazilian politics.

To answer this question we must investigate before and after conditions.

Only in this way can the period between 1930 and 1964 be placed in meaningful perspective. For example: What has happened to the Brazilian party system? What role, if any, is now performed by the parliamentary bodies? How does an orderly transference of power take place in the absence of democratic electoral procedures? What has the military tutelage of Brazil done to and for economic development? Who now rules Brazil — at local, national, and international levels? The political sociology of Brazil cannot be reduced to survey data on peasant aspirations, or to mechanical "left-right-center" divisions based on voting analysis. When the formal, procedural aspects of democracy are erased by political fiat, then attitude questionnaires become empty, devoid of sociological content. The study of Brazil has become increasingly plagued by methodological dilemmas precisely to the extent that acquisition of *real* data, in contrast to *formal* data, is difficult to accomplish by any standard survey procedure. It is a curious but real fact that many sociological techniques depend upon mass democracy for their validity. And when such techniques prove neither effective nor feasible, we have good grounds to assume that democracy itself is neither effective nor feasible.

A book is a living entity. It arouses passions no less than reason. It elicits an emotive response to act no less than a call to hard thinking. It invites the reader to participate as a critic or colleague. It appeals to different readers differentially: in my case, a warning to Brazilian businessmen to be more responsive to poverty in the country; to North Americans not to be deluded into thinking that anti-communist slogans will suffice; to workers not to imagine that the State is the gigantic father who takes care of all needs.

A book is a living entity in another sense — in the sense that it is history by the time it is read. For example, in the case of Brazil, within one year since the book has appeared, the country has had outright military domination for the first time since the Vargas period. It has witnessed the breakdown of the labor-aristocracy and government-tinged patronage system. It has witnessed class confrontations rather than traditional class compromises. Above all, within one year, Brazil has become very much part of the Latin American syndrome. This is horrifyingly clear-cut in the same way that one can now speak of Chile, or Argentina, or the Dominican Republic. Indeed, perhaps this stunning breakdown of Brazilian exceptionalism is precisely what is necessary for the ultimate completion of the Brazilian revolution. That as it may be, the fact is that things have changed significantly, enough to warrant extensive reconsiderations about what should be removed from the first edition and what should be included in the second edition, if such an optimistic outlook concerning the book's future is at all realistic.

There is yet a third sense in which a book is a living entity. Besides serving as a response to the world it examines, it may have an effect on the world. In the case of *Revolution in Brazil* this was most dramatically revealed in its Spanish language edition, published by the most widely respected publisher in Latin America, *Fondo de Cultura Económica.* The book served as the strain which finally broke the delicate thread connecting the publishing house to its liberal Director, Arnaldo Orfila Reynal. And in a deeper sense the snapping of this linkage signified the decline of the publishing house itself.

A considerable portion of the funding of FCE came through the *Banco Nacional de México,* and hence there was strong feeling that FCE was a national, governmental publishing enterprise of Mexico, not just a private enterprise. Because of this assumption, great pressure was brought to bear by a number of foreign governments on the Mexican government to make this prestigious publishing company reflect "all points of view" and not just the viewpoint of the editorial board and its Director. Orfila Reynal took the position that ultimate responsibility for what is published remains an editorial function, and that the Board of Directors should be concerned exclusively with profit-making and profit-taking.

The issue was joined on a number of books: FCE published C. Wright Mills' *Listen Yankee!* but refused to publish (under considerable pressure) Theodore Draper's powerful critiques of the Castro Revolution. The Director's position was that no book defaming the Cuban experience would be published by his firm. Oscar Lewis' *Children of Sanchez* was published, only to involve its author and the FCE editor in a legal suit over "defamation of Mexican national character." In this case the sensibilities were not so much political as cultural, but again it was felt that since FCE was a national firm, it might be better if the best-selling work were dropped. Subsequent editions of Lewis' book were published by another, far less potent, firm. FCE had issued a contract for Pablo González Casanova's brilliant book, *Democracy in Mexico,* only to find the book so furiously attacked by conservative Mexican authorities that the contract had to be canceled and the book given over to another small firm.

Treatment of *Revolution in Brazil* was similar to that given the Casanova book. After the contract for the book was issued, during a trip by Orfila Reynal to Europe, word was sent to my literary agents that the book would not be published. No reasons were given. I notified the FCE Director of this while he was in Spain, and was reassured that there must be some mistake and that the contract would be honored. Upon his return to Mexico, he pointed out that the precedent set in the Casanova case of breach of contract was an intolerable situation, and that it could not be allowed to happen again. While he was upheld in this view by the editorial board, it clearly triggered a movement of the conservative, bank-dominated Board of Directors to solicit Orfila Reynal's resignation — which in fact took place in late 1965, several months prior to the publication of *Revolution in Brazil*. The book thus has the honor of being the last work published by FCE under the leadership that transformed FCE from an exile press in the thirties to Latin America's greatest publishing empire.

Sociology, even a politically saturated and conflict oriented sociology such as my own, is still not historical writing. Social forces are ordered; social problems change; social classes dwindle and emerge. If any book is to be considered significant, it must be so viewed by its intellectual consequences. In this, *Revolution in Brazil* has fared well. There are now several graduate students working to either replicate, or use as a point of departure, parts of the book, and also some who are working to fill in the gaps left by the book. Thus one young Brazilian is working to supply a quantitative account of the mobilization process of Brazilian labor; an American Jesuit sociologist-priest is studying the factions and schisms in Catholicism in the Northeast; and yet another student of mine is examining the diplomatic aspects of the steel industrialization process under Vargas. All these themes are either neglected in the book or treated in such a way as to create a felt need for something more and better. This in itself has helped to make the study of Brazil exciting as well as challenging.

Then, one must not forget the emotional "pay-offs" involved. The warmth with which the great Jesuit Churchman Ivan Illych greets my students, no less than myself. The letters from Brazilian people of all kinds, from all classes, thanking me for the book and offering their services for future editions, translations, corrections, etc. The visit from a Mexican sociologist assuring me that the book is being treated seriously among experts on the rural situation in his country. Finally, there is the affection, no less than the respect, offered from the most serious minds and noble men of Brazil — some of whom are in prison, in exile, in hiding; while others survive and endure in the "open."

Diderot once remarked that the knowledge entailed in serious writing encompasses the art of being a good politician. For him, the pen was the chief weapon of the intellectual, the weapon of criticism. Marx, for his part, set out to upset this French Enlightenment applecart by noting that the real task of the social scientist, unlike that of the *literati,* is not to use the weapon of criticism but to engage in a criticism of weapons. In writing this book I tried to bridge these two standpoints, with what success I myself am not in the position to determine. It is enough for me to know that I have made the attempt and, as Max Weber once remarked, "What I have not done others will."

NOTES TO THE CHAPTER

1. Irving Louis Horowitz, *Revolution in Brazil: Politics and Society in a Developing Nation* (New York: E. P. Dutton, 1964).

2. Cf. Irving Louis Horowitz, *Three Worlds of Development: The Theory and Practice of International Stratification* (New York and London: Oxford University Press, 1966).

3. Charles Wagley, *An Introduction to Brazil* (New York: Columbia University Press, 1963), 267–97.

4. I have tried to explain these structural continuities in a follow-up essay to the book, see Irving Louis Horowitz, "Revolution in Brazil: The Counter-Revolutionary Phase," *New Politics, 3* (Spring, 1964), pp. 71–80. Another effort in this direction has been made by Juarez Ruben Brandão Lopes. *"Some Basic Developments in Brazilian Politics and Society,"* in Eric Baklanoff (ed.), *New Perspectives of Brazil* (Nashville: Vanderbilt University Press, 1966), 59–77.

5. One of these alternative routes was suggested to me by David E. Mutchler. His work on "Roman Catholicism in Brazil," in *Studies in Comparative International Development,* Vol. I, No. 8 (1965) led me to reconsider the role of the Church in developing areas.

6. See in particular, Edwin Lieuwen, *Arms and Politics in Latin America* (New York: Frederick A. Praeger, 1961), and *Generals vs. Presidents: Neomilitarism in Latin America* (New York: Frederick A. Praeger, 1964). Also see John J. Johnson, *The Role of the Military in Underdeveloped Countries* (Princeton: Princeton University Press, 1962); *The Military and Society in Latin America* (Stanford: Stanford University Press, 1964); Lyle N. McAlister, *The "Fuero Militar" in New Spain,* 1764–1800 (Gainesville: University of Florida Press, 1951); and "Civil-Military Relations in Latin America," *Journal of Inter-American Studies, 3* (July, 1961), pp. 341–50.

7. Gino Germani, *Society and Politics in Latin America,* ed. by Irving Louis Horowitz. Scheduled for publication by Prentice-Hall, Inc., 1968.

8. "Uma descoberta, um Furação e um livro de Valor," *Diario de Noticias,* May 26, 1964.

9. *The New York Times,* June 29, 1964.

10. "Brazil's Continuing Revolution," *The Nation,* 198 (June 22, 1964), pp. 630–32.

11. "The Social Revolution Continues," *The Christian Science Monitor*, September 3, 1964, p. 9.

12. "The Brazilian 'Revolution'," *The New York Review of Books*, 3 (November 19, 1964), pp. 25–26.

13. *The National Review*, 15 (October 6, 1964), p. 878.

14. *Social Forces*, 43 (March, 1965), p. 453.

15. *Journal of Politics*, 27 (May, 1965), pp. 420–21.

16. *Midwest Journal of Political Science*, 9 (February, 1965), pp. 103–04.

CHAPTER TEN

Political and Ethical Problems in a Large-Scale Study of a Minority Population*

JOAN W. MOORE

Any researcher who explores a massive violation of American norms and examines the consequences of this violation is sure to encounter political and ethical issues. As Gunnar Myrdal pointed out, the study of American minority groups tends to bring these issues to the fore. In a general way, any minority sits inside a delicate and complicated structure of political and moral postures. Imbedded in this structure are the group's deepest aspirations and frustrations. To enter this fabric, no matter how gently, means that this structure of frustration and aspiration is somehow altered.

Although the issues always exist, they become manifest problems to the researcher only to the extent that the scope and goals of his study explicitly raise them. They may, for example, remain dormant and unimportant in a study where minority group members show up randomly in a sample of the total population. And, they may remain latent in a small-scale or narrowly focused study, even though such a study may emphasize the minority status. In our study of the Mexican-Americans in the Southwest, both the scope and purposes of the project meant that the issues were active and important problems from the beginning.

What follows is largely a natural history of the first year of our work. It is an attempt to chronicle our initial plans and their modifications and to indicate the rationales on which our dilemmas were resolved, or at least dealt with at the moment. Since the research is still in progress, much may occur that will cast doubt on the validity of the interpretations and wisdom of the decisions discussed here. Though efforts have been made in the paper to conceptualize the junctures at which ethical problems may occur for the social researcher, these must remain tentative: even our one illustrative case has not been completed.

The Grant

The grant itself (from the Public Affairs Division of the Ford Foundation in December, 1963) was almost surely made in part to meet a need for information created by the significant emergence of Mexican-Americans on the national political scene. The first consequential national political activity of Mexican-Americans was probably the well-remembered "Viva Kennedy" movement of 1960.[1] Kennedy's Civil Rights Bill was pending. The U.S. Civil Rights Commission investigations of that year demonstrated that this national concern with the basic rights of all minorities extended specifically to Mexican-Americans. Also, in 1963, Lyndon B. Johnson, who was then Vice-President, met exclusively with Mexican-Americans from the Southwest, acting in his capacity as chairman of the President's Committee on Equal Employment Opportunity. Though this attention may seem limited, in the three years between 1960 and 1963 Mexican-Americans (comprising 11% of the population in the five states of Arizona, California, Colorado, New Mexico, and Texas) received more signs of national political concern than they had during many previous decades.

Our grant was relatively large. It provided $450,000 for our proposed "comprehensive study of the socio-economic position of Mexican-Americans in selected urban areas of the five Southwestern states (Arizona, California, Colorado, New Mexico and Texas) in which this population is concentrated."[2] The project director (a well-known urban land economist and former senior staff member of the Council of Economic Advisers with experience in several Washington agencies) proposed to assemble an interdisciplinary staff. He also proposed to establish collaborative relations with faculty members both at the University of California at Los Angeles and at other universities.

The ultimate political goals of the project were quite explicit. Our primary purpose was to do a baseline study of the socio-economic status of this population so as to make the "problems and prospects of the Mexican-Americans known to the nation and to help in the development of better action programs." We were, as a second point, to identify strategic factors conditioning the current status of Mexican-Americans in the Southwest as a whole and in different local settings. These factors, of course, could exist within the

Mexican-American population or within the larger society. We were to examine the processes leading to their current position and then, by analysis, we hoped to get some insight into conditions promoting or retarding change.

We were to analyze the results of the study in the context of existing findings about other ethnic or racial groups in the United States. We hoped to make general contributions to the literature on the processes of acculturation and assimilation by our study of this least known of all minority groups in the United States.

These goals were stated very broadly in our proposal to the Ford Foundation. Because we were dealing with a private foundation, we were permitted a great deal of flexibility in specifying our research plans. In fact, our original application had been for a small planning grant to design a larger study: the actual grant allowed nearly a year to be spent in planning the study and assumed there would be considerable modification of our plans as initially stated in the proposal.

The material presented in this paper is a report on one aspect of that year's work, that is, on the political and ethical considerations that arose in the course of exploratory research which shaped our final research design. The Mexican-American Study Project was born in an essentially political atmosphere: out of the endless complexities that our subject-matter presented to us, we had to select those aspects for description and analysis that could have positive consequences for the entire ethnic group through the influence of the research on social action. Both in its scope and in its purposes, the project was involved in manifest political and ethical concerns.

The Implementation of Our Goals: Our First Research Design

From the very beginning we had curious problems in the design of this research. Our early attempts to build a design on previous research on Mexican-Americans was next to impossible, since relatively little such research literature exists. A brief survey of the existing texts on minorities illustrates the problem. Of the half-dozen texts on minorities on my shelf only one contains more than a paragraph or two on Mexican-Americans.[3] These textbooks accurately reflect the nature of the reported research. (We were to discover later they do not reflect the amount of the research.) A handful of books and a handful of articles represent the extent of current scholarly knowledge of America's second largest ethnic minority. Reluctantly, we had to conclude that a severely depressed population of nearly four million people with a distinctive culture and appearance had existed in the United States for many decades, relatively unknown to social scientists generally, despite the latter's stated interest in ethnic groups. This rather sobering discovery made us recognize our own responsibilities even more dramatically.[4] And at the moment, it meant that the analytic portions of our research design must be based on hypotheses drawn from the study of other ethnic groups.

Our principal research strategy was to be the comparative analysis of local variations. Such a strategy would permit us both to test hypotheses regarding acculturation and assimilation and to cover the range of subcultural variation in the population: we could meet our descriptive and our analytic goals with the same procedure. Explicit comparisons would be made not only between ethnic groups but between communities within the region.

These comparisons, we realized, were implicitly political and we anticipated some reaction from our early interviews. We were not disappointed. Not only was there some resentment at our comparison of Mexican-Americans in different cities and subregions, but it appeared that many Mexican-Americans regard themselves as a unique group. Virtually any comparison, even rhetorical, with other ethnic groups tended to threaten their self-esteem and security.

Our tentative design called for the comparative analysis of data on several levels. Some data would come from the Census (which tabulates data for "white persons of Spanish surname" in these five states); we would arrange for special Census tabulations and collect state and local statistics to match Census data for multivariate analyses. There would be questionnaire surveys of six Southwestern cities, chosen analytically for as salient variations as possible. Important in this choice of locations for field study (which we planned to range from Los Angeles to south Texas) were variations in the characteristics of the "host" social and economic systems and in the number and characteristics of the Mexican-American population such as their length of residence in the "host" system, the modal social class of Mexican origin, and so on. These surveys were to be administered by local academic investigators who would also be responsible for their interpretation in the local context. Also planned was a group of special studies relating to the Mexican-American experience in the U.S., covering such areas as education, religion, and history.

In addition to the inter-disciplinary, inter-university structure, an important element in the planned structure of the study was the establishment of a group of citizens' advisory committees in each research locale. These committees were planned to include both Mexican-Americans and "Anglos" (anyone who is not Mexican-American). They would both advise the researchers and also (we hoped) help translate our new-found knowledge into action programs. Mexican-American participation in some form had been urged by our sponsor, and we chose this formal device.

In addition, we planned for a group of scholarly conferences to involve not only our direct collaborators but a broad cross-section of social scientists from all over the nation. We hoped to sow seeds of scholarly interest wherever and whenever possible and to build upon any existing research now under way.

Specifying Our Plans: The Field Tours

The first steps in specifying and implementing these general plans were tours of the Southwest to gather local data, to seek out potential collaborators, and to gather first impressions of local variations. None of us was native to the Southwest nor even very familiar with the regional culture. And, as it happened, this naiveté turned out to be very useful — it imposed effortlessly and reliably the norms and ideas of a national perspective. Against this naiveté, each respondent felt it incumbent to "explain" the situation in fairly basic terms. As a result we succeeded in getting not only a great deal of objective information but also a number of different sub-cultural definitions of the Mexican-American. These definitions are matched in the research literature by some basic differences in the way in which Mexican-Americans are conceptualized, e.g., as "a conquered people" (as by George Sánchez), a depressed racial minority (as by Carey McWilliams), one among many ethnic groups (as by Warner and Srole). The scholarly differences reflect the dissensus in the population itself.

We found ourselves, for example, the target of a probably honest, certainly politically vested, effort on the part of the Anglo informants to define the social position of Mexican-Americans. In Texas, for example, we arrived during the Democratic primary (in Texas, the equivalent of an election) and Governor John Connally assured us, in elaborate detail, that Mexican-Americans were happy Texans and had few problems of consequence not well on the way to solution.

Elsewhere, for example, in California, the friends of large growers (heavy users of *bracero* Mexican labor) told us of the serious problems of motivating "domestic" Mexican laborers to work in the fields. They told us how far superior the *braceros* were in both attitude and productivity to "spoiled" American citizens of Mexican or other descent. We were even told (by a State Department of Labor employee) about the genetic intellectual inferiority of "Mexicans" leading, by happy coincidence with certain physical characteristics, to superior performance in the harvest fields. Union organizers, on the other hand, discussed with us the living conditions for both domestic and *bracero* workers and explained the elaborate and profitable tie-ins between growers and suppliers of the labor force. (This controversy later received national airing when in 1965 Secretary of Labor Wirtz terminated further extensive use of *bracero* labor.)

In the state and local bureaucracies, we often found that such local definitions — and prejudices — were embodied in statistics. For example, a state agency staffed with intelligent, educated, and progressive professionals tolerated a clerk's definition of "Mexican" which was discriminatory by class and reproduced almost perfectly the mode by which Mexican-Americans "pass" as "Spanish." Often such a definition has been taken as the symbolic target of reform among Mexican-American leaders, with rather ironic results. Throughout the Southwest, we found ethnic leaders boasting that they had "succeeded" in having the designation "Mexican" or "Latin" removed from official statistics. Such a symbolic victory may actually entail the erection of further barriers in the struggle against discrimination: although it precludes attacks on the Mexican-Americans because of their over-representation in statistics of pathology, it also makes it much more difficult to evaluate, analyze, and ultimately to treat their problems. Though statistics collected according to local biases may be of scholarly interest only to those concerned with the kind of distortion we found, they do tend to indicate problems which are of concern to action people. We felt that despite their questionable validity and lack of comparability from one locale to another, such statistics were preferable to none at all. (We may note here that there are some indications that the "objective" Spanish-surname technique used by the U.S. Bureau of the Census may also have some systematic biases.)

Among Mexican-Americans, we interviewed local leaders and found very early that we had not fully anticipated the group's recent discovery of themselves as a national minority. Our first exploratory interviews coincided with a turmoil of intra-group redefinition and local and regional quarrels which entailed, among other things, competition for group leadership. While we did not represent "national" attention as directly as did the investigators of the United States Civil Rights Commission, our tours through the Southwest implied that we, sponsored by the "Eastern" Ford Foundation, were defining the population in a particular way — as a national minority. For highly localistic Mexican-American leaders in some regions, such a definition posed a threat, both by implicitly classifying them with their least acculturated ethnic compatriots and by suggesting that the era of local autonomy might be drawing to an end. (Our standard questions about the existence of local action programs threatened both Anglos and Mexican-Americans in this regard, but especially those Mexican-Americans whose leadership rested on accommodation to local powers.) Among other kinds of leaders, defining Mexican-Americans as a national minority implied comparison with Negroes, and although few Mexican-American political and action programs were performed in coalition with Negroes, such a comparison was more often seen as pejorative. It was somewhat offensive in terms of traditional Mexican culture. It was also offensive in terms of the normal ways in which many Mexican-American leaders who are upwardly mobile men habitually relate as persons to the dominant system. This comparison was also distressing in terms of the radical differences in tactics used by members of the two minorities to gain access to power.

While all interviewing sensitizes respondents to the peculiar and special aspects of their identity on which they are questioned, we began our interviews at a time when members of this population were unusually sensitive — not only because of some impact our findings would ultimately have but because of the process of research itself. We were Anglos and academics. We would appear to some of the population to be the escorts, if not the holders, of national power and thus to carry the prospect, however dim, of recognition and amelioration. Not all respondents seemed to feel this effect to the same degree. Sensitivity seemed to vary by city, by social class, and by other factors. Nevertheless, we soon began to feel that our study itself would be an element in the course of the group's struggle for identity.

We were also researchers, and there had been many before us. Like the Negroes, Mexican-Americans — and particularly their leaders — have been studied, surveyed, interviewed, and analyzed to their very considerable boredom and suspicion. The end result seems to be an inclination to deliver something of a set piece: the "Anglo investigator" produces a well-thought-out polemic. (It was still easy to get beyond this polemic; the population was still relatively lacking in major defenses, and we came prepared with personal references that guaranteed our intentions and qualifications.) But experience has taught the Mexican-American leader that he may never see the results of his responses: there will probably be no books, magazine articles, noticeable reaction from governmental agencies or local projects having any real meaning.

So serious is this effect among Mexican-Americans, and particularly among local leaders, that we began to feel that non-publication raises an important professional issue. Does not the researcher's invasion of the respondent's privacy set up an implicit bargain between interviewer and respondent that some useful purpose will be served by this invasion and exposure? This argument seems all the more valid when respondents represent a disadvantaged group. As with many other groups, the disinterested pursuit of science is not a particularly meaningful goal to most Mexican-Americans. Some of our predecessors made it even less meaningful.

Deciding Where to Conduct the Field Surveys

One of the major purposes of the initial field tours was to gather enough information about the principal cities in the Southwest to decide which six would be our best candidates for local surveys.

Our pragmatic criteria for selecting a city included the presence of competent local researchers and earlier studies to get at, if possible, changes in the community.

The analytic considerations included the characteristics of the total community — the nature of the industrial base, the rate of growth, the presence or absence of competing ethnic or racial minority populations, and so on. We gave as much weight as possible to the characteristics of the resident Mexican-Americans although at this early stage we knew little about them. We hoped, for example, to vary the relative size of the settlement and its social class origin. We knew, in this regard, that while Tucson is supposed to have sheltered many middle-class refugees from the early Mexican revolutions, Stockton, Fresno, and other California Central Valley cities had a primarily working-class population with no history of an early-settler group laying claim to higher status. Pinning down these variations would permit us to test hypotheses derived from earlier studies of acculturation of other ethnic groups. And, we felt, if the hypotheses didn't pan out — for example, if Tucson Mexican-Americans were no better off than San Diego Mexican-Americans — our local collaborators could retrieve our studies by explaining the peculiarities in local conditions that kept the hypothesized factors from being decisive.

One of our first problems was that locales on the less-industrialized end of our continuum tended to lack local research resources. We found research facilities extremely rare in the long stretch of cities running from Brownsville to Laredo, Texas. Analytically interesting cities like Pueblo, Colorado (an industrialized area within a traditional subculture) and Corpus Christi, Texas (an industrialized area relatively close to the Mexican border) also tended to lack local research resources. The practical problems of conducting and interpreting surveys in such areas began to loom very large.

Still another problem emerged when we began serious discussions with ethnographers who had done some research on Mexican-Americans and who questioned the validity of applying hypotheses derived from the study of acculturation of other ethnic groups to understanding acculturation — or lack of it — of the Mexican-Americans. Apparently, factors exist in the experience of Mexican-Americans that had not emerged elsewhere, for example, proximity to the mother country, involvement in isolated, labor-intensive industries, special relations with Federal law-enforcement officers. These (and still other factors whose effects were relatively unknown) might be as important in understanding the attainments of Mexican-Americans as were the more traditional variables uncovered in earlier studies of ethnic groups. Our strategy ran the risk of verifying a series of null hypotheses. We might discover the scientifically interesting but politically sterile fact that current theories about acculturation and assimilation were not valid for Mexican-Americans. And, we reminded ourselves, although all of us on the project wanted the opportunity for scholarly contributions, we were not mainly concerned with the testing of theory in this project.

We were led to the conclusion that ethnographic work should be done formally, rather than being left to "informed" local researchers, and that it should be much more exploratory in character. This would increase our expenses for each local study. We decided also that more exploratory research should be done around the central problem of our study: achievement and failure to achieve in the larger society. This research threatened to be expensive. We would need depth interviews of individuals and family members of both mobile and nonmobile families throughout the survey areas. Reluctantly we concluded the field budget would have to be reduced in another area.

Accordingly, we decided to reduce the number of cities to be studied. Knowing we had enough funds to study only two, or at most three, cities fully with survey, ethnography, and depth interviews, we decided to let some of the analytic concerns go in favor of a qualitative emphasis. The problem of selecting locales for study changed. We were no longer concerned with an analytic criterion, but with a sampling criterion. Partly to counteract the stereotype of Mexican-Americans as a rural population, we decided (and here enters one political concern) to focus attention on the far more important urban component. We knew that a quarter of the entire Mexican-American population lived in only two cities, Los Angeles and San Antonio. Increasingly these two cities (and others) assume symbolic and political roles in Mexican-American life. In the larger population, on the contrary, the stereotype persists of the Mexican-American as a simple, land-loving rural peasant.[5] Full-scale studies utilizing a range of data from Census to depth interviews in these two "capital" cities would accomplish many of our goals. We would be studying a large proportion of the total population rather than a small, though analytically significant, proportion. These large populations would encompass a wide enough range of variation to test many of the hypotheses we had hoped to test in cross-city comparisons.[6]

But although these two cities presented a wide range of problems confronted by Mexican-Americans, they presented neither the worst nor the best situation for this ethnic group. Both were large and relatively modern cities. We felt it desirable, for analytic as well as rhetorical reasons, to present a broader range. We would present this range in less elaborate detail than the "heartland," and describe a "good" city and a "bad" city as milieux rather than analyze a large sample of Mexican-Americans living in them. The best researchers for such study, we felt, would be Mexican-Americans themselves.

At the very beginning of the project we had decided to use as many Mexican-American researchers as possible. Not only do they possess special insights that we as outsiders lack, but with an anxious and suspicious population they could communicate confidence as well as perform the role of participant observers. (A complaint in the population is, "Why is it always Anglos who study us — why can't it be one of us?" After we added a full-time senior staff member of Mexican descent, we felt that the atmosphere improved.) We had not anticipated the full extent of suspicion and community defense against Anglo authority. In a lower-class community, periodically visited by Immigration officials, police, F.B.I. agents, and other authority, techniques of evasion are well developed, and research procedures may well need to be adapted to getting around them. One Mexican-American researcher suggested, for example, that if we confined ourselves to the use of a questionnaire technique we ran the risk of setting in motion the defensive communications network of the *barrio* and of eliciting collective rather than individual statements of attitudes in response to our questions. "No matter who asks, always say you were born in the U.S.," another Mexican-born researcher recalled his mother saying. Though we did not abandon survey procedures as a result of these insights, the addition of the formal ethnographers — Mexican-American and others — was partly a response to such considerations.[7]

But even when we had decided to use participant-observers, we had to decide just where they would be used. This, again, was a decision with political overtones. When we thought of a locale that would represent the regional and traditional past, the cities of South Texas were immediate candidates. But few have any resident research resources. Meanwhile we discovered that Arthur Rubel was about to publish a study of Mexican-Americans in Weslaco, a south Texas town. This would largely meet our needs for a study of a "poor" or traditional area, and we could then shift our efforts to some other area.

A critical decision on location had to be made — that of a "good" city. Our choice here was unanticipated. We had been planning a study of Mexican-Americans that was limited to the urban Southwest. We were, of course, well aware that perhaps a quarter of a million Mexican-Americans lived outside the Southwest and had moved into cities like Kansas City and Chicago well before the Depression. A visit to Chicago by one of the investigators brought the Southwestern focus into question. Most remarkably, there were an estimated 90,000 Mexican-Americans within the city limits of Chicago and they were very much like other ethnic groups in that potpourri of ethnic groups. (There were still certain resemblances to their Southwestern fellows: for example, they were relatively unknown and uninteresting to local sociologists; they failed to participate in the local political structure.) In general, as our exploratory tours continued, it seemed to us that nowhere in the Southwest were Mexican-Americans as well integrated as they were in Chicago. We began to feel that only *outside* the Southwest did the Mexican-Americans come in contact with a subculture that did *not* accord them a special niche as "our minority." In fact, we could quite reasonably guess that only outside the Southwest were Mexican-Americans fully in touch with the national experience.

Our somewhat slow realization of the new and important "national perspective" gave added weight to a possible field study in the urban North.

The Chicago area (far from the mother country and heavily industrialized) was a top candidate and became decisive when we succeeded in finding nearby an able Mexican-American sociologist to undertake the research.

While the choice of the Chicago metropolitan area was largely dependent upon analytic considerations, we were also very sure that a careful study of Mexican-American life outside the Southwest might be illuminating to both Mexican-Americans and Anglos in and out of the Southwest. It might offer a new or different goal to the minority.

The limitation of the number of direct research sites was thus in large part an "economic" decision, constrained by considerations of time, money, and personnel. We had increased the expenses of research at each site by amplifying and enriching our basic research design. Our difficulties in finding researchers who could rapidly penetrate the defenses of the more traditional Mexican-American communities had reinforced our decision to use a relatively standardized though more expensive research procedure. We felt that our sites and our procedure would yield maximum returns with minimal problems.

This limitation, of course, meant that we would not study some communities whose Mexican-American and/or Anglo leaders had hoped for or urgently requested such studies, as well as some communities of special analytic interest to us. It was a difficult decision to take, and it also exposed the study to criticism from some local leaders. Our rationale lay in the anticipated improvement in quality of each study, and the inclusion of a large proportion of the Mexican-American urban population in the sites we were considering.

One final locational decision faced us. From the first announcement of our project, we were made aware that the terminological split referred to earlier reflects a real social split in what we call the "Mexican-American" population. That is, the people of New Mexico and southern Colorado who call themselves "Spanish-Americans" are in many ways different from the descendants of more recent immigrants from Mexico and many of them resent being categorized as part of the same population. But our entire research design, from the analysis of Census data on "white persons of Spanish surname" through the analysis of family structure and personality which we hoped to undertake, assumed a basic cultural and structural similarity. The test of this assumption affects not only the validity of our conclusions, but also the extent to which they will be found plausible by Mexican-Americans. A general study of the "Hispanos" of New Mexico was commissioned, both to attack this assumption and to describe and analyze the rapid changes in the traditional culture of the area.

The Problem of the Community Advisory Board

Early in the research planning, we began to establish an advisory board of Mexican-Americans to communicate with our group. This function they served admirably, but not until the composition of the board posed for us yet another set of political issues. While the Mexican-American lives in close proximity to Negroes in many cities and his life is, of course, shaped by the dominant power structure, it seemed impossible to achieve any degree of comfortable harmony in the committee unless it were restricted to Mexican-Americans. We were told that we were the first researchers to ask for the organized advice of the Mexican-American community. This was pleasing, but we were told further that the Mexican-Americans, while flattered, would feel at least at the beginning that the addition of Anglos and Negroes would undermine the helpfulness of this committee. We had hoped other officials and influential people might ultimately translate some of our research work into action. Our Mexican-American leaders agreed that these were desirable goals but they wanted the group to be an "inside" group until at least the first research findings were available. After all, they told us, they wouldn't feel qualified in planning research in the Negro community.

Our decision to make this purely a Mexican-American group had immediate benefits. Intra-group differences of opinion were aired that most surely would have been suppressed otherwise. Further, the close in-group nature of the committees kept the action plans practical, realistic, and imaginative. We can trace at least one action plan to the suggestions of this group. Better yet, it tended to alert us to sensitive areas of research. Like any other minority group, the Mexican-Americans have been frequently "exposed" in terms of their more sensationally interesting peculiarities. The Los Angeles "Zootsuit riots" during World War II and, most particularly, the delicate subject of Mexican-American narcotics addiction are fine examples. As one of our informants put it, "Until 15 years ago narcotics addiction in the Los Angeles area was defined by the police as strictly a Mexican problem." On these, and other sensitive topics, the Committee alerted us to the degree and nature of sensitivity and gave us important clues on just how to handle the topic with the population, both in gaining access to data and in later presentations of data on a popular level.

Many Anglo groups — study, action, and political — who have attempted to establish relations with a group of Mexican-American leaders have become targets of an attack whose weapons are the old charges of discrimination and exploitation of Mexican-Americans by Anglos. Our project has been no exception: the Committee has been used as such a forum, by a leader apparently motivated at least in part by a desire to reaffirm the legitimacy of his leadership to the audience of other Committee members. Though we would reject the relevance of the manifest content of this attack on our project, its latent content may have considerable validity, and it calls into question the underlying nature of the bargain between researcher and subject.

Quite apart from specific guidance and advice, this committee has served a function for the project that cannot be overestimated in this type of research. Just as it may frequently be an effort for its members (who tend to be exceptionally active community leaders) to attend its sometimes boring sessions, so it is frequently an effort for the staff to leave our research involvement for yet another attempt to communicate with our population. Yet this very effort underlines its importance. Left alone, we might easily tend to forget the ultimate goals of our study in the fascination — and frustration — of immediate research issues. The bi-monthly confrontation of these two cultures reminds us continuously that somebody quite concrete is waiting for our results.

But this function may be bought at a price — the price of possibly implying that the study will have direct, immediate, and important results for the betterment of the population and that these results will be controlled in part by members of the committee. (It should be remembered that these are people who have been working in and on behalf of the Mexican-American population for a good part of their lives, against originally very high obstacles of prejudice and disdain.) On a motivational level, it seems to me that this is the incentive we hold out to them in return for their willingness to legitimize politically our essentially voyeuristic activities — to function as our public conscience. On a conscious level, of course, nothing of this sort is intended probably by either set of participants in the encounter.[8]

In another community where the advisory committee was called into being after the research was in the field, two other problems arose. One was a functional question, much like what has been discussed above: some committee members declared themselves not interested in research in whose planning they had no part. Here, where they were being asked primarily to learn about an ongoing study and apply its results, the issue of control of the research content became clear. The second important problem related to the symbolic significance that membership on the board had to members of the leadership group. Willingness to serve on the board also meant willingness to appear in public with other leaders of different political ideologies and alignments with the Anglo system. Under these circumstances, membership on the board became — even more clearly than in the case of the original committee — a symbol of political recognition and stance in the community. The study began to be associated with one rather than another faction in the community, to the detriment of what effects the results of the study might have.

Organized "community participation" in research with action implications clearly has important functions — both in general and specifically. But it is bought at a price. The project developed two other devices for reaching interested people throughout the Southwest. The first, a periodic Progress Report, has more limited impact but a far broader audience, numbering over

1000 after the first three issues. The second device was to ensure the continued availability of all staff members, and especially the Mexican-American staff member, to informal contacts in the Mexican-American community. Though this device could effectively inform the community about our research, it did not perform the feedback function that is met by organized group interaction. And its scope was limited to the scope of our staff members' travels and energies — both increasingly restricted.

In short, the problem of community participation in research with action implications entails conflict in frames of reference, in goals and in meanings. Its benefits can be real, but so are its hazards.

The Scholarly Conferences

All of us on the project were fully socialized to scholarly norms, and we felt little need of a scholarly counterpart to our public conscience as embodied in the community advisory committee. However, we had undertaken a task that was both conceptually and administratively complex, and we wanted as much scholarly *advice* as could be brought to bear on our problem. Accordingly, after the completion of our preliminary research design and field tours, we held four research seminars, with approximately 15 participants in each. The research plan we had designed and presented to them called for a broad, partly descriptive study, with considerable analytic potential in many disciplines. A number of questions were raised in areas that lay outside of our own fields of competence.

A large number of well-known social scientists took part. Most had done research on similar phenomena. We received much helpful comment, advice, and ideas but we also became aware of two recurrent critical themes that seem to reflect as much on the nature of social research itself as on our special and peculiar research effort.

The first of these themes was criticism for a premature focus, for a lack of exploratory work. We were told that it would not be adequate for us to build our research design on the studies of other ethnic groups for reasons discussed above, nor would it be adequate to extract hypotheses from these other studies.

The second critical theme flatly contradicts the first. We were told that our plan lacked focus, that we had not narrowed on a central theme. In short, we had no problem and without a problem we could not focus a truly scientific study.

So inconsistent and so mutually contradictory were these two ideas that it seems impossible to resist the conclusion that we are dealing here with a special rhetoric of the social sciences. Perhaps naively, we had hoped that the urgencies of the problem, the existence of the minority, the massive violation of American norms could be accepted as a social fact and the approach to the problem be considered in terms of the problem. Equipped as we were with an inter-disciplinary staff, we had expected some internal friction between disciplines which rarely appeared. The problem was massive enough and, after our field tours, impressive enough to occupy the fullest attention of all the staff members. We all became eclectics in one sense. And, perhaps naively, we expected a similar approach from *all* social scientists. The inter-disciplinary and inter-university character of our research plans also seemed to militate against an overly detailed plan of procedure, which, we felt, could not effectively be carried out by distant researchers of somewhat dissimilar orientation.

There were times during these conferences when we felt that we were in the presence of the academic institution rather than in the presence of a scholarly reference group. Interchanges between conferees along the lines indicated were often made dogmatically, and tended to be revelations of personal style — in most cases, to be sure, personal style that had paid off in professional eminence — in disciplines where style is still a very significant element of the scholarly output. Notably, the economists among our conferees were the *least* prone to such rhetoric. Personal style — or approach to a problem — may be a less important element of an economist's work than of work done by sociologists, psychologists, anthropologists, and researchers in other fields of "chronic *Methodenstreit*."[9] It may well be that in complex fields of inquiry, where theoretical guidance is largely lacking, professionals become overcommitted to the continuity (and psychological security) afforded by a personal or "school" approach to problems, to the neglect of significant aspects of the phenomena they are dealing with. In short, we encountered at these conferences many of the problems of professionalization that today plague the sociologists.[10] Though we are no nearer a suggested solution than are other sociologists, the revelation that this problem exists across disciplines, as well as in an intra-disciplinary context, may open avenues for discussion.

Discussion

The history of the exploratory phase of our project is one of modification of structure, techniques, and locations for research in the course of nearly a year's communication with our subjects and their neighbors, and our fellow academics. The focus of the chronicle above has been on this modification. Its secondary goal has been to show how the research process itself is involved in the political process and has moral consequences.

As suggested at the outset, these facets of all research may have been particularly pronounced in a large-scale inter-disciplinary study of a minority, financed for ultimate use in social action by a foundation which encouraged an unusual degree of flexibility in research development. But much empirical research passes through the same crises and turning points, even though professional socialization and its attendant rigidities in perception of social reality may often obscure them to the investigator. For example, any research involving direct contact with the subjects tends to elicit *their* definition of themselves and/or the situation being studied. In our study, we were compelled to take our subjects' comments seriously: but most sociologists have had experience with studies in which such comments were dismissed as irrelevant or as betraying the subjects' lack of understanding of research in the social sciences.

It was suggested earlier that all direct research sensitizes respondents to certain aspects of their identity and probably leaves a more or less significant, even if not always conscious, residue. As professionals we might profit from both a technique and an ideology that permit us to cope with our effect on our subjects. It seems unrealistic to continue assuming that this effect is either nil or benign. The ultimate political goals of our study gave us an immediate ideological basis for justifying whatever disturbance we caused in the pursuit of the ultimate good of our subjects. In this respect our project was unusual; though we were not engaged in action research, we had available the same ideology as do action researchers.

Our project was also unusual in that it represented a means for both collective and, in some cases, individual social mobility to many of our subjects. This problem, not explicitly discussed above, is endemic in research with action implications. At its least attractive it presents the face of near-blackmail, with the claim implied by some subjects that the project will be jeopardized unless their unique contributions or criticisms are utilized. This kind of claim can be made by subjects in any relatively closed population, whether formal group or subculture with a well-developed network of communication. At its most poignant, the researcher may be presented with subjects' despair that the project isn't doing *more* to foster collective mobility directly.

As researchers, in short, we not only asked respondents to verbalize perhaps suppressed definitions of themselves and their situations; we also, in ourselves, presented a new object for their definition. At the outset, when we were most ignorant of our population, we were inclined to excessive worry about the former kind of problem. As for the latter kind of problem, we have maintained consistently that ours is entirely a research task, and that direct action is outside our purview. The line has not always been clearly drawn, however, and many of our decisions have been made in the light of the latent functions that alternative "pure-research" procedures may have for collective mobility of our subjects.

In many respects, such as in our relations with state and municipal bureaucracies, our project was one of a very small class. In other respects, as indicated above, it was one of a large class, differing from much social research only in degree. In this final discussion I have emphasized the interaction of researcher and subject. The license we are given by our subjects to collect a great deal of information — much of it confidential — entails in our case an almost explicit bargain with them that this information be used discreetly and presented expertly in such a way that they will collectively benefit. This bargain also implies that we may not be able to afford — either ethically or financially — the kind of theoretically oriented research that runs the risk of accomplishing little more than the verification of null hypotheses. Recognition of the potential social effect of one's research need not generate a "social problems" orientation in the social scientist.

The immediate possibility of a social effect presses a scholar's conscience. He must be accurate and, perhaps at a cost, he is committed to a search for conclusions that can be potentially helpful.

A Personal Postscript

A year after writing (and a year before the end of this project) there seems little to change but much to emphasize in this paper. The potential political and ethical problems have become more acute.

Although at the moment our problems are largely confined to the Mexican-American political community, they mean that no large-scale academic study can take place for some years without being affected by our actions as well as our findings.

It is particularly clear now that political validation of the researcher is essential for good research among ethnic groups in the United States. Validation is important not only during the actual research but also upon completion when conclusions appear in the form of tables, statistics, and correlations. The academic's preoccupations — broad abstractions, alternative interpretations, cautious conclusions, and competitive colleagues — are emphatically not those of the ethnic activist. Nor is the activist particularly interested in or sympathetic with the means by which the conclusions are reached. Thus not only must the activist trust the researcher with "inside" interpretations of life (which many ethnics hold to be something of a family secret) but he must also accept and promulgate research conclusions on no basis stronger than faith. Pure research does not ordinarily inspire this kind of loyalty. There must be a political context for this loyalty. This, unfortunately, is a problem for which the ideological background of academic sociologists fits them badly. Possibly the modern ideology of research is obsolete for research in a contemporary urban ethnic setting.

Nonetheless there are many paths to validation: our project was helped by its sponsorship, its Mexican-American staff members, its community advisors — and by attacks from prejudiced Texans. Later, as the reports and results are more widely circulated, the effective and important reference groups will change. Perhaps also, in time, a new generation of activist ethnic leaders will be better prepared to utilize and understand modern sociology.

Notes to the Chapter

*I am indebted to Peter M. Blau, Leo Grebler, Ralph Guzman, and Frank Mittelbach for comments on earlier versions of this document. Though I have often reported staff decisions as if they were all consensual, I must emphasize that I alone bear responsibility for the interpretations and analyses presented here. My occasional use of an editorial "we" should not obscure this fact.

1. Notably, these clubs emerged outside of local Democratic party organizations, as the political scientist Ralph Guzman commented in verbal communication.

2. The quotation is taken from our *Proposal,* October, 1963, 2–6. The population we call "Mexican-American" is actually a group of Americans of Spanish and mixed Indian descent. It is variously termed "Spanish-American" or "Hispano" in northern New Mexico and southern Colorado. "Latin-American" is the term most frequently used in Texas, "Mexican-American" in California and Arizona. Often the variations reflect differences in the speed of the group's attachment to the United States and attempts to evade local prejudices.

3. One new text devotes a single chapter to each of the six major minority groups in the United States, among which Mexican-Americans are not included. Joseph B. Gittler, *Understanding Minority Groups* (New York: John Wiley & Sons, Science Editions, 1964). A second new text has two references to "Mexicans" in the index — one noting in a single paragraph why they and other groups are slow to develop a middle class and the other noting segregation of

Negroes and other minority groups within the Catholic Church. Milton M. Gordon, *Assimilation in American Life* (New York: Oxford University Press, 1964). Still another text has four references — three to lists in which Mexican-Americans appear and the fourth to a brief discussion of "Latin-Americans" which implies strongly that Mexican-Americans are predominantly rural and predominantly Mexican. (Neither of these implications is near the truth.) Peter I. Rose, *They and We* (New York: Random House, 1964). Another widely used text makes ten references to "Mexicans in the United States," and twelve to Japanese and Japanese-Americans, a far less significant group. George Eaton Simpson and J. Milton Yinger, *Racial and Cultural Minorities* (New York: Harper and Bros., 1958).

4. Since most national decisions affecting minorities are made outside the Southwest, this problem of neglect was particularly salient to our project, as Frank Mittelbach has pointed out.

5. See supra on contents of textbooks.

6. Full use of the comparative method will continue with our analyses of Census data and special tabulations from the Census. The remarks above apply only to our direct field efforts.

7. We were also cautioned against the use of any technique, or any mode of presenting our findings, that could be interpreted by action workers such as teachers or social workers as implying a social norm. Well-planned and well-executed studies had often lost their effectiveness or actually been misused in schools, for example, as a result of the "propensity of educationists to turn a statistical norm into a classroom or individual norm."

8. I am indebted for this analysis to discussions with Ralph Guzman, Frank Mittelbach, and Louis Schaw.

9. Joseph J. Schwab, "What Do Scientists Do?," *Behavioral Scientist,* 1 (Jan. 1960).

10. See, for example, the recent discussion of a related set of issues by Amitai Etzioni, "Social Analysis as a Sociological Vocation," *American Journal of Sociology,* 60 (March, 1965), pp. 613–22.

CHAPTER ELEVEN

Role Emergence and the Ethics of Ambiguity*

FRED H. GOLDNER

This paper describes the strains and strategies — both political and ethical — involved in the creation and subsequent emergence of a research role within a large business corporation.

For over three years I was "permanently" employed as a full-time research sociologist in a large industrial corporation. I was hired to perform what appeared to be a specific task — the study of middle and higher management. But within a few months I realized that the rights and duties of my job were undefined, except within broad limits. Like any entrant into an ongoing organization, I thought I had simply to get to know the limits of behavior by observing others. I assumed that the manager of my unit spoke for the organization and that there would naturally be consensus concerning my rights and duties. If he was able to hire me to "study" higher management, I could also assume he possessed some power to arrange for my research activities. All these assumptions were incorrect.

In order to understand my role, let alone the roles of others in the organization, I had to understand what was involved in establishing a role. In so doing, I quickly discovered that playing politics was not only a natural organizational phenomenon but a necessary one as well.

The sociological literature on roles[1] — despite its volume — was of little aid to me in understanding either my job or the organization as a whole. The literature on roles discusses the expectations of behavior that go to make up roles as if a role-incumbent has but to step into any position to find already

245

established expectations. Although writers have acknowledged the complexity of these expectations and the strains involved in role change, they have said little if anything about how roles emerge or are created.[2]

My personal experience was an example of the general phenomenon of role emergence. Here I will discuss the strategies employed in creating and controlling this role from the vantage point of the occupant. These strategies are particularly important because the lack of discussion about emergent roles has resulted in little if any acknowledgment of the active part played by an incumbent in shaping his own role. Actually, the incumbent plays an active and inevitable part in defining his own role; in an emergent-role situation there is an especially strong relationship between the role and the incumbent's own personality. The process of role emergence is much like the development of one's personality — the expectations about an individual are heavily influenced by his own actions.

Although I am using a setting appropriate for the study of role emergence, I shall not deal with the structure of emergence — i.e., the situations where it is likely to occur and the conditions of its initial development. Nor will I deal with emergent roles that are occupied by large numbers of persons. Hence I ignore the problem of how the expectations that develop around each individual occupant coalesce to form a more general role in society.

Setting

I was employed by an industrial organization with over 50,000 employees and facilities throughout the nation in manufacturing, research, and sales. The company was divided into a number of major operating divisions but also had the usual central staff group.

I worked in a social research unit that formed part of the central personnel department. This unit was at the time of my employment a relatively new creation. Previously the company had not engaged in social science research except for carrying out some simple "morale" surveys and the usual industrial psychology tasks of testing and counseling.

When I entered the research unit it had a manager and two research assistants. Soon thereafter I was joined by another senior (Ph.D.) researcher. There was also a social psychologist (Ph.D.) who identified with our group although he was in one of the operating divisions of the company. His research assistant later joined our unit soon before obtaining his own Ph.D.

My manager, who had successfully lobbied to set up this unit, occupied a position two levels below the head of the personnel department who, in turn, was three levels below the President of the corporation. The notion of "levels" may be misleading because relative rankings shifted from time to time and because the occupants of the top three levels usually had easy access to one another.

The Problem of Access: Expectations of Others

The company (over 4,000 managers) was too large for me to study all of it at once. In looking for some part of it to analyze I immediately encountered the problem of access. At the time this rather surprised me. The anticipation of ready access to the study of management was a major reason for my taking the job, and I had assumed that any access problem would be solved when I entered the company. But no social scientist in this company had studied its management, so that there were no institutionalized guidelines for me to follow.

My first step was to find a head of an operating division who would allow me to carry out my research. I felt that if I attempted to study top corporate management my presence would lead to questions and doubts that would threaten the very existence of my position. For at that time the top management was still not aware of the existence of my manager and his unit's activities, much less of me.

A denial of access to study the top executives would not be disastrous if they first came to accept my existence in the organization. But I had no assurance that if they knew about me or my unit they would approve of our endeavors. An executive below the top level had already taken the risk of creating our research positions without explicit clearance by the topmost management. It was thus hazardous to have our activities open to scrutiny before we had produced any results.

The point is that, through a process that is rather unclear and rarely discussed in the literature, change can originate from the bottom in large complex organizations. I learned about the kind of tactics essential for operating in this kind of system from the process through which I obtained access to study top management. For despite my relatively low status in the organization I was in a position to manipulate or control certain aspects of my own environment. My very presence in the organization, though not formally recognized by the topmost group, was sufficient to legitimize my functions in the eyes of other members of the organization. An outsider seeking this same access would have had to approach the top management for permission to study the lower levels, and very likely this permission would have been denied.

Because my boss did not have the power to grant or obtain access for me,

I had to devise my own strategy and to determine to whom I should make a proposal and under what conditions. I felt that formal proposals were likely to be rejected out of hand. Executives of operating divisions in the company were neither accustomed to being approached in this way nor likely to approve a formal proposal that promised little in the way of immediate results. It was necessary to establish contact with these persons in some other manner. I felt that if I could gain their attention and establish a degree of confidence I might then secure permission to do my research even though they had only a vague notion as to what it was. For the more unstructured the situation and the more unique the issue, the more dependent one is on personal contacts and friendships.

I had to carefully lay the groundwork for such contacts and bide my time. The academically based researcher usually has a number of other organizations to approach if he is rejected by one. However, there are a limited number of operating divisions within a given organization. A few rejections and my universe would have been exhausted.

The necessity of establishing personal contacts in order to meet the problem of access revealed the limited extent of my power and the tentative nature of my position. It also demonstrated that personal contacts are part of the definition of power in unstructured situations. I was finally able to gain access to two operating divisions of the company. Access to one division was obtained through contacts made with an executive at central staff headquarters who was subsequently promoted to the position of general manager of that operating division. I had provided him with the framework and data for a successful presentation that he made to top management. I obtained access to the other division through contacts made while accompanying my manager as he interviewed a number of executives to obtain evaluations of their experiences at a particular out-company management training program. Those who ran this program had approached the company to secure support to extend their program as a solution to international political conflicts.

Interaction with Respondents. Most of my contacts were with my respondents — managers and executives whom I observed in their day-to-day activities and with whom I conducted intensive interviews. As with most researchers who utilize interviews and observational techniques, I had to initiate the interaction. I had to define for them their expectations of my role. There was, of course, no guarantee that they would be willing to accept my definition of myself and my role. It therefore became important to control the context in which they first encountered me as well as the plausibility of my definition. For example, when interviewing field managers I had to prevent them from defining me as just another headquarters official sent out to gather information that might be used to evaluate them or to threaten their autonomy. Fortunately, many of them first encountered me as I sat in the back of the room taking notes during a series of meetings where the two levels of management above them were also present. This provided evidence that I was observing their bosses as well as them — something which they had not seen done before. Higher management's lack of caution in front of me plus the uniqueness of my behavior made it easier to distinguish myself from those who were seen as agents of headquarters and, hence, left me freer to define myself to the field managers.

As is common with other sociologist-researchers I repeatedly had to define myself to those who had never met a sociologist. Perhaps this process could be said to involve the researcher in an *asymmetrical role,* for the researcher is totally socialized into the role of interviewing a succession of respondents who are likely never to have been respondents before. However, I could only partially utilize the techniques of social researchers who carry out such a role for I was part of the same organization as my respondents who, being in communication with each other, were able to take part in defining my role. For example, I wanted to obtain observational as well as interview data. The respondents could have objected to my presence at meetings. They did ask me to leave meetings prior to the entrance of top corporate officials whenever these officials were expected to be critical of the division. But they did permit me to remain at most meetings including those where profit figures were discussed.

I was not an academically based researcher who is perceived as a temporary entrant into the organization or society he studies, rather I had a unique and undeveloped job as a permanent member of the organization.[8] However, my respondents not only took my permanence for granted but also assumed that I had an already established role. They insisted on trying to define my place in the organization because they were more comfortable with someone who was part of their system. Thus, my position differed from that of the anthropologist who spends time with his tribe or the sociologist involved in a community study — for they are perceived as sojourners in the system.

Managers and executives tried to ascertain my place in the organization by asking "Who do you work for?" It was not enough for members to know my title or the name of my department. Interestingly, the organization was so complex that interpersonal relations were almost as important here as in a very small organization. For the power of an organizational unit was frequently determined by the personal power of its leader, not just by the function the unit performed. This diminished the usefulness of the role concept in analyzing the organization. It may also have made it easier for a person with an "undefined role" to get around.

The high frequency of the question, "Who do you work for"? is an index of organizational complexity, for the question was posited most often in those parts of the organization where there were many relatively undefined roles. Also the higher level members of the managerial hierarchy tended to use it more frequently than the lower-level ones. Many persons also asked this question (as well as "Who do you report to?") in order to find out where the information I obtained would be going. They assumed that everything that was studied would be reported to persons above them.

Over time I found that to succeed I had to be defined as someone: a) who was a member of the organization, b) who was in a neutral position, c) who could be trusted, d) who was knowledgeable about the organization, and e) who had "inside" information.

It was an important advantage to be seen as a member of the organization. The management members identified closely with the corporation and did not wish to "wash dirty linen in public." But they made complaints to me about company policies and about specific officials, complaints that they would not voice to outsiders.

Quite naturally they were suspicious of anyone who came around asking questions. Not only did they identify closely with the organization but they were members of a hierarchy and therefore carefully guarded their responses to others both above and below. It was acknowledged, although not quite accepted, that the executives "managed" the information they sent to the lower levels. In addition the top management made continual requests for information from below. What was not so widely recognized was that those at the lower levels "managed" the news that went up. Although the top management knew they lacked certain information from below, they did not realize the amount of distortion that entered into the information they did receive.

I was able to gain the trust of respondents over time in part through the use of certain tactics. For example, respondents frequently asked me about the effectiveness or motivations of other persons in the organization. Or they asked what these others thought of them. By refusing to answer and by chastising them for asking such questions I was better able to convince them that I would keep their confidences. This was especially effective when I refused to comment on the questioner's subordinate, for such was contrary to normal hierarchical expectations. On one occasion I did go so far as to indicate to higher management that there were some managers who had not cooperated. When questioned I refused to be more specific, again reinforcing my claim to neutrality in their eyes.

I tried to extend my neutrality by remaining free of any hierarchical identity. I tried to maintain the undefined nature of the level of my role whenever dealing with higher executives. This was one of the reasons I was evasive when asked about who I worked for. Similarly, although sponsored from above I was frequently able to gain acceptance at lower levels of management because of the undefined nature of my level.

But to get the information I wanted I needed to be more than trusted — I needed to be respected. Respondents simply would not "open up" to someone they did not think competent. Competence is, in fact, probably the most overlooked variable in the study of interpersonal relations. I had to indicate that I knew a good deal about the area I was studying. I had to prove that I was knowledgeable about the organization, that I possessed "inside" information, and that I could give the respondents new insights about themselves or their organization.

I was able to demonstrate my competence through the use of questions that "got to the heart of the matter" and that could only be asked by an insider. It was also important that I showed that I knew when the respondent's answers were evasive or unclear. For example, when a field-service manager responded with the infrequent reply that his relations with the sales manager were excellent I would ask him about specific maintenance codes. One such set of codes was used to distinguish repair work necessitated by improper factory performance from that of an installation adjustment requested by the customer. In the former case the charge would go against factory costs and in the latter against the sales manager's budget. The sales manager could put subtle pressure on the service managers, who were located far from the factory. It was a key question that indicated I knew one of the areas of strain between sales and service.

Patterns of Avoidance and Noninteraction. One's perspective in an emergent role is partly formed through patterns of avoidance and non-interaction. The incumbent of a potential role soon learns to be especially careful of those whose work might overlap with his or of others who might be threatened by his existence.

I tried, for example, to avoid any confrontation with the organization department of the corporation. This group had the responsibility to recommend alternative organizational arrangements and the movement of key management personnel throughout the organization. The organization department exerted more power and authority than I could cope with effectively. I was located in the relatively weak personnel department, whereas the organization department was an autonomous unit reporting directly to the president.

Instead, then, of confronting a powerful and established department I attempted to by-pass it and gradually establish myself within the system as a whole. I met with the organization department in an early attempt to gain support for my efforts. But it became clear that they were antagonistic and would offer no support. They at first said they were concerned with my " . . . stirring things up — unlike the physicist who does not affect what he studies." I then attempted to make sure they would at least remain neutral and not block me. Thus, I did not discourage their depreciation of social science: "There is a gap between behavioral scientists and what goes on in organizations." I was satisfied that they saw me as harmless. For instance, one of them said:

> We're working in different areas . . . . we're making operating decisions about organizations and you are research; we're too busy to do that.

Managers in one part of a complex organization seldom make an effort to get rid of another unit if the unit does not directly affect these managers — even if they think the unit is a waste of money.

It was not enough simply to avoid obvious confrontations. I learned that the corporation was a complex one with characteristics of a plural society. The information I provided would, at times, help one group but be a threat to others. For example, I avoided pushing my views about a controversy over the creation of an incentive scheme for executives. Whatever I said was bound to antagonize one of the adversaries. I could not avoid getting caught in all controversies but I did attempt to select those issues on which I would take a stand. I was quite willing, for example, to struggle for the right to choose the problems I would study. At times I had to state an opinion and to carry out some applied research. But I did not want my applied efforts to threaten anyone who, in turn, could affect my basic research. As my manager warned me:

> Avoid speaking or collecting data about events within our own department. It puts people on the defensive and may jeopardize both you and my other research projects.

The Process of Research: Additional Strains and Strategies. Strains are inevitable in any emerging situation, and a variety of strategies must be developed to handle them. So far I have discussed the strains and strategies involved in obtaining access to data; I will now deal with additional ones involved in the ongoing research process.

An Emergent Role in an Emergent Unit. The strain of role emergence was intensified because I was not just an individual researcher; I was also a member of a research unit — a unit whose role was as experimental and emergent as my own. The unit as such was more visible than any individual researcher. The management immediately above our unit was more concerned with the activities of a group of individuals than with those of a single individual. They had to account for a unit with an important budget line.

Each of us in the unit was simultaneously aware of the problems of our unit as an entity and of our relations to the unit and to each other. We had to pay attention to the problematic existence of the unit as well as to the existence of our individual roles. It was, for instance, possible for the unit to disappear but for the members of it to remain in the organization, although dispersed to other parts.

My choice of research problems was affected by my membership in a specific unit, for my universe was limited to the population of this organization. Moreover, each member of the research unit had to choose a different group to study. We had to divide up our areas very carefully in order to avoid internal conflicts within the unit and to avoid overlapping areas of study. Several persons studied workers, one studied salesmen, and I studied management. Those who studied workers each took a separate division to study. Each then tended to become an area specialist rather than a specialist on a social process.

We might have combined forces to work on the same organizational problem, but in all probability our efforts would not have been successful. We had joined the organization at different times, and we were uncertain enough about our role and status without having to cope with the task of combining our efforts effectively. There was no one who could assume direct professional authority over the group and coordinate the various efforts, for our credentials were rather evenly matched. And we had no guidelines that could be used to organize the work of the group as a whole.

Reference Group Conflicts. In attempting to forge a role for myself I was under the constant influence of groups with whom I identified and others with whom I had to deal in order to succeed. My relationships — to my superiors in the organization, to sociology in both its concrete and its abstract forms, to my respondents, and to my colleagues in the research unit — were all interdependent and in conflict with one another.

Although I had some problems in my relations with respondents, this relationship proved to be an easy one: perhaps because I formally owed them nothing or perhaps because as a knowledgeable and neutral observer I offered them an opportunity to discuss hierarchically sensitive matters with impunity. For example, during an initial meeting with a plant manager he maintained that plant goals were set by the plant with division headquarters holding a veto power. As I established my neutrality, he revised this statement to say that they set goals jointly. Finally, when I questioned him about a goal that appeared to me to be set from above he replied: "That was a hold our nose and swallow kind of situation." He then followed with a long account of his problems with headquarters and of his attempts to maintain autonomy.

My most difficult relationships were those with my immediate superiors and were mainly caused by the way these relationships clashed with my relationships to my respondents. For example, although I was paid to do research I was once accused of devoting too much attention to the division I was studying to the neglect of my "responsibilities" to my parent unit. However, as befits an emergent role, the nature of this "responsibility" had not and could not have been clearly defined. My research was supposed to be of benefit mainly to the operating units I studied. Actually my superiors, as part of the normal management hierarchy, were eager to advance themselves in the organization and looked to me and my colleagues for data that would initiate or back successful programs with which they could identify. As one old-time manager advised my own immediate manager:

> You're working for a succession of salesmen [top managers usually came from marketing] who come and go but each tries to use a new gimmick and research is now that. So just sit tight and you will get raises and bigger staffs and bigger offices. And when it all settles down you will have your function and be better off.

An example of the emergent nature of my role is provided by contrasting the above accusation of irresponsibility to an incident that occurred much earlier in my employment. I had been accused by my manager of not getting "out" into the organization enough and not making sufficient contacts to establish myself. But, whereas I was first thought to be too dependent upon my superior for establishing myself, I was later considered by my superiors to be too well established with other persons.

The better my relationships with the persons I studied the more independent I could become of my superiors. But this kind of independence went against the expectations of a hierarchical organization. For example, one of my colleagues was invited by his informants to be an observer at a high-level conference that included these informants. This led to resentment on the part of the higher management (located in the personnel department) because the invitation did not go through proper channels. The head of personnel saw this as a negation of his position, for he was unable to separate the role of a researcher from that of a member of his department who would represent the unit's operating responsibilities.

My task was further complicated because the interests of the personnel department overlapped with those of all operating divisions. It was difficult for me to study the structure of the organization and yet neglect a unit that had so much to do with the rest of the organization. But it was more difficult to study the higher personnel managers if these were the very persons who evaluated me and my colleagues.

Conflicts with my superiors also arose over my identification with sociology. Although one of my specified responsibilities was to keep abreast of my field, my professional orientation led to uneasiness on the part of my superiors. A professional orientation implies an attachment to work uniquely identified with the "self." To my superordinates, work aimed at a professional audience meant that I was "out for myself" rather than loyal to the organization. Consequently, I had to lean over backwards to show concern for the needs of the organization as my superiors saw them, although these might be different from the needs as I saw them.

In any case I had sufficient personal motivation to ensure that I would try to provide useful material to the organization. As I indicate below, I did have a problem of over-rapport with the respondents. However, I felt free to define for myself what was for the good of the organization and to employ criteria that were different from those used by others above me in the organization. As a member of the organization I considered myself as legitimate as anyone else to specify the relationship between my responsibilities and the goals of the organization.

The academic community served as more than just a reference group for me. It not only provided alternative career opportunities that gave me a base from which to bargain within my employing organization, it also enabled my colleagues and me to utilize outsiders to impress upon the corporation the need for our kind of research and the need for providing the proper setting for it. We tried to acquaint academics with our problems whenever we thought these persons might be retained as consultants by the company. We did not directly ask for their help but simply made sure they were favorably disposed toward us in case an opportunity arose for them to "put in a good word" for our efforts.

There was a good deal of ambivalence over this use of consultants, however, because it left our "turf" open to encroachment by outside researchers. Although formal requests from outsiders to do research in the organization were normally referred to us, there was always the chance that an outsider might establish informal relations with our top executives and by-pass us.

An awareness of the effects of socialization processes enables one to pick the group into which he wishes to be socialized. For example, I had the choice of increasing or decreasing my contacts with outside professional colleagues. I was aware that the internal discussions about the necessity of publishing and of obtaining favorable conditions for writing occurred whenever one of the social scientists in the unit returned from an academic meeting. This knowledge spurred me to attend such meetings in order to sustain my scholarly values. I made a concerted effort to attend sociology conventions and to present papers there. Contacts with academics also helped me to maintain a degree of vocational freedom by providing me with the opportunity to "bank" the results of a socialization process whose values I could call upon if I wanted to leave the organization. However, other persons avoided such meetings for, by cutting themselves off from former groups, they were able to identify more strongly with the organization for which they now worked.

My colleagues and I were also subject to pressures from various conflicting groups within the organization. Our data were always susceptible to use by different factions, and there was little we could do to avoid certain power clashes in the organization. For instance, because of his studies of workers and of work standards one of my colleagues became involved in conflicts between the manufacturing and engineering departments. Specifically, one executive's career was hindered because survey data results slowed up a work standards program that he had advocated. As one nonresearcher said: "Few people are anxious to get in the middle of work standards now. It doesn't take a Ph.D. to tell that." In my own case, some of my findings confirmed certain claims made by advocates of an early retirement program. And my data on marketing management resulted in changing the way salaries were distributed among managers of different-sized offices.

The process of studying the organization causes some change in it. This raises serious questions about the possible permanency of basic social research roles within any one organization. It is significant that many students of management have become more interested in accomplishing change than in doing research. And where they have concentrated on research it has been mainly to study the processes of change in management.

Basic Research as a Strategy. Because of the emergent nature of our role my colleagues and I got directly involved in the struggle over the merits of basic vs. applied research. The members of management wanted researchers to do work having immediate or obvious applicability. But most good researchers, given their academic background and the present market for academic employment, are interested in basic research and will not enter industry. Under these circumstances it is irrelevant that basic knowledge can flow from applied research.

The personnel department was divided into two units — basic research and applied research. We defined ourselves as basic researchers in order to maintain control over our activities. We consciously used the terms "basic" and "applied" as ideological weapons and tried to maintain the split between the basic and applied units in the department despite the lack of theoretical merit in making such a distinction. For instance, our unit was under constant pressure to help solve day-to-day personnel problems; therefore, we urged management to provide themselves with adequate staff to deal with these problems. But in trying to clarify the distinction between basic and applied research, we probably made some tactical errors at this point. For we depreciated the efforts of the applied researchers instead of praising them and urging the organization to utilize them more often. We might have gained more autonomy if we had done so. But this is an ex post facto judgment. We were afraid the applied workers, if they became more influential, might narrow the scope of our research. And if they had been able to better serve the organization we might have become expendable.

Basic research implies long-range research without any immediate results or benefits. We wanted to make this "range" as long as possible. To this end, we tried to free ourselves from constant evaluation by persons above. They were unfamiliar with our work and its ultimate benefits; they were certain to become uneasy if they evaluated us too often. It is difficult to evaluate someone engaged in long-range projects, especially when the work may never produce measurable results.

In summary, then, my basic research orientation proved useful in three ways: This was the kind of research I wanted to do. It was also useful as a tactic in gaining autonomy. And it helped convince my respondents of my neutrality. They could see that whatever the results of my research, it was a long-range activity that was not likely to affect their present position.

Strains of Total Involvement. There was constant danger of over-rapport with individual respondents, with the respondents as a group and hence with the organization as a whole, or with the solution of certain problems. Social researchers have frequently pointed out the problems of over-rapport with respondents.[4] The chances of this happening are greater, however, when one is totally involved within an organization. The isolation from professional colleagues heightens this danger, for it throws the researcher back into the organization for interpersonal involvements. For example, during the course of my study a manager bitterly complained to me about his inability to see the vice-president about a program that had seemingly just received complete support from the president after three and a half years of equivocation. I then indirectly reminded the vice-president about seeing the involved manager by asking the vice-president if he had been following up on the newly approved program. I am not sure I did it as part of my research in order to hear his reply and observe his behavior or whether I did it: a) because of my identification with the manager, b) because I identified with the division and thought this was the best course of action, or c) because I became interested in an organizational problem as such and wanted to see if I could solve it.

As a member of an organization, the sociologist becomes subject to the norms of the organization. I gained access to my data because of this membership. Thus, any deviation from the norms of the organization threatened my rapport with respondents and my legitimate position in the system. Total involvement, then, provides a continuing subtle pressure for compromise and even for distortion of what the researcher observes. That strategy of neutrality becomes necessary if one is to acquire the "proper" amount of rapport as well as avoid intra-organizational conflicts.

A peculiar and subtle strain resulted from my constant involvement as an observer in the organization. My entire world view became that of a neutral. I tended to become an "observer" of almost all aspects of my own life. My university-based colleagues could immerse themselves in the activities of their university when they were not actively observing another organization. I had no such dual organizational involvement. To discuss or express opinions about some political and social subjects was to risk the loss of rapport with my respondents. And opinions to exist, must be expressed. I suddenly found that my approach to, for example, international problems was one of neutrality. I had to exercise a special effort to become involved in social and political affairs while "off-duty."

The cultural disparities between academic life and the world of big business lie behind many of the strains I encountered. There are striking differences in political beliefs, in social life, in leisure activities, in income — in the whole way of looking at life. An illustration of a small but irritating difference is that of time dimensions. There is no semester system in industrial organizations and none of the breaking points that are normal to the academic researcher. Definitive beginnings and endings produce a kind of stability that is not present in industry.

There is an attraction to becoming an active member of the organization rather than attempting to maintain a neutral role as a researcher. For the insider (or activist) the monetary rewards and power are clearly greater. The relatively low income of the researcher is one thing when it is relative to those he does not associate with — it is another thing when it is low relative to those by whom he is surrounded. And I was living in a situation where money and power were highly prized. Moreover, the skills of the sociologist are not much different from those required of management. Many of the rewards in large industrial organizations are for intellectual capabilities. Much of management has become oriented to problem solving rather than the older tasks of directing men in accustomed routines. The opportunities for much higher remuneration and the consequent chance for real participant-observation increase the pressures seducing the sociologist from his self-appointed pursuits.

An additional strain was produced by my presumed continuing relationship with the organization. Although an individual sociologist may feel a responsibility to other researchers who may someday study the same organization or community, he frequently does not let this deter him from arriving at conclusions which are antagonistic to the organization and which may limit future sociological research. But I felt constrained by my commitments to the organization and by the presence of other researchers who probably would remain after I left.

Introspection and Choice. In order to construct a role and thereby reduce uncertainty I came to rely upon increased introspection. Psychoanalysis aims at providing us with greater control of ourselves by making us more aware of the "forces" within us. Sociology, and especially the sociology of knowledge, seeks to clarify the manner in which our ideas and actions are affected by our values, our status, and our various reference groups. Inasmuch as we are then better able to pick and choose the pressures we wish to be subjected to, we can attain greater freedom of choice.

When I asked members of management about their future careers many answered with pride: "I just do my work and let the future take care of itself." But I could not, in an emergent role, "just do my work"; there was no self-defined job to do. Whether I wanted to or not I could not live indefinitely with uncertainty. I had to take an active part in creating specific expectations about my role if I was to function adequately. I believe these patterns hold for almost all emergent-role situations.

Introspection should be easier for a social scientist who carries out an emergent role. He is trained to recognize the effects of social interaction. And the more factors an incumbent is aware of the more planning he can do. This, too, heightens the process of introspection.

It is quite apparent that the degree of introspection varied from one researcher to the next within this organization, although it would be difficult to measure such variation. But an index of introspection might be available if groups rather than individuals are studied. My colleagues and I met about once a month to discuss the strategies and tactics that would enable us to better establish our roles in the organization. In addition there were frequent informal discussions. This activity was not peculiar to us, for some nonresearch groups in the organization met to discuss the lack of definition in their jobs.

Introspection was necessary for me because I was continually faced with choices provided by the conflicting alternatives thrust up by various reference groups. For example, at one point I had to decide to either stop my interviewing in order to produce an immediate report for my superiors or risk their great displeasure and continue interviewing in order to insure that I had an adequate sample to satisfy the needs of the division I was studying. I chose the latter course because I considered it to be the right one and because it was necessary for the kind of role definition that I was seeking. My conscious identification with my profession made it easier to take whatever risks were involved.

With so many divergent groups — all with different reward systems employing different criteria — there was a good deal of personal ambiguity but also a greater opportunity to gain control over the definition of my role. In the incident cited above I was able to insist on completing the interviews and to risk my superior's displeasure not only because of the ties to my profession but also because of the many contacts I had made throughout the organization — particularly with my respondents. It was possible not only to be many things to many people but to choose which people and, sometimes, which things.

The Effects of My Emergent Role on Research

Effects on Methods. I have already indicated that the research designs of my colleagues and myself were limited by the nature of our group. Our research designs were also affected by the structure of other groups in the organization. But detailed knowledge concerning these groups or "publics" was not available to us at first. And questionnaire surveys, for example, can be carried out within an organization only if the researcher knows which publics are relevant. For this reason and because there was a paucity of knowledge about business management, my studies initially had to be exploratory. It was only after two years of observing and interviewing that I used a questionnaire survey.

The need to report the results of our studies to management also affected the kinds of research techniques I employed. The results had to be interesting and clear to a lay audience and presented in such a way that the audience could see "action potentials."

Although I could employ factor analysis for analytical purposes I was in no position to present my data in this form. Using scales with two extreme anchoring points was satisfactory for correlations and multivariate analysis, but such scales did not produce the clear marginals one obtains from individually labelled response categories. However, if my presentation was simple and understandable, it then appeared that I had spent too much time on the analysis of my data.

Many executives tended to be dubious about social science. Since they considered themselves to be experts on their own organization, any findings only confirmed what they had "known all along." For this reason, I sought to "trap" them in my presentations. Before flipping over a chart I would ask them to guess what the findings were. Quite often they were unaware of certain contradictions in their knowledge, of the different ways data could be put together, and of new ways of looking at customary facts. This is of course not to deny that I learned more from them as a group than they from me.

But these examples are trivial compared to the distortions and unanalyzed data caused by the pressure for results and restrictions on time. Because our relationship to the organization was both an emergent and a continuing one, the results of any study directly affected the possibility of further studies by the involved researcher as well as by the rest of us. This led us to examine the data in order to uncover problems that management had not been aware of. The more difficult it was to secure permission for a study or to include sensitive questions in a questionnaire the more we felt we had to justify ourselves by providing results that had a payoff.

We were under great pressure to forego analysis and to conduct surveys that would provide immediate feedback to the corporation. Although we were allowed more time to do our work than is the case with most management projects it was still less time than in the academic community. For this reason we were led to neglect the literature in our field. Indeed there was even pressure not to use such literature unless it could be shown to be directly relevant to a *current* company problem. Executives were not willing to give much time to any particular report. Reports had to make a major point and make it "soon." Witness this communication from a superior of mine to his superior:

> I have received a draft copy of Dr. Goldner's report. In view of our interest in this particular subject, we asked him to speed up its preparation. I have attached a copy for your review. The reading time is about 18 to 20 minutes.

To achieve our goal of promoting basic as opposed to applied research we had to discover some means of translating the results of basic research into an applied form. Our unit therefore initiated a search for someone who could bridge the gap and serve the role of intermediary. But we were never successful in finding someone with the requisite skills and interests. Actually this was an attempt by persons in an incumbent role to create viable relations with other persons and groups in the organization through the creation of another role.

My relationship to respondents also affected the reporting of my research results. I had to categorize data so as not to reveal the identity of respondents or of units. If I was describing a particular position in the organization I could not actually identify that position unless there were enough incumbents to mask personal identities. Whenever the research involved data about particular levels in the organization my colleagues and I would first make it clear to the interviewees how the information would be reported. Those of my colleagues who were studying company plants regularly communicated the survey results to the plant manager before reporting them to his superiors. This gave him the opportunity to study the data and to prepare action programs before being confronted by his superiors. Nevertheless it inevitably involved the researcher in the general evaluation processes of the organization. In summary, there was great opportunity to obtain knowledge and data but great pressures to forestall analysis.

Effects on the Dissemination of Results. The code of ethics tentatively drawn up by the American Sociological Association further illustrates the uncertain nature of my emergent-role situation. The code failed to gain acceptance from the membership, in part because it is possible to stipulate the details of an ethic only after most of the probable situations have been encountered and dealt with.[5] Sociology has simply not reached that stage. The peculiarities of my own undeveloped role certainly would seem to make the code inapplicable. The inability of the proposed ethics code to treat situations other than the most obvious ones was illustrated by the use of the academically based researcher and teacher as the role models for the code.

For example, the code stipulated that questions of publication rights should be settled between a researcher and an organization before the research is initiated. In my research, no one in the organization with whom I dealt had the power to make any commitments about publishing. All they could say was that they were in favor of it. Such a commitment could only be made by the head of the corporation.

As I indicated earlier, no rules concerning my work procedures existed in the organization. There were company policies relevant to publication by physical scientists, but it was clear that there were sufficient differences between physical scientists and social researchers to make these policies inapplicable to my situation. The major focus of such policies was the protection of technical information that might provide a competitive edge vis-à-vis other corporations. My work dealt directly with the "image" of the organization — something about which most organizations seem to be highly sensitive.

I could, of course, have insisted that the question be resolved before I entered the organization. But this would have been an "unfair" demand, for almost no one in the organization had knowledge about social science, about me, or about the purpose of the role I was to create. Also, to have pushed the issue of publication might have killed the role before it even took form.

If commitments concerning the matter of publication could not be made until all aspects of the situation were clear, then it was up to us, the researchers, to try to shape the situation. We attempted to do so by establishing a series of precedents that would make publication of our social research data seem a natural phenomenon.

I started by delivering a paper at an academic convention. But I carefully refrained from submitting the paper to the press section at the meetings. Soon after that, my colleagues presented a paper to an academic group that publishes its proceedings. They had, however, rehearsed their answers to certain questions that might have proved embarrassing to the organization. They also assured their superiors that the meeting would be unattended by newsmen.

Nevertheless, a minor crisis developed. My paper inadvertently received some publicity, prematurely raising the issue of publication. A semi-academic magazine secured a copy through academic channels and, without informing me, built a lead article around the paper. It was picked up by a reporter from a national news weekly who then tracked me down. I stalled him as best I could, but at this point my immediate superior decided to raise the issue with our public relations department. Fortunately the reporter was kind enough to honor a request not to mention the company involved. The public relations department, although charged with responsibility for ties with the press, was really the last unit of the organization we would have wanted to involve; it was their responsibility to control the company's image — clearly a censor's role. It could have resulted in the public relations department demanding that our emergent unit submit all reports to them in advance of publication. This, of course, would have been untenable.

Our attempt to establish a series of precedents is another aspect of the process of role emergence. Thus, I sought to defer publication until the situation was ripe, just as I had earlier deferred calling my existence to the attention of top management until the appropriate time.

Implications: The Ethics of Ambiguity

On the basis of my experience with an emergent role I can now draw certain implications for the ethics of social research. I begin with the premise that it makes little sense to talk about relations with other persons within an organization without stipulating particular individuals or groups. Ethics, then, is an especially interpersonal concept. Peculiarly enough, it seems to be a "subject-involving" word implying one-sided action. What word exists for the recipient of ethical action? What expectations do we have the right to entertain about the ethical behavior of others? And how do these expectations arise? For example, I frequently encountered respondents who expected me to give them information that would involve my acting unethically toward others in the organization. They expected me to be ethical in my dealings with them, but to break other persons' confidences. This was particularly true in the case of superordinates vis-à-vis their subordinates. Although those below welcomed information about those above, they did not "expect" it. This is an example of a more general phenomenon in professional-client relationships, where the client expects the professional — e.g., doctor or lawyer — to depart from norms of impartiality and impersonality when dealing with him.

There is not just the problem of the ambiguity of ethics. More important is the question of the *ethics of ambiguity*. The incumbent of an emergent role is constantly forced to take ethical positions in the face of ambiguity.

Throughout this paper I have dealt with ethical problems and most of them have been shrouded in ambiguity. There was, however, one issue that illustrated the ease of taking an ethical stand when the issue is clear cut. I accepted a position in this company with the stipulation that I would never study the blue-collar work force. For whatever the reasons, I did not want to take part in what I conceived to be a technique for worker manipulation. I had no such fear for managers — I believed they could take care of themselves and, in any case, I was more interested in horizontal than in vertical relations.

It was easy to take a stand on one "side" or the other of this problem. The issue had already been explored at length and all the factors had been exhaustively discussed.[6] I remained firm on my initial stand, but I am not now so sure of my bland assumption that managers can take care of themselves; for in this organization they have increasingly become the work force. My data were inevitably more available to those above than to those below. Although I did try to feed data about those above to those below my only opportunity to do this was in the management school run by the company and even there my effort was an innovation.

How does one determine what is proper or improper when involved in undefined situations? The answer for my colleagues and myself was to keep the question in the forefront and to participate in defining the situation. The sociology of knowledge enabled me to better define ethical issues and to make ethical choices, just as it helped me to understand the various pressures involved in my emergent role and to decide to which I would be most responsive.

The profession of sociology, in my judgment, is at present in no position to lay out a detailed code of ethics. But we can and should encourage a continuing dialogue. We can and should collect "situations" and problems and consider as many alternatives as can be raised. A set of ethics for our profession will eventually emerge and perhaps become codified. There is no reason why we cannot consciously have a hand in shaping it.

Notes to the Chapter

*This paper was prepared as part of a continuing program of research on career mobility in organizations. Partial support for this program has been supplied by the Faculty Research Fund of the Columbia University Graduate School of Business. I owe a debt of gratitude to Gideon Sjoberg who fortunately served as a working editor rather than as a compiler. R. R. Ritti made a number of helpful comments on an earlier draft and Arthur Stinchcombe provided initial encouragement to develop the emergent role concept.

1. The sociological literature on roles is voluminous. For one of the most comprehensive studies, with references, see: N. Gross, W. S. Mason, and A. W. McEachern, *Explorations in Role Analysis* (New York: John Wiley & Sons, 1958).

2. For one of the recent studies of role conflicts, with an extensive bibliography, see: Robert L. Kahn *et al., Organizational Stress: Studies in Role Conflict and Ambiguity* (New York: John Wiley & Sons, 1964).

3. For a recent summary of articles that have dealt with the problems of research in organizations see: W. Richard Scott, "Field Methods in the Study of

Organizations," in James G. March (ed.), *Handbook of Organizations* (Chicago: Rand McNally & Co., 1965), 261–304.

4. For example: S. M. Miller, "The Participant Observer and 'Over-Rapport'," *American Sociological Review,* 17 (February, 1952), pp. 97–99.

5. A brief history of the A.S.A. code of ethics is presented in the *American Sociological Review,* 29 (December, 1964), p. 904. Two letters from Howard S. Becker and Eliot Friedson protesting the proposed code appear in the *American Sociological Review,* 29 (June, 1964), pp. 409–10.

6. An example of this debate is provided by the following: Clark Kerr and Lloyd H. Fisher, "Plant Sociology: The Elite and the Aborigines," in Mirra Komarovsky (ed.), *Common Frontiers of the Social Sciences* (Glencoe, Ill.: The Free Press, 1957), 281–309; Conrad M. Arensberg and Goeffrey Tootell, "Plant Sociology: Real Discoveries and New Problems," in Komarovsky, *ibid.,* 310–37.

CHAPTER TWELVE

The Low-Caste Stranger in Social Research*

ARLENE KAPLAN DANIELS

In the study under discussion, I, as a woman sociologist, did research on subgroups in the U.S. Army for three years. I entered some facets of the lives of officers, received confidences, and obtained information in depth about certain officer groups. If women can study male societies from which they are specifically excluded, it may be that other groups can be studied by individuals visibly alien — or in subordinate status — to the subjects: Negroes can study white colonials or southerners; recognizable Jews can study anti-Semitic organizations. It is not argued that such observers will learn the same things that less alien persons might. Some perspectives will be lost, others will be gained in the mutual assessment by the group and the researcher. The thesis presented here is that under such circumstances of clear separation or alienation from those observed, the researcher comes to the group as a stranger in purest form. Unlike the stranger who is an immigrant coming to stay,[1] the stranger in this instance encounters a situation fraught with all the opportunities for confidences and intimacies which Simmel describes.[2]

The compromises and the resolutions of conflict between the researcher and the researched indicate that, contrary to many of the accepted understandings,[3] researchers can penetrate a society even when they do not fit into traditionally acceptable categories. The description of tactics and strategies used by the subjects to resist entry and the countertactics and strategies employed to overcome such resistance are discussed here, not so much to present the mistakes and pitfalls to be avoided, but rather to show some

267

of the inevitable difficulties and creative possibilities that arise when the researcher seeks close contact with a resistant group.

The Initial Shock of Recognition: "Breaking and Entry"[4]

When I first began research under military auspices, it was generally expected by the sponsors that I would confine myself to a questionnaire survey of Army recruits, administered for me by Army officers. Secondarily, the sponsors hoped that members of the various officer corps with whom I came into contact would observe my behavior and that some research skill and interest would accrue to them in the process.

At first there were no particularly serious problems connected with conducting the survey. A pre-test was administered satisfactorily and we began data collection. Soon, however, it became clear that the military officers assigned to administer the questionnaire would require considerable supervision. Preliminary results showed that questionnaire administration was not uniform, and that the groups selected for administration did not conform to the principles of sample selection originally established.

At this point, the discrepancy between the position I felt I had and the position that others accorded me in the situation became evident. The military officers resented the introduction of a sociologist, a civilian, and a female into their midst. Resentment wavered between the active and the passive, depending upon the amount of pressure I exerted to get the tasks accomplished in a manner satisfactory to me.

From the officers' point of view, the situation was complicated by difficulty in assessing how much power I actually had and what that power meant when translated into military terms. In other dealings with civilians operating in the military structure, they were accustomed to the understandings which put civil service ratings into the military framework. Further, military officers are familiar with the civilian as consultant — where the civilian appears as adviser or lecturer with little formal control.

But I came as a principal investigator on a research grant sponsored by the officers' own headquarters. It was difficult, at first, for them to determine how far this headquarters organization might be willing to support me. Also, they were ignorant of the exact terms of my contract: how much time, money, and staff I could have at my disposal.

In my view, I had a clear mandate from the "home office" in Washington and initially imagined that the office providing liaison officers also offered complete support. The liaison office chief had indicated enthusiasm for the project; in addition he had gone out of his way to inform the Washington office of this enthusiasm and his personal desire to help. When instances of inefficiency or appalling omissions in agreed-upon procedures came to my attention, I felt the original commitment to the project should be firmly recalled. The force of my argument, unfortunately, was considerably diminished by factors not at first known to me. The liaison chief was counting heavily on his declaration of research interest to spare him from an unpleasant assignment which loomed as an alternative. Once this shadow was dispelled, much of his enthusiasm for the research evaporated. A noticeable, parallel decline could also be observed among his junior officers. My difficulties were compounded by my inability to see that keeping my helpers in the dark about the terms of my contract might be useful. When approached for this information, I promptly gave it. Strong support from the granting officers would have been indicated by a five-to ten-year commitment. I freely acknowledged that I had a three-year commitment. Since their appreciation of the military context was keener than mine, this information indicated to them that I was not in a powerful position.

I had imagined that a clear understanding of the conditions would spur them on to more earnest endeavors so that we might all finish within the agreed time. In the view of the liaison chief and his officers, my attitude was overbearing, demanding, and all too aggressive. Possibly, they felt, it was indicative of a character and behavior disorder — that is to say, I must be rash to the point of madness to behave in so imperious a fashion when I had so little power.

In addition, from their perspective, habits of secrecy or caution in divulging any information not strictly necessary were an important part of their "armamentarium." Concern for protection of vital secrets is, naturally, salient to any responsible official in the military system. Such concern, however, is sometimes diffused into a general air of suspicion and caution in many areas little related to the protection of secrets vital to the general welfare. The rationale is, of course, that habitual discretion will prove useful during moments of difficulty. Accordingly, my readiness to communicate the terms of my contract indicated to them a foolishly trusting nature. In my view, no secrets of any importance were involved. The information was available to these officers upon application to the granting office had they been inclined to ask.

But the behavior which these officers found most difficult to tolerate was my assumption that I was the director in the situation. In their view, they were at most interested consultants and advisors. In my view, they had volunteered to act as my assistants. The contradictions in perspectives were sharply revealed as some of the drudgery of the project became apparent. The terms of service do not permit officers to receive additional payments for work connected with military or federal concerns. Consequently, I could not smooth over the difficulties through that one traditional method of accommodation.

The problem was eased when I hired additional assistants from the university community. But much of the checking and interpreting of official records could only be accomplished by persons within the system. Accordingly, I befriended a number of enlisted men in the military organization who performed some of the necessary tasks voluntarily.[5] From the enlisted man's position, my own apparently seemed enviable and my presentation as a director of research was acceptable.

Although I managed ultimately to resolve most of the data-processing difficulties, interpersonal problems with the officers were exacerbated at each contact by my initial obtuseness about and resistance to the demeanor they thought I should exhibit. My manner tended toward the brisk, businesslike, and friendly. I usually entered offices quickly and in an assured manner. I looked each officer directly in the eye, presented my hand for a firm grasp, and proceeded to an agenda for the meeting which I had drawn up and distributed in advance. I never hesitated to interrupt, contradict, or control the conversation, pulling it back to the agenda when necessary. If any jokes or pleasantries were introduced, I initiated them.[6]

I came to understand that their views of the situation were not in accord with mine as time passed and my directives were politely ignored; letters went unanswered and had to be supplemented with phone calls and exhortatory visits. Two main lines of opposition in response to my demeanor developed. One line took the form, in Army psychiatric terminology, of "passive aggressive" behavior. My military colleagues would be tardy for appointments with me, cut them short, or postpone them without notice.[7] Sometimes they would miss appointments entirely. When we met, they would refuse to meet my glance, and they would make perfunctory excuses or evasive remarks about why some phase of the research could not be kept within a schedule.

The other main line of opposition was to respond in a frankly seductive fashion. Glittering eyes and roving glances would force me to conclude that my colleagues were not willing to cooperate about the business on hand by offering it their full attention.[8]

I finally understood that the pattern of resistance was becoming fixed and could not be attributed to the vagaries of any one officer. I interpreted both sulky and seductive responses as expressions of hostility and resentment against a woman exhibiting inappropriate behavior to a man.[9]

In addition, they were indicating that my behavior was inappropriate for an outsider — a civilian, and one trained in a profession different from theirs. Resistance was an indication that I expected to be "in" and accepted much faster than they were willing to move.[10] It is difficult, at such moments, for persons "in the know" not to haze the newcomer. Scheff discusses this tendency as a tactic to neutralize or discredit the newcomer in case he should also have aspirations to be an innovator.

> On one occasion a social worker was asked his opinion of a matter being discussed in staff meetings. Since the worker had been on the ward only a week at the time, he was flattered to be brought into the discussion. He proceeded to give his opinion. He later learned that he had been taken in by a ruse. He was purposely asked a question about a problem which the staff knew to be an intricate one, in the hope that he would make a fool of himself.[11]

Unfortunately, relations had deteriorated badly by the time I became aware of these aspects of the situation and it was, at one point, questionable whether the survey could be completed. Furthermore, before I developed mediating and soothing strategies, I exacerbated the conflict by finding means to sidestep the organization formally appointed to help and advise me in accomplishing the research. My fear was that the survey would not be successful. Either the data would be incompletely collected or else the inefficient and haphazard methods used to collect them might result in a collection of unremarkable and indefensible results. At first I considered an interview in depth of a sample from the test group. However, because of resentment at my manner, fear of repercussions, or a genuine belief that it would not be permissible under Army regulations, my liaison officers explained that it was impossible for me to have any systematic — or unsystematic — interviews with troops in basic training. I could not be present in the barracks, in the stockade, in the field, or during classes. I managed to make some limited observations in mess halls, in the dispensaries, and during mass troop dispersions for leave at holiday time. But I could not arrange to speak, directly and privately, with troops or their non-commissioned officers. Consequently, I felt I had no way of knowing how to evaluate answers the subjects would make on questionnaires.[12]

To anticipate possible difficulties in interpreting results, I began to seek out key informants on the post and in other military installations who *were* accessible. I turned from a consideration of how to get around the respondents' gatekeepers to an examination of the gatekeepers themselves. It was at this time that I shifted the orientation of my study from a survey to that of more formal interviewing (and in time this led to giving up my role as director of the project for a more strictly research role as an investigator).

At this point, when it became clear that the liaison officers had become subjects rather than collaborators, my relationships with my military colleagues hit rock bottom. In my view, I was seeking to answer their reasonable question: "What can *she* ever know about the military?" In their view I was setting myself up as a superior in a new way, no longer as director of a joint research effort, but as their observer, casting them in the "specimen" role. In addition, I by-passed them, as channels of authority, as I roamed around the post, meeting new informants and occasionally interviewing people of higher rank and in more powerful or crucial positions, within the military organization, than the liaison officers. If I were to get into any difficulties, raise any embarrassing questions, or "make waves" the liaison officers felt they might be held responsible. And they stopped calling me Mrs. Daniels and started referring to me as "that woman from Palo Alto" or, more simply — and with a shudder — "her." At the same time, the number of seductive gestures also increased.[13]

The sex and status base of contention was forcibly and explicitly outlined when I called for a showdown with one of my laggard military helpers. At first he jested and was evasive about certain of his derelictions in the data collection. As I persisted, however, in calling him to task, he became mocking. "Why should he pay any attention to my admonitions?" I told him I was in charge of the study. "And why did that give me any authority over him?" Formally, of course, he was part of the Army hierarchy and not in my employ. Doggedly I reviewed the history of the collaboration: he had earlier professed a desire to learn something about research and I had agreed to teach him, since independent research by military personnel was a professed hope of his own and of the "home office." And I explained again my professional qualifications for this task. Still mocking however, my collaborator remarked: "These qualifications are all very well; but I happen to be the post bowling champion." I told him that his remark had no bearing on the discussion. He saw that I was getting angry, but rested his case, stating: "Well, I think that it does." I then forcibly expressed my personal views on the proper tone and style for professionals. I stressed the importance of the obligation to do good work in a disinterested and ethical fashion. And I summarized all his deficiencies with regard to these matters. My antagonist also became angry and laid aside his mocking tone to address me quite seriously. As proof of his good faith in our collaboration he pointed out that he had already "taken more" from me than he ever had before from any woman.

As I began to move in a larger circle of military officer informants, I learned the necessity for changing my tone. And, once I was in the field, I abandoned my picture of myself as the director of a research project and returned to the role of student and humble observer. In the transition it was fortunate that I already possessed a low or ambiguous status in the military society. Many persons were eager and able to show me any error of my ways. I learned, for instance, that too friendly an assumption of equality with informants at a dinner table or officers' club bar might result in my getting stuck with a large check when the informants blandly assured me they accepted the privilege of being treated. Or I might receive a lengthy ogling and invitational approach from an officer who knew time was short for conducting an interview. Then, often enough, that same man would be palpably indifferent to the view of gallantry which would require him to offer assistance while I fumbled with the tape recorder, briefcase, purse and umbrella in an attempt to get out a door and down a steep flight of poorly lit, ice-covered steps.

Not all lessons were in the "trial by fire and ice" category, however. Some officers were favorably impressed with my research interests and general demeanor. They would take me aside and give me "tips." One officer, for example, volunteered that his wife was a professional woman also, and so he wished to take the liberty of interesting himself in my welfare. He very kindly suggested that it might be quite inadvisable to slap certain field grade officers on their eagles and call them "colonel, baby," even after being forced to buy them rounds of drinks.

On another occasion, my marginal or subordinate status was brought home to me by an informant who was a military officer. We had appropriated the office of an absent departmental director for our interview. In the course of the interview, another officer, Captain X, known to us both, knocked on the door and came in. The interview was temporarily discontinued. When the intruder showed evidence of staying a long time, I made tentative dismissal gestures: rising, mentioning that soon we must talk together again, and indicating by tone of voice that the interruption ought to be ended fairly quickly. As Captain X still showed no sign of leaving, I walked toward him and said: "I'm afraid you must excuse us; Captain Y can give me only a brief interview this afternoon." Before resuming the interview, however, the informant stopped to remark that I must feel a lot of hostility toward Captain X to "throw him out of the office that way." In his view, so great a command of the situation would not otherwise arise except through feelings of personal animosity. In my view, I was operating on a tight schedule and wanted to capitalize on the opportunity for the interview to the fullest. But the informant did not see how a woman could be so directive except from a wish to degrade or to humiliate a man (and an officer-professional of higher status than a sociologist).

Although my marginal or inferior status was sometimes a handicap, at other times it appeared to make little difference. Some officers, perhaps through boredom or some other disaffection from the system, took an active interest in the content of my research and volunteered extraordinary amounts of time and information. These officers became my first close friends in the military setting. They were not, however, always the most reliable or disinterested informants.[14] Yet, through this group I met other officers who apparently felt that my research would be genuinely useful. One such officer even undertook the responsibility of formal collaboration on some technical reviews of his military specialty which I felt would be useful to me as background for more sociological interests of my own. The collaboration bore some resemblances to that described by Whyte in *Streetcorner Society* as existing between him and Doc.[15] But, of course, status positions were reversed: Doc won his right to equal status with Whyte as his informal collaborator even though he was just a corner boy. I had to struggle for equal status with my informant as his collaborator, since I was just a woman. Even though I initiated and directed our small project, it is really open to question if I ever achieved equality.

The Process of Accommodation

Despite an unpromising beginning, my salvaging and restructuring of the original research program was surprisingly successful. The military organization gave me official, if unenthusiastic, permission to expand the study greatly and also to redirect the research away from a primary concern with the survey. In expanding the study and getting out into the military community, my position changed from that of a director to that of a student. In this role I found more tolerance and acceptance of my presence.

As I moved through various social worlds in pursuit of the information I needed, I learned what I might expect from the inhabitants through a variety of sanctions. One of the main informal sanctions was the "snub direct." For example, I agreed to meet certain officers from my home base of field research in an officers' club bar at an early hour, on the first evening of a convention in Washington, D.C. They had promised to review parts of the program with me and introduce me to persons who should be interviewed. I felt that this was an important appointment and arrived at the bar in good time, before them. Noticing that I was the only woman in the room, and being somewhat uncertain about appropriate cocktail lounge behavior, I sat down at a table and began looking over notes. After some time had elapsed, I glanced around and saw the men I was supposed to meet. Since they almost ostentatiously did not see me, I was in a quandary over the best way to enter the circle. I solved the problem by leaving the bar and re-entering it in a few minutes, going directly to their table.

What I began to learn was that certain kinds of deference to the idea of superior male status had to be paid. Many months later I became friendly enough with one of these men to ask him about his behavior that night. He candidly admitted that he knew I was there, and even that he knew I must be uncomfortable. But he felt that since I had shown I was prepared to move in the company of men as an equal, he and his friends were prepared to let me take whatever discomfort or embarrassment might be attendant — or leave the situation. On that occasion I got "points" for being "plucky."

Certain behavior was considered inappropriate or even insulting from women: a firm hand clasp, a direct eye-to-eye confrontation, a brisk, businesslike air, an assured manner of joking or kidding with equals were all antagonizing. Most galling of all was my naive assumption that, *of course,* I was equal. It was important to wait until equality was *given* me. When I learned to smile sweetly, keep my eyes cast down, ask helplessly for favors, and exhibit explicitly feminine mannerisms, my ability to work harmoniously and efficiently increased. Close and, for me, somewhat ex-aggerated attention to feminine behavior paid off because it showed I was willing to be a "good nigger." I learned the equivalents of the tugged forelock, the shuffle, and the "yassuh boss" of other minority groups.[16]

In addition to what I could learn from my own sometimes painful trial-and-error experiences, I was fortunate in having the active assistance of some friendly informants. One high-ranking officer advised me on how to deal with another high-ranking officer who might, or might not, give me permission to collect some crucial data.

> Under no circumstances should you talk to Shelby before Martin. Martin is very status conscious and resents any interference in his operation . . . The best approach would be a nice cooing little letter to Bix Martin and if he seems willing — a visit with all the semitic charm you can muster. . . . As to Martin, I would play him very cool indeed. As I have indicated before,

flattery will get you everywhere. He is very status conscious and loves attention . . . I wouldn't get into word one of a discussion as to the details of your project until you get your feet in the door and are in a position to flap your eyes at him.

When I found that "flapping my eyes" worked, when I found the permission for collecting data unexpectedly easy and rapid, I really *was* sweetly smiling and grateful.

In addition, I had the advantage of time. As two and then three years passed without my research interests causing the military any embarrassment, the fear that I would "make waves" began to recede. Furthermore, they became accustomed to my oddity: the personal eccentricities that I never managed to eradicate and the sex difference began to fade as novelties.

Understanding the Natives

The literature abounds with descriptions of the process of learning for the social scientist and the mistakes and misunderstandings which arise during that process.[17] When I began Army survey research, long before the possibility of field work arose, I believe I made two serious mistakes. First, I underestimated the extent of the defensiveness which many military officers feel about scrutiny by civilians. My general working assumption, that good or competent professionals would not want to make a career in the military seemed reasonable, and therefore I saw no reason to hide it. After all, there is evidence that long-term careers in the military are chosen at a declining rate by officers who have equal or better advantages outside.[18]

Through my continued interaction with military officers I came to perceive how my view of the situation jarred and unnerved them. Many regular Army officers do debate long and anxiously about whether or not to commit themselves to a military career. Even once committed, other possibilities may arise. On occasion, occupational contingencies may become so unacceptable that resignations are offered and job openings in the civilian market are taken in mid-career. As an indication of the interest in this topic, much Army gossip centers on speculation about who will stay in or get out upon completion of obligated pay-back time for professional training or other advantages. And time is also devoted to gossip about why officer A or B decided to resign, what effect one man's decision might have on another, and so on.[19]

Further, career officers in professions for which there are highly paid civilian equivalents (physicians, lawyers, psychologists) are often ambivalent and resentful about conditions of practice in the military as compared to the more lucrative fields outside. Consequently, certain kinds of questions or mild jests about this topic from an outsider may be very ill-timed. These subjects can be broached only when the informant feels sure that the questioner is not critical of the service; indeed, a neutral attitude is often not sufficient. An inquiry on these topics must come from one who shows evidence of real sympathy for and interest in the plight of the military in the modern world — one who can appear to give genuine respect to the idea of the military mission. The more I could present such interest, the more openly informants revealed their views on this topic. It was a long time before I collected concrete evidence on just how delicate the subject was, as indicated in the quotation below

> Behind the criticism of military people by civilians, those of us who are in active service frequently detect a kind of envy or even jealousy of the privileges and recognition offered to the career soldier. It is more difficult to get a career soldier to discuss in detail the feelings that he has about his service than it is to get him to talk about his relations with his wife.

Through trial and error one could learn not to tread on toes, to turn a sympathetic ear, to ask questions in a way which was acceptable. One demonstrates in a number of ways — certainly not all known to oneself — that an informant's position is considered reasonable by the interviewer; that even where there is no agreement, there is understanding. In my case, some of the explicit demonstrations of knowledge and friendliness were: 1) the development of friendships with officers and their families, a fact which became known in the circles with which I dealt; 2) a show of detailed knowledge of the complicated and technical problems arising in their work — gained through reading special military journals; 3) a willingness to consider and seriously discuss military problems even when these from my point of view had no relevance to the research. Among the inexplicit demonstrations was, no doubt, the reduction in expressions of contempt, despair, anger, boredom, and disgust which show in one's face when one listens to long statements couched in terms of values which are alien or repugnant. A growing fondness for those who were friendly, lively, and interesting in this setting made me more inclined to abate judgment and show sympathy, even when dealing with others who were not so appealing.

The second area of obtuseness on my part was the proper governing of male-female encounters in this setting.[20] Until I learned the special rules governing such encounters, I could never tell what would "put off" an informant. Since the interviews were organized in terms of a schedule, the central part of the interaction presented little problem. The real areas of difficulty centered around arrival and departure. Inappropriate entrance behavior frequently limited or even ruined the value of the interview itself.

In one instance I was more or less saved by the nature of the questions I asked. One informant told me that he had been prepared to throw me out of his office but decided to wait and see what the interview would actually entail. Since he found the questions interesting, he answered them all. In another instance, the informant, a high-ranking officer, indicated he would give me an interview if I first told him all about my study. After I had done so, he told me my interview would have to wait until another appointment, which, later, he refused to grant.

The military fraternity bears some resemblances to a secret society. Simmel remarks that the secret society group may be known "while the membership, the purpose, or the specific rules of the association remain secret."[21] As in the case of any other fraternal orders, the secret may not be so much a substantive one as a device to protect the organization and to repel intruders. The main point of a secret society — or of the secret aspects of a fraternity — may be to emphasize the exclusive nature of the group so as to make it more valuable, both to members and to outsiders.[22]

It is apparent from the foregoing descriptions of my difficulties in adjustment and accommodation that problems stemming from defensiveness about the value and stability of the organization and a wish for exclusiveness as a male fraternity are present. Despite the recent introduction of feminine branches into the military, with their own officer corps, the privileged, separate position of the male officer remains substantially unchanged, at least in the American military service.

Important considerations to keep in mind about fraternal societies with secret — and exclusive — aspirations, involve methods of approach to members and membership. Even when one is eligible for membership, it is important to remember that time is required to complete initiation into such a society. Rites are sometimes lengthy, painful or tedious — and there is no way to avoid progressive steps in advancement, as in the routine of the Masonic Order. In such a system it is not possible to sidestep a regulated order for advancement based on considerations such as age, time in grade, inherited position — any or all of which can outweigh considerations of efficiency or demonstrated ability. In general, of course, promotion in the military reflects consideration of talent and acumen, and inheritance of rank is impossible. Nevertheless, it is normally not possible to achieve meteoric career advancement; first there must be a prescribed minimum amount of time spent in each rank.

Aside from the importance of initiation and promotion through the ranks as necessary parts of a career, such moves also bear significance to the members in terms of their participation in a fraternity. The demeanor of junior officers to senior, and of senior to junior, can often be understood only in terms of the others' perceptions of common membership in a special society.

The following quotation from an interview with a recently promoted Major is an example of the awareness members can have of the significance of their participation in the military society.

> I went to Fort ————— as a captain. When I became a major, the difference was immediately apparent. Jokes about "when are you going to desert us and go out and make money?" A back-handed way of saying 'We're glad that some (professionals) want to stay in the Army.' When I got to be a major I began to be called by my first name by the Commanding Officer and he invited me to official functions: he told me dirty jokes. After I attained my majority, then I could say something like, 'I think we ought to have such and such a piece of equipment' . . . there is more tendency to listen.

One of the important characteristics of such a society is that it is closed to outsiders. Many persons are not eligible for membership. Civilians who have not served, for example, can never understand what the military society involves. A fraternity of this kind, then, is provided with a defense against criticism of its activities and a ready explanation for why some of its activities are inexplicable to outsiders. When I attempted to initiate a procedure for surveying basic trainees, a non-commissioned officer told me that it couldn't be done. When I pressed for reasons, he argued that one would have to go through basic training to understand why what I wanted done was too difficult to undertake. Once one understands something of the Army game, however, one knows that anything is impossible — or possible — in terms of how keenly someone of rank feels about it. When I had support from a commissioned officer, the doubts of the non-commissioned officer vanished.

Although one can minimize the difficulties of dealing with an exclusive, secretive fraternity, it is not possible to eradicate them entirely. Since membership in the fraternity is important to the members, it is extremely important to show by demeanor that one understands this, and to show, if possible, that one regrets one is not, and can never be, a member.

In the case of women observers upon the military scene, too much frank cheerfulness and interest indicates the wrong tone. An exhibition of awe and ill-ease puts officers at ease because it shows them that the woman has a nice understanding of her position. Then officers can have the satisfaction of putting the woman at her ease, allowing her to enter the situation in some degree. A feminine diffidence in shaking hands, entering a room, or finding a chair, provides reassuring cues to the officer. If a woman does not show such demeanor, she puts herself in the position of the guest who takes over, as if not waiting for hospitality to be offered before rushing to the refrigerator for a cold drink or a snack.

The handling of eye contact presents a good illustration of the problem. As Hattersley indicates,[23] women in the general passage of interactions must be careful to avoid challenging or inviting males at whom they look. Such considerations are of particular concern in the military setting. One important activity in many all-male societies is the recounting of amatory adventures and interests. An underlying expectation of this activity is that males are supposed to be constantly in search of sexual opportunities. When such opportunities arise, they are to be briskly and efficiently capitalized.

It is difficult in societies where such ideas are a dominant theme for participants to ignore them, even with good will on both sides. Sometimes, for example, I would find that officers would become remote if I remained in their offices after work hours ended. If I requested a continuation of the interview at another time or place outside the office they would often decline. They would "reject my offer." One officer was at some pains to inform me that he was happily married and "not interested." At first, I found such remarks inexplicable. Later, I understood that the circumstances in which I presented myself were such that informants felt forced into "rejecting my offer." Sometimes they felt pressured into making a counter-offer. Accordingly, the offer would be made with a certain amount of accompanying resentment or defiance. Such problems became particularly acute at dusk. In one instance, my informant and I sat in the gathering gloom of twilight until I found it too difficult to see to write. When I asked if we might have a light turned on, he arose and, with some show of embarrassment and indecision, switched on the lights.

In terms of the military context in which these incidents are embedded, it is necessary to understand two things. One is an assumption, presented above, about the nature of relations between men and women. But the other concerns the value and place of work. Among the professional officers I observed, working overtime — an excessive work orientation — has a negative value. Perhaps because military men may be (technically) on duty twenty-four hours a day, they strongly prize free time and off-duty hours. Staying in an office overtime is usually rated as a *serious* inconvenience.

And a request to stay on at work by a female researcher is often interpreted as a seductive invitation — for what else *could* it be?

A concomitant of the distinctions which are made between maleness and femaleness in identifying the unique characteristics of the military society is a pervasive interest in social drinking. Drinking is institutionalized as a significant part of formal-informal expressions of solidarity and "esprit" within departments of the military organization. Membership in the officer's club may actually be compulsory rather than optional; appearance at what are called "happy hours" or "hi and bye" parties (weekly cocktail parties and parties celebrating promotions and reassignments, respectively) is often considered mandatory. One hears complaints from unsocial or non-drinking officers about such responsibilities; but officers are usually not inclined to flout openly the understandings surrounding these activities. It is not surprising, then, that some of the clashes or difficulties with informants arose over the question of drinking, paying for drinks and, generally, participating in such occasions where civilians and women — even women officers — were not present ordinarily. Even though I came to understand something of the importance of this aspect of their culture fairly soon, it was difficult not to tease back and bait the informants if they hazed me about inability to match their drinking habits. Once, when pressed to order something, I ordered a "Shirley Temple" (a child's cocktail made of syrup and lemonade and dressed to look like a Tom Collins). This annoyed my drinking companion very much. He asked me to order a plain lemonade; however, I persisted, and caused something of a stir, since the bartender was unfamiliar with the practice of preparing a child's drink under that name. The amount of irritation and annoyance that I caused my companion, however, was directly related to the seriousness and importance of drinking in his social world. When I realized that I made informants uncomfortable by refusing to take seriously the ritual of drinking, I was able to resolve the problem in various ways: pleading a fictional ulcer, ordering a highball and nursing it for hours; passing my drinks to understanding informants who sympathized with my indifference to alcohol; throwing drinks into plants — and the whole gamut of tricks in which Victorian maidens were counseled.

The Social Position the Researcher Can Make for Himself in the World He Studies

Some of the problems already presented for the researcher are caused by the fact that initial entry occurs while he is bearing low status in the eyes of the observed, and observing, group. The group members are not only annoyed and suspicious about intrusion, they are also outraged in their sensibilities and understandings about propriety and decorum. But time, and the making of friendships in the group under study, mitigates status problems.

Blau, for example, mentions that once he was accepted as a social scientist his prestige rose, thus "increasing the value of *my* (italics mine) approval and respect for my respondents. . . ."[24] In my case, the problem of access to high-ranking officials could not have been resolved without the chance development of a friendship with one high-ranking officer who took some pains to provide personal introductions to his colleagues. Then, through an accumulation of introductions, accessibility to relevant officials became a simple matter. (In the beginning I would have the discouraging experience of learning that informants told prospective new informants not to bother with me if inconvenient. Once I got to know some higher-ranking officers — and it was known that I knew them — this problem disappeared.)

The major difficulty, as the group under study saw it, was that I would be likely to take out my "hostilities" and "aggressions" on them. Naturally I would resent an all-male society with secrets and prerogatives I was not invited to share. And, since they saw me as quick-witted and sharp-tongued, I would have an unfair advantage in depicting them unkindly. They, with little interest or skill in publishing, would have no manner of redress. In addition, as already noted, persons committed to the military for a career are defensive about how they are seen by civilian eyes. I was often asked if I intended to write an "exposé" of the military for the popular magazines. I would reassure the questioner that I was a serious researcher, interested only in serious publication directed toward a specialized audience.

One officer, who inconvenienced himself to give me interview time, explained his reason for doing so in terms of such fears. Although in some ways it was uncomfortable for him, he wanted to show himself to me as a reasonable man. He felt I would be less inclined to ridicule and portray negatively the special branch of the military in which he served if someone took such special pains with me. In the course of the interview, he told me that he had felt sorry for me at the military cocktail party at which we had met. He saw that I was snubbed and treated badly. He noticed that I became angry and ridiculed several officers who had behaved with what I took to be gratuitous rudeness. At that time, he resolved to show me that not all Army men behaved that way; that he, for example, was one of the responsible, hard-working family men in the military who took their professional careers seriously.

My own problems in handling my position *vis-à-vis* the group were recognized in the group. Some of these difficulties can arise for any observer. But they are intensified when the group under study anticipates and expects problems. Blau,[25] for example, mentions that it was a mistake to adhere rigidly to a plan for recording social contacts among officials. The members of the organization suspected his motives and thought he was trying to check on their use of time. When I took out a notebook during parties, there was a general outcry from the participants. At first, I bantered to turn aside what I took to be good-natured protests. Eventually I learned I was seriously annoying. The informants saw me as a spoilsport and a wet blanket, distracting from the ease and informality of the party atmosphere. I was able to correct these deficiencies at a fairly early point, but not until, at a party in an officers' club, I had provoked an informant, who was ordinarily quiet-speaking and well-mannered to me, into public ridicule of me and my note taking.

Another difficulty that is intensified for the female observer is one which Dalton describes as "knowing too much."

> Eager to learn more, he alarms some persons, even his fringe intimates, by accidentally disclosing bits of unofficial information they think it strange that he should have.[26]

In my case, I learned from one informant that another had counseled care in speaking to me, because I was a "dreadful gossip."

However, the study did not require any secret or confidential information about military matters. And informants came to accept and even welcome the opportunity to discuss the military setting and their careers within it. Also, as already noted, the appearance of a female researcher became less of a novelty as time passed. In some ways, feminine identity was a positive advantage. Papanek[27] reports that she had unique opportunities to participate in both men's and women's societies through her role as an outsider. Dressed in a sari, she could enter situations where no man could go. In Western dress, she could participate with men where no native woman could be present. While the parallel advantages were not quite so striking in my case, I was able to check on a number of observations through my friendships with officers' wives.

An aid in collecting information was that I was perceived as a person traveling in the main stream of certain Army communications channels. I could provide information to officers in outlying posts when I came to interview them. They would often ask me for the current news from

Washington. As the "price" of the interview, then, I would "swap" information on who had resigned, who had been transferred, who had divorced or remarried. Of course, it is not difficult to gain a reputation as a "gossip" in such circumstances, even if one sticks to publishable items. However, it is doubtful if any information on the scale that was actually collected could have been gathered without purveying some gossip. The offer of a piece of news is an act of good faith and encourages the informant to make his own revelations.[28]

Another reason interviews were cooperatively given was that the researcher was sometimes seen as a personage with power at the "home office" in Washington. And so, at times, I would be asked by persons who did not understand the nature of my marginal position to help them avoid an unpleasant overseas assignment.

Perhaps the largest consideration which served to outweigh the difficulties, scruples, and discomforts which officers felt in facing the research — and the researcher — was the nature of the study itself. Informants, both in scheduled interviews and informal discussion, were pleased to have an intensive interest shown in their work. Furthermore, they often saw the usefulness of the research project for explaining or organizing aspects of their work not previously considered by their own superiors and researchers. In the last analysis they were willing to take my presentation as a researcher on faith and accept my interpretation of my "mission" in the Army.

Wherever possible, friendliness was encouraged and personal acquaintanceships were made. Perhaps the establishment of such relationships was more crucial in this kind of study than might often be the case because of the organizational and structural difficulties in the collection of observations. The original understandings of the research contract did not allow for direct observation of the officers at their work. And actually, for the kind of work in which most were engaged, it would have been difficult to observe them without disrupting the ongoing activity. Furthermore, since some of the officers were engaged in activities which involved confidential matters, it would have been necessary to obtain authorizations to observe them. As relations with the granting organization were marked with some difficulties, it did not seem wise to press for such authorizations.

In consequence, personal friendships became the most important channel of information about the military setting. More formal meetings — the interview appointment, invitations to and participation in symposia and the military sections of professional association meetings—were extremely important. But they were put into context and made more meaningful through informal meetings—gatherings in clubs or in homes, and at lunches, dinners, at coffee breaks, and cocktail parties.

My problem, since officers resisted the idea of working after hours and were not available as they moved about their duties, was to be sufficiently friendly and interesting so that they would want to squander their free time with me. Naturally, it was difficult for some officers to understand this mode of operation, and even those without any disruptive intent could, in all reason, be expected to feel somewhat harried as I dogged their footsteps at conventions or persistently angled for invitations to spend free time with them.

The mutual efforts to work out a *modus vivendi* resulted in some surprisingly stable friendships. One main avenue of response from the subject group was to "adopt" me. Wood describes the phenomenon succinctly:

> Adoption is a device which has been widely used by both primitive and civilized peoples for the purpose of including an outsider within the social organization of the group. By means of adoption the newcomer is given a definite status in the group and his relations to the other members are determined by this.[29]

In her discussion, Wood makes the distinction between adoption as an honorary member without active duties and obligations (as in the cases of Morgan, Spencer, and Gillen in their adoption into the primitive tribes of Australia), which she calls ceremonial adoption, and formal (legal) adoption with all its consequences and considerations related to the inheritance of property and abandonment of the earlier membership group. In my own case, it is, of course, to ceremonial adoption that I refer. And, in my own case, the phenomenon occurred with a relatively small number of individuals within the military system rather than in the system at large. Nevertheless, it was clear to most that I had been adopted by some; and it was clear that they would have to take that factor into account when dealing with me. On one occasion I was at lunch with several field grade officers. One of them said jokingly to another: "Why don't we get (a very high-ranking officer) to make Arlene a civilian consultant to (our special branch)? Then she could review troops when she comes to visit us and we could do a parade inspection and it would be a lot of fun!" On another occasion, at a convention meeting, I joined a group of officers at a party. One member of the group was not known to me. He asked the person standing next to him who I was. That officer clapped us both on the back and said: "What? You don't know Arlene? Then you ought to meet her. She's a great girl. She's our mascot. She studies us."[30]

The other main avenue of response, which overlapped with adoption, was to accept me as a friend of the family. I began to receive invitations from officers, when I was working in their home area, to meet their families. Where home invitations were not possible, some of the officers would go to pains to introduce me to their wives and children in some other context. When such meetings were not possible, officers would tell me about their families and show me the pictures they carried. And I would be asked questions about my own family; regards to them would be included in meetings or in letters — even when the officers writing had never met my family.

The Ethical Problems of Exploitation and Manipulation

It is common for the researcher to be concerned with his own ethical problems; yet it became apparent, as the study progressed, that the representatives of the granting organization in the military were also concerned about the nature of their ethical responsibilities to the research.

The original understandings, when the contract was drawn, were that the research was "basic" rather than "applied." However, the granting organization did express the hope that some application for the research might eventually be discovered. Since I, as principal investigator, had to take no responsibility for such eventualities, I saw no reason to disagree. Yet, once I began to reformulate the original research design, the granting organization representatives became apprehensive about what I might be doing. Some of the major objections, I felt, were really related to a fear that I might discover something unfavorable about the organization. Still, the representatives of granting organizations didn't feel free to voice these fears.[31] Since the organization not only paid "lip service" to the idea of scientific neutrality, but also had written itself out of control by the terms of the contract, it was in no position to take decisive action. However, in the first discomfort at seeing the research take a different line from what had been anticipated, the granters attempted to pull my research organization (through which the grant was administered) into the fray. This move involved some discomfort for everyone. The director of the research organization pointed out to me that I was jeopardizing future grants from this branch of the military to his organization as well as the future of my own grant. And he questioned the professional propriety — as well as the reasonableness — of some of my research procedures. Fortunately, in the ensuing debate, I was able to persuade him that my professional concerns would be most appropriately managed at my own discretion. And the director was able to persuade the military organization that they might wish to terminate *my* support without washing their hands of his research organization.

In this sub-stage of the conflict, the resolution of self-questioning about just what, exactly, I *did* owe the administering organization was to help them find a replacement, suitable in the view of the granting organization, as principal investigator. When the candidate was found, I helped him with the granting organization's application forms and generally put my office at his service until his own project began. The administering organization showed its appreciation of my helpfulness by assisting me, in some degree, in continuing the research I wanted to do under different auspices. The new investigator showed *his* appreciation by naming me as formal consultant in his research proposal.

In the major conflict between myself and the granting organization, we agreed to separate without hard feelings, though there was some ambivalence. One officer of the granting organization wrote me a bitter, curt, dismissing letter. The other officer wrote a more gentle "let's be friends and agree to disagree" letter with hopes for some other research affiliation in the future. The personal difficulty I experienced in this resolution was that the granting organization refused the renewal of the third year of what had been understood in the beginning to be a three-year grant. The effort at partial amends by the granting organization was the offer of a small sum to terminate certain aspects of the research.

It was never too clear whether the granting organization representatives felt my research was not worth supporting or whether they wished to stop my line of enquiry by cutting off funds. The final resolution of the difficulties came in the form of benign intervention from a less personally involved federal granting organization. When the representatives of the military granting organization saw that I was not to be shaken from my research interests — and that other organizations would support them—they resumed friendly relations; or at least they became resigned to my continued presence in their group.

Difficulties faced by members of the organization who volunteered to be subjects and helpers were discomfiting for them, and for me. From their point of view, the officers had an amorphous desire to help in the research and to show good will. But they were constantly embarrassed and made uncomfortable, or angry, when my demands for assistance or information became pressing. One officer told me flatly that he thought I was a "bottomless pit of demands." He said he was not surprised when another officer, whom we were discussing, refused further assistance on my project. Still another officer was moved to satiric remonstration when my requests for his time could not be met.

> Alas . . . my tongue is hanging out and I am on the ropes. You, who live in the rarefied atmosphere of academic endeavor, seem not to realize that those of us in the workaday world, carrying on the business of our great nation, are somewhat pressed for time. Thus it is that additional efforts must be, of necessity . . . carried on without recompense, and in the odd moments here and there . . .

At the same time, as collaboration and information contacts continued, many of the officers involved showed some ambivalence or sheepishness about exploiting — or trying to exploit — the researcher for advantages or "treats." On one occasion, I remarked mildly that it seemed odd that an officer needed to submit bills for postage fees (connected with mailing packets of questionnaires) when he could use the government frank on his mailings. The officer responded quickly, assuring me that he had collected enough "beer money" and that he would submit no further bills. Furthermore, some of the officers with whom I established stable contacts attempted to equalize the costs of dining and drinking. They would point out that I had been "standing" a series of drinks or lunches and it was now their turn.

In relation to the main concern, officers showed an interest and a commitment in the success of the research and tried to offer special help, particularly after exigencies of their own work had caused them to hinder or delay some phase of mine. In short, despite some exploitative and resistant responses to the idea of the research project, and to me in particular, the situation was complicated for the informants by the fact that some of them genuinely desired to be of help and were willing, on occasion, to face some inconvenience to do so.

For the researcher, the necessity to maintain a position against the granting organization and against the real wishes of the recipient organization created considerable self-doubts and difficulties. The granting organization representatives, after all, had some right to feel nettled and bewildered when the direction of the research changed drastically. While it is reasonable to assert that the sociologist often has to define the problem — or redefine it — for the sponsor of the research, it may also be true that such definitions or redefinitions can be alarming or painful to vested interests within the organization. In my own case, my resolution of the dilemma was to court disaster: that is, to let the sponsors know early in the project how the research was changing and to give them the opportunity to terminate the grant. This move was neither as high-minded nor as considerate of the organization as it might first appear, however. By the time the organization could mobilize to terminate, I had already collected most of the data I needed. Their alternatives were limited to decisions about whether or not there would be support of further research and/or the writing of the reports on the initial research. My resolution of qualms in this area was to return to the original aims of the study, indicate how I had fulfilled them and what my right was to contribute something beyond that in my research on the military.

In addition, the conviction has grown upon me that inviting researchers into an organization is equivalent to the sorcerer in fantasy tales who calls up the demons and permits them to enter the charmed circle. Once invoked, demons have a logic and a direction of their own. The moral in such tales is that one is supposed to consider this aspect of the matter before the invoking. To the extent, then, that sociologists have a calling or a perspective of their own, they have the responsibility to follow it in whatever situation they conduct research. If the researchers' affiliations and interests become so closely allied with the organization studied that they cannot view it in any disparaging light without severe discomfort, they are in danger of changing professions — becoming organizers, lobbyists, personnel officers, or some other kind of official responsible to the organization. The organization also has a choice — either to close itself off from access to researchers who might view its processes in a disparaging light, or to resign itself to the possibility that research findings may be both useful and discomfiting. The situation is felt most keenly on both sides, I believe, when the organization is supporting the researcher. In my case I was often made to feel "how sharper than a serpent's tooth a thankless researcher . . . whom we have been supporting in high style." My alternative was to answer: "If you don't like it, don't pay for it . . . and I will take the consequences."

A less readily resolved ethical problem was posed by my realization that some of the hand-to-hand battles with the military in which I engaged during early phases of the research were not a background conducive to a dispassionate assessment of the area. To add to my discomfiture, many of the officials responsible for my entry into the field were well aware of my initial difficulties and encounters (the gossip channels in the system worked both ways; I learned a lot from the officers about one another and they learned from one another about me). Accordingly, any reproaches which

I met about my neutrality were keenly felt because they matched my own doubts and misgivings. I did feel resentment against the status and sex barriers which I felt impeded my work, and I did resent the time, trouble, and effort required to break these barriers down. However, the difficulties which multiplied in the initial phases of Army research faded as emphasis switched from directing a project and teaching participants in it to observation and interview.

The most serious ethical problem — and the one for which there is no permanent resolution — is the fact that friends in the group studied may be displeased or discomfited when research reports reach publication state. This problem is combined with the realization that, inevitably, one's own main interest in the group members is an exploitative one. Unless one moves from ceremonial to legal adoption (to become a lobbyist or "company" man in one form or other) by the group, one inevitably approaches all relationships with informants from the specialized perspective of one who eventually will withdraw. Sometimes this realization colors one's interactions to the extent that it draws reproaches from one's friends. One officer's wife, in writing a friendly letter to me, asked me if I didn't think I was too hard and too critical of the military folk. I tried to apologize for my criticism and explain how, in addition, an outsider may appear more critical than he actually is.

Although I answered this wife's letter with amicability — on personal stationery rather than office letterhead — I nevertheless filed *her* friendly letter to me as part of the data under an appropriate category in my field notes. The relationship between us, and out of which the letter stemmed, illustrates the difficulties involved in the growth of friendships between the observer and the studied.

The Creative Possibilities of the Role of the Stranger in Research

Some of the ethical difficulties for the researcher considered in the foregoing invoke putting aside questions of the status differential between observers and the subjects of their study. One of the conditions mitigating status inequalities is that the introduction of a stranger into their normal routine is often an exciting and interesting event for subjects. In the military setting, for example, much of the daily work routine can be boring and monotonous. The advent of a new person with new questions and new ideas to break this routine is sometimes welcomed. Schuetz points out that some of the difficulties which arise for a stranger stem from his objectivity and doubtful loyalty. But there are also positive values to the difficulties.

He also mentions some of the adventurous or exciting aspects of the meeting from the stranger's point of view.

> The approached group is to the stranger not a shelter but a field of adventure, not a matter of course but a questionable topic of investigation, not an instrument for disentangling problematic situations but a problematic situation itself and one hard to master.[32]

Schuetz's observations might well be applied to the group which observes the stranger observing. For members of the group the exciting aspects may be highlighted and the dangerous or nerve-wracking quality to the meeting minimized. The piquancy of the situation with all its possibilities for learning new things — as well as the opportunity for watching a newcomer make a fool of himself — yields many attractions to those observed. For those who care to be friendly, here is also the opportunity to do a good turn: offer information or advice, and lend a helpful hand.[33]

Under such circumstances it is not surprising that so many social scientists report difficulty in keeping distance from subjects who befriend them. Limited or transitory friendships, however, have a poignancy or charm of their own; for all parties generally understand the circumstances of meeting. In Simmel's perspective, revelations are possible *because* everyone understands that true intimacy does not exist.

> . . . 'intimate' content, although we have perhaps never revealed it before and thus limit it entirely to this particular relationship, does nevertheless not become the basis of its form, and thus leaves it outside the sphere of intimacy.[34]

This is a reasonable view if one allows as friendships or intimacy only a stable, regularized pattern of interaction. Alternatively, one may observe, with Renard[35] that "there are no friends; only moments of friendship." For those who "find moments of friendship" binding in many of the same ways as stable friendships, the development of these patterns of interaction in the research setting are difficult to accept:

> There follows for many a fieldworker the unsettling recognition that, within very broad limits, it is precisely when his subjects relate to him . . . in his 'out-of-research role' self . . . that the *raison d'être* for his 'in-role' self is most nearly realized; they are more themselves, they tell and 'give away' more, they supply connections and insights which he would otherwise have never grasped.[36]

However, in the research experience described in the foregoing sections, the difficulties presented for both researcher and informants in separating exploitative and friendly responses to each other were not insurmountable. The main avenue for resolution of such difficulties was a common interest in the collection and organization of the data.

The peculiar advantages in this situation for a stranger who *must* remain alien; who *cannot* be integrated into the system are many. If members of the group are willing to give information and to build a friendly relationship with the stranger, they are prevented from too unrealistic an emotional investment by the facts of the situation. In the same way, the stranger is always aware that participation in the group is temporary. In my case, for example, I was charmed by the efforts to incorporate me into the society as a mascot. But it was impossible to conceive of the mascot role as a serious or permanent one which I would be interested in maintaining as a career.

The realization which all parties come to is that friendship and intimacy carry a "hands across the seas" flavor. All parties in the relationship find themselves making a conscious effort to bridge the gap. Through their efforts they discover, in the research situation, what Simmel observed in any interaction between an outsider and the group he enters — areas of similarity in a universe of strangeness. Many bonds are created between persons who consciously overcome difficulties together. In my participation in military society, I found that some of the strongest bonds of friendship were formed with officers who were least similar to me in their personal tastes, interests, and values. In this connection, I should note that although I am a pacifist, my best key informant and closest friend in the military is one of the most warlike participants in the group of officers studied.

The aim of this paper has not been to argue that a position as a clearly visible stranger — and one in a low-status position — is the best way to study a group. There are many disadvantages to the worm's eye view of an organization. However, if the social scientist can resist the opportunity to rise within the organization he studies, or if — as in my case — the opportunities for mobility are strictly delimited, he may profit from his circumstances.

NOTES TO THE CHAPTER

*This paper was prepared while the author was principal investigator of a study entitled "A Study of Social Factors Affecting Acceptable and Unacceptable Responses to Army Life in the Trainee Population," U.S. Army Research and Development Command, Contract DA-49-193-Md-2396.

I would like to acknowledge the help of Richard M. Colvard. Without his sympathetic ear when this material was still a loose collection of anecdotes, and without his insistence that this material should be published, the chapter would never have been written. In addition, I owe much to friends and well-wishers who offered valuable advice, encouragement, and substantive criticisms through various stages of the writing. Among many in this group were Howard Becker, Sally Cassidy, Roy Clausen, Richard Daniels, Joan Emerson, Neil Friedman, Erving Goffman, John Seeley, Leonard Schatzman, Thomas Scheff, and Paule Verdet. Finally, I am grateful to W. Richard Scott for providing me with a pre-publication of his "Field Methods in the Study of Organizations," in James March (ed.), *Handbook of Organizations* (Chicago: Rand McNally & Co., 1965), 261–304. Without this excellent review of the literature I would have been quite at a loss to place my problem in perspective.

1. See Alfred Schuetz, "The Stranger," in Maurice R. Stein, Arthur J. Vidich, and David Manning White (eds.), *Identity and Anxiety* (Glencoe: The Free Press, 1960), 98–109.

2. *The Sociology of Georg Simmel,* trans. and ed. by Kurt H. Wolff (Glencoe: The Free Press, 1950), 404.

3. Stephen A. Richardson, Barbara Snell Dohrendwind, and David Klein, in their *Interviewing: Its Form and Functions* (New York: Basic Books, 1965), 31, 92, take the view that certain personal characteristics of an interviewer may make such a project inordinately difficult.

4. I am indebted to Leonard Schatzman who acquainted me with this use of the term.

5. I regret that I cannot indicate by name those persons in the military who are concerned here. The most altruistic — and efficient — help I received in managing the clerical tasks of the study came from the enlisted men who waded through the drudgery for no gain except warm gratitude.

6. Although I was familiar with Coser's work on laughter in a collegial group, I did not catch its relevance for my position. Since I did not see myself as a subordinate, I didn't at first grasp the inappropriate control of the situation I indicated by cracking jokes and making pleasantries; nor did I notice how disturbed my colleagues were becoming. See Rose Laub Coser, "Laughter Among Colleagues," *Psychiatry,* 23 (February, 1960), pp. 81–95. Coser demonstrates that the display of humor follows a hierarchical pattern.

7. See Edward T. Hall, *The Silent Language* (Garden City: Doubleday & Co., 1959), 23–24, for an analysis of the relation between promptness or lateness to the cultural context.

8. An interesting parallel to my problem — women interviewing police officers — is reported in Richard Blum *et al., The Utopiates: The Use and Users of LSD-25* (New York: Atherton Press, 1964) 12.

9. See the excellent review of appropriate and inappropriate behavior for minority-group persons in marginal situations which is contained in Bertram Wilbur Doyle, *The Etiquette of Race Relations in the South: A Study in Social Control* (Chicago: University of Chicago Press, 1937).

10. Researchers rarely have the patience or resignation required to remain comfortable during the initial period before they receive signs of acceptance from the persons under observation. See Rosalie Hankey Wax, "Twelve Years Later: An Analysis of Field Experience," in Richard N. Adams and Jack J. Preiss (eds.), *Human Organization Research: Field Relations and Techniques* (Homewood, Ill.: Dorsey Press, 1960), 175, and her "Reciprocity in Field Work" in the same volume, pages 90–98.

11. Thomas J. Scheff, "Control Over Policy by Attendants in a Mental Hospital," *Journal of Health and Human Behavior,* 2 (Summer, 1961), p. 99.

12. Selvin ran into similar methodological problems in using questionnaires constructed and administered by Army officers. Hanan C. Selvin, *The Effects of Leadership* (Glencoe: The Free Press, 1960), Appendix B.

13. Male psychiatrists often discuss seductive gestures toward them from female patients. Sometimes they call it transference and sometimes they just consider it realistic. See discussion of the case "I Love You, Doctor," in Stanley W. Standal and Raymond J. Corsini (eds.), *Critical Incidents in Psychotherapy* (Englewood Cliffs: Prentice Hall, 1959), 95–97. In this discussion, Mowrer suggests that seduction of authority figures carries possibilities for considerable non-sexual gains.

14. Peter Blau, "The Research Process in the Study of *The Dynamics of Bureaucracy,*" in Phillip E. Hammond (ed.), *Sociologists at Work* (New York: Basic Books, 1964), 30, reports on the dangers of becoming too closely affiliated with marginal or disaffected informants. However, I did not find, as Blau warned, that these early contacts impeded the development of other contacts.

15. William Foote Whyte, *Street Corner Society* (2d ed.; Chicago: University of Chicago Press, 1959), 291–93, 301.

16. E. Y. Harburg and Fred Saidy, *Finian's Rainbow* (New York: Random House, 1946), contains an amusing and ironic statement about how subordinate mannerisms may be learned quickly and efficiently so as to promote smooth relations with the superordinate group.

17. There is no more interesting or poignant description of the process than that contained in the fictionalized account of field work: Elenore Smith Bowen, *Return to Laughter* (New York: Harper & Bros., 1954). See also Hortense Powdermaker, *Stranger and Friend* (New York: W. W. Norton & Co., 1966).

18. See Morris Janowitz, *The Professional Soldier* (Glencoe: The Free Press, 1961), 116–23, and Meyer N. Zald and William Simon, "Career Opportunities and Commitments Among Officers," in Morris Janowitz (ed.), *The New*

Military: Changing Patterns of Organizations (New York: Russell Sage Foundation, 1964), 257–86.

19. Howard S. Becker, "Notes on the Concept of Commitment," *American Journal of Sociology,* 66 (July, 1960), pp. 32–40, provides a theoretical framework for a consideration of the influence of "side bets" on commitment.

20. In study and even when collaborating with members of other professional groups I had not run into any similar problems. See, for example, my "Ideological Response to Social Pressures on the Profession: A Study of Dentists." Unpublished Ph.D. dissertation, University of California (Berkeley), 1960.

21. *The Sociology of Georg Simmel, op. cit.,* 346.

22. Camilla H. Wedgewood, "The Nature and Functions of Secret Societies," *Oceania,* 1 (July, 1930), p. 132. "A secret society may be defined in its widest sense as a voluntary association whose members, in virtue of their membership, are possessed of some knowledge of which non-members are ignorant."

23. Hattersley has developed some preliminary rules applicable to any social encounter for playing the eye game. In his rules for women he says: "1) Looking too long at a strange man will make him think you are sizing him up sexually or laughing inwardly at him. 2) Never stare a man down unless you wish him to feel impotent or to believe you are trying to prove youself a better man than he." Ralph Hattersley, "The Psychology of People-Pictures," *Photograph* (November, 1963), p. 177. I am indebted to Erving Goffman for this reference.

24. Blau, *op. cit.,* 31.

25. *Ibid.,* 27ff.

26. Melville Dalton, "Preconceptions and Methods in *Men Who Manage,*" in Hammond, *op. cit.,* 88.

27. Hanna Papanek, "The Woman Field Worker in Purdah Society," *Human Organization,* 23 (Summer, 1964), pp. 160–63.

28. I am indebted to Warren Hagstrom for this comforting observation.

29. Margaret Mary Wood, *The Stranger: A Study of Social Relationships* (New York: Columbia University Press, 1934), 34.

30. The type of adoption offered to me is a further indication of the limitations of status opportunities within the group when one enters as a low-caste stranger. Whyte became a significant force or leader after his adoption into Cornerville society. I became, after three years, an amusing and ornamental mascot, treated with friendly affection but little respect. I am indebted to Neil Friedman for bringing this distinction forcibly to my attention.

31. See Alvin W. Gouldner, "Explorations in Applied Social Science," in Alvin W. Gouldner and S. M. Miller (eds.), *Applied Sociology* (New York: Free Press, 1965), 5–22.

32. Schuetz, *op. cit.,* 503.

33. One must not forget that the stranger may be a nuisance or even a danger; though dangers in befriending him may add to the attraction. The difficulties and obstacles presented by the granting organization in this presentation indicate the possibility that the new arrival may be feared as a danger. Especially when an institution is not the strong indomitable edifice it might appear, the stranger can do it much harm, causing insiders worries and doubts. I am indebted to Professor Paule Verdet for this cautionary observation.

34. *The Sociology of Georg Simmel, op. cit.,* 127.

35. *The Journal of Jules Renard,* trans. and ed. by Louise Bogan and Elizabeth Roget (New York: George Brazillier, 1964), 58.

36. Fred Davis, "Comment on 'Initial Interaction of Newcomers in Alcoholics Anonymous,'" *Social Problems,* 8 (Spring, 1961), p. 365.

CHAPTER THIRTEEN

Ethical and Political Dilemmas in the Investigation of Deviance: A Study of Juvenile Delinquency

RICHARD A. BRYMER AND BUFORD FARRIS

We shall examine various ethical and political issues that arose during the course of a research project whose primary goal is to evaluate an action program aimed at reducing the incidence of delinquent behavior.[1] In order to understand the problems involved in this study, we must first consider the setting in which the action and the research have taken place. We shall then discuss the ethical and political dilemmas that have arisen as a consequence of (1) the theoretical framework, (2) the research design, (3) the role of the researcher, (4) the collection and storage of the data, and (5) the presentation of the findings of the project. The decisions relative to these issues — which we have reason to believe arise in other similar projects as well — have affected the whole course of the action and research program. In fact, these issues seem to have relevance for any researcher who attempts to study deviant behavior (especially that involving the violation of legal norms) within American society.

Setting and Background of the Study

The project is being carried out in a small community center in San Antonio, Texas. It began in September, 1964, and is scheduled to terminate in June, 1967. The experiences reported in this paper are primarily those which emerged during the first year of the project.

The staff of the research and the action project includes the administrative

297

staff, the action staff (social workers and gang workers), the researcher (a sociologist), and the research advisers and consultants. The gang workers, who are attached to the center, have functioned in lower-class neighborhoods with Mexican-American delinquents and non-delinquents and their families in an effort to improve the "life-chances" of these young people. The researcher's task has been to evaluate the effectiveness of the gang workers and to formulate certain generalizations about the development of delinquency within the context of a lower-class urban ethnic group.

Even in the early stages of our study we sought to cope with the ethical and political issues that influenced the development of our research. Although we found little or no guidance in the literature, we soon came to recognize that sociologists who study juveniles are aware that these issues arise in their work. The senior author, in particular, raised the question regarding the impact of ethical and political decisions upon the research design with a number of specialists in the field of juvenile delinquency. In these conversations, a variety of opinions were set forth which, for heuristic purposes, can be used to construct a set of polar types. Most researchers undoubtedly will insist they fall somewhere between the polar extremes.

On one end of the continuum are the opinions or views held by the social scientist who defines himself as a rigorous empiricist, studying the world as it actually is. According to this position, values should not affect scientific research. Although the scientist with these views recognizes the inevitability of ethical issues he tends to regard them as obstacles to good research, as something to be overcome. Ethics are seen as problems of strategy rather than of morality.

At the other end of the continuum are the views held by the social scientist who defines himself as non-objective because he argues that the researcher's actions affect the lives of the persons he studies. For him, ethical issues are inevitable. The issues are not mere obstacles to research but are an integral part of the research process. Ethics, in this view, are a matter of individual conscience and as such must be worked out by each individual researcher according to his own values.

Both types of researchers do not deem public discussion of these issues as essential. However, proponents of the first position see publicity as a threat to the future of good research, whereas followers of the second hold to the view that ethical issues are matters of private, subjective conscience. We would agree with both of these positions to the extent that to us, ethical issues appear to be inevitable. However, we would also argue that public discussion of these ethical issues is necessary. And it is to this end that we present this paper.

Problems Resulting from the Theoretical Framework

At the beginning, we were not aware of any particular ethical consequences that would stem from our theoretical framework. But since our theory committed us to a particular methodology and a given set of data-collection procedures, various ethical problems soon became apparent.

We took a symbolic interactionist position. From this position delinquency — and deviance in general — is seen as the result of the cumulative consequences of a person's interaction with various sets of other persons. These sets of persons are crucial in that they participate in defining both acts and individuals as deviant or delinquent. Now, these definitions may not necessarily be congruent with one another. A boy may have certain definitions of himself and his world, whereas the persons with whom he interacts may have different sets of definitions. Each set of definitions, and the boy's response to them, influences the development of either a delinquent or a non-delinquent career. With this frame of reference we were, therefore, obliged to gather chronological data about a boy's relationships with the neighborhood and the community, the way that he defines them, and the way these systems in turn define him, as well as the actions based upon these definitions. Obviously we could not study all persons in the community and neighborhood, so we narrowed our focus to those persons — family, friends, police, teachers, social workers, etc. — who were in a position to intervene rather directly in the boy's behavior. Although the police may not be an accepted part of the boy's world, they are nonetheless an acknowledged part of it, for when the police define a boy as delinquent, and take action based upon that definition, this definition and action have consequences for the boy's future behavior and career.

In order to gather relevant data, it was necessary that the researcher interview persons in these crucial positions concerning their interaction with, and definition of, the boy. In order to obtain further information on how these definitions developed, and how these might be related to changes in the boy's behavior, interviews were required at a minimum of two or three points in time.

At least three kinds of ethical issues appeared to be involved in this type of interviewing. The first was the question of the invasion of the boy's privacy. We did not have his permission to interview other persons concerning his behavior, and thus we were gathering data about him over which he had no control. And, by logical and legal extension, we could have been violating the rights of the parents of the boy, because we did not have their permission to gather either data about their son or data about themselves. This latter problem occurs frequently in investigations of minors.[2]

Second, we were using a type of "hearsay" evidence in that we were asking for a person's opinions about a boy, rather than for established, hard facts about him. However, if people do in fact act in terms of their opinions and beliefs about someone, we should attend to this type of evidence as well as to the more or less "hard" data.

Third, by repeatedly interviewing a person about a particular boy, we may have called attention to a situation that might otherwise have gone unobserved. This may have led the respondent to change his definition of the boy and to act in terms of this new definition. Thus, our research action may have created consequences for the boy over which he had no control. This would be especially true where the interviewee knows that the researcher is working with a delinquency control project. The respondent may then assume that all the subjects of the interviews are delinquent, when in fact such may not be the case.

Other ethical problems arose in a series of depth interviews that we undertook with the families of the gang boys. We knew, for instance, that certain boys were delinquent, and that their parents had been required to visit the probation office with the boys. Yet, in interviews with a few of these parents, they denied that their sons had ever gotten into trouble. As a consequence of this denial, we were deprived of information about the parents' perception of, and relationship to, official institutions. In order to elicit this information, the obvious step would have been to apprise the parents of our knowledge of their son's delinquent status. But this act would have indicated our prior knowledge to the parents — and constituted possible invasion of their privacy — which in turn might have terminated the interview and created hard feelings. Therefore, we did not tell the parents of our knowledge, but relied upon further interviews with the parents in which a closer relationship was developed. In retrospect, it would appear that this problem involved not only ethics, but politics, i.e., how to use previously gathered data in order to obtain further information, without revealing this prior knowledge and without disrupting the interview relationship.

This is not to suggest that the symbolic interactionist framework we have employed is the only theory that creates problems of ethics. For example, serious ethical and political issues may, and do, arise when one develops and uses scales for predicting juvenile delinquency.[3] Ethical issues seem to be inevitable, and perhaps are a by-product of all research studies. However, the form and content of these issues may well be a function of the particular theoretical framework which one carries into his research. But perhaps the issues that arise from a symbolic interaction framework and the method of participant observation are more immediate and obvious than issues arising out of other theoretical perspectives.

Problems Resulting from the Research Design

Ethical problems were also created by the research design. Ideally, the experimental method requires that a sample should be divided randomly into two groups, and that the treatment variable should then be administered to one group and not to the other. Comparison of the control and the experimental group after administration of the experimental variable makes it possible to isolate the effect of the treatment variable.

We first thought that it would be ideal to select gang groups randomly and allow the social workers to work with some and not with others so that we might approximate an experimental design. To achieve an even closer approximation, we also thought of dividing an entire neighborhood into two parts, working with one half and letting the other half serve as a control group.

However, practical difficulties militated against the development of any experimental design. First, it would have been virtually impossible to split the neighborhood because it approached a unitary social system, and, further, the residents were not under our direct control. Second, any attempt to create an ideal research design would have contravened certain tenets of the ethical perspective held by the social workers, for this perspective holds that everyone in a neighborhood who needs the attention of a worker should receive it. Once, at a planning conference, the researcher, half in jest and half in seriousness, suggested that we remove all of the social workers from one neighborhood to see if social conditions would cause it to revert to a gang neighborhood. The social workers viewed this plan as highly unethical and were shocked that anyone would be so Machiavellian.

Other aspects of this issue may be more political than ethical. The public sponsorship of the project, and the laws regarding the distribution of federal money without regard to race, creed, etc., lead to the question of whether it is legal to withhold federally sponsored services from a population so that it may serve as a control group. At first glance, this issue might seem to be easily dismissed — for example, with the argument that it is difficult to deprive a group of something it never had. But as the interest in civil rights grows, more and more actions that were once defined as privileges rewarded to a deserving few are now being defined as rights due to all. Geis suggests, for example, that experiments in the field of corrections and penology, where one group of prisoners is paroled under certain conditions while another group is kept in prison, may violate the right of all prisoners to parole.[4]

The attempt to follow an ideal experimental design may then provoke questions regarding the legitimacy of depriving a group of something potentially helpful in order that it may serve as a control group. This is perhaps a reversal of the usual ethical problem wherein the experimental group may have its rights violated by being subjected to an experimental treatment which is as yet untested, and perhaps potentially harmful. In any case, as the amount of public money for demonstration programs of an applied nature increases, the ethics of using control groups will loom increasingly large.

Problems Resulting from the Role of the Researcher

One of the ideal norms of science is that the role of the researcher should be as neutral as possible so that his findings will not be biased. Our efforts to adhere to this ideal, however, led to the creation of a number of ethical and political problems. Our task was made more complex by the presence of several distinct groups with whom the researcher had to maintain relations: (1) the action staff, whom the researcher was both evaluating and working closely with, (2) the neighborhood, including the juvenile gang groups, and (3) institutional officials whose actions impinge upon the neighborhood and the gang boys.

Initially it was thought that the researcher would move into the neighborhood itself, adopt a neighborhood identity, and thereby maintain a "secret" role with respect to all three groups. This presumably would have minimized the possibility of bias in the responses he received. However, it would have been difficult for the researcher to develop any close relationship with the gang workers, and because the project was supposed to document what it is that the workers do, this plan was quickly discarded. Moreover, a secret role would also have made it difficult for the researcher to gain access to certain crucial institutional positions in which we were interested.

It was then decided that the researcher would have to be known to the action workers and to the relevant organizations in the community, but not to the neighborhood. But this position did not solve a highly important and perplexing problem that has recurred numerous times. The researcher would still have to live in the neighborhood, and because delinquent groups in the neighborhood were our primary interest, presumably the researcher would have to develop some contacts with them in his neighborhood identity. There was a danger, then, that the researcher would be placed in a peer position with respect to these gang groups, and might therefore have to countenance delinquent acts. At the same time, he would be in contact with institutional officials and workers. And were the delinquents themselves to discover his dual role, the researcher's position would be a difficult one. The research advisor was arguing for secrecy at this point, with respect to the role of the researcher, whereas the researcher and director were arguing for a more public role.[5]

The next alternative proposed (and the one that was finally adopted) was to identify the researcher as a university professor who was merely spending some time at the agency headquarters. This would allow the researcher to develop a relatively close association with the action workers and be identified to them as a researcher. With respect to the neighborhood and persons in crucial positions, e.g., police, teachers, etc., he could remain an "outsider." It was felt that it would be advantageous for the researcher to remain something of an outsider because he would be trying to ascertain the relationship of the neighborhood and community institutions to the community center and the action workers. An identification of the researcher as a staff member of the agency might introduce some form of bias in favor of the community center. Or at least we would not know where the bias might lie.

As the project progressed, difficulties began to develop. For example, the staff knew that the researcher's function was to carry out an evaluation of the action program, and there was initially some discussion of concealing the staff's activities from the researcher's scrutiny. The researcher has, however, played down the evaluation aspects, and, as of this writing, a relatively close relationship has been established between the workers and the researcher. Such would in fact have been difficult to avoid, because the researcher is involved with the action staff in almost all activities — both on the job and off. This close relationship has, however, resulted in some ethical problems, as we shall discuss later.

With respect to persons in the neighborhood, the set of multiple identities has been difficult to maintain. Initially, we failed to consider the close working relationship that the agency has had with this group. The gang boys for instance were in and out of the agency continuously, and some performed part-time work there. When they observed the researcher's office, with its air of permanence, his complete set of keys, his familiarity with the agency and its facilities and personnel, the "university professor" fiction became tenuous at best. The researcher has also spent a large proportion of his time at the agency, and if one spends much of his time at a place, it becomes difficult to maintain the notion that he works full-time at another job.

The fiction of "university professor" was also difficult to sustain with leaders of the formal organizations. As a part of the action program, the members of a relatively large citizen's advisory group, most of them leaders in the community, have met periodically at the agency. In addition, the action workers have had frequent contact with these officials. The latter also have noted the researcher's air of permanence and have come to the same conclusions as the gang groups.

Probably the most serious problem stemmed from the fact that the researcher was not solely responsible for maintaining a particular identity. The gang workers, for example, knew about the researcher's actual research role; yet in interaction with gang boys and organizational figures they presented him as a university professor. When these persons observed the close camaraderie between worker and university professor, it was difficult to maintain the notion that they belonged to separate social systems. Maintenance of this identity required a consensus among action workers which was difficult to obtain, for each had his own particular ideas as to whom the "university professor" image must be presented. Also, we initially did not consider the impact that the researcher would have on the lower echelon staff members, i.e., clerks, maintenance workers, etc. They saw the researcher not as a professor, but as a fellow staff member, and because they have contacts within the neighborhood, the researcher-as-staff image was then communicated to the neighborhood.

The maintenance of multiple researcher identities in order to minimize bias was very difficult and created both ethical and political problems. Ethical problems arose when some respondents discovered these multiple identities and assumed that the researcher was gathering data under false pretenses. This problem is also political in that it can disrupt the research relationship and cut off an avenue of information for the researcher. In order to counter the strains involved, and the ethical and political dilemmas posed, we began to shift the public image of the researcher to his true role as a researcher.

However, presentation of the researcher as a researcher has not magically overcome all the ethical problems regarding his identity. When one tells a potential respondent that one is a researcher carrying out a sociological investigation, that the findings will be written up, but that the respondent's name will not be used, one gains entrée and simultaneously protects the anonymity of the respondent. But at the same time, this public announcement has the result of "putting the respondent on his guard," so that he can control the nature of the information he reveals. The researcher is in effect setting up a *caveat emptor* situation in which the respondent must take the full burden of protecting his own privacy. After such an announcement, the researcher usually attempts to gain as much information as he possibly can by "building rapport," and "putting the respondent at ease." In our experience, at least four factors have affected the relationship between the publicly defined researcher and the respondent. These factors are: the respondent's sophistication, his knowledge, his power and status, and the duration of the relationship between the researcher and the respondent.

Taking Goffman's *Presentation of Self in Everyday Life*[6] as an instructive case in point, we see that there are variations among actors in the degree to which they can manipulate an audience, and among audiences in the degree to which they can withstand, or "see through," the actor's presentation. Specifically, there are differences in the sophistication of both actors and audiences. If, for heuristic purposes, we substitute researcher for actor, and respondent for audience, we can see similar differences among researchers in the extent to which they can manipulate respondents and among respondents in the extent to which they can withstand the seductive onslaughts of the researcher. Time and time again it has been observed that respondents tend to give information more easily to the researcher who appears to be a "good guy."[7] And certain types of persons are more likely to define persons as "good guys" than are others, depending upon their sophistication. Lower-class persons, for example, are more likely to define others in a personalistic manner and perhaps, therefore, as "friends."[8] What may occur then, is a situation which further works against the maintenance of privacy for lower-class persons. For sociologists, the ethical problem is whether the researcher has the right to use information given to him by a lower-class person — or any person for that matter — under the assumption that the researcher is a "good guy," even where the researcher has made his research identity known.

Related to the degree of sophistication is the extent of knowledge the respondent has about sociologists and about the kinds of consequences that are likely to ensue if he provides information. Again, middle-class persons are more likely to possess this kind of knowledge than are lower-class persons, if only because of the former's higher level of education. Even if the respondent is aware of the sociologist's role, there is still an ethical question in those situations where the sociologist is more aware of the possible consequences than is the respondent. In one instance, where the researcher was interviewing a person who had had research training in social science, the respondent began revealing his participation in a series of deviant activities, along with the locations and the persons involved. These revelations were made in spite of the researcher's prior and repeated warning that "Perhaps you (the respondent) had better think about whether you want me to know that or not." These kinds of situations raise the question of the sociologist's obligation to educate the respondent in terms of the consequences that may result from revealing certain kinds of information.

Thus far our discussion of the implications of various relationships between respondents and interviewers could apply to either single or multiple interviews with a respondent. In our research, the tendency has been to establish long-term relationships with respondents rather than to conduct single or multiple interviews. And as the acquaintance process has developed, the researcher has come to be viewed as "good guy" or an "insider" and thereby has gained access to certain kinds of information that are not otherwise available. Social "after-hours" interaction also has developed which has produced additional privy information — in many cases welcome in the sense that it concerns relationships between the neighborhood and the personnel of formal organizations in the community. This type of data gathering has been a special problem for the researcher vis-à-vis the action staff, for the division between public and private roles has vanished as friendships have flourished. For the researcher, then, an ethical problem arises as to whether he should continue to "draw the line" for the respondent in each and every social interaction or whether he should rely only upon his initial public declaration of intent.

Still another factor in the relationship between respondent and researcher which creates ethical and political problems concerns the respondent's potential to create adverse consequences for the researcher and for his study. If the respondent possesses such power, the researcher is likely to be very circumspect in his dealings with the respondent. For example, in a city the size of San Antonio, there are perhaps hundreds of lower-class neighborhoods, and if the sociologist commits an error in one of them which precludes further data gathering, it is a relatively simple matter for him to shift to another neighborhood. But if the researcher commits an error with the Police

Department, the entire city is off-limits to him. The sociologist in his efforts to acquire additional data may be much more cavalier toward a powerless group than toward a powerful group, because he knows that the former cannot seriously disrupt his research. Discrimination of this sort between the more powerful and the less powerful may be considered an ethical problem, as well as a problem in the accumulation of knowledge, for it certainly channels the researcher into some areas and not into others.

In summary then, the researcher seems to gather much of his data via methods over which he lacks firm control. Just as the actor in normal social interaction cannot control completely the definitions that others make of him, so too the researcher is unable to control the definitions that his respondents make of him. And the data that respondents provide the researcher tend to be in terms of their own definitions of him. Therefore, the ethical issues that arise may also be uncontrolled by the researcher. Because he may be unable to anticipate ethical questions beforehand, the researcher should perhaps shift his ethical concern to those aspects of the research process where he does wield relatively full control — namely the storage, interpretation, and publication of the data.

Problems Resulting from Collection and Storage of the Data

There are other data-collection methods that create ethical issues. Some of these stem from the use of informants, paid or otherwise, who have had experiences that give them access to information which would otherwise be unavailable to the researcher. The nature of the data itself poses ethical problems in that much of the data consist of documentations of deviant and illegal acts, and possession of such knowledge creates ethical and legal problems for the sociologist because he does not have the immunity of privileged communication and, moreover, because of the hazy and ambiguous legal status of persons possessing such knowledge. In this section, then, we would like to document some of these problems as they have arisen in our research project, and our tentative responses to them.

By chance, the researcher met a young man who came from an area bordering on the two gang neighborhoods in which we were interested and who was distantly related to members of one of these gangs. He was also a college student, majoring in sociology, and thus was out of the neighborhood area for long periods of time. These factors, plus his values and orientation, made him somewhat marginal to his original subculture. They also made it possible for him to be an excellent interviewer or informant.

The research staff began discussions of the possible roles that this student might play in our research. There were essentially two dimensions to these discussions: (1) whether he should play an active role, i.e., interact with the gang and report on current phenomena, or a passive role, i.e., report on experiences that he had had with the gang in times past; and (2) if he played an active role, whether he should be publicly known to the gang as a research assistant or as a "returned gang member."

In these discussions, as in many like them, essentially two points of view developed. This fact, perhaps more than any other, illustrates the impact that ethically based decisions can and do have on the course of research projects. The research adviser took the position that to have an active, secret informant in the gang would violate the autonomy and privacy not only of the gang boys but also of the group workers. In addition, it would put the research project in the tenuous position of supporting, albeit indirectly, deviant and illegal behavior. The point was made that if, as a secret observer, he reinstated himself as a gang member and resumed his previous status, he would then be subject to the social and situational pressures that led the other gang members to engage in delinquent behavior. Should the observer get into trouble, and perhaps become officially defined as a delinquent, what would the project's responsibility be toward him? There was also the possibility that the gang members would discover the observer's identity and the fact that he was reporting their activities back to a third party (the researcher) and take action against the informer.

In this matter, the research adviser was arguing for an open, publicly defined research role, which was, of course, a reversal of his original position on the role of the researcher in the neighborhood. This reversal of positions was, however, typical of much of the development of the project, for there have been numerous disagreements and shifts in viewpoints. This pattern is itself cogent evidence of the confusion concerning the role of ethics in research decisions.

The other position, one taken primarily by the researcher, was that such a secret, active role would, in principle, constitute no greater violations of privacy than those resulting from other research techniques. The researcher further maintained that it was possible to create a "secret observer" role so that gang members would still be able to maintain some degree of control over the information they allowed the observer. Moreover, the researcher would still retain control over the ultimate use of such data, and with him would rest the final responsibility for the protection of the gang member's privacy and autonomy.

The researcher contended that such a secret activist role would, in the long run, be no different from the situation wherein one seeks to develop a long-standing "good guy" relationship with an informant. It was recognized, however, that it would be easier for the observer to acquire information about illegal activities than for the researcher to do so. Finally, such an observer would allow us to cross-validate certain types of information; this in turn would enable the researcher to make more accurate assessments of the social world being studied. And with more accurate assessments one is in a better position to judge what might and might not infringe upon the individual's anonymity and autonomy.

After several discussions of the possible consequences of different roles for the student observer, a compromise between the aforementioned positions was worked out. The researcher hired the young man as an active, secret participant observer, but with the understanding that he was in no way to engage in any delinquent or illegal activities himself. The social and situational pressures that would be involved were discussed, and the young man agreed to remain a marginal rather than a full-fledged member of the gang. It was recognized that this arrangement would perhaps decrease the amount of information that he could obtain, but it would produce a situation which was more congruent with the research staff's ethical orientation. In order to ensure this marginality, the observer was to take a job which would legitimately keep him out of the gang area except during certain odd hours. In general he was to play the role of "ex-gang member who is back in town working for money to go back to college." Also, if he got into any trouble, it was understood that the researcher would not be able to help him out, because this would jeopardize other facets of the project. For the first month of the anticipated three-month observation sequence, the observer was to have no explicit instructions; rather he was to observe from his own perspective as an ex-gang member and report back to the researcher every two to three days. After this one-month period and after examination of the data gathered up to that point, more structured and directed observation was to be undertaken.

After about ten days of observation two difficult situations arose; one was anticipated, the other completely unanticipated. The anticipated situation occurred when the young man got into trouble on his own time. He was reinvolved in an inter-family feud and participated in a "shoot-out." No one was seriously injured, but the student felt that he should leave town for a while. The climate was, in his estimation, ". . . too hot to hang around!" It is significant, however, that this situation did not happen as a result of his observation of the gangs per se, but more as a consequence of his own ethnic, class, and familial background — precisely those characteristics which made him an excellent observer for our purposes.

The second difficulty was quite unanticipated. In the course of the last interview that the researcher had with the observer prior to the latter's hasty departure, the observer described a fight that had occurred between a clique of one of the project's gangs and a gang clique in a rival neighborhood. The observer felt that the first-named gang clique was attempting to rally the rest of the gang in its behalf for a retaliation excursion.

There were several alternatives as to what the researcher might do with the information that a large-scale gang war might occur. Each involved an ethical problem. In fact, the question of whether to do anything at all involved an ethical commitment. Since the researcher understood that a group of boys had the apparent *intention* of a revenge battle, there was the possibility that the researcher could do something to stop it. If the researcher turned this evidence over to the police, the fight would perhaps be stopped, but such an action would be a violation of the autonomy of the gang boys. There was also the question of whether it is legitimate to judge a person by a statement of his intention to commit an act, rather than by his actual commission of such an act. Also, turning such information over to the police might bring questions from the police as to how the researcher came into possession of such information. If the information was turned over to a gang worker on the agency staff, it would let the worker know that he was being observed without his prior consent and perhaps rupture the relationship between the researcher and the worker. Also, the social worker might feel obligated to provide the gang with his source of information. Although the observer had already left town, it would then be difficult for him to return because gang boys have relatively long memories about *relajes* (informers). Finally, from an ideal-design point of view, if the researcher turned this information over to the workers or to the police, the treatment variable — the natural course of events in a social work agency — would be changed, however slightly. On the other hand, if this knowledge were not acted upon, there would be the possibility of a gang fight which might result in injuries or deaths and potential legal stigmatization of the boys.

The researcher's course of action was based upon his unique relationship with the project director, who is administratively responsible for both the action and the research phases of the project. In consultation with him, a plan was worked out whereby the director would pay close attention to workers and gangs in this particular area and, by means of indirect counseling, would alert the workers to the possibility of some trouble occurring.

Later in the week, the gang workers independently obtained information about the fight, but by that time the episode had cooled down. Or at least we interpreted events in that way. The boys may have been misleading the worker about their intentions, or they may have "cooled it" as a result of the interest the worker displayed in the subject. In any case, because of our particular ethical commitment, the course of the research project was altered and the impact of that alteration may never be determined.

We have suggested that the nature of the data gathered also creates ethical problems, and the above example partially supports this. Because we have been investigating gangs, and because the social workers are in daily contact and dialogue with these gangs, knowledge of deviant and illegal acts comes to be an everyday affair. For example, a worker while driving home one evening happened to see two of the gang boys rolling a drunk. The worker stopped and intervened by suggesting to the boys that they could get arrested for such activity. He did not, however, determine whether the boys had already robbed the man or were preparing to do so. The worker wrote up this incident — as is done in such instances — and turned the report over to the researcher. Now, the researcher had at least hearsay knowledge that the boys had committed such a crime, that the worker had witnessed it, and that he had not called the police.

In another instance a social worker was contacted late at night by one of his boys, who was a drug addict. The boy was scheduled to go on a voluntary commitment to the federal narcotics hospital, but his bus did not leave until the next morning. His supply of drugs had been raided and he had no money. If he was to get through the remaining twelve hours, he needed a "fix." In San Antonio at present, there is no way for an addict legally to get a fix. On the other hand, if he didn't get it the withdrawal symptoms would become "unendurable," at which point he might try to steal some money in order to get more drugs. This would place the boy in jeopardy, and if he were caught, it would lead to imprisonment, a criminal record, and possibly involuntary commitment to a hospital.

The social worker was in an extremely delicate ethical position. Moreover, he was the one who had originally made the arrangements for the voluntary commitment to the narcotics hospital, so he felt some moral responsibility to the boy. The worker's resolution of this problem was to place the boy in a situation where he could get a fix, although the worker was not present when the boy bought and used the drug. The worker stayed with the boy part of the night and met him in the morning to get him on the bus and on the way to voluntary withdrawal from drugs. The boy stayed in the hospital until his release and has been off drugs ever since. Had these events led to some unfortunate consequences for the worker or for the boy, we might have had to view the ethical issues in a somewhat different light.

These are only two examples of many such incidents that we have encountered in the course of the project. And from conversations with researchers and action personnel in other projects, we are convinced that they are by no means unique. They may, in fact, be relatively common. Further, these incidents stem from gang work methods, and, as such, they form the experimental variable of the research and demonstration project. Therefore, these incidents are data, and according to scientific methods, should be collected systematically. The ethical problem in collecting this sort of data stems primarily from the lack of privileged communication for both the social worker involved and the sociologist engaged in related research. The social worker knows that some of his gang members have engaged in certain illegal acts, yet he does not have the protection of privileged communication in a legal sense. The researcher also has knowledge of these illegal acts of the gang members — although mostly by hearsay evidence — and also of the fact that the social worker had knowledge of these acts and did not report them. Indeed, records of these incidents are in the researcher's files as part of his data. Although sociologists usually insist upon the importance of maintaining the anonymity of their respondents and attempt to guarantee it, it is clear that they have no legal justification for doing so.

Because the sociologist does not enjoy privileged communication, we must interpret his actions in terms of his "duty" as a citizen to report or make known to legal authorities the commission of illegal acts. A legal summary of this aspect of the citizen's duty has been set forth by Broeder:

> Flippant modern assertions that a citizen is under no circumstances currently obliged to inform on the criminal or at least the felonious activities of third parties simply cannot be justified in terms of the statutes and case law of many jurisdictions. While there are few places where one must affirmatively seek out a policeman — and perhaps there is no such place when constitutional considerations are given appropriate weight — the situation in many states becomes quite different when one is asked by a policeman to speak out and refuses.[9]

Perhaps the central feature of Broeder's article is the documentation of the hazy and ambiguous nature of this obligation. Yet, cases indicate that in certain situations persons who have failed to inform the police of illegal activities have been accused of misprision (failure to inform) and of being accessories after the fact. The sociologist who studies deviant and illegal behavior is, therefore, placed in a difficult legal and ethical situation. In addition the sociologist may endanger his respondents by acquiring data about them that could possibly incriminate them. The situation is all the worse when we consider that many times we do not have the explicit permission of the persons involved to collect such data about them.

Another problem in collecting information on illegal acts relates to the storage of records. Such information must be written down and filed. If information sheets are not carefully controlled they can be easily seen by visitors. One begins to spend more and more time worrying about the "security" of his information — with whom he can discuss such information, which clerks can handle the information, which janitors can clean which rooms, and so on.

In effect we are arguing that the adherence to scientific norms can produce ambiguous ethical and legal situations. Ideally one should keep daily systematic records of on-going events so that one can objectively interpret these at a later stage. Yet keeping such records concerning illegal acts without privileged communication for the sociologist makes it difficult for him to insure the anonymity of his respondents.

Our attempts at resolving the issues involved have had two dimensions: a practical, strategic one and a moral one. In practical terms, we have made it a point to tell only a few people what we are doing. We also have kept the files locked behind locked doors with only the researcher and one clerk having keys to either. Moreover, we have retained a lawyer to whom we can turn for advice on particular issues. In fact, we have sought advice from him on the writing up and publication of this paper.

In an even more practical vein, we have bargained with some persons in the legal system. As a result of past experiences of this kind, a working agreement of a sort has developed so that both we and certain legal officials recognize that there is a wide area of behavior in which both the legal system and the social workers (and by extension, the sociologist) are involved and that is both legally and ethically ambiguous. Both parties recognize that there are acts which are not strictly legal but which can hardly be tested or explored in public and legal encounters. There is, then, a private area between the two systems in which problems common to both systems can be discussed.

In moral-ethical terms, we have come to the conclusion that one needs an ethic which transcends the groups, persons, or situations involved in the ethical issue. We have come to view "ethical problems" as a result of the collision of groups or persons having different interests. In such a situation, the researcher or gang worker needs an ethical orientation to guide him in making decisions that will affect both or all of the groups or persons involved. Actually what we have developed is not so much a set of ethical precepts as a set of ethical procedures. First, one should seek a commonality of interests which transcends the parties involved as well as the immediate situation in which the collision of interests occurs. There is the assumption that these sorts of common interests can be found, or created, among all human groups. Further, this set of ethical procedures accepts the legitimacy of the values of every human group. Obviously, one must go to an extremely general level in order to find, or create, this commonality in many instances. This commonality of interest can then serve as referent for a decision. Second, in creating such commonality, one must attempt to take into account as many divergent interests as possible. That is, one must ensure that all divergent interests are included, for if they are not, the ethical decisions stemming from this commonality, as well as the actions based upon it, may conflict with the unincluded interests. One must note that creating a commonality of interests is radically different from saying that one or the other interest is right or wrong; rather, he seeks to develop a commonality that leads to decisions which, ideally, all parties will accept as right. Third, in establishing commonality, one does not assign weights to various divergent interests, i.e., one does not necessarily emphasize the interest which has the backing of the majority or which is held by the socially powerful person. In fact, we would argue that care must be taken to ensure that the minority and the powerless are represented in the establishment of the commonality.

We would note that this transcendental procedure is not synonymous with the universalism-particularism dimension. We would argue that the basis of the universalistic procedure is to treat all persons involved equally — or to pursue an action in terms of what is the greatest good for the greatest number. A transcendental procedure would not consider the absolute numbers of all participants, nor would it assume that everyone involved in an interaction sequence is equal. Rather it would attend to the interests and goals involved, and attempt to establish a common frame of reference to which all participants could agree, and then work from there.

Perhaps an example would serve to clarify these distinctions. When a gang worker is working with a gang, and the gang is making some "progress" toward less delinquent behavior, he is frequently faced with the problem of the "back-slider," i.e., the person who slips back into delinquent activities. If he punishes the boy by preventing him from using agency facilities, the boy is then pushed outside of the worker's influence. Yet if he keeps the boy in the group, this may not be fair to the other boys who have been on their best behavior. The problem the worker is faced with, then, is how to reward the boys who have remained on their good behavior, and at the same time avoid punishing the back-slider so severely that he is placed beyond the reach of the social worker. This is usually done by devising a level of punishment which suits the boy's particular background, explaining this action to the other boys in the group, and giving them some reward. In any case, an attempt is made to take the interests of both the back-slider and the rest of the group into account, as well as the goals that the gang worker has for *all* of the boys concerned.

Problems Resulting from Presentation of the Findings

Even in the writing-up stage of the project, problems of an ethical and political nature have arisen. One key problem stems from the traditional usage of the composite case — the fictional-but-representative case — as a means of protecting the anonymity of informants. Consider the cases cited in the body of this paper. On the advice of a lawyer, we have modified and fictionalized cases, and we have constructed hypothetical and composite cases. However, in seeking to protect ourselves and our respondents from possible adverse consequences, we have violated a series of scientific norms. First, we have effectively precluded any other social scientist from replicating our study. Second, although we have tried to select the relevant characteristics for the composite cases, the fact remains that we have still presented some data and not others. The logical possibility exists that we have failed to present the very data which are needed by other scientists.

The laws of scientific evidence may in this instance conflict with legal norms regarding protection of the researcher and the respondents. This is a strange paradox. Logically and legally it may be that sociologists are simply unable to guarantee the anonymity of respondents. Of course sociologists pursue research projects of this type quite frequently and without adverse consequences. But we would argue that this is more a matter of "probability" than of "possibility." And if there is a possibility that the sociologist cannot guarantee complete anonymity for his respondents then this factor should be taken into consideration in designing research projects.

A related problem in the construction of composite cases concerns the implications of attributing certain actions and statements to particular informants. There is a choice as to the number and specificity of descriptive adjectives that one can use in identifying an informant. For instance, one might attribute a statement to a "social worker" or "a Mexican-American social worker" or "a Mexican-American social worker with the leading social agency in San Antonio." To the extent that one constructs general categories, exact replication becomes impossible and the relevancy of certain variables is obscured. And yet for the specific groups in which the research was done, even a very general description is often sufficient to identify an informant.

Finally, there is the question of the effect of this very article on the situation in which the research was undertaken. Particularly important is the degree to which this paper violates implicit agreements that were made with respondents. For instance, the social workers at the agency have not been, up to this point, aware that the researcher hired a secret observer. When this becomes publicly known via this article, it may have some effect on the relationship between the researcher and the social work personnel. In any case, it is clear that the publication of this and similar articles may have an effect upon the latter stages of the research project as well as on the continued operation of the agency.

Conclusions

It would appear from an examination of this case study that ethical and political issues do arise in a research project, that they drastically affect its course, and that they are almost unavoidable. This is perhaps so because we are performing research in a pluralistic society. In a pluralistic society different sectors operate more or less autonomously and develop their own special values and ethics. Because these sectors are only loosely articulated, relatively little conflict occurs between them. Yet such conflict is possible, because to the extent that any one sector insists upon the rigid application of its own values in other sectors it questions the legitimacy of these other sectors.

Scientific research is one sector and it has its own set of values, ethics, and goals. Yet rigorous adherence to scientific ideals infringes upon the rights of other groups or persons. Conversely, if, say, the legal system insisted upon rigid application of the law, then science, or at least research on deviant behavior, would become virtually impossible; science would become merely an extension of the legal system.[10]

Perhaps the infrequency of direct confrontation is due to adaptations that the research sector has made — either implicitly or explicitly — with respect to other sectors. One adaptation is engaging in research that (1) does not explicitly appear to controvert the values of any other group, or at least not the rights of powerful groups, and (2) does not draw the researcher into direct interaction with these other systems. Studies of individual characteristics of delinquents are perhaps an example of this type of adaptation.

Other theoretical traditions — for example, the symbolic interactionist, which emphasizes the impact of systems upon one another — draw the researcher into direct interaction with these other systems in the data gathering process. In this situation, obvious ethical dilemmas arise, and the adaptation seems to be one in which the research sector bargains with the others in a more or less private arena, so that compromises are made and each sector is allowed to achieve certain of its values and retain its legitimacy and autonomy.

This sort of private inter-sector bargaining is probably very common in our society. What has not often been recognized is that the research sector must also make its private arrangements. And if such accommodations are necessary, the techniques of making private arrangements should become an accepted and examined part of our methodology. As it is now, it is privately recognized, yet relegated to the status of a "skeleton-in-the-closet."

NOTES TO THE CHAPTER

1. The data in this study were collected in connection with the Wesley Youth Project under the support of the National Institute of Mental Health (Grant number R11-MH-1075-02 and 02S10) and the Hogg Foundation for Mental Health, Austin, Texas.

2. "HEW Blasted in N.Y. Pupil Personality Test," *San Antonio News,* February 11, 1966, p. 6-A. Shortly after this, many persons and institutions holding grants under the Department of Health, Education, and Welfare were instructed to set up committees which would safeguard the privacy and autonomy of the subjects or respondents. Special emphasis was placed upon the rights of children under college age.

3. Alfred J. Kahn, "The Case of the Premature Claims: Public Policy and Delinquency Prediction," *Crime and Delinquency* (July, 1965), pp. 217–28.

4. Gilbert Geis, "Legal and Ethical Aspects of Experiments in Correctional Research," Unpublished paper presented on August 29, 1965, at the Fifteenth Annual Meeting of the Society for the Study of Social Problems, Edgewater Beach Hotel, Chicago, Illinois.

5. The research adviser referred to here and elsewhere in this paper is Gideon Sjoberg, Associate Professor of Sociology, The University of Texas, Austin, Texas.

6. Erving Goffman, *The Presentation of Self in Everyday Life* (New York: Doubleday Anchor Books, 1959).

7. Art Gallaher, Jr., "Plainville: The Twice-Studied Town," in Arthur Vidich, Joseph Bensman, and Maurice R. Stein (eds.), *Reflections on Community Studies*

(New York: John Wiley & Sons, 1964). *Cf.* William Foote Whyte, *Street Corner Society* (rev. ed., Chicago: University of Chicago Press, 1955).

8. Herbert Gans, *The Urban Villagers* (Glencoe, Ill.: The Free Press, 1960).

9. Dale Broeder, "Silence and Perjury Before Police Officers," *Nebraska Law Review,* 40 (December, 1960), p. 102. Cf. Margaret K. Rosenheim, "Privilege, Confidentiality, and Juvenile Offenders," *Wayne Law Review,* 11 (1965), pp. 660–75.

10. For social workers, this sort of adaptation has already been suggested. See Mary E. Blake, "Youth Workers and the Police," *Children,* 8 (September-October, 1961), pp. 170–74.

CHAPTER FOURTEEN

Interaction and Identification in Reporting Field Research: A Critical Reconsideration of Protective Procedures

RICHARD COLVARD

It is in preparing a manuscript for formal publication that the field researcher most fully realizes how much his insight has depended on his identification with others, and how much his interest in accuracy might affect them adversely. Assessment of his rights and responsibilities in such final writing is a complicated process of considering informants' expectations, and those of editors, publishers, sponsors, and the public at large, as well as self-expectations and the anticipated reactions of other scholars, who are often the author's main audience, and jury.

In such interaction, the integrity not only of individuals but of institutions[1] is on trial. There are many parties of interest in research and its public presentation. And in this society, the author of a field study continually encounters competing values: the advance of scientific knowledge, the protection of personal privacy, and the preservation of political responsibility.

Choice is inevitable, and always partly personal. But while considering such values, and the social relations supporting them, the man with the manuscript before him is influenced by his particular theoretical perspective, and its arbitrary assumptions about reality, validity, and reliability. He can also be both supported and constrained by the editorial customs of special interest in this essay: reporting statuses and pseudonyms instead of actual names, paraphrasing quotations rather than presenting them verbatim, withholding information obtained more personally than officially, and obtaining post-research permission for publication.

Such protective procedures are obviously important means of accommodating many conflicting rights and interests in social research. But the analysis of complicated case evidence here suggests that they often neither protect privacy adequately nor preserve knowledge accurately, and they can also blur political accountability — to a degree undesirable in a society still stressing personal responsibility for acts affecting others. The larger implication is that the responsible scholar is not necessarily one who avoids personal identification *with* others during actual research, and personal identification *of* them in subsequent writing for formal publication.

Editing an Article about "The Colleges and the 'Arkansas Purchase' Controversy"

The case evidence below comes from extensive editorial correspondence about an article on a major battle in the liberal arts — professional education war still being waged in American higher education. The Arkansas Experiment in Teacher Education (or AETE) was originally conceived as a state-wide conversion to a fifth-year internship program. All fifteen public and private four-year institutions then training teachers would remove education courses from their undergraduate curricula. All prospective teachers would first obtain a regular arts or sciences degree (B.A. or B.S.), then have another year of concentrated professional education — organized cooperatively by colleges in particular regions, and closely tied to supervised practice teaching in selected public schools. Initial costs of conversion to the new program — estimates went up to $10 million — were to be covered by a philanthropic foundation, which was already sponsoring similar efforts in other states — but on a smaller scale.

Those especially interested in the sociological aspects of what some at the time (1951–52) called the "Arkansas Purchase" controversy should refer to the article as finally published.[2] It deals with them in considerable detail, and also with the eventual decision to develop fifth-year programs which were optional rather than required — ones lasting in some form from 1952 to 1959.

A sufficient sense of the AETE controversy can be obtained from the correspondence here, which concentrates attention on "protective" issues in the editing process. The letters have been shortened where logically possible and are presented without interstitial comment, in order to invite the reader to consider the case in his own way. The following overview of issues is far from exhaustive. But it is important as a more specific introduction, especially to the final section, which contains a critical reconsideration of the author's original decisions about accuracy and anonymity — and much evidence of his persistent ambivalence about the desirability of deleting actual names.

The following related issues, recurring through several series of letters, will receive special attention in the eventual analysis:

. . . whether additional permission to publish the field evidence on AETE should have been obtained from the academic and philanthropic sponsors (and subjects) of the field research on which the article was being based;

. . . whether selective reporting of statuses and pseudonyms (e.g., "President X of College Y") rather than real names provided sufficient anonymity, and sufficient accuracy as well;

. . . whether quotations from interviews (in which fairly prominent educators and politicians expressed themselves in provocative and/or profane ways) should have been paraphrased, rather than presented as verbatim as possible;

. . . whether any use should have been made of information which some informants had specified, and others implied, was offered more personally — e.g., more "off the record" — than in official researcher-respondent roles.

Another issue that eventually emerged concerned whether a libel suit would be likely, if the author and the editors agreed to rely on the original permission for publication, despite the probability that some individuals would still be indirectly identifiable. And finally the analysis here will include extensive discussion of the larger implications of even more general issues about protective procedures in social research — especially in American Sociology.

The Case Evidence

[Editor to Author: London 7/31/62] Dear Professor C————:

I am currently editing a book of papers on the processes involved in educational innovation[3] . . . The range is wide . . . The intent is to open up the area of educational innovation for further inquiry.

The book ought to have . . . a chapter on the innovative role of foundations in relation to research and demonstration. . . . [Recently I learned] that you had been working on a project via Russell Sage on the inter-relations of foundations, research people, and educational institutions. I would be very much interested in knowing more about what you are doing, and whether you would be interested in contributing to the book . . . .

As you might expect, I think the book has a lot of potential impact. Mostly this area has been ignored or treated polemically, or examined only from the point of view of the content of innovations. An approach which looks systematically at change *processes* can, I think, be very helpful in illuminating the area as a legitimate one for inquiry. It might even be useful in some of the current spate of attempts at educational reform.

[Reply to Editor: Austin 8/21/62] Dear Professor M————:

I hope you will excuse the delay in replying . . . But it seemed the only way I could tell whether I might have something of possible value for the very interesting book you're working on was to sit down and rough something out . . .

As you can tell, the manuscript is based on work which led up to my current larger study on risk capital philanthropy and higher education.[4] The latter is still so very much "in process" . . . and the early parts which I have in very rough draft form deal so much with foundations and so little with higher education — or innovation, really — that it seemed to be a better idea to work with what is really more of a single, although extremely complex and unprecedented, case of foundation-college interaction in a controversial experiment in teacher education.

Though it all started over ten years ago now, practically nothing of an analytical sort has been published about the Arkansas Experiment in Teacher Education, or the fight which preceded it, the latter really being the main subject of the enclosed manuscript. Everybody has "heard of it" sort of vaguely. But nobody really knows much about it, one reason being that the Executive Committee (in Arkansas) which sponsored the Evaluation Report has apparently not been anxious to circulate it, nor has the foundation which ultimately paid for the evaluation.

[The] director of the evaluation assured me a few years ago, however, that under the terms of the contract he had with the Executive Committee I was free to publish anything I wanted to from the field study material, part of which I helped gather during 1956–57 and used for my 1959 dissertation.

[Author to AETE Evaluation Director: Austin 10/5/59] Dear Professor ————:

[The field director] tells me that you are now in Europe, but I am sending this letter along anyway, hoping that your office will know where to get in touch with you . . .

I'm wondering whether the 11/13/58 memo which I received from you, the one indicating that we were "now free to publish articles relating to the evaluation of AETE," still holds. I ask this because since that time I have received several cryptic notes from Little Rock, notes indicating that there was some delay and ambiguity about publication of the final report. . . .

Though I'm naturally somewhat tired of working over that material we gathered, I'm still interested in the AETE developments and would appreciate being brought up to date. Must confess I was disturbed to see what seemed to me to be some of the more interesting sections condensed or eliminated in the version of the final report sent to me. Though, as you may recall from the long memo I sent you several years ago, I had some differences — both of fact and of interpretation — with some sections, especially the ———— chapter, I felt that many of those chapters would be of interest to a wide audience in education.

[Evaluation Director to Author: The Hague 10/16/59] Dear Dick:

. . . The report of evaluation of AETE was published by the Executive Committee and a copy was supposed to have been sent to you by them. Accordingly, you are now free to publish anything which you can get printed.

The story of why the report was published in mimeo rather than as planned is long and complicated, but essentially the Fund was able to prevent a printed report coming out, if my hunches are correct. A full story would occupy many pages.

[The field director] may have an extra copy of the final report, if you wish to use it.

[Author to AETE Executive Committee Member: Austin 9/26/62] Dear Dean ————:

I appreciate your help on these matters of dates and developments subsequent to the field study, and your patient cooperation in the past. I also want you to know that, in accordance with the contractual arrangements . . . I am making full use of interviews and other data gathered during the evaluation which bear on the sociological questions in which I am interested.

The dictates of documentation require that I identify the Fund and the University, but it seemed both desirable and legitimate to me not to refer to specific individuals by name, or even by unequivocally identifiable position. If I could in good conscience go further in that direction, I would. But, as it is, those familiar with the situation will know that you are the "University representative" somewhat ambivalently trying to bring the various factions together, that ———————— is the "president of teachers college X" whose vigorous letter to the *Arkansas Gazette,* e.g., is cited, etc.

There seems no honest way to analyze the events without using such somewhat transparent designations of the positions of major actors involved. I worry about this but see no way around it . . . However, I have made every effort I could to show all sides of the issues, and have been very explicit on the point that I am not interested in trying to assess "heroes, fools, and villains," but, rather, in suggesting what sociologists and others can learn from AETE.

[Editor to Author: New York 10/5/62] Dear Professor C————:

I am currently copy-editing your chapter and am as pleased with it as ever. If I have any more questions as I proceed I'll certainly be in touch with you promptly. Otherwise you can expect to see galleys within a month, I should think.

I really applaud, by the way, your continuing interest in the sociology of foundations, and hope you continue with it. One of the striking things I encountered during plans for the innovation book was the alacrity with which people shy away from doing anything on foundations as a legitimate subject of inquiry. I don't think people were "frightened" of the topic — only a little uneasy and uncertain as to how to take hold of it, perhaps. Still, there are undoubtedly forces pushing scientists away from examining the sources of manna. More power to you.

[Editor to Author: New York 10/19/62] Dear Professor C————:

Among other requests for clarifying details . . . The professional reader would be enormously gratified if you can give more bibliographical data on the Evaluation Report, which is widely assumed to have been suppressed. As it stands, all we have is "undated, mimeographed," which doesn't help much, and simply confirms the notion that the Fund is against inquiry, etc. Can you give more?

[Reply to Editor: Austin 10/23/62] Dear Professor M————:

On the bibliographical reference to the Evaluation Report: this is a long story and one I have been checking on since I got your letter yesterday afternoon. Since I was a little hazier than I wanted to be about the subsequent fate of that report, I finally called the Evaluation Director about it last night. He told me:

a. That 100 copies of the report (mimeographed) were prepared under the auspices of the [AETE Executive Committee] and subsequently distributed both to the colleges in Arkansas and elsewhere. Note: the enclosed copies of letters from the State office of AETE indicate, at least to me, that the Executive Committee itself was not anxious to have the sections dealing with college conflicts . . . widely distributed. According to the Evaluation Director on the phone, however, such sections (in which pseudonyms were used) were included in the copies distributed.

b. The Evaluation Director, on his own initiative I suspect, had a pretty complete set of the interviews and other basic evaluation data deposited in the University of "Midwest" library.

c. Again according to the same man on the phone, the Fund hired ———— at "West Coast" University to write a presumably condensed version (and appraisal?) of the Evaluation Report . . . This was apparently published, but after hunting all morning through the normal bibliographic sources I have been unable to find a reference to it. I will write to the man at West Coast today, but I think the quickest way for you to get a reference (and I think one should be included as at least a "cf." in the notes referring to the Evaluation Report) would be to call the Fund in New York and ask them for a reference.

From the way the Evaluation Director talked there was a published report, and the foreword, as he recalled it, indicated that in the West Coast man's opinion the Evaluation Report had included a lot of irrelevant information. What this means I'm not sure, but I recall that as the Evaluation Director explained it during 56–57, the Fund, from the outset, had been interested in the evaluation of the "product" (i.e., the abilities of the 5th year graduates) and not much interested in the "process." It is my personal opinion that one of the Fund official's personal convictions about the basically inconclusive nature of much educational research entered into this attitude; perhaps a reluctance to expose the Fund's effort, the conflict, etc., was also involved but I have no evidence of that.

[Reply to Author: New York 10/26/62] Dear Professor C————:

Many thanks for your prompt help on the ms. I'm enclosing for your interest a copy of the West Coast man's report (no publisher — no date — no wonder you couldn't find it) which the Fund sent me. Please keep it, and I'll get another.

It's an interesting document; I'd love to know what the "non-germane" material in the Evaluation report was.

I have followed your suggestions on footnoting the fate and availability of the Evaluation Report, added this other report, and mentioned that the data are at the U. of Midwest Library. When you see galleys (about a month, I estimate) you can fix whatever doesn't look appropriate.

[Second Report Writer to Author: West Coast University 10/28/62] Dear Professor C————:

I have your inquiry about the report on the Arkansas Experiment. Through some oversight I never received a copy of the final report. I believe you can secure a copy from the Arkansas State Department of Education . . . If you are pressed for time, it might be useful also to write immediately to the Fund . . . with the same request.

[Editor to Author: New York 2/10/63] Dear Professor C———:

My optimism as to when you could see the galleys seems to have been about as unfounded as most optimism. Sorry! I have just gotten some queries from the [Publisher's] editor, who has just — finally — gotten through copy-editing. Can you send me back responses? Then you really will see galleys soon afterward.

The most central query focuses around the interview material. The editor says:

1. Can anonymous quotes be identified by looking into files at Midwest or in Colvard (1959), etc.? If so, and if they are published anywhere, we must either have the speaker's permission (in writing) to quote, or the quotations must be replaced by brief and to-the-point paraphrases.

2. Have any of them been published? If so, we must have permission of copyright holder(s) to quote. Or paraphrase . . . .

My guess is that the [Publisher] is being a little over-cautious, perhaps because the quotes themselves are fairly salty, and it wants to be sure that it won't get into trouble. There is ordinarily no difficulty in quoting respondents directly in a study. The special touchiness here is that a number of respondents are themselves public figures.

I would appreciate your comments on the questions above. I am very much for keeping as much of the verbatim material as possible, because of the flavor it conveys. In a way the issue is whether the public fiction of protected anonymity has been successfully maintained.

And finally: is a copy of the original Evaluation Report on file anywhere? The citation now reads . . . .

I think that's all. Yours for fearless truth. As soon as I have your help on these queries we can march ahead.

[Author to Director of University of Midwest Library: Austin 2/26/63] Dear Dr. ———:

The Evaluation Director has suggested that I contact you directly . . . I have a chapter dealing with some of the early and controversial stages of AETE which is due to appear . . . in just a few months. The editor . . . . recently raised a question about the degree of protection provided informants, some of whose statements in interviews (made by myself, by the Evaluation Director, and several others) are cited anonymously in the manuscript.

There is little doubt that I have permission to cite anonymously: several records in my possession make that clear. The problem is whether the anonymity is really adequate if the informants can be identified by their real names in the documents . . . under your control there at Midwest.

This is one of those almost impossible situations in which — to be scrupulous in your responsibilities to informants it is important to maintain a public fiction of anonymity, even though those familiar with the circumstances can easily tell the identities — and to be thorough in your documentation you need to make the documents accessible to others. I urged the Evaluation Director to have some sort of arrangement whereby the documents stored at Midwest would not contain the real names in some easily accessible way — particularly since some of the interviews contained "off the record" speculations and similar remarks intended only for researchers' use. There must be some way to maximize the extent to which the obligations to informants and to other scholars can be met without undue compromise.

[Reply to Author: Midwest U. 3/1/63] Dear Professor C————:

In response to your letter . . . I would like to report that the Arkansas survey material is in the University of Midwest library. The collection is contained in the original nine boxes in which it was received, and for safety is kept in our closed stacks. I believe that yours is the first request to consult it [sic] since the material was deposited . . .

In answer to your specific questions: (1) the collection is not classified or catalogued, though I believe that the items you want are in Box 5, containing the interviews; (2) our general policy is to make such materials available to qualified faculty members and graduate students, but since the documents in the particular instance appear to be highly sensitive, perhaps we would need a statement of approval from the Evaluation Director before granting access; (3) there is no way of separating the names of interviewers and interviewees, judging from an examination of the records; (4) it would be appropriate in your footnote reference to locate the documents at Midwest — we have made no secret of their presence here.

[Author to Editor: Austin 3/3/63] Dear Professor M————:

I finally heard from the University of Midwest today, and can go ahead and answer almost all of the questions reported in your welcome — if somewhat frustrating — letter of February 10. It is not surprising that the [Publisher's] editor raised the questions he did about adequacy of protection: I have been aware of the moral and political problems posed by some of that Arkansas data for much longer than he has.

Some of them are simply not possible to resolve in a completely satisfactory way. But I think this letter and its enclosures will indicate that the precautions that have been taken during and after the original research, and in the manuscript itself, are more complete than usual in work of this sort, in which it is impossible to be accurate without referring to the positions of otherwise anonymous persons.

Perhaps I am wrong, but I felt the requirements of documentation, particularly in this case where newspaper accounts for example, were important kinds of data, made it illogical (and a little ridiculous) to disguise the period of time, the state, and the state university, and the positions, e.g., editor, governor, etc., of some key actors, whose statements and general roles could not adequately be understood if they were changed or further blurred.

Well, enough of general comments: let me try to answer the various questions in the order in which they appeared in your letter:

p. 1 . . . Since the anonymous quotes cannot be identified by looking into my dissertation (1959), and since it now appears that they can also not be identified by patrons of the University of Midwest Library, it would not seem necessary to paraphrase the quotations (something I would hate to do not because some of them are pungent, but because they are more accurate in their present form, and give — as part of their accuracy — an important sense of the mood and tone of the controversy), or to track down and secure written permission to quote from each person.

A blanket permission to use anonymous quotations from the academic people interviewed was secured as part of the contractual arrangements in the original research (see enclosures), and similar permission was obtained orally from the Arkansas newspaper editor (who was interviewed by myself and one other colleague) and the governor (again a person who I personally interviewed). There comes a point in work of this sort when one must simply rely on the integrity of the scholar involved, who surely must also have some rights to be considered . . .

Re your suggestion about a standard insertion, e.g., "in an interview with an evaluation team member" etc. It seems to me that the over-all footnote makes it clear that statements not footnoted are from interviews. Repeating that, even in some standard form, would get boring, I believe, as well as making the thing more turgid than it should be: it's hard enough to keep the action flowing . . .

p. 17 [I] thought the time sequence . . . would make it clear that the University's president had already left and that a School of Education official took his place as the chief representative in the negotiations. I realize that the sequence is much clearer to me than to the average reader, however, so might suggest the following rewording. Note: I would very much like to be able to avoid (as I have in present ms.) the use of the S of E man's actual title: it seemed unavoidable (for accuracy) in the case of the presidents, but perhaps I'm being very inconsistent and irrational here. . . .

p. 18 [I] suggest the following rewording. Note: again, this matter would be clarified if I used the man's actual position, but I would rather not. It is quite definitely true that he was "long familiar": his own work brought him in direct touch with accreditation matters in the state, and his father had known and worked with many of the principal actors in AETE, or their institutional predecessors — as an educator himself. This man was very helpful in providing some historical background on the financial and administrative problems of higher education in the state . . .

p. 26 . . . The sense of the passage in question here might be clearer . . . if it read:

> fearful that, *whatever* they decided about the fifth-year program, these just-buried bones of contention might rise again: if these administrators went along with the University and the private college people advocating a state-wide fifth-year program, the coordinating machinery necessary for the new program might naturally serve as an eventual nucleus for a comprehensive state control system: if they didn't go along, the legislature might become alienated enough to force such a system on them anyway.

If I've missed the point, or the problem, here — please let me know. I'm willing to defend the line of argument, or I wouldn't have written it up that way.

p. 27. "Trite" is the way this was taken down in the [attempted verbatim] interview: that's the way I think it ought to appear. I deliberately attempted to show the mood on the other side with the "it's just a blank check" quote which follows shortly after.

p. 13. Apparently this was one of the many excerpts which I took from the [*Arkansas*] *Gazette,* and in this one case I neglected to get the complete page and date reference: didn't even notice it that way in the dissertation. I have sent for microfilm copies of the *Gazette* and will have the date etc. for you probably in a matter of a few weeks. They will only release 3 microfilm reels at one time, but I know the approximate period within which that editorial appeared.

Incidentally — or maybe not so incidentally — I should probably tell you that, in what may have been an excess of protective caution in the dissertation, I referred to the *Arkansas Gazette* as the *Arkansas "Clarion,"* but gave correct page and date references. That is probably no longer as necessary (if it ever was) since the editor involved is no longer in the state.

My thought was that in formally published work it would be vital to use the actual sources in a complete way. I think in the case of this particular footnote you could just leave space for a complete reference . . . then I can change it on the galley proofs . . . I don't mind tracking this one down because I want it to be accurate . . . .

"Final query": According to my telephone conversation with the Evaluation Director a few months ago, copies of the original report were distributed to: 1) all the participating colleges and universities in Arkansas; 2) the University of Midwest library (note that pseudonyms were used, not real names, in the Evaluation Report sections dealing with the aspects of AETE I deal with); 3) the University of Northwest library, and 4) "many other places."

I also have a personal copy which I would be willing to let any professional person with a legitimate interest peruse. (I don't know of a succinct way to put all that — at least not at this time of night!)

Sorry about the delay in replying, but I thought I would wait until I got some definite word from Midwest. If the word presented here is not definite enough, let me know. I'll send along anything else that turns up.

As I say, I'm sympathetic on the "protection" problem, which bothers me a lot in much social research. I do feel, however, that the protection is adequate — or even more so — for all concerned. There is no perfect way to do this sort of thing. I have enclosed some supporting documents which might ease your editor's mind. I would like to know if he has subjected all such work to the same degree of scrutiny. I'm not advocating irresponsibility here, but rather feel that I've handled the material in a responsible way, with a minor exception or two which I was glad to have detected . . .

P.S. As of next June, I'll be associate professor in the Department of Sociology, State University of New York at Buffalo . . . Also: Learned a few months ago from my mother-in-law that you were also from Antioch — should have known anyway . . . I graduated in '52, my wife Pat in '53. It would be fun to compare notes sometime.

[Reply to Author: New York 3/13/63] Dear Dick C————:

Many, many thanks for the careful work you put in on the ms. queries I passed along. Antioch blood will show! At any rate, I think all the problems have been disposed of and we can rest easy. Final OK from the [Publisher] is still pending, but it looks positive, judging from my talk with the editor yesterday.

I think your over-all position as expressed on the first page of your letter is excellent, and gives a good underlying rationale for the handling of quotes, identification, etc., throughout . . .

I'll look forward to getting the AETE address, and the *Arkansas Gazette* reference. Both can be caught at the galley stage. I would agree that there is no point in calling the *Gazette* by an assumed name.

[Author to Editor: Austin 3/14/63] Dear Professor M————:

As I indicated in our telephone conversation this morning, I have gone back over the whole manuscript to make doubly sure that every possible effort to maintain accuracy, while protecting anonymity as much as possible, has been made. There were quite a few places in which it seemed to me that improvements on both scores were possible, some being fairly minor corrections of a word or so left out or garbled somehow — either within my dissertation or in the excerpting from the dissertation, some being more major corrections of that sort.

In one case I had inadvertently combined quotations from two different people — one of those things where the bottom of one page ends and the top of another begins. Another case is the one I mentioned to you, where, as I went over the interview summary made by another researcher, it seemed more clear than I had previously realized that the respondent had been attempting to keep some of the remarks he made "off the record."

Clearly if all responsible officials kept all of their statements in the latter category it would be impossible to do research of the sort I am attempting. But, even as in the publication of this manuscript, it is equally impossible to control the consequences one statements might have for others. And the researcher must be obliged to recognize and accept that fact as much as he can without jeopardizing his effort to be accurate.

If I had made the interview in question myself, and was therefore more definitely sure which statements were made only on the condition that they not be recorded (in this situation, the use of the material was just plain ambiguous), and which were clearly intended to be usable if anonymity was maintained, I might feel more legitimate to use at least a "later paraphrase" type of quotation. Since the actual situation was different, I have decided to simply include the points made — the most important ones — in the text, as a way of trying to maintain accuracy without undue use of imperfectly categorized interview material.

If you feel strongly that I have bent over too far in the direction of protection, please let me know and I will reconsider the matter, which I have been brooding about for quite awhile since I last wrote you.

The enclosed carbon copy of the manuscript contains several kinds of changes: Many pages, for example, contain interview indented material, and I have marked these (at the ends) either AV . . . or LP . . . An explanatory footnote could be put at the place where the first use is made of this sort of material, indicating that "AV" ones were either taped and transcribed, or the attempt was made to write down the exact words at the time of the interview, and that "LP" ones were written up shortly after interviews, from notes made during the interviews. (This distinction, to my knowledge, is not usually made in most social research, but perhaps it is time we did something like this).

[Reply to Author: New York 3/28/63] Dear Dick C————:

Last letter before we go to the printers, I hope. I've incorporated all your additions and corrections, including the AV-LP notation, so we are in good shape . . .

I've reviewed the problem of identification of respondents, etc., with ———————————, the [Publisher's] director. If I understand his concern correctly, it is not so much being sued as such, but the possibility that a suit might succeed in getting an injunction to stop sales of the book, require removal of the material, etc., which would be inconvenient and costly.

What's needed at this point is some probability estimating on your part. There is no real way to be 1,000% sure that an identity has been successfully concealed, particularly in the case of the public figures involved. The question is, are any of these people (see below) likely, in your opinion, to be bothered enough to make an issue out of it? There is also the possibility that a disgruntled person, not really caring about the quote as such, would bring suit in order to foul up the book for other reasons. . . .

If you'd like to talk this over by phone, please call me collect . . . any day next week. Better make it a person-to-person call.

My hope, of course, is that you will say: fine, none of them is at all likely to do anything — because I think the chapter a rich, flavorful account with a lot of learning for the reader. It would be the poorer (for example) with the School of Ed. guy's quotes out. But if there is a strong possibility that the book would get held up, then I'm concerned.

One funny problem exists here. It's possible that if we ask permission for some of the quotes, this would raise problems in the respondent's mind which might never appear otherwise, even if he saw himself in print after the fact.

So what do you think? Let me know as soon as you can and we will proceed. . . .

These seem to be the most identifiable people. The pages listed give quotes that they might (or might not) be bothered about seeing in print. Can you make a rough estimate of the likelihood that each guy would be moved to act? If it looks high in any particular case, then the cue is to moderate the quote, or get permission. If none of them look high to you, then let's go ahead. This is all very iffy, of course, but is an attempt to draw on your understanding of the situation. . . .

> Editor: 24, and added material you sent, beginning, "There is something you have to consider here . . ."
> Governor: 23, 24, 34.
> Foundation official: material you sent earlier, enclosed (" 'Arkansas Purchase' charge was stupid . . .")
> University president: 23.
> School of Ed. official: 14, 17, 33, 37, 38. I just love him; the quotes are earthy as hell.
> SDE [State Department of Education] official: 26, 27, 33, and 35.

There were a lot of assorted quotes from presidents and deans of colleges, but my assumption was that they were largely unidentifiable. However, if I'm wrong, the saltiest or most actionable are probably those on 18, 35, and 19.

[Reply to Editor: Austin 4/2/63]

[Notes on telephone call] First indicated generally that: 1) prior permission to use all field data had been part of original agreement with Director and sponsors; 2) positions but not names had been used in the Evaluation Report and in the author's dissertation, and the written preface to the U. of Northwest's team's interview schedule had indicated that the evidence would be "collected and reported in such a way that no individuals will be named" — their respondents had read that statement and followed a copy of the schedule during the interview; 3) another consultation requesting additional permission might be ideal, but would give officials on both sides of the controversy another opportunity to abrogate the original agreements; 4) political controversy among the state institutions was perennial and familiar, and well-covered in the press already. Next indicated more specifically that the:

> Editor: was out of the state now and, in any event, had clearly indicated in the interview that he was even willing to have his name used.
> Governor: was not Faubus. Had run again recently but was a political realist who probably couldn't care less about such a small storm as this.
> Foundation official: couldn't imagine his protesting very much; it would make him look silly. He might mumble and grumble, and maybe write a rebuttal, but the accounts were accurate, and the stuff in, e.g., D. Macdonald's *The Ford Foundation* was much stronger.
> School of Ed. official: had already written him 9/26/62 as an informant

and Executive Committee [of AETE] member, informing him that the interview material would be used but as anonymously as possible to also protect accuracy. He had not squawked. Had supplied some dates and other needed facts on the demise of AETE, and later developments in the state. Was a smart, blunt-speaking person.

It would be possible to include some other quotations that would make the latter points more evident, but the ones already included seemed accurate and honest, as the man himself had seemed, and indirectly been shown to be.

SDE official: was out of the state now. His former colleagues would recognize his role and statements, but my own colleague's interview with him gave the clear impression that he would not be offended by such indirect identification.

Assorted presidents and deans of colleges: fifteen colleges and universities had been involved. The dean of one of the two teachers colleges might be more identifiable than he would like: it would not distort the analysis unduly if he were referred to as an "administrative official" rather than as a dean.

The president of one teachers college had made many similar statements in the press; had been cooperative, if a little evasive in an old administrator's way in the interview; and, although he would probably not prefer to be so evident, he would probably respect an objective analysis — now that AETE has already been over for several years.

The private college dean quoted on p. 19 was one of seven, and thus not readily identifiable anyway — as was just as well, given the accurate quote that the college had earlier put more emphasis on football than education.

We ought, in short, to go ahead: the issues and events were important, the analysis defensible, and the odds at this point were that none of the people the Publisher's editor was worried about was actually very likely to sue.

[The latter agreed, and the book went ahead with the chapter intact.]

[Publisher's Editor to Author: New York 5/27/63] Dear Professor C———:

You will be happy to know that the manuscript for your chapter for *Innovation in Education* is ready to go to the printer. But before sending it off, we thought we should give you an opportunity to look at it one more time. We say this because the cost of making changes in galley are so high that we must keep changes to an absolute minimum.

You may answer by checking the appropriate space on the copy of this letter and returning it to me in the enclosed envelope . . .

___ Send it to the printer.

× Better let me have one more look.

[Author to Publisher's Editor: Buffalo 6/13/63] Dear Mr. ———:

In haste, I am sending you the manuscript, and what I regret to report is a rather lengthy set of suggestions for final revision. I think [your] editing improved the admittedly cumbersome manuscript a great deal. But there were a few places where the sense of the passage became obscured, and some others in which changes were made in original source material without the use of brackets.

In general, I feel pretty strongly that the original material should not be changed. I also feel pretty strongly about the minor suggestions made in the enclosed material, but am certainly willing to compromise on some of them, and am very much aware of the time pressure.

[Editor to Author: New York 9/4/63] Dear Dick C———:

Here finally are the galleys of your piece . . . . As you know, resetting is costly, so please inhibit the impulse to "improve sentences" unless your soul cries out deeply . . .

As things stand now, we'll have the page proof in late November and books in January. I'm really pleased with the book, and with your chapter as one of the more vivid parts of it. Reading galley, I got delighted all over again with the wonderful counterpoint between "the real facts" and the official pronouncements which alluded to them.

[Author to Editor: Buffalo 12/3/63] Dear Matt:

A quick congratulatory-critical note. I was pleased to get the table of contents and concluding chapter, have read the latter fairly carefully, and, although I could sense your dissatisfaction with what it was possible to do with the disparate chapters, I feel you are more deserving of praise than of censure, and need not apologize at all . . . Unlike the authors of many collections of works on broadly related subjects, you made an intelligent effort to try to pull the threads together. . . .

Now, for whatever their worth, and I hope it is not too late to suggest some things, let me make some constructively (I hope) critical comments, under the slogan "No conclusion without confusion." . . .

"My main point, from a personal viewpoint.) I am not happy at all with your arithmetic and related conclusions from my chapter . . . Its definitely critical undertone may have contributed here to oversimplification, and "in the absence of evaluatory evidence," actual distortion of an extent which I am reluctant to go along with, even indirectly. On to more specifics:

1) There were two fifth-year programs ("regular and alternate"), rather than one. So the calculation of an average direct cost per teacher which takes no account of that fact is a pretty dubious figure, I believe, especially so when the second program was set up partly in an attempt to reduce the costs involved, and also when no comparative figures on similar kinds of costs for other programs (experimental or otherwise) are offered.

I would much prefer that the gross figures be used without the cost per teacher arithmetic: It is legitimate to attempt the latter, of course. But, without the presentation of many more details, I think it is a slippery effort, which might better be foregone — not out of cowardice, but out of a cautious consideration of the complexity concealed by the bare figures . . .

2) To say, "Thus over $3 million was spent in six years *to produce*" (my emphasis) is again seriously to confuse a much more complicated issue. There is a possible confusion about motivation, for example: in my own abbreviated overview I tried to make clear that the advocates were much interested in multiplier effects, not just in the situation in Arkansas. And there is a fairly clear confusion of conclusion-evaluation (again one I may have tipped you toward). For example, there *were* other products. Much as I think they were probably exaggerated by the Fund people, I would agree there were stimulation benefits within the system, and multiplier effects outside it — to mention just two.

3) (In the same sentence) to say "improved programs" within quotation marks is to imply-conclude-evaluate that they were not improved at all. If the reference to programs (really unclear) is to those in general education, as seems the most likely, I believe it is a matter of singular consensus, among all participants-evaluators-advocates, that these were very definitely improved.

As I tried to affirm by using the words "strengthened" and "enriched" (only without quotation marks), the evaluation reports clearly pointed to improved faculty, libraries, integration of courses, etc. It is true that the Fund was led to do much more financing of this sort of thing than it had originally intended. But it is equally true that they did it, and that they did it in part on recognition of the real need for it. They could afford to be generous; I am not urging generosity here, but accuracy again.

You are certainly entitled to your own conclusions about AETE. But on the points I have just raised (about the particular paragraph on page 3) I don't think I'm just being a complaining author, who feels no one understands his manuscript but him. I think you do understand it, but were led (perhaps partly by me) to succumb to the temptation of the sort mentioned at the beginning of your chapter, i.e., to pontificate — especially in the "improved programs" passage.

Perhaps I protest too much. Would appreciate your reactions anyway. Thanks again, and again — congratulations.

[Reply to Author: New York 12/20/63] Dear Dick:

Thanks very much for your note with comments on the concluding chapter; they arrived just in time for me to hit page proof with them so we are in good shape.

First on your comments on the arithmetically outrageous statements I perpetrated; I think your points are well taken. You, after all, were closest to the situation and have a feeling for what is justified or unjustified commentary. I have substituted the following for the material you had doubts about:

For example, an experimental statewide program in teacher education, though it did appear to strengthen the participating institutions and may have influenced teacher education programs elsewhere, nevertheless only produced 194 teachers during the experimental program, and cost over $3 million.

I hope this is okay. I tried to take into account the various reservations you had as well as I could. I will assume that this is okay, unless I get a phone call from you by this Monday, December 23rd, when the page proof is going back to the printer forever . . .

Now I am breathing a sigh of relief and the book is 99% sewed up. Mid or late February still looks possible; we are a little ahead of schedule. [sic]

In return for your congratulations, let me add mine to you for what is undoubtedly one of the most punchy chapters in the book. I do hope we can have a chance to meet some time before too long . . .

[The call did not seem necessary, but the opportunity to meet occurred as hoped. It was many months after the book was actually available, but it was pleasant in itself and also helped make this subsequent study possible.]

The detailed case evidence can end abruptly here. But the file folders on the AETE article include: a later note from the Publisher's editor saying that the letter thanking him for the clear layout and clean typography of the printed chapter was a "splendid tonic for a Friday afternoon"; and a still-later set of reviews of the book as a whole. The reviews were generally favorable, and several singled out the AETE chapter for special attention. One reviewer, for example, called it especially "carefully researched,"[5] and another said it was a "minor gem in the history of American education."[6]

Surely it was, and maybe it is. But there is still a sour after-taste from such otherwise pleasant professional tonics for its author. One reason is that there was not one reply when chapter reprints were sent to all key respondents. It is hard to believe that they found it not worth reading. But if they did read it did they simply not care enough about the issues, so long after the actual events? Or did they still care too much? Were the protective procedures (finally decided on) professionally defensible but ethically and politically suspect? Were they even scientifically sufficient?

The reader may have ready answers. The "Author" is still not sure, but will now review such issues much more personally, and indicate some of their implications. The present section has been primarily a dialogue with anonymous others; the next one is essentially a dialogue with myself — as a sociologist and as a person. But it also deliberately exemplifies the style of research reporting — of identifications and identities, of values and value-conflicts — eventually recommended as preferable to present protective procedures.

Issues, Decisions, and Implications

1. *Requesting Post-Research Permission for Publication.* If indirect but intensive documentation leaves individuals still identifiable by others familiar with the situation studied, should the researcher renew his initial permission for publication? Should he especially do so if he already has evidence that some research participants are apt to regard accurate findings as embarrassing or otherwise injurious?

Before writing the AETE article accurately was itself an issue, my general position on the question of "final permission" was approximately this: if subjects had a right of initial informed consent to investigations, then scholars had a related right of informed dissent if disagreements developed about what evidence to include in a published manuscript and how such evidence should be interpreted. To argue otherwise would be to accept a degree of censorship seriously antithetical to objective social science.

The same line of defense was evident in the actual decision not to seek additional permission in the correspondence just reviewed. (8/21/62,

9/26/62, 4/2/63) But later reflection has led me to see that such a customary "professional" defense was quite arbitrary, as I suspect it often is.

If I could make the decision again, I would still try to preserve the initial agreements about evidence and its interpretation. But I would make more of an effort to see to it that, if my dissent were still desirable, it be more fully informed — especially about the feelings and preferences of persons importantly involved and particularly identifiable. Sending the manuscript for review for that purpose itself, not simply as an additional check on accuracy, would be an important if still imperfect procedure. It would still be difficult, and arbitrary, to decide whether a gain in accuracy was worth a loss in anonymity. But to avoid direct assessment of respondents' reactions now seems to me to amount to an uncritical subordination of personal responsibility to the rights, obligations, and privileges assumed in particular professional roles.

The common temptation to which I succumbed was that of trying to resolve value conflicts — my own and others' — by separating professional roles from whole personal identities.[7] Graduate training itself encourages such "solutions," by tending to make professional commitments central to individual identity. But decisions are moved in the same direction by personal identification with those who, for whatever reason, become researchers' "significant others" in a particular study.

In the case here, for example, I did actually notify one key informant far in advance of actual publication (9/26/62). And all through the final writing, I was better able to accept my ambivalence about the decision because this particular informant proved especially co-operative, because I realized that he was the one person who had been in close contact with all the academic and foundation people involved (as both informants and sponsors), and also because I had long since come to respect his frankness and considerable objectivity about the controversy I was analyzing. Encouragement from the Evaluation Director, and other AETE researchers who reviewed the manuscript for accuracy, was similarly helpful. And so, especially, was the advice and support of the Book editor, whom I came to regard as especially able in that role, and also — despite his partisan interest in the article and in teacher education — as a person unusually appreciative of both the scientific and nonscientific issues involved in writing simultaneously for sociologists and for educators.

Still, the ambivalence returned, as it apparently has for other American field researchers[8] long after they have decided that their main obligation was to their professional readers. And, to understand that more than role conflict is involved in such situations, it is important to realize not only that all field researchers can very easily acquire either positive or negative identifications with particular informants (or other participants), but also that American researchers are often personally committed to contradictory values — ones which transcend the professional parts of their lives.

The first such value to be discussed could correctly be termed that of *beneficent objectivity*. For the social scientist who self-critically strives to be as objective as possible is often simultaneously assuming that, on balance and in the long run, his study will be of benefit to his own society and to mankind.

But neither objectivity nor accuracy is ever complete. And there is never any guarantee that a study will be put to purposes the scholar personally approves.[9] A published study may itself be neutral, simply arbitrary symbols on carefully printed pages. But when read with any kind of comprehension it affects imagery and overt action, or inaction.

What the writer intends is rarely irrelevant altogether, for he often selects and always interprets the topic he studies. But "neutral" objectivity is itself a political posture, and "science itself" is only abstractly separable from the rest of society. Scientific and nonscientific meanings alike are established in men's minds; and both "on balance" and "in the long run" the impact of a study is the action it prompts in an audience.[10]

The too-simple faith that research will be beneficial beyond science gets symbolic support, in American society especially, from the idea of progress, persistent now as a belief in the value of *progress through knowledge*.[11] And because the importance of open opportunity for social mobility gets special stress in American ideology generally, researchers in this society are particularly apt to be sensitive about the risk of doing economic injury to the people participating in their studies. Protection of "career chances" is itself reinforced in the social organization of science, which is supposed to be stratified more by achievement than accident and to progress through the confrontation of ideas and cumulation of intellectual wealth.

Such a commitment was evident in the AETE case in my own concern to give the more vulnerable colleges more anonymity, wherever this appeared compatible with the "dictates of documentation." (9/26/62) And it seems implicit, for example, in many of Becker's recommendations about preparing informants in advance for the various possible impacts of publication.[12]

Another cultural aspect of American researchers' ambivalence about making field findings public property can be seen in the common reluctance to jeopardize informants' *right to privacy*. Such reluctance is revealed, for example, in the norm of requesting permission for interviews, a procedure followed in the AETE case and one apparently much more common than that of asking for formal authorization of final publication.

Social scientists here and elsewhere continually study subjects' attitudes and social relations. They often also scrutinize their files, record their furnishings, and analyze their values for inner consistency. But to do so without informed consent is itself inconsistent with the right to privacy, now fairly firmly established in American mores despite its fairly recent and still incomplete institutionalization in law:

> The right of privacy is not rooted in our centuries old custom of common law like many rights, but is a relatively new concept which first made its appearance in 1890 in the now famous law review article by Louis Brandeis (later Justice of the Supreme Court) and Samuel Warren.
>
> They envisaged a broad right to be let alone — to be free from intrusion by others into our personal lives.[13]

Yet the right to privacy is itself even in increasing legal conflict with that of *free speech* — a value more obviously supportive of social science. The trend in libel law has been "in the direction of greater and greater freedom of speech"; but there is now a counter-trend which could become "a kind of Frankenstein doctrine which really cuts down our first amendment freedoms:"[14]

> There has come to be a belief that a person has a right not only to prevent the use of his name and likeness to exploit commodities or works of fiction about him, but also a correlative right or ownership in the *facts* of his life — even though his name is not used . . . A whole new constellation of problems arise, if in addition to the right to be free from libel or slander, a person also has the right to claim exclusive ownership in the things that have happened to him.[15]

Already, both public and private financial aid to science and education are being politically defended as investments in economic opportunity and growth. So it is not inconceivable that the facts in research findings — both of the kind the Publishers' editor was worried about and less personally "sensitive" ones as well — could eventually be considered "commodities," and full permission for publication become even more of a problem in American field research.

My present position on this first important issue is this: American researchers' personal commitments to competing values — which in the field situation show up in selective identification with particular participants —

will make some one-way streets inevitable in the ideal "moral community" of social scientists and their subjects.[16] But the undeniable importance of a scholar's freedom to present and interpret his findings — in writing, or orally — is inadequate in itself to justify acceptance of the following blind-alley beliefs: that to be objective is to be apolitical, that scientific knowledge will inevitably spur social progress, and that pre-research consent is a sufficient protection for personal privacy or other rights or interests at stake in formal publication.

A science checked only by the limits of investigators' intellectual curiosity would be a morally barbarous institution, as some of the recent history of physical science shows all too clearly.[17] Open recognition and as full as possible prior communication of the problems posed by publication of field studies would not eliminate conflicts of interest. But it could check the uncritical tendency to separate professional roles from personal identities, and professional rights from personal responsibility for acts affecting others.

2. *Deleting Names.* For discussion next are the reasons why — aside from the field agreement that particular persons would not be named — I decided against identifying any individuals and most groups involved in the AETE events. The larger issue is whether such incomplete documentation is scientifically defensible. And again, the main implication will be that such decisions are personal, not just professional and scientific matters.

To review this aspect of the editing more specifically: names of individuals were always excluded, but reporting of groups, while not wholly arbitrary, was clearly inconsistent. The state, for example, was identified specifically. So were the single state university, the foundation, and several state and national professional organizations active in the educational controversy.[18] But names of the fifteen private and public colleges involved were always disguised.

Various letters show that the rationale for direct identification of the former groups was the same as that for identifying the newspaper from which some important accounts of events had been taken. It was not simply that such identification had already been made — in the press, professional journals, and several dissertations — but that it seemed essential to accurate, traceable documentation of important statements, especially those taken from organizational records still in existence. (9/26/62, 2/26/63, 3/13/63, 3/3/63)

But no letters show that concealing the *colleges'* names was a less professional decision. It is true that citing them specifically seemed less essential to the analysis. For with a few exceptions — evident in the article despite the disguises — the colleges' actions were more patterned, less distinctive, than for example, those of the state university. But it is also true that I used that defensible sociological difference to help rationalize my personal feeling that the colleges deserved and require more anonymity than the other groups involved.

The kinds of actions the colleges took were often as controversial as those of the more distinctive and economically stronger organizations identified by name, and the evidence reported did not obscure that fact. But the colleges names *were* obscured, and partly because their particular — often impoverished — circumstances seemed to make them already overly vulnerable to political and economic injury. Whatever degree of protection this particular decision provided, and anonymity was still slight for the somewhat more active colleges, I was clearly protecting my own conscience at the same time.

One obvious alternative would have been to disguise all identities — individual or group — equally. But I was unwilling to do that, and probably would be again. Another would have been to offer, perhaps in a footnote, to provide full identification to scholar-readers especially interested in the subject and willing to help keep such information confidential. This is sometimes done. But I was reluctant to do it in the AETE case, because many of the informant-sponsors were themselves academic men, and some of them seemed quite capable of using such information in their own local and national wars. I arbitrarily decided not to openly offer anyone that particular opportunity.

The best bet would have been to try originally for permission to report real names, and have it reaffirmed prior to publication. If such final permission had been denied, however, I would probably have still resorted to the selective identification already described. In my role as a social scientist, however, I would remain ambivalent about that decision too.

It was only after this first serious field work of my own was over that I began to realize that the custom of withholding names was a professional and political norm, rather than one supporting scientific ideals. Any such procedure is actually a form of censorship. Vidich has already implied as much,[19] but missed the larger implication: that *no* such convention in publication can logically be defended as a short-run means to the long-run end of advancing scientific knowledge. To consider one's work as fully scientific "in principle" despite such self-censorship is, as Burke has convincingly argued, to perpetuate a fallacy frequent not only in American field research but in social science generally.[20]

The ideal in scientific documentation is that of full disclosure of evidence essential to critical interpretation and, ultimately, replication. The burden of proof that names are not essential to social science field reports should be on the investigator. And whether made in advance, or after permission has been sought and rejected, a decision to withhold names forecloses that obligation.

Even in survey research based on probability premises, if accuracy of evidence became an issue, access to specific informants would have to be the final check. The AETE article was based on different theoretical premises but it bent the same scientific ideal. It did so more for educational researchers than for readers who were sociologists. But it was addressed to both, and the former readers could not only have better understood but also better criticized and possibly extended the analysis if some informants had been more fully identified. For such readers could then have drawn on their own professional knowledge of the backgrounds, biases, and work styles of the key actors in the crucial situations analyzed in the article. The same argument would apply to the colleges whose identities I also disguised. In short, if familiarity can breed contempt, it can also raise reliability.

And on the latter issue of scientific credibility alone, it is irrelevant that, in the AETE case, the publisher would probably have been unwilling to let me report individuals' names anyway, perhaps even those of all the groups involved. And it is beside the same theoretical point that the "Northwest University" (i.e., University of Oregon) research group with which I had worked had already agreed to withhold individual's names. Such voluntary or expedient censorship has considerable precedent, and undoubtedly often supports social science as a profession. But neither consideration makes any decision to withhold evidence which is important to replication any more compatible with the scientific ideal. Such decisions are moral and political acts, and should be recognized and reported as such.

Lest the last idea be misinterpreted, I am not making only another plea for identifying one's "own values" in conducting and reporting research.[21] The researcher who approves disclosure of his personal preferences is still forced to choose among norms which support some values more than others. And he cannot accurately represent the deletion of names or any other norm supporting censorship as "in principle" supporting science.

3. *Reporting Statuses.* Attention now turns to the sociological, political and ethical wisdom of the related practice of reporting statuses but excluding the identities of the individuals involved. In writing the AETE article, I followed this third protective procedure, but again not completely consistently. In a few cases, for example, rather than referring to someone fairly specifically as

"Dean Q" or "Provost B" I deliberately applied the more ambiguous title of "administrative official." Once more this was a personal as well as a professional decision, made wherever it appeared — even without the consultation earlier recommended — that the individuals involved would be more identifiable than others and than they themselves would probably prefer to be. 3/3/63, 4/2/63)

My general position on reporting statuses was this: when done with reasonable precision, such reporting did not seriously endanger either scientific accuracy or the academic freedom, personal privacy, or other rights and presumably legitimate interests of those studied. Now, however, I have come to believe that reporting this way is not only sociologically suspect, it can also insufficiently protect the public interest in a society in which individual political responsibility is still an important ideal.

It is not necessary to review details of the decision to drop the bomb, or of price-fixing conspiracies in American industry, or even of the Eichmann case to call attention to the widespread tendency to claim that politically questionable acts were done under "others' orders" — or in response to role-expectations deemed central to professional practice. For the same kinds of compartmentalization and rationalization were common in the AETE evidence, and in most of my own representation (and defense) of that evidence as well. And a style of analysis which stresses statuses over identities not only reduces credibility and replicability; it also reinforces a similar trend in American social science to consider social systems the principal actors in the recurrent dramas field researchers study.

When a scholar puts his own name on a published paper he assumes some moral and political as well as professional responsibility, at least for that penultimate act itself — perhaps even for some of its uncertain consequences. But when he removes individual informants' names from his findings and reports their statuses instead, he is, in effect, if not excusing at least shielding them from individual accountability for the acts analyzed.

The same result would be evident whether such shielding was done, e.g., as a means to sponsorship and information (for "reciprocity" is probably the most common rationale) or as a result of personal identification with certain participants, or from a respect for privacy, or from a desire to be beneficent by protecting informants' economic interests. And it is almost equally irrelevant that many social science authors at present pay careful but special attention to contrasts between the ideal and the actual in some sector of human life.[22] For even when their political-critical aims (and hits) are apparent to all, but statuses are reported shorn of names, this still reinforces the trend to consider men mostly in roles, and man as primarily a creature of the circumstances of the systems in which he is arbitrarily set.

The degree to which such reinforcement occurs, and blurs both scientific accuracy and political accountability, is obviously difficult to determine. But surely this is true in part because this particular protective practice and this particular view of man are both so prevalent in American social science.

Since most social research is neither primarily clinical in aim nor fully value-free in actuality, even the legal warrant for such shielding is clearly questionable. At present, apparently only in official census surveys can field researchers lawfully consider their findings either as privileged communication or as unequivocally "expert" evidence.[23] Whatever the legal future may hold, as long as some political pluralism exists, and social scientists continue the commendable trend to study the wealthy and powerful as well as the poor, there will be increasing pressure to provide the public with verifiable dates and names. Some of such pressure will be self-induced. But if an increased interest in specificity could contain a threat to the ideal of objectivity, it would also hold a promise of greater validity and reliability in research, and a hope of an increase in researchers' personal political responsibility as well.

The difficulty of protecting privacy, when privacy was legally or morally warranted, would probably increase. But there is already considerable ambiguity about what privacy is and extensive political and moral hypocrisy about its protection in social research.

The names I agreed to withhold in the AETE study, for example, were usually those of persons on college or university faculties. Are such men's actions in an educational-political-economic controversy their official actions, their personal actions, or often both at the same time? When some academic men study others, what incest taboos should be honored? If there is a special honor among all academicians as among thieves, does it apply to college and university administrators to the same extent that it applies to faculty? Should the same privilege of protection from identification apply in private institutions as in public ones? Are faculty and administrators in public colleges as accountable as the governor of the state supporting their work? And, somewhat similarly, where does the official role of a foundation official end and his private status start?

As other social researchers have done, from Middletown to Monkeytown, I partly avoided such ambiguous questions by concentrating on the role of an impartial investigator interested in accuracy. That allowed me, as I realized in part at the time (4/2/63), to feel that I did not have to honor the probable objections of people who were presumably officially committed to the advance of knowledge as well as to the protection of their own careers and organizations. But it was only later that I realized how much better it would have been to have been able to report real names.

I am not arguing here that the conscientious field researcher should never report statuses without names. But I am suggesting that he should be aware of both the scientific and the political consequences of that choice in considering protective procedures. And I am also asserting that it ordinarily *is* a choice, and one that is considerably personal. Statuses and roles are far from irrelevant in human affairs, including the AETE events and my own dealing with them. But statuses and roles do not determine behavior: they are taken into account in considering and constructing lines of action from perceived alternatives.[24]

The evident alternatives may, of course, be unacceptable in a particular situation, and this is often the case in American field research. The social scientist's "license"[25] is not yet even as firmly established as that of the journalist. And the journalist still often reports information from unidentified sources, partly to maintain communication with people who have power over the evidence he needs.

The same "boundary role"[26] reasons often develop in social research. But the essentiality of the work of the social scientist is not so easily demonstrated, in a democracy or elsewhere. The irony is that this is probably true in part because so much published work is so abstract and impersonal as to appear politically innocuous, except to those familiar with the events and persons involved. Moreover, many respondents' fears of political exposure seem to me to be mirror-images of many researchers' own protective commitments, commitments not only to their own careers, to the too-cautious custom of initiating decisions about leaving real people out of published reports, to the quest for respectability through a rigorous objectivity (erroneously) assumed to exist in the "real sciences," but also to a view of man not completely compatible with either professional accuracy or personal political accountability.

To make the latter polemical point more explicit: for many of the reasons already reviewed, I sharply disagree with Shils' argument that the system theory of social action, which he has helped develop, is both scientifically valid and morally valuable — seeing man as "neither beast nor machine."[27] I can still agree with his implication — in the same important essay — that any protective procedure should be compatible with the informed conscience of the man with the final manuscript to prepare. But my main argument here has been that an increasing part of the problem of reconciling the demands of conscience with conventions of documentation is that the contemporary emphasis on statuses and roles discourages identification *with* and identification *of* both the self and the other — as something more than role players on society's stage, or interdependent units responding to the requisites of any social system.

4. *Paraphrasing Quotations.* The specific question here was whether it was desirable to paraphrase interview statements included in early drafts of the AETE article. The larger issue is that of the scientific wisdom of such a protective procedure. And the implication of most interest is that a researcher's theoretical premises affect the character and consequences of his editorial preferences.

As the correspondence indicates (3/14/63), I did finally decide to paraphrase some minor issues and decisions in the AETE controversy. But, when similar treatment of what I considered crucial interview excerpts was suggested, I resisted, and the book editor successfully backed me up. After they had all been double-checked for accuracy, none of the thirty-six such statements was excluded or altered.

Paraphrase was not being suggested for reasons of space limitations or style — as often happens — but because the Publisher was worried about libel. That was one reason why, while still resisting a paraphrase "solution," I insisted on categorizing nine of the excerpts as LP (for "later paraphrase"), and the remaining 27 as AV (for "attempted verbatim"). I recognized that the exigencies of research collaboration had meant that the former statements had actually been written up from skeletal notes; only the latter had been taken down in deliberate detail during the interviews. And if it was correct, as I had earlier read somewhere, that "the truth" was the "one sure defense against libel," it seemed more politically responsible to distinguish clearly the different degrees of literal accuracy represented in such evidence.

That makes even more sense to me now — although like many social researchers, I suspect — I still know less than I should about how legal differentiations of fact from hearsay, for example, would apply in formal field studies. But the most important reason why I felt strongly about presenting interview statements as "verbatim as possible" was that such a style of reporting was the one most consistent with my commitment to a particular theoretical perspective — Median symbolic interaction, especially as interpreted by Blumer.[28]

Fichter and Kolb have already observed that different "images of science" have different *ethical* implications in social research.[29] But their discussion deals with whether the scholar sees science in general as a game, for example, or as a service to mankind. The idea here is that the different ontological and epistemological premises in various sociological perspectives lead researchers to consider certain forms of evidence more *valid* than others, and thus more important to obtain and to present precisely in publication.

Social scientists of the more positivistic persuasions, for example, stress chance and central tendency in the determination of events. Respondents' actual statements — the "indicators" from which such scholars derive their statistical data — are seldom deemed important to present precisely, or seen as significantly altered if it proves necessary to "collapse categories" to make the main evidence — the numbers — large enough to fit probability premises. But the researcher's own meanings and measurements are ordinarily stated quite explicitly, to reduce subjectivity.

Although it is well known that symbolic interactionists regard reality as emergent in the process of action, it is less widely recognized that to be consistent with their premises, such scholars must attempt — in both investigation *and* publication — to reconstruct their respondents' own special worlds from their special words (or other gestures). And they must do so without unduly distorting such realities, as would happen if they were fitted into other forms — whether those the researcher himself expected to find or those which have become traditional or fashionable elsewhere in social science.

Partly through elaborate coding and cross-checking procedures worked out with the other Oregon researchers, I had managed (in my dissertation) to reconstruct as much of the crucial interaction process as was possible to do accurately so long after the actual events and interviews. Then, in the still-later preparation of the AETE article itself, I had to take some of the interview statements out of that complex context. But it proved possible to do so without doing serious violence to the respondents' definitions of the situations to be dealt with — e.g., inter-college rivalry, fear of foundation domination, and economic and political pressures on teacher preparation — and teachers' salaries as well. So, when paraphrase was seriously proposed by the Publisher's editor, I was well aware that some of the evidence was "sensitive," but I still considered it central to accurate analysis. The interview statements at issue, then, did not simply (as the other editor expressed it) give some of the "flavor" of the controversy. Instead, both in the order *and* in the particular form presented, they represented much of its objective substance, as intersubjectively verified. In other words, to paraphrase — i.e., literally to use "other words" in actual reporting — would have been to make the most empirically valid and theoretically valuable data disappear from the article altogether.

Quite conscious of Cooley's emphasis on understanding "personal ideas,"[30] I was, in short, much less worried about libel (which seemed unlikely anyway) than about losing the distinctive imagery in statements such as these (which in the article were presented without the real names):

> Ex-governor Sid McMath: At that particular time we were also trying to establish a state board which would be the board for all the colleges and [the] University and have an integrated and planned educational program for the whole state. There was opposition because it was felt that this [foundation-financed "Experiment"] would be a step toward your over-all planning commission. That would be more advantageous but I don't know when you'll see it come, because each college is politically autonomous. They are kind of like a state in a way. They don't want to lose any of their sovereignty.
>
> The senators and representatives from those areas: one of their primary jobs is to protect that institution against encroachment. They did this but they also combined against the University or whatever group [was] getting the upper hand. It is a kind of check and balance. It's got nothing to do with education. It is a log-rolling proposition. A pork barrel. That was the big argument for your central board. . . . (AV)
>
> Editor Harry Ashmore: The . . . [Commission recommending the central board] was set up by the Legislature, which was damn sick and tired of the squabbling and jockeying for positions and appropriations. They had [had] a bellyful of that sort of thing. (AV)

To "catch" others' interpretations and report them accurately is obviously difficult. But such role-taking is neither impossible nor undesirable in social science, for reasons well summarized by Blumer. Ontologically:

> From the standpoint of symbolic interaction, social organization is a framework inside of which acting units develop their action. Structural features, such as "culture," "social systems," "social stratification," or "social roles," set conditions for their action but do not determine their action. People — that is, acting units — do not act toward culture, social structure or the like; they act toward situations.[31]

Thus, methodologically:

> To try to catch the interpretive processes by remaining aloof as a so-called "objective observer" and refusing to take the role of the acting unit is to risk the worst kind of subjectivism — the objective observer is likely to fill in the process of interpretation with his own surmises . . .[32]

The philosophical controversy at issue here will probably continue indefinitely in American sociology. But the major "sociology of knowledge" implications of interest now are these: Initial decisions about styles of investigation are based in part on the desire to make analyses of data consistent with theoretical commitments. But research perspectives differ in their very premises — about validity, reliability, and reality itself. Acceptance of different premises leads to different editorial preferences, and, eventually, to different possible political consequences from final publication.

The direction and degree of such consequences would vary with the situation studied and with the author's eventual audience, as well as with the style of investigation and formal presentation. But it is partly the arbitrary personal choice of a research perspective which makes the range of probable consequences run from the (initially) impersonal "impact" of statistical tables, through the semi-personal results of stress on statuses and roles, to the very personal political accountability possible if living informants are quoted literally and personally identifiable.

5. *Reporting Personal Knowledge.* The final protective procedure to be reconsidered in this essay is that of the editing of evidence acquired more personally than in the researcher-respondent roles initially assumed in field studies. The larger issue for summary consideration is that of the limits of objective knowledge. And the concluding implications will all be based on an argument that now must be made more explicit: that, in the more comprehensive sense stressed by Polanyi, all scientific knowledge is a form of "personal knowledge."[33] Neither theories nor formal factual findings acquire either significance or validity apart from the interpretations made by the particular persons whose intersecting actions create and sustain science as a social institution.

As Bramson has recently stated this concluding contention more specifically for social science:

> We should acknowledge the extent to which acceptance of 'truth' in social science is determined in part by an agreement among social scientists as to the warrantability of beliefs. And we should perhaps acknowledge that it is in the nature of social science that it may be influenced in its methods and results by the character of the observer . . . The positivistic dictum concerning subjectivity — that it must be extirpated root and branch — has passed its period of usefulness in some areas of social science. Many sociologists are still clinging to methodological notions concerning "science" which have been questioned by scientists for decades.[34]

An even stronger statement would now be acceptable to me, from the general standpoint of symbolic interaction and also from my specific experiences in writing and reviewing the AETE article.

It was during the delicate process of deciding which interview excerpts were crucial to include that I became most fully aware that the "warrantability of beliefs" is inevitably based on subjective role-taking. For it was then I remembered that, in the field work itself, I had vaguely realized that both empathy and insight had been increased whenever respondents — whatever their "sides" in the AETE controversy — had tended to "open up" to me (and other researchers) not in our official access roles as neutral investigators, but as informed and sympathetic persons.

And as I thought about it more, I also realized that even when writing my dissertation about AETE I had begun to wonder whether the development of that sort of rapport didn't carry with it the unspoken stipulation that information was being offered in a spirit of at least fleeting friendship or common-human trust, rather than of official or scientific accountability. And even then I had not been sure that it made scientific sense to link such more personal statements only with the informants' own official statuses, and, indeed, whether it was morally correct to include such statements at all in a published paper.

Later on, even more such questions came to mind. What should I do in cases where informants more openly requested that certain information be kept "off the record"? (3/14/63) Was that an inviolable request in a society valuing privacy? Couldn't both the offering and the honoring of such requests amount to avoiding public accountability, also valued in the society? If, as in the AETE interviews, there was no advance agreement about allowing such reservations of evidence, should researchers tactfully reject requests as they occurred? Should they do so even at the risk of thus failing to get important evidence? And if (as some of my associates and I did) they tactically accede instead, how should the forthcoming "confidential" information be handled in writing for publication? Would researchers in such a situation be free only to use such evidence as "background material" for their own enlightenment? Or could another journalistic convention apply, that of either quoting or paraphrasing such statements — with the printed reservation that they were from anonymous but authoritative sources? And could evidence so reported ever actually be authenticated?

My final decision was, again, a partly personal "professional" choice. As already indicated, in a few instances I blurred even the formal status of my own interviewees by referring to them only as "administrative officials." And in another instance, where a close reading of the interview suggested that another researcher's respondent had probably intended to have his remarks be "off the record," I paraphrased the points necessary to include in a paragraph about an interesting if fairly minor aspect of the controversy.

Those few omissions of evidence did not slant my analysis toward either the liberal arts or the professional education "sides" of the AETE struggle. The "critical" cast of the article (12/3/63) came primarily from the "warts and all" picture I had presented, and regarded (and still regard) as an accurate portrayal of the contrasts between expressed aims and what the antagonists had finally decided to do at various crucial points. I had respected some respondents more than others (in the field), but the different degrees of anonymity I tried to achieve in the article had less to do with that than with greater visibility and vulnerability. In short, I tried for "beneficent objectivity," and even made what I then regarded as my major polemical premise apparent in the actual writing, by citing Tawney with approval:

> The disputes which matter are not caused by a misunderstanding of interests but by a better understanding of diversity of interests.[35]

But it was necessary, of course, to interpret the evidence sociologically. And even though I tried as much as possible to report in respondents' own idioms, how they themselves defined situations and made critical decisions, the interpretive emphasis I gave — to issues of autonomy, for example — were the ones which I had been most interested in originally and been encouraged to study by colleagues and dissertation advisers. So the analysis was much more subjective than I either recognized or admitted until the article was in galley proofs. At that point of no return, the reflections reported at such length here really began to seem both sociologically and personally important.

The initial implications of interest here are that subjective role-taking is inevitable and essential to interviewing and interpretation alike; that values transcending science are involved, e.g., the value of neutral objectivity itself; and that objectivity cannot accurately be considered as some simple "matter of degree": it is a complex and continuing kind of agreement among particularly interested and informed observers and readers. Whatever his theoretical perspective, and whatever "rules of evidence" he tries to honor, both in investigation and in writing for publication the social researcher's insight comes from his own empathic interpretations of his own and others' actions.

Access situations in the field, for example, become subjectively structured in some emergent way, however the researcher proceeds. An effort to avoid involvement itself affects informants' perceptions, and responses to questions.[36] And methods texts themselves attest to the frequent importance of establishing rapport. But what is less recognized (or perhaps admitted) is that establishment of effective rapport often removes the masks of researcher and respondent. Manifest identities change and interaction moves to a more personal plane: one in which the expression of feelings, belief, and speculations are not only permissible but expected. And what is missed most of all is that the (accidental or deliberate) development of such more personal situations has important scientific, moral, and political consequences.

To be more specific: positivistic models of science (and of social research) often especially discourage the interviewer, for example, from being more than a neutral questioner — a task-oriented object — to his subjects; or (where the expediency of rapport is recognized) no more than a friendly stranger keeping his personal feelings at home. And my present argument is that such advice is not only scientifically and politically suspect — in conception and consequences — but morally blind as well; and not just because neutrality is defined by respondents, not researchers alone.

The interviewer is always a stranger to an important degree. But he is never just a stranger, for a stranger has his own preoccupations, while the interviewer's preoccupations are those of his subject — at least those deemed important to study. In sociology, the participant-observer (with his open-ended inquiries) is at one extreme here, the opinion-surveyor (with his standardized questions) at the other; but neither is simply a neutral stranger.

To me it seems both more accurate and more honest for the researcher to try as best he can to consider himself at least a temporary member of his subjects' moral community, whatever the values may be. For his findings will probably be no more valid or reliable than the accuracy of that empathic impression, however arbitrary his eventual theoretical interpretations become. And as long as his ultimate aim is to complete his study and leave, he will at best be an invited guest, doing well-explained detection which he is permitted to report with full identification. At worst, he will be an anonymous voyeur, compounding professional investigation with social self-deception.

When eventually wrestling with "what to publish" and "how" he should critically assess, and compensate for, as best he consciously can, how his positive or negative identification *with* others — i.e., how his feelings of sympathy, antipathy, or something in between — are probably influencing his interpretation and presentation of evidence. But "as best he consciously can" is not meant here in a narrow professional sense. I mean that he should ordinarily encourage and honor such feelings, rather than try to squelch them "in the interest of science."

To be even more specific: I think he should honor them even to the point of withholding or otherwise obscuring evidence, including evidence indicative of identities — even though such use of protective procedures is counter to the scientific ideal of frank and accurate communication. But I also think that he should include all pertinent evidence, and make identities as visible as he can, if he feels personally that to do otherwise would be morally dishonorable and politically irresponsible. He should openly defend what he is doing. But to do less is — if not to be less than human, for man can be beast as well as machine — at least to be less personally responsive and socially responsible than men ought to be, whatever their work and its cultural setting. Or so it seems to me. For as Cooley saw so well, it is not cultural ideals that men have in common: all cultures are different. It is common human feelings, moral sentiments — of love, hate, and all the intermediary shadings — that constitute the social reality to which all men are capable of responding.

Surely one *strength* of the contemporary distrust of reason[37] is its recognition of the arbitrarily narrow concepts of man and reason employed in so much social research at present, conceptions of role-expectations which lead scholars and subjects alike to distrust and discourage the emotional empathic processes which help men know who they are and what the world is. It is to be hoped that a fuller recognition of the subjective basis of all scientific knowledge will lead social researchers especially to realize the importance of making their own work logically and morally reconcilable with what Cooley called men's "personal ideas" of each other:

> The man is one thing and the various ideas entertained about him are another; but the latter, the personal idea, is the immediate social reality, the thing in which men exist for one another, and work directly upon one another's lives. Thus any study of society that is not supported by a firm grasp of personal ideas is empty and dead, mere doctrine and not knowledge at all.[38]

My own "grasp of personal ideas" in the case reconsidered here was at times far less than firm. But it was a sympathy for such an intuitive and human form of social research that attracted me to sociology originally. I may distort it at times, but I will affirm it again now, over the interest of an "impersonal" science unaware of its arbitrary presumptions and methodological and moral pretensions.

Summary and Final Conclusions

The protective procedures at issue here have been shown to be something less than professional customs completely compatible with accurate analysis, something more than political condoms making scientific intercourse sterile, though still enjoyable. And various sections of the discussion have suggested that, however and whenever applied, they should be consistent with the scholar's own image of science, his particular theoretical perspective, and his assessment of the whole situation he is in. An act of personal choice is involved and should be made as evident as possible to all other parties of interest in a particlar investigation and forthcoming publication.

If permission for full identification proves impossible to obtain, and the prospective author honestly feels that publication in that ideal form would do other persons, their worlds, and the world at large more harm than good, then it would be morally obnoxious to go ahead; he should censor his findings instead. If he finally comes to believe that scientific inquiry and scientific knowledge — which are both subjectively based — are inherently destructive of values he thinks it more important to preserve, then he should leave the field to others and fight its growing force with other weapons.

The soul-searching shown in this essay has left me a less "happy Meadian" than I at one time was. But it has not yet led me to the latter step: I still cannot accept an argument which reifies science, or any other institution, as an abstract social force impossible for man himself to control.

In recent decades, and in American society especially, social research has shifted its attention from the contrasts between sacred ideals and secular practices to the discrepancies between public ideologies and privileged deliberations and decisions. Such study can be intellectually rewarding and socially valuable, although neither result is inevitable. And there is clearly a place in such work for protective procedures, in investigation as well as in publication. But that place is often misconceived, as scientific rather than political and moral. It is also often misrepresented, as protecting informants' personal rights more than researchers' professional interests. As a result, much social research has become misanthropic, making scholars themselves distrust and discourage the very sort of empathy which gives all men a personal sense of human identity.

NOTES TO THE CHAPTER

1. Philip Selznick, *Leadership in Administration* (Evanston, Ill.: Row, Peterson Co., 1957).

2. Richard Colvard, "The Colleges and the 'Arkansas Purchase' Controversy," in Matthew B. Miles (ed.), *Innovation in Education* (New York: Columbia University, Teachers College Bureau of Publications, 1964), 117–55.

3. Miles, *op. cit.*

4. Richard Colvard, "The Foundation and the Colleges: A Study of Organizations, Professions, and Power in the Arkansas Experiment in Teacher Education," Unpublished Ph.D. Dissertation, University of California (Berkeley), 1959.

5. Review of Miles, *op. cit.,* Cyril Sargent, *Journal of Teacher Education,* 15 (September, 1964), pp. 337–38.

6. Review of Miles, *op. cit.,* Rychard Fink, *Saturday Review,* 48 (July 18, 1965), p. 57.

7. Robert K. Merton, "The Role of the Intellectual in Public Bureaucracy," *Social Forces,* 23 (May, 1945), p. 408.

8. Cf. William F. Whyte, "The Slum: On the Evolution of Street Corner Society," in Arthur J. Vidich, Joseph B. Bensman, and Maurice R. Stein (eds.), *Reflections on Community Studies* (New York: John Wiley & Sons, 1964), 3–70.

9. Jessie Bernard, "The Power of Science and the Science of Power," *American Sociological Review,* 14 (October, 1949), pp. 575–84.

10. Cf. John R. Seeley, "Crestwood Heights: Intellectual and Libidinal Dimensions of Research," in Vidich *et al., op. cit.,* 157–206.

11. Richard Colvard, "Risk Capital Philanthropy: The Ideological Defense of Innovation," in George K. Zollschan and Walter Hirsch (eds.), *Explorations in Social Change* (Boston: Houghton Mifflin Co., 1964), 728–49.

12. Howard S. Becker, "Problems in Publication of Field Studies," in Vidich *et al., op. cit.,* 267–84.

13. Harriet F. Pilpel, "What Price Privacy?" *Civil Liberties,* No. 225 (April, 1965), p. 2. Cf. Oscar Ruebhausen and Orville G. Brim, Jr., "Privacy and Behavior Research," *Columbia Law Review,* 65 (November, 1965), pp. 1184–1211.

14. Pilpel, *op. cit.*

15. Pilpel, *op. cit.*

16. Cf. Edward A. Shils, "Social Inquiry and the Autonomy of the Individual," in Daniel Lerner (ed.), *The Human Meaning of the Social Sciences* (New York: Meridian Books, 1959), 114–57.

17. Cf. Hans F. Morgenthau, "Modern Science and Political Power," *Columbia Law Review,* 64 (December, 1964), esp. p. 1387.

18. Cf. Samuel Halperin, "A University in the Web of Politics," Case 14, Eagleton Institute Cases in Practical Politics (New York: McGraw-Hill Book Co., 1960).

19. Arthur J. Vidich, "Freedom and Responsibility in Research: A Rejoinder," *Human Organization,* 19 (Spring, 1960), p. 4.

20. Kenneth Burke, *A Grammar of Motives* (Cleveland: Meridian Books, 1962), 510–11.

21. Cf. Gunnar Myrdal, "A Methodological Note on Facts and Valuations in Social Science," in Gunnar Myrdal, *An American Dilemma* (New York: Harper & Bros., 1944), 1035–45.

22. Cf. Becker, *op. cit.,* and Gideon Sjoberg, "Research Methodology: A Sociology of Knowledge Perspective," Unpublished paper presented at the meeting of the American Sociological Association, September, 1965, esp. 16–21.

23. Cf. Hans Zeisel, "The Uniqueness of Survey Evidence," *Cornell Law Quarterly,* 45 (Winter, 1960), pp. 322–45.

24. Herbert Blumer, "Society as Symbolic Interaction," in Arnold M. Rose (ed.), *Human Behavior and Social Processes* (Boston: Houghton Mifflin Co., 1962), esp. 186–87. Cf. Ernest Nagel, *The Structure of Science* (New York and Burlingame: Harcourt, Brace & World, 1961), esp. 447–502.

25. Everett C. Hughes, *Men and Their Work* (Glencoe, Ill.: The Free Press, 1958), 78–87.

26. Cf. Fred H. Goldner, "Organizations and their Environment: Roles at their Boundary," Unpublished paper presented at the meeting of the American Sociological Association, New York, 1960.

27. Shils, *op. cit.,* 153.

28. Blumer, *op. cit.*

29. Joseph H. Fichter and William L. Kolb, "Ethical Limitations on Sociological Reporting," *American Sociological Review,* 18 (October, 1953), pp. 544–50. Cf. Edward Gross, "Social Science Techniques: A Problem of Power and Responsibility," *Scientific Monthly* (November, 1956), pp. 242–47.

30. Charles H. Cooley, *Human Nature and the Social Order* (New York: Charles Scribner's Sons, 1902), Chap. 3.

31. Blumer, *op. cit.,* 189–90.

32. *Ibid.,* 188.

33. Michael Polanyi, *Personal Knowledge* (London: Routledge & Kegan Paul, 1958).

34. Leon Bramson, *The Political Context of Sociology* (Princeton, N.J.: Princeton University Press, 1961), 152. Cf. Llewellyn Gross, "Values and Theory of Social Problems," in Alvin W. Gouldner and S. M. Miller (eds.), *Applied Sociology* (New York: The Free Press, 1965), 383–97.

35. R. H. Tawney, *The Acquisitive Society* (New York: Harcourt, Brace & Co., 1920), 40.

36. H. H. Hyman, *Interviewing in Social Research* (Chicago: University of Chicago Press, 1954), esp. 75–76.

37. Reinhard Bendix, *Social Science and the Distrust of Reason* (Berkeley: University of California Press, 1951).

38. Cooley, *op. cit.,* 89. Cf. T. Shibutani, *Society and Personality* (Englewood Cliffs, N. J.: Prentice-Hall, 1961), esp. Pt. I; also Adam Smith, *The Theory of Moral Sentiments* (London: George Bell & Sons, 1880), Pts. I, III, V.